D1010799

Fortunate Son

Fortunate Son

George W. Bush and the Making of an American President

J. H. Hatfield

ST. MARTIN'S PRESS NEW YORK

For

my wife, Nancy, a fifth-generation Texan
from a long line of Republicans who taught me that
a biography must be more than dates, facts, and quotes—
it must convey the person's heart, soul, and thoughts.

And to the memory of my favorite Uncle Cobe,
a war hero, lifelong Democrat, and union activist.

"Many good men should weep for his death . . ."
—Horace, *Odes*

THOMAS DUNNE BOOKS.
An imprint of St. Martin's Press.

FORTUNATE SON: GEORGE W. BUSH AND THE MAKING OF AN AMERICAN PRESIDENT.

Design by Maureen Troy

ISBN 0-312-24268-9

First Edition: November 1999

10 9 8 7 6 5 4 3 2 1

Contents

Author's Note

When a man assumes a public trust, he should consider himself as public property.

—Thomas Jefferson

I tried several times to interview George W. Bush for this book. Beginning in the fall of 1998, I not only wrote Karen Hughes, his longtime communications director, but I also e-mailed the Internet-savvy Texas governor. In each letter, I offered to meet with him at his convenience, any time or anywhere, or if he chose because of his busy schedule, I would fax or e-mail a series of questions for him to address in writing. After several attempts went unanswered, I finally received the following curt, one-paragraph response from Ms. Hughes on the governor's official State of Texas stationery:

Dear Mr. Hatfield:

On behalf of Governor George W. Bush, thank you for your request for an interview. Unfortunately, he will not be able to accept due to the high volume of requests and many demands on his time. He remains focused on Texas issues and is busy preparing for the upcoming legislative session. We appreciate your understanding and your interest in the Governor.

Sincerely,
Karen Hughes
Communications Director

It is certainly regrettable that the governor declined to be interviewed for this book. In an effort to write an in-depth and objective biography, I had wished to offer him the opportunity to provide his response to comments attributed to others whom I had interviewed and also to present him with a forum to give his side of the story on the many controversial issues I raise herein.

This book could not have been written without the help of hundreds of Bush's friends, college classmates, business associates, political colleagues, employees, acquaintances—present and former—and family members who graciously contributed their time, knowledge, and experiences. To all of them, named and unnamed, I am grateful.

Because George W. Bush wields sizable power, especially in Texas, and has a reputation for aggressively contesting those who cross him, researching this biography posed a problem. Some individuals central to the life story of Bush agreed to be interviewed only under the condition that they not be identified in the book. Not everyone is willing to put careers (especially political ones) on the line or to jeopardize relationships. The information they provided was often important enough to use despite this restriction. As a result, quotations sometimes appear without attribution in this biography. In no case, however, did I use material from one of these interviews unless I independently corroborated its accuracy through another person or documentary source. For example, in providing the account of the newly-elected governor calling his parents from the master bedroom of his hotel suite, I used well-placed campaign aides and friends of the elder Bushes who provided virtually identical accounts of the telephone conversation to the author. These sources opened doors to the governor's private world which could never otherwise have been opened.

In addition, I consulted, and in some cases quoted from, unpublished material garnered from several interviews I originally conducted with Bush, his family, associates, and others throughout the eighties and early nineties when I was a freelance journalist and frequent contributor to the *Dallas Times-Herald, Houston Post, Dallas Observer*, and *The Texas Women's News.* Other Lone Star State journalists who previously had done research on Bush and his family were also generous and collegial in sharing their insights, voluminous notes, contacts, suggestions, and source material. They have my deepest appreciation.

Librarians, curators, and archivists contributed immensely to this project, and I'm eternally indebted to the Texas State Archives, Austin, Texas; Permian Basin Petroleum Museum, Midland, Texas; Midland County Historical Museum; Texas Room, Houston Public Library; Mary Finch, archivist of The George Bush Presidential Library, College Station, Texas; Wes Gamble of the operations staff at the *Houston Chronicle*'s archives department; *Midland Reporter-Telegram* librarian, Diane King, who also deserves a special thanks; Center for American History, the University of Texas at Austin; Texas Historical Society, Houston, Texas; Public Service Archives, Woodson Research Center, Rice University; Haley Library and History Center, Midland, Texas; Yale and Harvard University Libraries; University of Connecticut at Storrs; Center for Archival Collections, Bowling Green State University, Bowling Green, Ohio; Eugene C. Barker Texas History Center, Austin; Columbia Oral History Research Office; Curtis Wilcott, photo editor at the *Midland Reporter-Telegram;* Regina Greenwell, archivist, Lyndon Baines Johnson Presidential Library; the Library of Congress, Washington, D.C.; the National Archives and Records Administration, Washington, D.C.; John Broder, archivist at *Texas Monthly;* Jeff Cronin, Common Cause, Washington, D.C.; writer and retired teacher Jerry "Politex" Barrett of Austin, who collects and archives every article ever written on George W. Bush for his exhaustive Web site "Bush Watch" (www.geocities.com/CapitolHill/3750/bush.htm); and The Bush 2000 Network electronic mailing list, a joint venture between political writer Patrick Ruffini and veteran New Hampshire politico David Colburn, which gathers the latest articles on Bush, poll numbers, and insider information about the governor's White House aspirations.

A tremendous amount of research is necessary for any comprehensive biography, and this was especially true in the case of this book. I am particularly grateful to Ed and Judith Echols, whose Texas connections and assistance helped me uncover a treasure trove of invaluable source material. I owe them so much.

To research my subject as thoroughly as possible, I began by trying to read everything ever written about George W. Bush and his family, an enormous task considering the political legacy that spans several generations. My wife, Nancy, working in the capacity of an underpaid research assistant, spent months tirelessly gathering the mountain of newspaper and magazine articles, Web site printouts, and television interview transcripts, which she diligently copied, filed, and cross-referenced. I cannot thank her enough, for helping in a thousand ways big and small, for putting up with it all, and for inspiring me every step of the way.

Although she wasn't my editor on this book, I cannot adequately express my heartfelt thanks to Martha "Yodette" Bushko for her unselfish and rock-steady support and for prodding me when I was suffering from a severe case of writer's block ("Write, you will!"). I also wish to thank author Ruby Jean Jensen for her encouragement and wise counsel over the years; Scot and Jane Hundley and Scott and Kelli Eccleston (the "S & S boys" and their *very* pregnant wives), whose sincere friendship, genuine concern, and emotional support during this project was most appreciated; Texas hospitality and generosity are always exemplified by Tommy and Sue Isaac, two very special people whose unconditional love and family support knows no bounds; for legal advice, my publisher handed me over to Celeste Phillips, who's a treasure both professionally and personally; my dear friend Susan Bradshaw's contribution to a clearer and more accurate text was indispensable; Dr. Mark Rubertus and his wife, Kitty, for making my back more bearable after hours of categorizing chapter source notes; and, of course, I cannot fail to mention George "Doc" Burt, my former writing partner and blood brother for life, who was the driving force in making certain that my dreams became reality. As they say in Texas, "May your horse get fat from eating the grass off your enemies' graves."

Additional thanks go to the A-Team of Lena Lewis and Dale Sands for transforming that old barn on the corner of the property into a rustic office with an inspirational view (I especially enjoyed the "christening" party); Bruce Gabbard for once again arriving just in the nick of time to get me back on-line, overhauling my Web site, and making my life a hell of a lot simpler; and my ol' beer-drinking, crab legs–eating buddy, Dusty White, for reconnecting me to the world. Thanks, gang, for giving me your time and energy and, more importantly, for beating the clock.

I would also like to extend special appreciation to Laura Tucker of Richard Curtis Associates, who's not only my literary agent but one of my dearest friends. Ever since she came into my life in early 1998, it has been an exhilarating adventure of one book after another, and if I have learned anything along the way, it has been to listen to her and trust her professional judgment.

My sincerest thanks to my editor at St. Martin's, Barry Neville, a selfless man of letters who had enough faith in my writing abilities to assign me the task and then allow me to do a Houdini-inspired disappearing act for several months. His quiet wisdom and example have taught me to shun mediocrity and strive for excellence in my writing while attempting to go beyond the "clothes and buttons of a person," which is how Mark Twain defined biography. Barry believed in me as a wordsmith and in this book, and for that show of support I shall always be grateful.

I am forever indebted to my "Eufaula Connection," who was exceptionally helpful—especially during the last quarter of this project—with his time, information, recollections, and insightful perspectives into Bush's persona.

And finally, to my mother, who passed away a decade ago. Always unfailingly helpful and supportive of my desire to be a writer, she advised me to follow the creed of the preacher in John Steinbeck's *The Grapes of Wrath* who abandoned the ministry: "There ain't no sin and there ain't no virtue. There's just stuff people do. It's all part of the same thing. And some of the things folks do is nice, and some ain't nice, but that's as far as any man got a right to say."

Words to keep in mind when writing a biography, especially the life and times of a politician.

J. H. Hatfield
Lake Eufaula, Oklahoma
August 17, 1999

I hope you will judge me by what I'm about . . .

—George W. Bush, a week before he was elected
governor of Texas

I have said many times that there's nothing in my background that would disqualify me from being governor of Texas, much less president.

—Governor Bush's response when asked by CNN
if there was a "lapse in judgment" in his past

Character is like a tree and reputation like its shadow. The shadow is what we think of it; the tree is the real thing.

—Abraham Lincoln

It is easier to pretend to be what you are not than to hide what you really are; but he that can accomplish both has little to learn in hypocrisy.

—Charles Caleb Colton
Lacon 1825

Prologue: Curious George

. . . Bush is something quite rare in today's presidential politics: a front-runner who has become the darling of his party's establishment even though most voters don't know much about who he is or what he stands for.

—Kenneth Walsh, *US News & World Report*

Governor Bush is in an enviable position. He is well-liked without being well-known.

—Harry Smith, host of A & E's *Biography*'s "George W. Bush: The Son Also Rises"

Ever since the 1770s, when colonists of the first "Thirteen United States" renounced their allegiance to Great Britain and its ruling monarch King George III, Americans—despite their democratic pretensions—have periodically attempted to create political dynasties based on family lineage. Decade after decade, U.S. voters have assumed that subsequent generations of Adamses, Tafts, Roosevelts, Rockefellers, and Kennedys—basically heirs to the throne—were entitled to power and genetically preordained to lead their country.

Now as a new millennium dawns in the United States, Texas governor George W. Bush—son of a former president and brother of Florida's chief executive—seems destined to inherit the White House simply because he is viewed as a member of what is essentially a political aristocracy. Propelled by instant name recognition, a ready-made political network of his father's contacts, and a record-setting war chest of millions of dollars in campaign contributions, Bush (known as "W" to his friends and pronounced "DUB-ya" in Texas) is enjoying the kind of surge in momentum that his father used to call "Big Mo."

Although unemployment stands at an almost thirty-year low, the resurgent economy has sent the stock market soaring, and crime is plummeting, a popular groundswell—the likes of which hasn't been seen since Dwight Eisenhower returned home a World War II hero—has made Bush the prohibitive Republican front-runner and the GOP's strongest candidate by far in the 2000 race.

But the Texas governor has reached this point in spite of the fact that most of the country knows virtually nothing about him as a man or where he stands on the political issues. Even in the Lone Star State, where Bush has built an approval rating higher than any Texas governor in modern times, voters indicated in an April 1999 poll (conducted five months after he was reelected to a second term) that his popularity was based more on name and image than substance and accomplishment. Almost half of the Texans surveyed could not answer the following questions:

- What have been Bush's top three achievements as governor?
- Can you name three programs the governor has initiated in the state legislature during his first term?
- What is Bush's stance on Social Security privatization? Abortion rights? Gun control? Health care? Juvenile crime?
- Can you identify some of his stated opinions that you agree with?
- What is it about the way Bush approaches the day-to-day governing of the state that appeals to you as a resident of Texas?
- Do you know anything about his economic, military, or diplomatic philosophy?

In another indication that Bush's popularity is anchored in brand name recognition rather than any single achievement, an independent poll of New Hampshire Republicans showed that his lead evaporated when a short biography was substituted for his name.

The Reuters/Zogby Poll in New Hampshire was conducted two ways, first with names and then without. When candidate names were used, Bush piled up a huge lead, picking up 38.4 percent of the support among 309 likely GOP voters contacted in late April 1999. Two-time Cabinet officer Elizabeth Dole was second at 14.9 percent. Widely-respected Arizona Senator John McCain was third at 8.9 percent, and former Vice President Dan Quayle was fourth at 8.4 percent.

But the picture changed dramatically when names were removed and short biographies were used. Bush dropped to 24.1 percent. McCain shot up to second at 19.2 percent which, because of the 5.7 percentage point margin of error, put McCain and Bush in a statistical dead heat. Dole dropped to fifth place at 7.7 percent.

"That's a clear message. A lot of his support at this point in time appears to be name recognition support, and there are other people with biographies that can be very appealing to the public," asserted poll director, John Zogby, whose firm conducted the survey with the Reuters news organization.

"The advantage of George W. is he represents a fresh face in a new generation of leadership, but with a little bit of reassurance that he has good connections or ties to the last generation of leadership," explained Republican pollster David Hill of Houston, noting that the Texas governor certainly wasn't handicapped by having the same name and a distinct physical resemblance to a former president of the United States whose recent Gallup Poll popularity ratings had shot up to seventy-one percent from the fifty-six percent he received just before leaving the White House.

History has demonstrated, however, that American voters almost always recover from periodic lurches toward family dynasties. Former New York governor Nelson Rockefeller was an unsuccessful candidate for the Republican Party's presidential nomination in 1964 and 1968, losing to GOP standard-bearers Barry Goldwater and Richard Nixon, respectively, after delegates began taking more stock of his political views than his famous genes.

In 1980, Senator Edward Kennedy was the favorite of the Democratic Party, which had already given up on a remote and inadequate President Jimmy Carter. For months, the political spin touted Kennedy as his party's popular savior, but when he finally ran, he couldn't articulate why he chose to take on an incumbent Democrat and eventually lost the nomination to Carter. And so, the decade and a half-long pining for a second Kennedy presidency ignominiously died.

There are now signs that many Americans are beginning to ask, "What has George W. Bush done to deserve such early exaltation as the future of the

Republican Party, the political messiah who will hopefully lead his people back into the White House after eight years in the wilderness?"

In 1993, Bush was the managing general partner of the Texas Rangers major league baseball team, living in a state whose governor, Democrat Ann Richards, was enjoying unbelievably high poll numbers and appeared unbeatable for reelection in 1994. Then the son of the former president traded the ballpark for the political arena and went into the family business.

Five years after defeating Richards, the only thing most voters know for certain about Bush is who his parents are. It's way past time that, not only Texans, but the rest of America begins to learn more—a lot more—about the younger Bush, the man who would be a second-generation president.

But the mystery lies not so much in the man himself, but in how the path to power can often be the path of least resistance, as in the case of George W. Bush.

★ 1 ★

The Founding Father

The story of the son is not wholly separable from the story of the father. For John Quincy Adams was, as Samuel Eliot Morrison has described him, 'above all an Adams'; and his heartwarming devotion to his father and the latter's steadfast loyalty to his son regardless of political embarrassment offer a single ray of warmth in that otherwise hard, cold existence.

—John F. Kennedy
Profiles in Courage

Branches

Although George Walker Bush has always felt uncomfortable discussing his prestigious pedigree, his ancestral line can be traced back to the fourteenth century, making him a fourteenth cousin of Queen Elizabeth II and a relative of the entire British royal family. Bush, who considers himself a product of West Texas, prefers to ignore the aristocratic branches on his family tree, but never hesitates to boast about his American heritage in the last two centuries, which includes the fourteenth president of the United States, Franklin Pierce (on his mother Barbara's side of the family); his paternal grandfather, U.S. Senator Prescott Bush; and, of course, his father, George Herbert Walker Bush, America's forty-first president.

Just as his father did before him, George W. graduated from Andover and Yale—Ivy League schools in the East; and journeyed to West Texas in hopes of striking it rich in the oil fields; lost and won political races in the Lone Star State; and eventually ran for the White House.

If George W. Bush himself takes the oath of office as president of the United States on January 20, 2001, the two men would join John Adams and John Quincy Adams as the only father-and-son presidential teams in the history of American politics.

And, like the younger Adams, it can also be faithfully recorded that the story of George W. is not wholly separable from the story of the father.

Tales of the South Pacific

On January 6, 1945, Barbara Pierce, wearing her mother-in-law's long-sleeved white satin dress and veil, married George Herbert Walker Bush, a genuine war hero attired in his Navy midshipman's dress blues, at the First Presbyterian Church in the comfortable upper middle-class New York City suburb of Rye. Although he tried to cover it up with his mother's makeup before the ceremony, "Poppy" Bush, as he is known to close friends and family, was still sporting a gash on his forehead, a slow-healing battle scar leftover from a bombing raid accident four months earlier.

Bush's plane, a Grumman TBF Avenger (which he had named *Barbara*), was hit by Japanese antiaircraft while he was on a World War II mission to destroy a radio transmitter on Chichi Jima, one of the Bonin Islands in the Pacific theater. "Suddenly there was a jolt, as if a massive fist had crunched into the belly of the plane," Bush later wrote in his 1987 campaign autobiography, *Looking Forward.* "Smoke poured into the cockpit, and I could see flames rippling across the crease of the wing, edging towards the fuel tanks. I stayed with the dive, homed in on the target, unloaded our four 500-pound bombs, and pulled away, heading for the sea. Once over water, I leveled off and told Delaney and White [the squadron ordnance officer and radio-gunner, respectively] to bail out, turning the plane starboard to take the slipstream off the door near Delaney's station."

In Bush's account, there was no further mention of White and Delaney until the bomber pilot himself parachuted safely into the South Pacific, inflated his raft, and began looking around for his two crew members. Bush wrote that it was only after he was rescued by the American submarine USS *Finback* that he "learned that neither Jack Delaney nor Ted White had survived. One went down with the plane; the other was seen jumping, but his parachute failed to open."

What *really* occurred over the skies of Chichi Jimi on September 2, 1944 is a matter of lively controversy. In the presidential candidate's 1980 authorized biography, author Nicholas King provided a cursory account of the same wartime incident, but noted that "Bush's own parachute failed to open properly," becoming momentarily fouled on the tail of the plane after he hit the water. Interestingly, King omitted any mention of Bush's injury in bailing out: a gashed forehead he sustained when he struck the tail assembly of the plane.

However, in award-winning historian and biographer Herbert S. Parmet's 1997 book, *George Bush: The Life of a Lone Star Yankee,* which was based on interviews with the former president and access to his personal papers and private diaries, the distinguished author described how Bush "jumped prematurely and pulled the ripcord," his head striking the horizontal stabilizer at the plane's rear and his parachute ripping in the process as it became snagged on the tail.

In direct contradiction, *Flight of the Avenger,* a book commissioned by Bush to glorify his wartime bravery, Joe Hyams wrote that the bomber pilot's "chute opened" after bailing out of the flame-enveloped plane at approximately three thousand feet "and he landed safely in the water."

Hyams' 1991 account was an attempt at damage control by Bush's political handlers after the *New York Post* printed an August 1988 interview with Chester Mierzejewski, the only person who has ever claimed to have witnessed Bush's plane struck by Japanese antiaircraft shells, and to have seen it violently hit the water. Mierzejewski, who was the rear turret gunner in the aircraft flown by Squadron Commander Douglas Melvin and had the most advantageous position for observing the events in question, had raised important questions about the haste with which Bush bailed out, rather than attempting a water landing.* Since Melvin's plane flew directly ahead of Bush's, Mierzejewski had a direct and unobstructed view of what was occurring aft of his own plane. He has repeatedly stated that his aircraft was flying

---

*On June 19, two and a half months before the Chichi Jima mission, Bush's torpedo bomber had lost oil pressure and instead of bailing out, the naval aviator skillfully guided the Avenger to an emergency landing in the ocean. In addition, Bush decided against jettisoning the plane's armament of 2,000 pounds of TNT. "We skidded along until the nose dropped," Bush later recalled. "Then it was like hitting a stone wall. The water cascaded over the entire craft."

approximately 100 feet ahead of Bush's plane during the incident, so close that he could see Bush's face in the cockpit. Incensed by what he considered were false claims of war heroics made by Bush during the 1988 presidential campaign (especially after watching his December 1987 interview with David Frost), the sixty-eight-year-old retired aircraft foreman living in Cheshire, Connecticut, decided to write the Vice President and inform him that his recollections were very different from his own. When he never received a letter in response, Mierzejewski elected to break a forty-four-year silence and tell his story to reporters at the *New York Post.* "That guy is not telling the truth," Mierzejewski said of Bush, denying his publicized account that the Avenger was actually on fire. "I think he could have saved those lives, if they were alive. I don't know that they were, but at least they had a chance if he had attempted a water landing." (The Avenger torpedo bomber had been designed to stay afloat for approximately two minutes, giving the crew an extra margin of time to inflate a raft and paddle away from the plane if it sank.)

When the newspaper's reporters asked former Lieutenant Legare Hole, the executive officer of Bush's squadron, about who might have best observed the final minutes of the plane, Hole replied, "The turret gunner in Melvin's plane would have had a good view. If the plane was on fire, there is a very good chance he would be able to see that. The pilot can't see everything that the gunner can, and he'd miss an awful lot."

Gunner Lawrence Mueller, who flew on the Chichi Jima mission, when asked who would have had the best view, responded: "The turret gunner of Melvin's plane." Mueller had also kept a logbook of his own in which he made notations as the squadron was debriefed in the USS *San Jacinto*'s ready room after each mission. Mueller told the *Post* that "no parachute was sighted except for Bush's when the plane went down" and that no one in the ship's ready room during the debriefing had mentioned a fire aboard Bush's Avenger. Mueller claimed, "I would have put it in my logbook if I had heard it."

Mierzejewski stated that he witnessed "a puff of smoke" emerge from the plane and then quickly dissipate. The decorated WW II veteran asserted that no more smoke was visible, that Bush's Avenger "was never on fire" and that "no smoke came out of his cockpit when he opened his canopy to bail out." Only one man exited the *Barbara,* and that was the pilot himself, Mierzejewski alleged. "I was hoping I would see some other parachutes. I never did. I saw the plane go down. I knew the guys were still in it. It was a hopeless feeling."

Airman Thomas R. Kenne, a pilot from another carrier, who had been picked up by the *Finback* a few days after Bush, was also quoted as being surprised to hear about an alleged fire onboard the future president's Avenger. "Did he say that?"

The "incident was a source of real grief" to Bush, according to former Congressman Thomas W.L. (Lud) Ashley, a close friend and confidant. After being rescued at sea, Bush penned a letter to his parents, in which he confessed " . . . and yet now I feel so terribly responsible for their fate. . . . Last night I rolled and tossed. I kept reliving the whole experience. My heart aches for the families of those two boys with me."

In an attempt at catharsis, Bush later wrote letters to the relatives of the two crewmen who had perished in the aircraft's crash. He received a reply from Delaney's sister, which read in part: "You mention in your letter that you would like to help me in some way. There is a way, and that is to stop thinking you are in any way responsible for your plane accident and what has happened to your men. I might have thought you were if my brother Jack had not always spoken of you as the best pilot in the squadron."

Evidently the U.S. Navy agreed and awarded Bush the Distinguished Flying Cross for completing the bombing mission against the Chichi Jima radio transmission tower.

Bush's return date to stateside was repeatedly delayed due to the ongoing war with the Japanese, thus forcing his bride-to-be, Barbara Pierce, to reschedule their planned wedding date from December 17, 1944 to January 6, 1945, nineteen days later. Bush's older brother Prescott, who had himself married just a week earlier on New Year's Eve in Miami Beach, interrupted his honeymoon to be best man. Most of the ushers were "whoever was around" because so many of Bush's friends were fighting in the Pacific or Europe.

The young couple's honeymoon on Sea Island, Georgia was cut short because Bush was in line for special combat training that would prepare him to take part in the final Allied assault on Japan scheduled for later in the year. For the next eight months, while Bush's new torpedo plane squadron, VT-153, was formed and trained, the newlyweds were relocated to military bases in Florida, Michigan, Maine, and Virginia.

On August 14, 1945, they were living in Virginia Beach while Bush was stationed at the Oceana Naval Air Station, when President Truman announced on the radio the unconditional surrender of Japan. While America collectively celebrated in the streets, Barbara was particularly grateful that her new husband would not be forced to "ship out" for the anticipated final attack on Japan. For several "eye-opening" months filled with uncertainty and fear, she had constantly prayed that God would end the war before she lost her husband. After joining other young couples cheering in the streets of Virginia Beach, the Bushes went to a nearby church to give thanks.

Baby Makes Three

A month after the war ended, the twice-decorated Bush was discharged from active military duty and the young couple wasted no time moving to New Haven, Connecticut, where he enrolled at Yale University (alma mater of his father and other relatives) under a special program for veterans that enabled them to graduate in two and a half years. Five thousand of the eight thousand newcomers to the Ivy League school that year—Yale's largest freshman class ever—were returning servicemen whose tuition was paid for with government benefits designated by the GI Bill for veterans.

The Bushes took up residence in a small apartment on Chapel Street, the first of three places they would live in in the Yale community. A veteran of numerous wartime relocations, Barbara would not have minded the packing and unpacking had she not been pregnant at the time. Complicating matters was the fact that the landlord "liked dogs, but not babies," so they moved to an apartment on Edwards Street, where their first child, George Walker Bush, entered this world on July 6, 1946, the first year of the Baby Boom.

"The baby did not come and did not come," Barbara Bush recalled years later in her memoir. "George's mother finally gave me a good dose of castor oil and the baby came all right—I'm tempted to say covered with glory."

The young family of three quickly outgrew the less-than-spacious apartment on Edwards Street. A few months after their son's birth, they moved into their third and final New Haven residence, a former single-family dwelling at 37 Hillhouse Avenue, next door to the one inhabited by the president of the university. The Bushes' new home had been subdivided into thirteen separate apartments, which were used as housing for nine married students with eleven children. The Bushes shared the first floor with two other couples and their families, but they considered themselves fortunate to have three small rooms and their very own bathroom.

It was difficult for Bush to study in an environment of communal living, but by the time of his graduation in 1948, he had been elected to the Phi Beta Kappa fraternity (an honor traditionally associated with academic achievement*), captained the Yale baseball team, played on the school soccer and basketball teams, was a member of the Torch Honor Society and the secretive Skull and Bones Society, and succeeded in winning the Gordon Brown Prize for "all around student leadership."

Although he interviewed with several companies, Bush told Barbara that he had "decided he did not want to work with intangibles; he wanted a product he could see and feel," which she interpreted to mean that he didn't want to work in the investment banking business like his father, Prescott, or maternal grandfather, George Herbert Walker, the forces behind Wall Street's Brown Brothers Harriman, the largest private banking house in America at the time.

After reading *The Farm* by Louis Bromfield, Bush considered moving his family to the Midwest and pursuing a career in farming, but the investment costs proved to be prohibitive. "If I really believed there was a solid business prospect to discuss, I wouldn't have hesitated to go to Dad," Bush wrote in his campaign autobiography. "No matter how we looked at it though, George and Barbara Farms came off as a high-risk, no-yield investment. . . . We were young, still in our early twenties, and we wanted to make our way, our own mistakes, and shape our own future." For one of Prescott Bush's sons, though, not following in their intimidating father's footsteps certainly didn't mean breaking away.

The tall, dignified, stern, and commanding elder Bush was a "terrifying challenge" to his children, especially his sons. This was a regal and imperious man who expected them to be properly attired with jackets and ties at the dinner table. Grandson, George W., remembered that in Prescott's home, "one always wore a coat and tie to dinner." He was, wrote one journalist, "a leviathan of a father, whom George could never get out from under," especially when he decided on a career choice after college.

Most published profiles of Bush have usually chronicled this phase of his life as that of a fiercely independent young man who could have gone straight to the top in Wall Street by trading on Prescott's name and his family's powerful associations, but who chose instead to strike out for the new

*According to former Congressman Thomas W.L. (Lud) Ashley, a fellow Yale graduate and one of Bush's closest friends, the future president was "not among Yale's young activists or its intellectuals," nor was he "terribly well-informed." The Phi Beta Kappa achievement reportedly surprised many of Bush's friends and former teachers. Although much is known about his social status at the university, his academic records have been sealed by the FBI, ostensibly because the federal investigative agency requires such documents to conduct background checks of important office holders.

frontier among the wildcatters, roustabouts, and roughnecks of the West Texas oil fields and become a self-made man free of his father's influence. As Bush himself recounted in a 1983 interview, "If I were a psychoanalyzer, I might conclude that I was trying to not compete with my father, but do something on my own."

Prescott, however, procured his son's first post-graduation job in the oil boomtown of Odessa, Texas, where the young Bush would be employed as an equipment clerk with the International Derrick and Equipment Company (Ideco), a subsidiary of Dresser Industries, a leading manufacturer of drill bits and related oil well equipment.

Dresser's significance to the Bush family began in 1928, when its directors decided that further expansion of the family enterprise required the company to raise new capital by issuing public stock. Prescott's investment house paid four million dollars for its corporate stock and sold securities against the company. Then, as the elder Bush later recalled, the banking firm refinanced Dresser in 1929 "so that we retained a substantial measure of control."

After the oil well equipment company was reorganized, Prescott became a member of the board of directors and, along with E. Roland ("Bunny") Harriman,* subsequently recommended that H. Neil Mallon, a fellow Yale graduate with close family ties to the Tafts of Ohio, became Dresser Industries' president and chairman of the board.

"I had heard stories about 'Uncle Neil' almost from the moment I met George," Barbara Bush later wrote in her memoir. "He and Prescott Bush were certainly about as different as two men could be. . . . Yet, both men were very successful in their own fields and were the best of friends. Every family should have an 'Uncle Neil.' "

With Mallon at the helm of Dresser, the company—with its chain of sixteen equipment stores that catered to the needs of the energy and natural resources industries—was well on its way in 1948 to becoming the leading manufacturer of portable rigs in a postwar country dependent on petrochemicals for the growing defense industry. When Mallon offered the equipment clerk job to young Bush, he immediately accepted, a move he later

*Bunny Harriman's older brother, Averell Harriman, another Yale graduate, would later become a prominent political figure on the world stage as an ambassador to the U.S.S.R. and Great Britain, a cabinet officer, governor of New York, two time unsuccessful presidential candidate, and U.S. representative at the Vietnam peace talks in Paris.

acknowledged as "being caught up in the romance and adventure of searching for black gold."

BOOMTOWN

Barbara Bush was initially apprehensive about moving with her baby son (whom she affectionately called "Georgie") to the tumbleweeds, sandstorms, blistering summer heat, and bone-chillingly bleak winters commonly associated with the West Texas cross-country prairie. "I didn't want to go at the time," she later acknowledged, noting that their flight from the East Coast took twelve hours. "But a day after I got there, I thought it was really exciting."

Her husband's first job with Dresser Industries was in Odessa, a blue-collar town located in the geographical formation known as the Permian Basin, the scene of an oil boom that developed in the years after World War II. Odessa in 1948 was populated mostly by oilfield laborers involved in working the drilling equipment, the derricks, and slow, repetitive pumping jacks that dotted the nearby countryside.

The Bushes lived in the rough and tumble prairie town for only a few months (sharing a house with a mother-daughter prostitution team). While the elder Bush worked long days sweeping out oil equipment warehouses and painting pump jacks while his wife looked after their boy in a house frequently occupied by the prostitutes' male clientele. Neil Mallon wanted his young protégé to learn the oil equipment business from "the bottom up" and briefly transferred him in 1949 to various towns in California where Dresser Industries had subsidiaries. Bush later claimed that he drove a thousand miles a week through the Carrizo Plains and the Cuyama Valley as a drilling-bit salesman.

In less than a year, he moved Barbara and Georgie from Huntington Park to Bakersfield to Whittier, Ventura, and Compton, where Barbara gave birth to their second child in December 1949. The blond-haired, blue-eyed Pauline Robinson Bush, whom they called Robin, was named after Barbara's mother, the victim of a fatal automobile accident just two months earlier.

Shortly after Robin's birth, Dresser Industries transferred Bush and his young family back to West Texas, but this time to the more white-collar town of Midland, twenty miles to the northwest of Odessa, where he worked for the Ideco subsidiary as a city salesman, calling on oil companies mostly headquartered in the town. "California was fine," Bush wrote years later in his autobiography, "but the oil boom was on in Texas. And Midland, the heart of the Permian Basin, had come into its own as the biggest boomtown of them all."*

In 1880, the Texas Pacific Railroad began to lay tracks westward from Fort Worth at about the same time that the Southern Pacific began building east from El Paso. The place where the tracks met became known as Midway, which was later changed to Midland after it was learned that there was another Texas town by the same name. Prior to World War I, Midland was a prosperous railroad town serving the surrounding ranching community. But on May 27, 1923, the future of Midland would drastically change with the discovery of oil beneath the surface of the dry, barren land. At 6 A.M., just eighty miles southeast of Midland, the Santa Rita No. 1, the "rankest of wildcats," blew. As oil action moved west during the ensuing decades, so did the headquarters of major oil companies.

"Oil proved to be a prodigious economic multiplier of Texas," wrote local historian D. W. Meinig, as the black gold became the magnetic pull for more money in the state, especially the Permian Basin area, and created a wealthy new class that formed "a distinctive kind of community, related in people, economy, and society more to others of its type than to older towns of its region untouched by oil."

Bush himself later wrote that Midland, with its new skyline of banks and other buildings rising from the plains, could be called "Yuppieland West." Nouveau millionaires were building mansions on newly-paved streets named after prestigious Ivy League universities such as Harvard, Princeton, and Yale. They drank late-afternoon martinis and spent evenings at the Petroleum Club. Many of these entrepreneurs had access to patrician fortunes back East for the venture capital they mobilized behind their various oil deals. Native Midlanders referred to this clique as "the Yalies."

"As the grunts of the oil business flocked to Odessa to work and service the fields, the majors and colonels and generals came to Midland," wrote H.G. Bissinger in his book about West Texas culture, *Friday Night Lights.* "They were men with the hearts of pioneers and teeth sharpened by years spent dutifully at the knees of their good daddy capitalists back east."

When they first arrived in town, the Bushes rented a motel room on Main Street in a place called, ironically, George's Court. They stayed there until

---

*Even at the beginning of the new millennium, only one state—Alaska—has produced more oil and gas than the Permian Basin alone.

they bought into the first mass housing development to be built in the West Texas town, using a $7,500 FHA loan to purchase an 847-square-foot house, which was identical to all the other tract homes in the neighborhood, except for the color. To compensate for the analogous floor plans, the developer had painted each one a different vivid color. The area eventually became known as Easter Egg Row. The Bushes' house was blue.

The Bushes easily settled into the new house, living very much the lifestyle of their contemporaries: taking turns having backyard cookouts and barbecues, watching each other's children, and playing touch football and softball games after services at First Presbyterian Church, where George and his wife taught Sunday school.

"We were all in the same situation," Barbara recalled later. "No one had any family. We were all newcomers and we came from all over the country. We formed really good friendships."

Martin Allday, a Midland attorney, remembered the days when he was dating his future wife, who happened to live near the Bushes on Easter Egg Row. One day, he said, "I went over to pick her up and Bush and Barbara and the kids came walking across the street barefooted, and sat down in the backyard to have a beer with my father-in-law."

This was the insular, Ozzie-and-Harriet world young George W. (who was now called "Junior" for the sake of convenience, even though that was not strictly accurate) grew up in during the Midland of the fifties. All the women spent their days tending young children, taxiing them to the doctor, dentist, birthday parties, baseball games, and so on, while their dauntless husbands worked long hours in one of the many oil-related businesses. The Bush family was no exception.

"I just feel a special relationship with my mother," George W. said of Barbara, who "fostered, nurtured and brought me up" while his father typically spent twelve-hour days selling drilling bits to oil companies in the area. "She was the front line of discipline. She was the sarge. . . . George Bush was more the goals and ideals setter, the ultimate enforcer. But Mother was the immediate enforcer."

Barbara made light of her role as the family disciplinarian years later at the 1988 Republican convention: "I remember I called George one day . . . and I said, 'I'm desperate—I don't know what to do. Your son's in trouble again. He just hit a ball through the neighbor's upstairs window.' And George said, 'My Gosh, what a great hit!' And then he said, 'Did you get the ball back?' "

Midland neighbors remember the hyperactive, precocious boy they called "Bushtail" as "just another pesky little kid" riding his bike around town, playing baseball, rooting for the Midland Bulldogs football team on Friday nights, watching Buck Rogers serials and cowboy movies at the Ritz theater on Saturday afternoons, and leading his gang of friends on "wild adventures."

"We'd crawl underneath the high school stadium and get up on the cross bars," recalled Bill Sallee. "We used to swing up there like a couple of monkeys. If anybody had ever slipped, they'd have killed themselves. Hell, you were a story and a half up. There were light poles that go around the stadium. We climbed all over those things, too."

"We were always playing—after school, during recess," said another of George W.'s childhood friends, Mike Proctor. "We'd head for the appropriate ball field . . . pick teams and play," adding that the future presidential candidate would always "jump out there to be captain."

"The Sky's the Limit"

In late 1950, Bush decided to leave Dresser Industries and go into business with his Easter Egg Row neighbor, John Overbey. "The people from the East and the people from Texas or Oklahoma all seemed to have two things in common," Overbey recalled. "They all had a chance to be stockbrokers or investment bankers. And they all wanted to learn the oil business instead."

Overbey made his living in the Permian Basin as a petroleum industry landman, an independent operator who attempted to identify properties where oil might be discovered, occasionally on the basis of leaked geological information, and sometimes after observing that one of the major oil companies was drilling in the same locale. The landman would scout the property, and then attempt to get the owner of the land to sign away the mineral rights in the form of a lease. Given the cost of drilling holes in the West Texas prairie only to find them dry, good money could be made by trading leases. Over cold martinis in his backyard, Bush offered to raise capital back East if Overbey would join him in a partnership.

The two men flew to New York to meet with Bush's maternal uncle, George Herbert Walker, Jr., in the oak-paneled boardroom of G.H. Walker & Company on Wall Street. Overbey later said that he still remembered "the dizzying whirl of a money-raising trip to the East with George and Uncle Herbie: lunch at New York's 21 Club, weekends at Kennebunkport where a bracing

Sunday dip in the Atlantic off Walker's Point ended with a servant wrapping you in a large terry towel and handing you a martini."

The result of the odyssey back East was a capital investment of $350,000 (including $50,000 from Eugene Meyer, publisher of the *Washington Post*) and the formation of the Bush-Overby Oil Development Company, Inc. More important than the money, however, was the advice of Dresser's president, Neil Mallon, who mapped out a blueprint, a sort of "crash course not only in how to structure but how to finance an independent oil company."

The Bush-Overbey company "rocked along and made a few good deals and a few bad ones." By 1953, the two partners merged with oil industry attorneys, J. Hugh Liedtke and William C. Liedtke, sons of the Chief Counsel for Gulf Oil, who saw there was more money to be made in large-scale drilling and production of oil than writing legal briefs and sitting in courthouses.

The name chosen for the new company was Zapata Petroleum Corporation, drawn from *Viva, Zapata!*, the Marlon Brando film about the Mexican revolutionary, which was showing at the time at the downtown Midland theater. The entrepreneurs later said part of the appeal of the name was the confusion as to whether Zapata, a rebel leader who fought for land reform in the early 1900s, had been a patriot or a bandit. "We couldn't afford a public-relations counsel," Bush acknowledged, "but if we had one he would have told us that was exactly the corporate image we were looking for."

Although one Midland observer complained to *Los Angeles Times* reporter Barry Bearak that "independent oilman" Bush "would've been just another carpetbagger if he hadn't rode [*sic*] in on a silk carpet," Johnny Hackney, who ran Johnny's Barbecue in Midland, had a different recollection of Bush and other well-heeled graduates of prestigious Eastern colleges who were attracted to the Permian Basin and the opportunities it afforded: "We had a bunch of Ivy Leaguers come to town then," Hackney said. "They were all hard-working, aggressive, ambitious. Those Yankee boys were something else. I remember George Bush when he worked on the big oil rigs, worked in the warehouses, when he used to come in here dirty and sweaty."

George W., who has always become visibly agitated by complaints that his father made his fortune trading on the Bush family name and its Eastern establishment connections, once remarked, "My dad didn't know anything about the oil business" when he came to Texas in the late forties, but lack of knowledge didn't hinder him. "He understood how to start from a modest position and work hard to get something. The slogan when I was out there [in Midland] was, 'The sky's the limit.' That meant for everybody, not just a few."

His Father's Eyes, His Mother's Mouth

During those years, Bush was away from Barbara, young Junior, and Robin much of the time, either working in the oil patch with his partners or traveling the state securing more deals. Hugh Liedtke, who eventually became head of Pennzoil, recalled the Midland period as "hard on the girls" because of their husbands' lengthy absences away from home. "We would sit up on an oil well all night, stay out in the field several days," Liedtke said. "Then we would come home, covered with grease."

Somehow, the Bushes found time to move from Easter Egg Row to a slightly bigger house, and in February of 1953, had another child, John Ellis Bush, whom they called Jeb. The family was expanding like most others in Midland during that era.

"We finally decided it was the water," said Marion Chambers, one of the Bushes' best friends. When she told Barbara that her fifth child was on the way, she confessed that she initially believed she had a tumor, "but that the doctor said 'the tumor has arms and leg.' Bar started crying. I said, 'I'm the one who should be crying.' "

Although there were times when Barbara resented "sitting at home with these absolutely brilliant children, who say one thing a week of interest," she firmly believed that mothers needed to be nearby during the early, formative years of their children's lives. She nursed young Jeb, played with Robin, and sat behind backstops at dusty Little League ballparks, scorebook in her lap, charting games of Junior, whose boyhood dream was to be the "next Willie Mays," although he joked later that he "couldn't hit a curve ball."

Although the elder Bush, like most fathers in Midland, was frequently absent from home, he spent what little spare time he had on the weekends coaching Junior's Little League team, the Cubs. The former Yale baseball captain was revered by the neighborhood boys for his athletic skills.

"If he was standing in the outfield when someone hit a ball, he could put his glove behind him at belt level, drop his head forward, and catch the ball behind his back," remembered Joe Neill, George W.'s oldest Midland friend. "We'd try to do it, too, but the ball would always hit us on the back of the head. We all had scabs on our heads from trying to catch the fly balls like Mr. Bush did."

George W., seizing on his father's passion at early age, used baseball as a way to prove himself to his father. Years later, he would admit that one of his proudest moments was when the senior Bush no longer needed to hold back on his throws.

While his father spoke East Coast English, Junior grew up amid the dry "yeps," "nopes," and "bidness pardners" of West Texanese. And in personality, he was certainly more his mother's than his father's son. "We're pretty much alike, people tell us," George W. now readily admits. "I don't mind a battle. She doesn't mind a battle. I've got my father's eyes and my mother's mouth." In her memoirs, Barbara called Junior "the son who pulls no punches and tells it like he thinks it is."

As a child in Midland, Junior was the smart-alecky and hot-tempered one of the Bush clan. He was a curious and incorrigible youth, who was a bit of a bully, according to Bucky Bush, a frequent babysitter. On more than one occasion, Barbara was called to Sam Houston Elementary School by the principal after Junior was punished for fighting or disrupting classes. She recalled another incident when the "class clown" was sent from music class to the principal's office for disciplinary measures for painting a false mustache on his face as a prank, but was spanked with a board after he "swaggered in as though he had been the most wonderful thing in the world."

But no measure of bravado would prepare the little boy for the heartache to come in the spring of 1953.

A DEATH IN THE FAMILY

One morning, three-year-old Robin woke up pale and lethargic and told her mother she couldn't decide what to do that day. "I may go out and sit in the grass and watch the cars go by or maybe I'll just lie in bed."

After taking the listless girl to the children's pediatrician, Dr. Dorothy Wyvell, for an examination and blood tests, the Bushes returned later in the afternoon for the results. The doctor, who was also a family friend, met them at the door with teary eyes.

"I'll never forget it," Bush said. "We walked in and the first thing, she pulled a Kleenex out of the box and just kind of wiped her eye. Then she said, 'I've got some bad news for you.' " Dr. Wyvell explained that their young daughter was suffering from an advanced case of leukemia—her white blood cell count was the highest she'd ever see—and would not live much longer.

"Then she gave us the best advice anyone could have given, which of course we didn't take," Barbara remembered. "She said, 'Number one, don't tell anyone. Number two, don't treat her. You should take her home, make life as easy as possible for her, and in three weeks' time, she'll be gone.' "

By that evening, the Bushes told everyone in the neighborhood, and were immediately comforted by their surrogate family in Midland. They also refused to accept the pediatrician's prognosis that Robin's cancer was incurable. The next morning they flew their little girl to New York, where Bush's uncle, Dr. John Walker, a former cancer specialist who was president of Sloan-Kettering Memorial Hospital, urged them to treat her in an attempt to extend her life, just in case of a breakthrough in medical research. She was immediately prescribed a newly developed cancer drug, which seemed to work, but not fully.

For the next seven months, Robin was in and out of the hospital. When she was in remission, they spent the time in Midland. The Bushes also decided not to tell Junior that his sister was dying. "We hated that, but we felt it would have been too big a burden for such a little fellow," Barbara recalled in her memoir. "On the other hand, there could be no more roughhousing since leukemia patients easily hemorrhage, so we had to keep a close watch on them when they were together."

Junior grew suspicious, though, when his parents' friends would come over to the house but wouldn't let their children get near his sister. Years later, he would learn that many people thought the little-known disease was contagious and others simply couldn't cope with a dying child.

Robin was a brave little girl, repeatedly undergoing agonizing bone marrow transplants and painful blood transfusions. "I remember her very clearly because she was one of those adorable children you can't forget," said Dr. Charlotte Tan, a pediatrician and one of the physicians who treated her at the hospital. "She always was a mature child. It takes a really big girl to tolerate an oxygen tent and all that when you're three years old."

Barbara never left her child's bedside while she was hospitalized in New York, forcing her husband to play the dual role of both parents to seven-year-old Junior and his infant brother, Jeb. He couldn't be away from the newly formed Zapata Petroleum company all the time, but he flew back and forth between Midland and the East Coast on the weekends, leaving the boys with neighbors until his mother sent a nurse to Texas to help. The immediate burden of caring for the dying little girl fell to Barbara, whose hair began to turn gray at the age of twenty-eight.

Eventually the medicine that was used to treat Robin's leukemia created life-threatening side effects. In October, while the elder Bush was rushing back to New York, his frail daughter, whose skin seemed almost transparent, began to hemorrhage. The Sloan-Kettering doctors decided to operate with Barbara's permission, but Robin didn't survive the surgery. With both of her parents standing at her side, Robin passed quietly away.

After a memorial service in Greenwich, Connecticut (the Bushes donated her body to research), the bereaved couple rushed back to Midland. They didn't want Junior to hear about his sister's death from anyone else. As they drove up the gravel driveway to the front of the elementary school, the boy spotted their familiar green Oldsmobile and ran quickly inside to ask his teacher, "My mom, dad, and sister are home. Can I go see them?"

"I remember looking in the car and thinking I saw Robin in the back," Bush said many years later. "I thought I saw her, but she wasn't there."

Barbara confessed later that she and her husband "felt devastated by what we had to tell him." Typically inquisitive, he initially asked several questions, but then began beating the car seat and crying uncontrollably when he realized they had hidden the truth from him about Robin's terminal illness for the past several months. When they returned home, Junior ran into his room, slammed the door shut, and destroyed half of his beloved baseball card collection before his mother stopped him.

"It was really hard for a little guy to comprehend," George W. admitted in an interview years later, stating that he knew Robin was sick but never dreamed she was dying.

"Why didn't you tell me? Junior repeatedly asked his parents, to which his mother would reply, "Well, it wouldn't have made a difference." Decades later, however, George W.'s mother, who still has trouble discussing her daughter's death, questions the decision not to tell her son that Robin was terminally ill. "I don't know if that was right or wrong," she has confessed. "I mean, I really don't."

Although the elder Bush cried quite often during that difficult time period, Barbara never wept, but after her daughter died, she surrendered to her pent-up sorrow. In a speech at the Republican Convention in 1988, Barbara told the 2,300 delegates how her husband became the rock of their family. "He held me in his arms, and he made me share it and accept that his sorrow was as great as my own," she said. "He simply wouldn't allow my grief to divide us . . . push us apart, which is what happens so often where there is a loss like that. And for as long as I live, I will respect and appreciate my husband for the strength of his understanding."

The other George in her life also refused to let her retreat into her grief, although he did so unknowingly at times. After Robin's death, Barbara became overly protective of her two sons, seldom letting them out of her sight. Then one afternoon she overhead Junior tell one of his boyhood buddies, "I can't play today because I have to be with my mother—she's so unhappy."

"That started my cure," she later wrote in her memoirs. "I realized I was too much of a burden for a little seven-year-old boy to carry."

Although he was only seven at the time, Junior was grieving, too, feeling cheated by his little sister's premature death. One time he asked his father if they had buried Robin lying down or standing up. Bush replied that he wasn't sure and asked why he wanted to know. Junior stated he had just learned in school that the earth rotated, and he wanted to know if she spent part of her time standing on her head.

On another occasion, he was attending a football game with his father when he suddenly commented that he wished he were Robin. When asked why, Junior answered, "Well, she has a better seat than we do! I bet she can see the game better from up there than we can here."

Junior also was plagued by nightmares about his sister's death. Once, while his friend Randall Roden was spending the night, Bush had a bad dream and his mother rushed in to comfort him. "It was one of the most realistic experiences I have ever had about death," Roden said in 1999, "and I am certain it had a profound effect on him because it had a profound effect on me."

Years later, when he was running for reelection as governor of Texas, George W.'s parents acknowledged that their eldest son's "back-slapping, wisecracking, occasionally teasing style" was developed as a child of seven, when his sister died, and he felt it was his responsibility to try and lift his parents out of their grief.

The loss of Robin had left a seven-year gap between their firstborn, Junior, and his brother, Jeb. Fifteen months after Robin's death, the Bushes had another child, Neil Mallon Bush, named in honor of the family friend who had brought the senior Bush to Texas in 1948. Marvin Pierce Bush, named for Barbara's father, was born in 1956.

"We need a girl," Bush wrote to his mother. "We had one once—she'd fight and cry and play and make her way just like the rest. But there was about her a certain softness. . . . Her peace made me feel strong, and so very important."

In 1957, the Bushes were still grieving, according to Otha Taylor, the family's twenty-four-year-old part-time babysitter, awakening "night after night in great physical pain." Every time the subject of Robin's death was broached, Barbara would say, "What I'm going to do . . . I'm going to keep trying until I get another girl."

Finally, in 1959, Barbara gave birth to their sixth and last child, Dorothy Walker Bush, named for her mother-in-law, but she grew up answering to "Dordie" and later "Doro." "Dorothy is enchanting," Bush wrote to his fellow Yale classmate and future U.S. congressman, Lud Ashley. "She is a wild dark version of Robin. They look so much alike that Mom and Dad both called Dorothy 'Robin' all last week when Bar went to visit . . . "

While the rest of the family was obviously quite taken with the newest addition to the Bush family, Junior was distant and, according to friends and family members, deeply resentful of the baby girl that seemed to have taken his dead sister's place. "I'm ashamed to admit it, but I actually hated Doro the first month or two after she was born," George W. later acknowledged. "No one in the family mentioned Robin's name any more and it seemed to me at the time that everyone was fawning over Doro like she was the second coming of the Almighty. You have to remember I was young back then and confused in my feelings and emotions, but I don't think anyone, including my mother, knew that a little of me died with Robin and seeing this new baby sister only served as a daily reminder for a while of my own personal loss."

THE ROCK OF GIBRALTAR

The Bush-Liedtke partnership of Zapata Petroleum concentrated its corporate attention on an oil property in Coke County, Texas called Jameson field, a "patch of sandy prairie" and sagebrush (even by West Texas definition) where six widely dispersed wells had been producing black gold for several years. Hugh Liedtke (called by one writer the "boy genius of West Texas oil") was convinced that the half a dozen wells were tapping into a single underground pool of oil, and that perhaps hundreds of new oil wells drilled into the same field would all prove to be gushers.

Acting where other investors hesitated, Zapata Petroleum drilled 130 wells without encountering a single dry hole. With an average daily production yield of 1,250 barrels, the price of a share of stock in the company rose from seven cents a share to twenty-three dollars, and the partners each became millionaires through the increased value of their stock in the company.

Although he wasn't superwealthy as defined by Texas oil standards, Bush had clearly provided for his family's financial securities in the late fifties. The family moved again, this time to an upscale subdivision, near McCall Park, where Junior often played Little League baseball and soccer. The Bushes also built the first residential swimming pool in Midland; traveled extensively throughout the U.S.; and, at Junior's encouragement, initiated a family tradition of going to Camp Longhorn in the Texas Hill Country for the entire month of July every summer. The Bush family was living the American dream.

Barbara devoted all her energies to her husband, her children, and her household. She was the traditional, supportive mother, who "always went the extra mile," her husband said, "every inning of their Little League game or every tear to be wiped away." In addition to providing the sympathetic hugs and words of encouragement, she also imposed the day-to-day discipline.

"Dad was the chief executive officer, but Mother was the chief operating officer," Jeb said, noting that "she let us know when we crossed the line, and the line never shifted." His older brother, Junior, agreed: "My mother's always been a very outspoken person who vents very well—she'll just let it rip if she's got something on her mind. Once it's over, you know exactly where you stand and that's it. She doesn't dwell on it or hound you or anything like that."

"I don't think George W. would ever be sassy or sarcastic with his father and if he was, it would certainly be within the foul lines," said cousin John Ellis, noting that Junior's blunt outspokenness and irreverence was inherited from his mother. "Bar will say to George W. something like, 'Oh, don't be ridiculous,' and they're off to the races."

In her 1985 speech at American University's Distinguished Lecture series conducted by Jihan el Sadat, the widow of slain Egyptian president Anwar Sadat, Barbara warmly described her early life in Texas, although her remarks seemed at times to be tinged with feelings of resentment:

"This was a period, for me, of long days and short years; of diapers, running noses, earaches, more Little League games than you could believe possible, tonsils, and those unscheduled races to the hospital emergency room, Sunday School and church, of hours of urging homework, short chubby arms around your neck and sticky kisses; and experiencing bumpy moments—not many, but a few—of feeling that I'd never, ever be able to have fun again; and coping with the feeling that George Bush, in his excitement of starting a small company and traveling around the world, was having a lot of fun."

In a sense, the Bushes were a matriarchal family. As an independent oilman venturing into offshore exploration, Bush traveled much more extensively than he did when he was a salaried salesman for Dresser Industries. As the oldest son and now a teenager at San Jacinto Junior High School in Midland (where he ran for class president of the seventh grade and won), Junior voluntarily accepted the role of his "mother's best friend" and surrogate father to his much younger siblings.

When he came home from school or baseball practice in the afternoon, he helped her clean the house, played catch with Jeb in the backyard, taught Marvin how to swim, and even changed his baby sister's diapers. It was also Junior who first noticed that Neil, the middle child in the family, had severe reading problems, which he was able to cover up until second grade. A battery of tests later revealed that Neil suffered from dyslexia, a neurological disorder that hinders the learning of literacy skills.

"Dyslexia, back in those days, was not well known," George W. later said. "Mother worked hard with Neil, disciplining, training, encouraging. She was the one who really spent the time making sure that Neil could learn to read the basics."

"I look back on those years in West Texas," Barbara recalled, "and I wonder how I would have ever made it without my oldest son. There was never any groaning or moaning on his part [although he did call her the 'Gray Fox' under his breath when she angered him]. I probably put more responsibility on him than I should have, especially for a boy his age," she confessed. "But whom else could I turn to, with his father gone so much in those days? He was my Rock of Gibraltar. Plain and simple, and because of that, we have a very special relationship."

★ 2 ★

Young and Irresponsible

When I was young and irresponsible,
I behaved young and irresponsible.

—George W. Bush

"The End Depends on the Beginning"

The elder George Bush and his partners had been very lucky with the Jameson field discovery of oil, but they could hardly expect a repeat performance. It wasn't the way the game was played. "You could only roll sevens for so long, and then it was time for the return of snake eyes," George W. later said when he followed in his father's footsteps and went into the oil business in West Texas.

During the mid-fifties, Bush and the Liedtke brothers concluded that the era in which large oil fields could be discovered within the continental United States were over. They believed that the new frontier of discovery could be found in offshore areas, located under hundreds of feet of water on the continental shelves, or in shallow seas like the Gulf of Mexico.

"We decided that offshore drilling was going to be a growing and major factor in the oil industry," Bush explained. "To get that business you had to take a risk. There were other companies that had built rigs that tipped over or just cratered on the first well, and that was the end of the company." The rigs that Bush and his partners ordered for drilling in coastal waters were a revolutionary tripod design by southern industrialist-engineer, R.G. LeTourenau that weighed about nine million pounds and cost up to six million dollars.

By 1959, however, Hugh Liedtke had grown impatient with the constant meddling of Bush's Uncle Herbie, who honestly believed he was running the oil company from his Wall Street office. In addition, the domineering and abrasive Liedtke wanted to compete with the majors by heading his own company. During the course of the year, Zapata Petroleum Company "amicably" split, producing a series of complex stock swaps, with Bush taking control of Zapata Off-Shore along with his Uncle Herbie.*

Bush was now the president of his own company, but there was only one problem: Midland was nowhere near the coast of Texas. He would have to move the corporate base to Houston, only an hour's drive from the Gulf of Mexico.

After a decade in West Texas, Bush fulfilled his dreams of becoming a self-made man. "He was the first of our group along with Hugh Liedtke, to make a million, and in that day a million was a bundle," recalled Earle Craig, a Midland friend of the family.

"I'll never forget the day we moved," Junior later said. "I was shocked. I was a small town boy moving to the big city. I learned to adjust, but it was hard. I had enough adventure in me, though, to also be excited about the move."

The Bushes built a "fancy" new, two-story brick home on an oversized lot in an exclusive suburb of Houston that was large enough to accommodate three houses. They had a swimming pool, a small baseball field, and plenty of trees for the children to climb. Two years later, though, Junior's parents—

---

*John Overbey, Bush's original partner, had stepped aside earlier when the direction of the company moved toward the risky business of offshore drilling.

who required him to learn twenty-five new words each Saturday before he could play baseball—demanded more out of his education than he was getting at the prestigious, private Kinkaid School (where he was elected a class officer) and packed the fifteen-year-old off to the strict all-male boarding school at Phillips Academy in Andover, Massachusetts, his grandfather and father's alma mater. Bush entered the New England school as a sophomore or "lower middler" in the institution's vernacular.

Andover, located on fifty acres twenty miles north of Boston, was one of the most exclusive preparatory schools in the country and was essentially a mirror image of Yale University. Still a conditioning field for "Americas' finest," its named derived from the founding Phillips brothers and dated back to 1778. The school's motto, *Non Sibi,* "Not for Self," and the reminder, *Finis Origine Pendet,* "The End Depends on the Beginning," was appropriate for such families as the Bushes, who committed their money, their sons and grandsons, and their own political ambitions for generations to come.

Andover, which emphasized Christian teachings and modeled itself on British "public schools," was more like a military academy and "tended to graduate homogeneous boys with no more originality than the products of a cookie cutter," with a "good attitude more valued than creativity."

As a product of West Texas, Junior initially underwent severe culture shock at Andover and quickly found himself at the bottom of the class. "In Midland, they don't ask, 'What's your pedigree?' They ask, 'Can you hit a baseball?' " Bush later recalled.

The few Texans boarding at America House dormitory (where "America," a patriotic hymn beginning "My country 'tis of thee," was penned by Dr. Samuel Francis Smith in 1832) quickly bonded, attempting to adjust to "cold, dark, faraway" New England and catch up with their better-educated Eastern peers. "We were way behind the curve," remembered Clay Johnson, a fellow Texan who attended Andover, later roomed with the younger Bush at Yale and served as the governor's appointments secretary. "All of a sudden we were at the tail end. There was an article about private schools in *Time* magazine our first or second year. The headmaster of Andover was on the cover, and the point was that Andover was the hardest school in the country."

The school's unofficial motto was "sink or swim" and with a long waiting list of applicants, it was considered a cardinal sin if a boy was just an average student who didn't strive for academic excellence. By his own account, Bush, who scored high grades in history and math but barely passed English, "learned to read and write" over the next three years. The school and its rigors changed his life, he has acknowledged. "I can remember trying to figure out how to catch up. The high standards lifted me up."

For his first English assignment—an essay on an emotional experience—Bush looked up the word "tears" in a thesaurus his mother had given him, hoping to find an impressive synonym. He wrote, "Lacerates ran down my cheeks," prompting his professor to give him "a big fat zero" for his grade and call Junior's paper "disgraceful." Although he would later confide to friends he was terrified of flunking out of Andover and the embarrassment it would cause himself and his family, Bush struggled to remain in school as an average student.

The campus day began when Andover boys, in mandatory coat and tie, attended a 7:05 A.M. breakfast, a "generally resented" 7:50 A.M. chapel service, and "work, work, work." Peter Pfeifle, a Bush classmate, recalled that "not very many people were happy to be there. There was a great deal of cynicism and unfriendliness in the air, people putting people down. It was like an old-fashioned English boy's school where you were watched all the time and weren't having much fun overall."

By his last year at the academy, Junior had gained a measure of independence from his well-connected family, and made new friends who saw the former class clown from Texas as an extroverted, likeable kid with a gift for two of the most-prized values at school: athletics and the reputation for being a "regular guy." One yearbook photo showed Bush among several students trying to squeeze into a phone booth.

Classmates also remember him as a "hearty partier." "George was not a goody two-shoes," said Tom Seligson, a CBS-TV producer in New York, who remembered a spring break at Fort Lauderdale. "He partied as much as anybody. I don't ever recall him being depressed."

Back home in Houston, Junior's mother was going through separation anxiety. "Every day I walked down the driveway to meet the mailman to see if he had written," Barbara later said. "I was homesick, but the child obviously wasn't." Finally she received a letter from her son, who raved endlessly about the school and how many new friends he was making on campus.

"Everybody knew George and George knew everybody," recalled Clay Johnson. "People just wanted to be around him . . . and this was before the name George Bush was known." Pfeifle agreed, describing Junior as "a natural-born leader and a very popular fellow."

The younger Bush earned a baseball letter, played junior varsity football and basketball, and was drafted by his fellow students to be "High Commissioner" of an informal stickball league (umpire of a street version of baseball), nicknaming him "Tweeds Bush" after Boss Tweed, the infamous New York political boss.

"He would give long talks, citing all these rules about what spectators could do and what players could wear," said John Kidde, one of Bush's closest friends, noting that he institutionalized the casual after-dinner pickup game.

After he decided not to try out for varsity football, the ever-popular Junior was also elected "chief cheerleader," although he had not campaigned for the job. "It's more of kind of a student leader position," he later explained, in a preemptive strike against the "blue-collar, gun-toting, pickup-driving" Texans' stereotypical view of male cheerleaders. "It was a hard thing to explain to my buddies in Houston when I came home." True enough, his chores as cheerleader had more to do with rallying student support before an event than leading cheers at it.

Friends at Andover state that Bush was always friendly and sociable, earning the nickname "The Lip." "I was quick with a one-liner," he admitted, although most classmates say he received the handle because he was never short on opinions.

In their final year at Andover, Bush and his buddy, Kidde, were appointed proctors of a tenth-grade dormitory, considered to be a high honor responsibility, and consequently the two seniors roomed together. Mid-year, Junior returned from a trip to Houston with Barry Goldwater's book, *The Conscience of a Conservative.*

"I said, 'What the hell is this?' " Kidde recalled. "We didn't have any time to read anything extracurricular. If we did, you would read a novel. But George seemed honestly interested in the book. He said his parents had asked him to read it. I remember him telling me what Goldwater stood for."

Around the same time, the Andover school dean asked Junior where he planned to attend college. When Bush told him he was considering Yale, his family's alma mater, the school administrator replied, "Well, you won't get in there, so where else are you thinking of going?"*

Junior's choice of Yale was a natural extension of his upbringing. His grandfather, father (who became a member of the board of trustees), uncles,

*As an alternate choice, Bush had also applied to the University of Texas. When he was accepted into Yale, friends say he was "shocked."

and several close family friends, such as Neil Mallon, had all graduated from the Ivy League college.

The Bush family, especially his grandfather Prescott, a U.S. senator from Connecticut, reportedly used their influence and connections to get Junior into the Ivy League school, although George W. still contends he was accepted into Yale in 1964 on his own merits. "It was my idea of trying to get as much out of life, and to do as much possible, made me want to go to Yale," he said years later. "It was also this whole notion of dealing with people from all different walks of life that you see on the East Coast. I enjoyed the whole atmosphere. I was no fantastic genius at Yale, but there was always a challenge to do well."

Frat Brat

In the autumn of 1964, George W.'s grandfather, Prescott, physically exhausted and crippled with arthritis, retired from the U.S. Senate after serving for over a decade; George senior, chairman of the Harris County Republican Party in Houston, unsuccessfully ran for the Senate against liberal Democrat, incumbent Ralph Yarborough (losing by 300,000 votes); and a year after President John F. Kennedy's assassination, Lyndon Johnson began his first elective term by deploying tens of thousands of young Americans to South Vietnam in a U.S. effort to prevent a Communist takeover by the North Vietnamese.

Yale University, like many college campuses across the country served as well-publicized battlegrounds between the administration and cynical, rebellious students who protested America's involvement in the war.* By his own admission, Junior spent his college years gratefully detached from campus politics, protests over the government's deceitfulness on the conflict in Vietnam, and the sixties counterculture. "I don't remember any kind of heaviness ruining my time at Yale," he admitted later. (Although Yale student body leaders signed an Ivy League manifesto saying they were "seriously

*The president's wife, Lady Bird Johnson, visited several college campuses, including Yale, where she saw the war polarizing the country. "I was speaking to the Young Democrats and realized that nothing was getting through to them," she later said upon returning from the Ivy League campus, "not conservation, not the cities, only the war."

considering or have already decided to leave the country or go to jail rather than serve in Vietnam," Bush was not among the signers.)

It was during this period of his life that friends say Junior first showed signs of being a natural politician. His inherited skills—subtle, like any personal touch, but distinct—were always evident, especially his photographic memory.

Clay Johnson, a Bush classmate at both Andover and Yale, recalled the time when he and Junior were fraternity pledges during their sophomore year at the university and the upperclassmen ordered them to stand and attempt to name the other fifty initiates. "The average person stood up and named about three," Johnson said. "George got up and named all fifty. He just has such an interest in people that he remembered their names, which is his medium, like writing numbers are for somebody else. He has such an interest in people. They sense that and respond to him."

Roland Betts, a friend from Yale and later president of Silver Screen Management of New York, which finances motion pictures, remembered similar incidents. "Someone may say that's just Bush the politician, something he learned from his old man," said Betts. "But I can tell you when I ran into George in 1964 . . . he would wander up to anybody, absolutely anybody, and stick his hand out and say, 'Hey, I'm George Bush,' and start talking. The name George Bush didn't mean shit to anybody. That's just his nature. In the twenty-five years we have known each other I don't think he's changed at all. He's not pretentious, not exploitive. George is a very disarmingly charming person."

Another former schoolmate, the New England-based fiction writer Christopher Tilghman, added his own recollection of Bush: "That's exactly what it was. He did have this certain ability with people. The way he'd look you in the eye when he'd shake your hand, the direct way he talked—it's hard to describe, but you just came away thinking he was more interesting than the average preppy."

Lanny J. Davis, a Yale classmate who later served as special counsel to President Clinton, noted that Bush "could capture somebody's essence very quickly. Was he a spoiled, wealthy kid? Absolutely not. . . . The one thing he conveyed was a lack of pretense. You never would have known who his father was, what kind of family he came from. There was nothing hierarchical about him."

Junior was, however, a very average student, majoring in history. His parents worried somewhat about their eldest son's attempts to prove his worthiness. "He was not the smartest," recalled Clay Johnson. "He was not the most athletic." Although he was tapped for Skulls and Bones,* the prestigious and secret campus society to which his grandfather and father had belonged, young Bush couldn't make varsity as a catcher on the school's baseball team and later switched to rugby.

Although he concedes he was "never a great intellectual" during his college years, Junior was nevertheless quite popular on campus, literally the life of the party, and was elected president of Delta Kappa Epsilon fraternity "sort of by acclamation," said University of Colorado law professor Robert Dieter, a close friend of George W.'s at Andover and Yale.

He is remembered by former fraternity brother, Don Ensenat, as an enthusiastic participant in a college party atmosphere, often mixing a garbage can full of screwdrivers before football games. "Did you ever see the movie *Animal House?*" asked Ensenat. "The DKE frat house was the site of soul bands and dancing and dates. There was a lot of alcohol," and Junior was "a high-energy guy, fun to be around."†

Russ Walker, a former classmate and Bush friend from Oklahoma City, recalled returning from a frat party one night when drunken Junior fell to

---

*This exceptionally morbid, death-celebrating order, its name unmentionable before outsiders, assisted Wall Street financiers in discovering young men of "good birth" for prosperous careers once they graduated from Yale. As one of only a handful of new members, Bush was initiated into the society's secret rituals in a triple-padlocked crypt where he was reportedly placed naked into a coffin and immersed in mud.

The Skull and Bones Society, which was first established among the Yale graduating class of 1833, was an inner sanctum where the truly elite could separate themselves from the merely privileged. Twice a week after six in the evening on Thursdays and Sundays during the academic year, Bonesmen met in the society's "Tomb," a windowless stone building resembling a mausoleum on High Street to "celebrate one's brief life on earth." Much like the members of California's Bohemian Club, they conducted their rituals in exclusive solitude.

A traditional session usually required one member to dutifully reveal his innermost thoughts and detail another chapter in his "sexual autobiography," holding the others in a state of "CB," or connubial bliss. The sexual histories helped break down the normal defenses of the members, according to Lucius H. Biglow, a retired Seattle attorney and a former Bonesman. "That way you get everybody committed to a certain extent," he remembered. "It was a gradual way of building confidence." The blackmail potential of such information, however, had obvious permanent uses in enforcing loyalty among the society's members.

As with Prescott and George senior, the younger Bush, made lifelong friends in the inner sanctum of the Skull and Bones Society, which along with the base that had already been built as early as Andover, formed the core of a network for his future careers in business and politics. As the years progressed, George W. and his fellow Bonesmen would periodically gather for a private dinner and Bush would "unburden himself" as he struggled with the life-changing decisions of whether to run for governor of Texas and president of the United States. After forming his presidential exploratory committee in March 1999, George W. tapped many of these now successful businessmen for substantial campaign contributions.

† A November 16, 1998 *Newsweek* profile of George W. noted: "He went to Yale, but seems to have majored in beer drinking at the Deke House."

the ground and started rolling down the middle of the street. "He literally rolled back to the dorm," Walker said.

Bush's friend, Tom Seligson, added, "I think George, like all of us, felt the constraints and probably wanted to make up for lost time. College is a time to explode." While Seligson never saw Bush use drugs, he said, "if he didn't use marijuana at that point, then he wasn't alive."

In 1966, while serving as fraternity president, Junior had his first brush with the law, involving the theft of a holiday decoration from a store display so he could hang it on the door of his frat house. "We evidently made a lot of noise," George W. said, recalling how the police responded to the theft scene, "because the local gendarmes came and said, 'What are you doing?' I said, 'We are liberating a Christmas tree wreath. Don't you understand the Delta Kappa Epsilon house is short of a Christmas wreath?' They didn't understand." The police booked him on a misdemeanor charge but later dropped it after the intervention of one of his father's friends.

Bush, the leader of the frat pack, got into more publicized trouble after Steve Weisman, a Yale student and occasional contributor to the *New York Times,* reported in a *Yale Daily News* article accusations that campus fraternities had carried on "sadistic and obscene" initiation procedures against pledges.

"The charge that has caused the most controversy on the Yale campus," Weisman wrote, "is that Delta Kappa Epsilon applied a 'hot branding iron' to the small of the back of its 40 new members in ceremonies two weeks ago. A photograph showing a scab in the shape of the Greek letter delta, approximately a half-inch wide, appeared with the article. A former president of Delta said that the branding is done with a hot coat hanger. But the former president, George Bush, a Yale senior, said that the resulting wound is 'only a cigarette burn.' "

"There's no scarring mark, physically or mentally," Bush told Weisman at the time, defending the practice to the *Yale Daily News.* The frat prankster stated that he was amazed that anyone was making a fuss about the branding, adding that at Texas colleges they used cattle prods on pledges.*

Another headline-making college experience for the legendary party boy occurred in his senior year after the Yale football team defeated Princeton

---

*Bush downplayed the controversy of the branding, claiming he once spent a weekend with a classmate driving through New York and New Jersey in an unsuccessful effort to find a tattoo parlor that would apply a Skull and Bones symbol, to permanently mark his membership in the exclusive campus society.

for the first time in five years. Junior called for an immediate celebration, though the game was played on their Ivy League rival's home field.

"A well-lubricated group of select Yale students decided to remove the Princeton goal posts," Clay Johnson said, noting that young Bush was the ringleader. A skirmish ensued and they were arrested and then released a few minutes later by the campus police, a transgression made more problematic by the fact that his father had just been elected to Congress.

"It was a college exuberance," George W. now says with a laugh, noting that he was "young and irresponsible," repeating the standard three-word descriptive phrase he would use countless times over the years. "I was escorted to the campus police place, and the guy said, 'Leave town.' So I was once in Princeton, New Jersey, and haven't been back since."

His father, however, never mentioned the embarrassing incident. "In Dad's case he never really tried to direct your life," George W. later said. About the worst the oldest son could expect from the senior Bush was for him to tell his namesake he was "disappointed" in something he did. That was his reaction upon learning that Junior had walked out on a summer job as an oil field roughneck in Louisiana a week early to be with his girlfriend before they both returned to college. Actually, Junior had abruptly quit a variety of summer jobs between his Yale school years—as a sporting goods salesman at a Houston Sears & Roebuck store, a clerk in a brokerage firm, a ranch hand in Arizona—but the oil field walkout was the proverbial straw that broke the camel's back.

"Before long I was called to my father's office in downtown Houston," George W. remembered. "He simply told me: 'In our family, and in life, you fulfill your commitments. You've disappointed me'—and that was it." Typically, the elder Bush did not stay angry for long. Three hours after the office confrontation, he invited his son—and his girlfriend—to a Houston Astros baseball game, "which says a lot about him and how he disciplines," George W. told PBS talk-show host Charlie Rose shortly before the 1988 Republican convention.

Although Bush outwardly excused his son's "youthful irresponsibility" at the time as mere frat-boy high jinks, family friends say that his father was the first to realize that Junior had a serious drinking problem.

"George's dad had a spy network of Yale teachers, fraternity brothers, and even his roommates, calling him in Houston with detailed reports of all-nighters, weekend binges, showing up at classes drunk, and driving way too fast while drinking way too much," said one of Bush's close friends who attended college with him. "When he suddenly quit his summer job as an oilfield roughneck, the old man knew he'd been out chugging beers all night long and just wanted to keep the party going with his girlfriend before they went back to school. He didn't say anything to George about his drinking, though, hoping instead that he would 'outgrow it' by the time he got out of college,* which was like leaving the landing lights on for Amelia Earhart."

THE WOMAN HE LOVED

Junior's girlfriend at the time, Cathryn Lee Wolfman, grew up in the same upper crust Tanglewood area of west Houston where the Bushes lived. A standout athlete at St. John's, the city's premiere private school, Cathryn lived with her mother and stepfather, the Jewish proprietor of a high-end clothing store that bore his name: Wolfman's.

The young couple dated occasionally during George W.'s visits home from Andover prep school, but their romance grew more serious after they both enrolled in college on the East Coast. She attended Smith College in Northampton, Massachusetts, like Barbara Bush, but after being injured in a sledding accident, she came home to recuperate and eventually transferred to Rice University in Houston, where she majored in economics and joined the Elizabeth Baldwin Literary Society. When Junior returned to Texas for summer vacation or holiday breaks from Yale, the couple were usually seen hand-in-hand at a pirouette of cocktail parties, tennis matches, and other social events associated with oil-town privilege.

Described by friends as "outgoing, happy people," it came as no surprise when the twenty-year-old college juniors' summer wedding plans were proclaimed in a January 1, 1967, *Houston Chronicle* society column under the headline "Congressman's Son to Marry Rice Co-Ed," with an accompanying fireside portrait of the couple: he in a suit, tie, and crewcut; she in a sleeveless dress, smiling, her hair cropped short. Like his parents had done twenty years earlier, they planned to live in New Haven, Connecticut during Junior's senior year. (Yale was still an all-male school at the time, and would not begin accepting female students until the year after Bush graduated.)

According to Bush, within six months of the engagement announcement, the young couple "just grew apart" due to their long-distance relationship. "I

---

*Barbara Bush, who never minced words, gave her drunken son a tongue-lashing during his Christmas break from Yale when he upset one of her dear friends at a cocktail party by asking, "So, what's sex like after fifty, anyway?"

was crazy about her, but we decided not to get married in between my junior and senior year in college," Bush later said. When they graduated in early 1968, they decided to delay the nuptials for a year, and then eventually cancelled their wedding plans completely.

Bush's ex-fiancée, who married a Harvard MBA two years later in Houston, was equally tight-lipped regarding the particulars of their breakup, saying only, "I loved him. But I have no thoughts of 'what if'—no regrets. I was engaged to him. I was glad I was engaged to him. The relationship died and that was that."

Friends of the couple surmised otherwise about the reasons for the couple's breakup, noting that in an essentially old-money social circle, there were some "nasty, snobbish whispers" about the young Wolfman woman's "merchant" family.

"Given her last name and her stepfather's prominence in the garment industry, the Bush family pressured their son to call off the wedding because the prospective bride had a Jewish background," even though they were Episcopalians, claimed one friend who knew the couple ever since the Bushes moved into the Tanglewood neighborhood. "They were very good friends and they both took it hard, especially George. He was always a wild and crazy party guy, but the losing of the woman he loved, combined with the fear of going to Vietnam, kind of pushed him over the edge."*

FLYING THE FRIENDLY SKIES OF TEXAS

In the spring of 1968, when Junior graduated from Yale with a degree in history, his father presented him with an education trust fund check for $17,000 (not "enormous piles of money" as the press later reported). Bush had hoped that his son would use the funds to further his education, either in business or law, but when he graduated from Yale, Junior lost his college deferment from induction into compulsory military service. Four years at Yale had helped him avoid the draft, but now he was suddenly faced with the possibility that he would join the ranks of the other half million American youth in Vietnam, who were dying at the rate of 350 a week.

The Tet Offensive and other memorable images of the unpopular war,

*As this book went to press, a representative of the Bush family called my publisher and said that the Bushes vehemently denied this explanation for the breakup. She said the family was "enthusiastic" about the engagement and did nothing to discourage it.

were being played out in graphic detail on American televisions and Junior didn't want any part of direct combat. Deciding that he had no desire "to be an infantry guy as a private in Vietnam," and "wanted to learn how to fly," he joined the Texas Air National Guard to fulfill his military obligation at the height of America's involvement in the war.

The National Guard is primarily a domestic military reserve but can be called to active service. From the time of Captain Myles Standish's service in the New England colonies to the late twentieth century and America's involvement in Kosovo, the United States has relied upon its militia to provide a ready reserve of young men to support its professional armed services.

During the 1960s, however, many of George W.'s generation who joined considered it an option to outright evasion of the draft. Overall, National Guard members had only a remote chance of ending up in Vietnam. Throughout the war, only fifteen thousand of the more than one million of the Guard and reserves were sent to fight in the Southeast Asian country.

Speaking of himself in third person, Bush later said, "Yeah, I mean one could argue that he was trying to avoid being the infantryman but my attitude was I'm taking the first opportunity to become a pilot and jumped on that and did my time." Although George W. has never directly addressed the issue of whether he joined the Guard to avoid the draft, he says that "had my unit been called I would have gone . . . to Vietnam. I was prepared to go."

"In a sense he was trying to remain a centrist in a time when there wasn't anything left at the center," said Craig Stapleton, who is married to Bush's cousin. "All of the sudden everybody moves and you're still standing in the center. He didn't dodge the military. But he didn't volunteer to go to Vietnam and get killed, either."

Junior told Roland Betts, one of his classmates from Yale, that while he wasn't particularly enthusiastic about enlisting in the Guard, he "felt that in order not to derail his father's political career he had to be in military service of some kind." The elder Bush had been elected to the U.S. Congress in 1966, representing Harris County in Houston, the first Republican ever voted into political office in the district.

Numerous questions remain as to whether then-Congressman Bush used improper influence to obtain a coveted slot in the military reserve for his son that allowed him to remain stateside during the war. In 1968, the national waiting list for Guard slots contained approximately 100,000 names. Although there are no records of how long the Texas waiting lists were at the time, Retired Major General Thomas Bishop, who was the state's adjutant general in the late sixties, stated there were lengthy waiting lists in Texas. "We were full," he flatly stated. In addition, Dale Pyeatt, associate director of the National Guard Association of Texas, was noted in the press as stating: "There were definitely waiting lists. There wasn't any question about that."

Although pilots were in demand in Vietnam, Tom Hail, a historian for the Texas Air National Guard, noted that records from the era did not show a pilot shortage in the Guard squadron. Hail, who reviewed the unit's personnel files for a special Guard museum display on Bush's service, stated that his unit had twenty-seven pilots at the time he initiated his application for enlistment. While that number was two short of its authorized strength, the unit had two other pilots who were in training and another awaiting a transfer. Hail asserted that there was no need to fast-track applicants.

George W.'s official and oft-repeated version is that he had come home to Houston two weeks before graduating from college and "heard there were pilot slots open" at a unit of the Texas Air National Guard at Ellington Air Force Base, and simply "signed up to fly a single-seat F-102 Interceptor," which provided him with a deferment. "Your options either were to avoid the draft or sign up," Bush acknowledged, "and I signed up."

Four months before enlisting, Bush reported to Westover Air Force Base in Massachusetts, a recruiting office near the Yale campus, to take the Air Force Officers Qualification Test. While scoring 25 percent for pilot aptitude on the screening test—"about as low as you could get and be accepted," according to Retired Colonel Rufus G. Martin, a former Guard personnel officer—and 50 percent for navigator aptitude in his initial enlistment test, Bush scored 95 percent in the "officer quality" section, compared with a current-day average of 88 percent.

His Guard application form asked for "background qualifications of value to the Air Force," Brush wrote, "None." Another question he had to answer was whether he was interested in an overseas assignment. Bush checked the box that said: "do not volunteer."

In a September 1998 profile of George W., the *Washington Post* asked his former Guard commander, Retired Brigadier General Walter "Buck" Staudt, who had previously met Congressman Bush while serving as a member of the Houston Chamber of Commerce aviation committee, how George W. gained entry into the military reserve in 1968 despite a waiting list.

Staudt told the *Post* that the young man was promptly accepted because there were five or six openings for pilots. "Most of the guys didn't want to be pilots because it was a commitment—there was a long training period," Staudt said. "He had to go through an interview process with the [pilot] board—they decide if you're the kind of person they want to fly with. And

I'll tell you, this kid was an asset. . . . Anyone who suggests there was family influence to get him in is a damn liar."

However, Staudt did admit to the *Houston Chronicle* in 1988 that George W.'s wealthy background indirectly helped him qualify for one of the hard-to-fill officer slots, noting that most young men didn't have the financial "flexibility that would allow them to take off for the training the positions required," which was typically more than a year.

Evidently Staudt was so pleased to have Texas congressman's eldest son in his Guard unit that he later staged a special ceremony so he could be photographed administering the oath, instead of the captain who actually had sworn Bush in. Later, when Junior was commissioned a second lieutenant by another subordinate officer, Colonel Staudt once again staged a special ceremony in his office for the cameras, this particular time with Bush's VIP father flying in from Washington to pin the bars on his son.

Ironically, when he was a campaign adviser to his father during the 1988 presidential race, George W. was forced to defend Bush's running mate, U.S. Senator Dan Quayle, the heir of a newspaper fortune, against media assertions that he had used the influence of either his wealthy publishing family or political friends to gain a slot in the Indiana National Guard in 1969 as a means of avoiding the draft.

The Quayle family-owned newspaper, the *Huntington Herald Press,* had incessantly attacked antiwar activists and draft dodgers who "enjoy all the comforts and pleasures and extravaganzas of the good, prosperous life" while American GIs were fighting "under such harsh conditions." At the Republican National Convention, Quayle, a conservative advocate of a strong national defense, suddenly found himself on the defensive and unprepared for a barrage of press questions about why he had joined the National Guard instead of fighting in Vietnam and accusations that he was a hypocrite who wanted others to go to war.

"He didn't want to face his real service. That's the bottom line," said Allen Gerson of Austin, Texas, a Vietnam veteran who was interviewed by the press during the political convention.

John DeCamp, another war vet and convention delegate, stated: "Back there in the sixties, you had boys with money and influence who didn't want to go to Vietnam finding a way to get into the National Guard," he claimed. "And then you had other boys without so much money, and some of them didn't want to go to Vietnam, but they volunteered or got drafted and they went. And some of them, like me, got shot at a lot, and a great many of them just plain got shot and killed."

Another interviewed delegate noted that the National Guard would fire on unarmed students like they did at Kent State University, but wouldn't go to Vietnam to shoot the enemy.

After the senior Bush refused to take questions and his campaign chairman, James A. Baker III admitted to CNN that Quayle "was assisted by his family" in joining the Guard, George W., in an attempt at damage control, met with the press and suggested it was enough that Quayle had not fled to Canada as was the case with multitudes of American draft evaders. "The thing that's important, I want you all to remember," Junior told reporters, "he didn't go to Canada. Let's keep it in generational perspective."

Quayle finally met the press and said that he "let a number of people know" that he wanted to "get into the National Guard. . . . Phone calls were made. . . . I don't know the specifics of that." Although he worked for the Indiana governor while he was in law school, Quayle stated that he was "almost certain the governor and lieutenant governor were not involved" in securing a slot for him in the National Guard. However, the senator did acknowledge that a family friend who was an employee of his grandfather's newspaper and a former commander of the Indiana National Guard more than likely interceded on his behalf.

Flanked by Senator Phil Gramm of Texas, George W. announced in a press conference that his father's running mate had adequately answered questions regarding his National Guard enlistment. "He made no attempt to deceive anybody," he proclaimed. "It [the allegation] was total bull. That's what it was."

Junior's public defense of Quayle, however, brought unwanted attention to his own military record during the Vietnam War and accusations that he, too, had used undue family influence to avoid the draft by obtaining a hard-to-get slot in the National Guard. After former Senator John Tower of Texas, who once chaired the powerful Senate Armed Service Committee, remarked to the media that the son of Democratic vice presidential candidate and Texas senator, Lloyd Bentsen, had also served in the military reserves at the time, it wasn't long before the press discovered that Lloyd Bentsen III and George W. were both members of the Texas Air National Guard at then Ellington Air Force Base in 1968.*

Within hours, the press was reporting that Bush had been a pilot with the 111th Fighter Interceptor Squadron and Bentsen had worked in the analysis

*Senator Tower's son also was admitted to the Air Guard.

management office of the 147th Support Squadron in the Guard, with both units under the overall command of Walter B. "Buck" Staudt, a colonel at the time. "These kids are clean," the retired Guard commander told the media when asked if the younger Bush and Bentsen had used improper family influence to pave their way to Air National Guard enlistments and thus avoid combat in Vietnam.

Since the National Guard is run by the state, with its adjutant general chosen by the governor, there are any number of ways that someone could have intervened on behalf of privileged young men like Bush or Bentsen. "Obviously, the governor, the lieutenant governor, and the speaker of the house had a lot of influence on the National Guard," said a former personnel officer in charge of a Texas squadron. "And if you look at that list, you'll see besides George W. Bush, many sons of politically prominent Texas families who just happened to get into the Guard—regardless of the waiting lists."

Former Texas speaker of the House Ben Barnes later acknowledged that periodically distinguished residents of the state would contact his office requesting assistance in obtaining Guard slots for their sons. Barnes stated that he never received such a call from the then–U.S. Representative Bush or anyone else in the family. But when asked if an intermediary or friend of the Bushes had ever asked him to intercede on George W.'s behalf, Barnes later stated that Sidney A. Adger, an influential Houston oilman and longtime Bush family acquaintance, requested his assistance in securing a spot for Junior in the Guard.

Several news outlets also noted during the 1988 presidential race that the elder Bentsen was a private citizen in 1968 and was not elected to the Senate until 1970, but the senior Bush was a congressman at the time his son obtained a highly sought after slot in the Texas Air National Guard. When asked how he got into the military reserves unit, Junior jokingly, but evasively, replied, "They could sense I was going to be one of the great pilots of all time."

One Vietnam veteran and delegate to the Republican National Convention in 1988, did not see the humor in George W.'s response. "While the Bush boy was busy defending the Texas-Mexico border from bandits in his F-102 fighter jet,* I was watching my buddies get their brains blown out by the VC

*One of Bush's rivals for the Republican nomination in 2000, Senator John McCain, also said he slept better at night as a POW in Vietnam for five-and-a-half years, knowing that George W. was protecting the coast of Texas from invasion.

[Viet Cong]," said James Johnson, a wheelchair-bound double amputee who lost both of his legs during the Tet Offensive in 1968. "As Terry Kent Reed, a former 'Nam vet and author once said, 'As a nation, you should never test your very best, while at home you leave the rest.' "

Veterans have also noted that Bush, who enlisted in May 1968 as an airman basic, received his second lieutenant's commission only a few months later, one of the most rapid rank ascensions in military history. Walter Staudt, Bush's commander at the time, classified him as prime officer material with "the interest, motivation and knowledge necessary" to become a pilot. In a separate report, Staudt added: "Bush meets all the requirements established for this appointment program," a special process that would allow the young recruit to become a second lieutenant right out of basic training without having to go through officer candidate school. A three-person examining board, of which Staudt was a member, approved the direct appointment in July.

An Adjutant General's Department manual from that time listed numerous qualifications required for commissioned officers, which for the most part, Bush lacked: a high school education, eighteen months of military service, including six months of active duty, and completion of officer training. A separate Guard pamphlet titled "Take Command, Apply for OCS," detailed three ways for Guardsmen to become second lieutenants: a twenty-three-week office training program, a nine-week training "reserve component special officer candidate course," or completion of eight weekend drill periods and two summer camps.

Charles C. Shoemake, an Air Force veteran who later joined the Texas Air National Guard and retired as a full colonel, noted that direct appointments such as Bush's, were rare and hard to obtain and required the extensive credentials. "I went from master sergeant to first lieutenant based on my three years in college and fifteen years as a noncommissioned officer. Then I got considered for a direct appointment," Shoemake said, adding that even then he didn't know whether he was going to get into pilot training. Of Bush's prompt entry, he asserted, "His name didn't hurt, obviously. But it was a commander's decision in those days."

"I'm not suggesting I was any great war hero," George W. later said, "but I want you to know that flying F-102 fighters, putting the thing in afterburner at the end of a runway, was something other than not being part of the military. I wouldn't necessarily call it risky, but we lost a couple of guys in our unit. I'm not the least bit ashamed of what I did." The F-102 aircraft, which were constructed in 1953, were being phased out for use in Vietnam by the late sixties, which meant according to Guard officials, Bush would have never been transferred overseas.

Almost two and a half million American men and women served in the Vietnam War, of whom 153,300 were wounded and 58,209 killed defending the South from the communist North. During the conflict—1964 to 1973—more than twenty-six million young men faced the possibility of being drafted and hard choices about whether to participate in the U.S. military. An estimated ninety thousand refused induction into the service or fled the draft by moving to Canada and other countries. Thousands of others, like Bush, opted to continue their personal lives and reduce the risk of seeing combat by joining armed forces reserves and the National Guard.

JET JOCK

Junior's stint in the Guard was one continuous party where he could "fly-hard, play-hard, drink-hard" and when he wasn't flying fighter jets, he spent, as he later confessed, "enormous amounts of time and energy courting women," the well-earned reputation of "being the wild Bush son."

"He basically continued the partying tradition post-college," said one former Yale classmate. "He graduated one day, enlisted in the National Guard the next, went to basic training in San Antonio for a few weeks, and then never let his foot off the accelerator of life. He flew jets, drove fast cars, screwed more women than Hugh Hefner and partied hardy."

In the fall of 1968, the newly commissioned second lieutenant packed up his "sporty little blue" Triumph TR-6 convertible and headed for fifty-three weeks of flight-training school at Moody Air Force Base in the piney woods near Valdosta, Georgia.* Junior had the unique distinction of being the only Guardsman among the seventy or so officers from other branches of the military who undertook the training.

Although his flight school classmates heard rumors that his congressman father had intervened to get his son in the Guard, foremost among their recollections of George W. were their impressions of him as an excellent pilot,

---

*In addition to his special commission, the Guard gave Bush immediate and considerable flexibility. After basic training at Lackland Air Force Base and his commissioning as a second lieutenant, Junior received what amounted to a two-month-plus vacation to Florida before heading to Georgia for yearlong flight school. During this time, Bush worked in the political campaign of Edward J. Gurney, a Republican candidate for the Senate and a close friend of the elder Bush. He occasionally returned to Houston for weekend Guard duty.

near the top of his class, that are validated by the exemplary ratings in the public portions of Bush's military record.

"I liked him a lot," recalled Colonel Ralph Anderson, who was in flight school with Bush and now commands a fighter wing in the Ohio National Guard. "He was a real outgoing guy, a good pilot and lots of fun."

The young trainees also remember their colleague as "a guy who could hold his own at the bar," when the would-be fighter jocks gathered after hours at the on-base watering hole. Valdosta was dry back in the late sixties, and the "Friday night social at the Officers Club was a big deal," said Colonel Anderson. "There was draft beer, and all the girls from town came in. Everybody got crazy," especially Junior, who, on more than one occasion, stripped off his uniform and danced nude on top of the bar while lip-synching to rowdy George Jones jukebox tunes such as "White Lightning."*

Bush later admitted he "worked hard and played hard" during his rigorous flight training days in Georgia. "I kept a level head in a time that was pretty chaotic," he said. "For me it was much more practical. I am not very good at psychoanalyzing myself, but I learned to fly jets. I remember telling people everywhere I went that it didn't matter where you've been, where you were going or what you were doing, when you put a burner on you are focused on the moment. . . . It took a great deal of concentration to fly those planes."

Although Junior never threw his political family's name around, his fellow pilots acknowledge, however, that it was impossible to forget they were training with the son of a United States congressman, especially after the time a government plane landed at the Air Force base to chauffeur George W. back to Washington for a date with President Nixon's oldest daughter, Tricia.

The elder Bush was reelected to the U.S. House of Representatives in 1968 without any opposition and presumably could have served in Congress for several more years, but the newly-elected Republican president was convinced that Texas Democratic Senator Ralph Yarborough was politically vulnerable. In an effort to "sweeten the pot" and persuade Bush to give up his congressional seat and run against Yarborough for the Sen-

---

*Only four days before George W. announced the formation of a presidential exploratory committee in March 1999, a well-placed Bush campaign source told the *Drudge Report* that the presidential hopeful's advisers were "very concerned" that there was a photograph—"a visual ticking time bomb"—of young Bush dancing naked atop a bar somewhere in existence. "Not that it matters what we've been through with Bill Clinton," the source explained to Drudge, "but we do need to know what could be used against us. We do not even know if there is a picture out there . . . we're getting to the bottom of it."

ate, Nixon attempted to play matchmaker between his daughter and Bush's son.

"We went to dinner," George W. vaguely recalled of his one date with the president's daughter. "It wasn't a very long date." Or evidently a very memorable one. When pressed by the media years later for details, then-Governor Bush could only recall that the date had been "arranged."

He also seems to have suffered a similar convenient memory lapse when questioned about a young, very attractive Georgia woman he was seen with regularly toward the end of his flight training. According to his classmates, Junior spent less and less time at the Officers Club after hours, choosing instead to leave the base and go to movies and dances with a woman whom he led them to believe was going to become Mrs. George Walker Bush. When it came time to graduate from flight school, however, he left Georgia for active duty in Texas without even saying "good-bye." Years later, he acknowledged that there had been such a woman, but that he could only recall her first name: Judy.

Although he has refused to shed any light on details of the relationship, Bush's classmates state unequivocally that he never had any intention of marrying the "Georgia peach" he repeatedly promised he was going to take back to Texas as his wife. "Oh, he was very much in love back then," confided a former Air Force officer and flight school drinking buddy, "but Junior wasn't about to settle down and raise a family, which is exactly what she wanted. He'd get drunk and promise her a big church wedding and all the trimmings, but when he sobered up he'd say, 'I must've been out of my goddamn mind when I told her that.' "

After earning his wings in December 1969,* Junior was assigned part-time to a National Guard unit that flew night maneuvers over the Gulf of Mexico from Ellington Air Force Base on the outskirts of Houston, where he attended Combat Crew Training School. "Lt. Bush is a dynamic outstanding

---

*Bush was criticized by the press and his opponents during his 2000 presidential run for claiming in literature for his failed 1978 congressional campaign that he had served in the Air Force. A pullout ad from the *Lubbock Avalance-Journal* on May 4, 1978, showed a huge photo of George W. with a "Bush for Congress" logo on the front. On the back, a synopsis of his career stated he had served "in the U.S. Air Force and the Texas Air National Guard where he piloted the F-102 aircraft." When confronted about the misleading ad years later, Bush claimed that while he was attending flight school from November 1968 to December 1969, he was considered to be on active duty for the U.S. Air Force. The military branch denied his assertion by stating that Air National Guard members were considered "guardsmen on active duty" while receiving pilot training. They were not, however, counted as members of the overall active-duty Air Force.

young officer," stated one of his performance reports. "He clearly stands out as a top notch fighter interceptor pilot."

Bush's release from active Guard duty after two years allowed him time to work in his father's unsuccessful 1970 Senate campaign. George W. traveled the state giving speeches on his father's behalf, assisted in coordinating college interns for the campaign and, on one occasion, strolled shirtless behind his father on a charity walk, smirking in the Houston heat and humidity.

According to New Mexico businessman Dan Gillcrist, who was the 1970 campaign's scheduler, George W. was supremely confident. "I don't know where you get that, but I see it in others. I had brothers who were fighter pilots. They just know when they get up there, they are going to kick ass. And that's one of the characteristics I would chisel in stone for Bush," Gillcrist said. "Some people see that as cockiness, but it's in the eye of the beholder. I just think he knows what he can do, and he has no reservations about it."

Junior leased a one-bedroom apartment at the time at Houston's Chateaux Dijon ("The Place to Live"), a four hundred unit complex dominated by young, upwardly mobile, single professionals, who remember George W. as a "Winston-bumming preppy with a disarming smile and an eye for young women and a taste for beer, Jack Daniels, and martinis."

Gillcrist also saw Bush take a hearty approach to his social life. "Would you want a president who was some kind of person who never left his room? He had fun and partied and raised a little hell like the rest of us."

"He did some night-flying as I recall," said Don Ensenat, a Yale classmate who lived with him in Houston. "No alcohol twenty-four hours" before his part-time weekend Guard duty. "They had to keep planes on alert at all time."

George W., who acknowledges he was "a hard drinker and heavy smoker" back then, was a frequent patron of the Mileau, a local nightclub where iced-down Budweisers ("red-and-whites") and cigarettes were the drugs of choice among the clean-cut crowd. But persistent allegations of marijuana and cocaine abuse during his self-described "young and irresponsible" years have continued to dog Bush since the late sixties, especially during the "meat grinder" level of scrutiny associated with his congressional, gubernatorial, and presidential campaigns.

George W. addresses his "reckless" years head-on, but not in detail. In response to direct questions from the media, he refuses to answer questions about possible illegal drug use, offering instead an all-encompassing mea culpa. "I have made mistakes," he has repeatedly stated during the presidential race. "I choose not to inventory my sins because I don't want anybody to be able to say, 'Well, the governor of Texas did it, why shouldn't I?' That's why I have been somewhat mysterious about my past. . . . I'm not going to talk about what I did as a child. It is irrelevant what I did twenty to thirty years ago."

"I must say I found his answer about whether he had used marijuana and cocaine interesting," *Newsweek*'s Eleanor Clift said of the undeclared presidential frontrunner on the syndicated TV news talk show *The McLaughlin Group*. "Republicans have a gift for redefining the life cycle. Childhood now goes through probably the early thirties."

Former Yale classmates and friends who partied with George W. in Houston during his stint in the National Guard, fill in the blanks beyond his vague, Clintonesque admission, saying that he occasionally smoked marijuana and snorted cocaine.

"We all experimented back then," explained one of his many girlfriends during that time period. "But you have to remember that George was just living for the moment.* He never dreamed or schemed of running for governor, let alone president, so he didn't worry in the sixties and seventies about protecting his future political viability. Poor George, it'll probably come back to haunt him when he runs for national office."

During the Y2K presidential race, the press and Bush's opponents warned that he would continue to face the speculation about drug usage until he spoke out. "This sort of talk is out there, and it's encouraged when he admits to having had problems with drink but refuses to answer questions on drugs," said Brian Kennedy, campaign director for Lamar Alexander, one of Bush's GOP rivals. "Until such time as he gives a full answer, the governor can expect that it will be an issue in the campaign."

YOUNG AND RESTLESS

After his father's 1970 campaign, Junior moved to a garage apartment on a tree-lined street close to Rice University, which he shared with Ensenat. When not flying "alerts" over the Gulf for the National Guard on weekends

---

*Ironically, a 1970 National Guard news release at the time, read: "George Walker Bush is one member of the younger generation who doesn't get his kicks from pot or hashish or speed. As far as kicks are concerned, Lieutenant Bush gets his from the roaring afterburner of the F-102."

(sometimes he flew his F-102 from Houston to Orlando and back), he worked part-time during the day for an agricultural conglomerate owned by Robert Gow, a Yale graduate and family friend who years earlier had been an executive at the elder Bush's Houston oil company, Zapata Off-shore.

Gow, who dispatched George W. to Pennsylvania, Ohio, and other states to do preliminary research on plant nurseries he sought to acquire, remembered the younger Bush as "a buttoned-down Brooks Brothers type." But Junior seemed restless, repeatedly saying that he wanted to contribute to society in "a nonbusiness way." Calling the job "dull," he quit the agribusiness company in less than a year.

After flirting briefly with the idea of running for the state legislature, George W.'s first notable full-time job was in 1972 as a youth counselor for the Professionals United for Leadership League (Project P.U.L.L.), an inner-city antipoverty program in Houston, of which his father was a "benevolent supporter" and honorary chairman. Mentored by P.U.L.L.'s director, John White, a now-deceased former player for the Houston Oilers and civic leader, George W. remained clean and sober for a few months while counseling the hardened black youth in the city's tough Third Ward, playing basketball and wrestling with them, and taking the teenagers on field trips to juvenile prisons.

"He was the first real white boy that all of the kids really loved," said Ernie Ladd, a retired Houston Oiler, who worked with Bush at the time and noted that George W. forged a special bond with boys whose Houston upbringing in no way resembled his own in affluent Tanglewood.

Bush so impressed his African-American coworkers with his dedication that they still speak highly of him almost thirty years later. "I truly remember like it was yesterday how he bonded with the kids so much they wanted to follow him home," recalled his direct supervisor, Edgar Arnold. Another coworker, Muriel Henderson, recalled that Junior was "so down-to-earth, to be honest, I just thought he was a poor kid trying to make his way in the world."

In a sense, he was. "I think George was really twisting back then," said Doug Hannah, a friend of Bush's from that time, "trying to figure out whether he could get away with doing something other than following in his father's steps."

Bush refers to this unfocused and troubled time in his life as his "nomadic period." For three months in 1972, he lived in Montgomery, Alabama, after receiving a transfer to the Alabama National Guard so that he could work as a paid political director of the ill-fated U.S. Senate campaign of another friend of his father, construction magnate and former Postmaster General Winton "Red" Blount.

Although he is collectively remembered by other staff members as a "party boy who couldn't keep his hands off the girls," they seemed to be more surprised that the Texan with a distinct twang acted like a Connecticut-born preppy Yankee. "He wore penny loafers without socks to the office," said one surprised campaign associate.

After Blount was "clobbered" in the Senate race, young Bush traveled to Washington, D.C., to spend Christmas 1972 with his parents at their new home on Cathedral Avenue. George senior, as one of President Nixon's loyal supporters, was expected to become chairman of the Republican National Committee within the next three weeks, although the position was considered a "dead end" for a politician. His son, likewise, was feeling frustrated, bitter, and questioning his own worth in the world. As David Maraniss later wrote in the *Washington Post,* George W. was faced with the burden of having to "overcome his father's name."

A man-to-man, in-your-face confrontation between Bush and his eldest son was way past due. After Junior arrived at the house, he took his fifteen-year-old brother, Marvin, to a friend's house, where they both drank too much holiday cheer. On the way home, Junior struck and dragged a neighbor's garbage can noisily down the street before turning into the Bush driveway.*

The elder Bush asked his son to step into the den. Junior, who recalls being drunk and belligerent as they entered the study, was ready to pick a fight. "I hear you're looking for me," he shouted at his father. "You want to go *mano a mano* right here?" Both men were suddenly in each other's face, screaming at the top of their lungs, until Barbara ran into the room and literally pulled them apart and sent them into opposite corners of the room like a referee in a boxing match. Tempers eventually cooled, but Junior's feelings of anger and animosity remained through the holiday visit.

Before leaving Washington, he announced to his parents that he had applied to Harvard Business School in hopes of obtaining a master's degree

*In 1996, Governor Bush was struck from a list of potential jurors in a DWI case in Travis County Court at Law, a development that allowed him to avoid potentially embarrassing questions about whether he had ever driven a vehicle while intoxicated.

and was accepted.* When the obviously joyful parents asked when he'd be enrolling, he snapped back: "Oh, I'm not going. I just wanted to let you know I could get into it."

Junior did go, however, after being allowed to end his National Guard service seven months early in October 1973. "I thought Harvard would open up more horizons," he said later. "It was a lot stricter environment than Yale.... What Harvard provided were some tools. I've always said it was a vocational training exercise in capitalism."

"He went there for the same reason a lot of us did," said Clayton Day, Jr., one of his Yale classmates. "I had a lot of degrees, but I couldn't do anything. It was like trade school."

As he had been at Andover and Yale, young Bush was unpretentious, hard working, hard playing, and popular while attending Harvard. He lived in an apartment in a three-story walkup near Cambridge's Central Square and jogged every morning along the Charles River. He also traded in his penny loafers for cowboy boots as he seemingly abandoned his rich playboy arrogance in favor of his true down home West Texas roots. Friends recall his carrying a spit cup to class for his chewing tobacco, and wearing a National Guard bomber jacket while he sat in the back of the room. While other students were drinking Chivas Regal, Bush was chasing Wild Turkey, and when they left to attend the opera, he would stay behind at his apartment listening to Johnny Rodriguez albums.

Nancy Ellis, George senior's sister, living in nearby Boston, remembered the turbulent early seventies and the Watergate scandal as a trying time for her nephew. "You know Harvard Square and how they felt about Nixon. But here was Georgie, his father head of the Republican National Committee. So he came out a lot with us just to get out of there."

"There were a lot of contradictions out there," the elder Bush said. "A lot of difficulty for young people. And they were schooled by people telling them our country was wrong in Vietnam. And yet they went to school, made friends, and came home."

---

*Project P.U.L.L.'s director, John White, urged George W. to apply for admission to Harvard Business School. "You ought to go," he told Bush. "You'll be a much more effective person if you have some net worth. [You'll] be able to help people." Bush had previously applied to University of Texas law school and had been rejected. "I think that got under his skin a little bit, because I don't think he was used to not doing what he wanted to," Barbara Bush later said.

But George W. didn't return to the fold. Like his father before him, he had no desire to work on Wall Street and was even more eager to leave the East Coast.

GO WEST, YOUNG MAN

In 1975, with the ink barely dry on his MBA, the thirty-year-old Bush rebelled against his starchy background, packed his belongings into his spray-painted five-year-old Cutlass and with "no job, no nothing," as he once said, sought "a new frontier."

On his way to Tucson, Arizona to visit friends, Junior stopped in West Texas to drink a few beers with his childhood buddy, James "Jimmy" Allison, a former Washington, D.C. political consultant and fourth generation newspaperman who had become president of the *Midland Reporter-Telegram* earlier in the year upon the death of his father.

Bush and Allison had worked together in 1972 in Alabama on the unsuccessful U.S. Senate campaign of Winton Blount. "We talked about the oil and gas business and how someone who wanted to work hard and who had a quick mind could advance on his own," recalled George W.

Bush continued on to Arizona, but the idea of Midland, the town of his childhood, stayed with him while he drove further west. "Cambridge, Massachusetts [Harvard's location] is a very heavy environment compared to Midland. People there don't realize that horizons can be broadened," he explained. "There is no growth potential there. West Texas is a doer environment. People can do things there."

Following once again in his father's footsteps, George W. repeated the journey the senior Bush had taken almost three decades earlier and returned to Midland and the oil fields in an attempt to carve out his own piece of the Lone Star dream.

★ 3 ★

Ties That Bind

He was dreaming about finding a big oil field and building a career and a family. He had the right stuff.

—Midland oilman and future chief fund-raiser for the Bush presidential campaign, Donald Evans

He's one of those guys who was born on third base and thinks he hit a triple.

—Former presidential adviser, Paul Begala

Dancing with the Devil

With Jimmy Allison's Midland connections, Junior located an alley-side garage apartment (that one friend described as a "toxic waste dump") and arranged an appointment with a respected oil field veteran, Walt Holton, Jr., to whom Bush impatiently said, "Just show me how to look up mineral lease records and I'll figure out the rest."

"He had only an inkling of the oil business," recalled Holton, noting that Bush ignored the advice to work for an established company a few years. "But he knew the terminology. Every kid from Midland has that."

George W. also had an entrepreneur's nervous intensity to succeed. Although he began his business career near the bottom of the oil industry's pecking order, he wasted no time in getting started, initially hiring himself out at $100 a day as a free-lance landman, researching titles and mineral rights for independent oilmen and large companies seeking leases in the Permian Basin.

"When George moved back to Midland, he bummed an office, he bummed golf clubs, bummed shoes," remembered Tom Craddick, a ranking Republican in the Texas House, who has known Bush for almost thirty years. "You were lucky if you saw him in a fresh shirt." (A prize was established in his honor at the Midland Country Club as the worst-dressed golfer.)

Holton recalled that Junior's 1970 blue Cutlass "looked like he'd painted it himself and drove it like it was going to boil over."

Don Evans, who first met Bush in 1975 and has remained a friend, adviser, and campaign fund-raiser ever since, noted: "He didn't have anything as far as I could see . . . He lived in a dump. He used to bring his laundry over to our house. We were just fresh faces dreaming about finding an oil field somewhere."

In a few short months, Junior ceased doing the equivalent of paralegal work and began buying a few small leases, selling off parts of them and keeping a share for himself. Then he began trading mineral royalties, generating income, hiring geologists and secretaries, and expanding his business.

Some of the "old-timers" who knew "Big George" took a liking to the cocky, curly-haired, fast-talking son they called "Little George" and the "Bombastic Bushkin." Oilmen from the era recall sitting on a pile of soft-drink cases as they talked business with Bush in his "closet-size office." He was also famously frugal—"so tight he damn near squeaked"—when he wore his rich uncle's hand-me-down black wingtips to meetings with his risk-taking peers who were hitting it big while the cautious Bush was doing only marginally well. Repeatedly he would tell friends and associates, "Don't borrow for anything that flies, floats, or fornicates."

George W.'s early years in Midland coincided with heady days for West Texas, touched off by the 1973 Arab oil embargo, as the price of crude eventually soared to more than thirty dollars a barrel and economists predicted it would go even higher. Junior desperately wanted a bigger piece of the action, to strike it rich like his father did years earlier, but without using any of his own money.

In June 1977, he formed his own drilling company, Arbusto Energy ("arbusto" means "bush" in Spanish). Like his father who made his fortune in the oil business with the money of others, George W. founded Arbusto with the financial backing of investors, including James R. Bath, a Houston businessman whom Bush apparently first met when they were in the same Texas Air National Guard unit. Tax documents and personal financial records show that Bath, an aircraft broker with business ties to Saudi Arabia sheiks, had invested $50,000 in Arbusto, granting him a five percent interest in two limited partnerships controlled by Bush.

In one of the most bizarre footnotes to history, *Time* magazine described Bath in 1991 as "a deal broker whose alleged associations run from the CIA to a major shareholder and director of the Bank of Credit & Commerce." BCCI, as it was more commonly known, was closed down in July 1991 amid charges of multibillion-dollar fraud and worldwide news reports that the institution had been involved in covert intelligence work, drug money laundering, arms brokering, bribery of government officials and aid to terrorists. An accounting commissioned by the Bank of England finally exposed the extent of BCCI's deficits and criminal offenses, forcing the bank's eventual collapse.

Bath was never directly implicated in the BCCI scandal, but according to *The Outlaw Bank*, an award-winning 1993 book by *Time* correspondents Jonathan Beaty and S.C. Gwynne, Bath originally "made his fortune by investing money for [Sheikh Kalid bin] Mahfouz and another BCCI-connected Saudi, Sheikh bin Laden," allegedly the father of none other than Osama bin Laden, the man accused by the U.S. government of masterminding the August 1998 terrorist bombings of the American embassies in Kenya and Tanzania which killed more than 250 people.

According to news reports, in a 1976 trust agreement drawn shortly after Bush's father was appointed director of the Central Intelligence Agency,* Saudi Sheik Salem M. bin Laden appointed Bath as his business representative in Texas. Bin Laden, along with his brothers, owned bin Laden Brothers Construction, one of the largest construction companies in the Middle East.

In a 1991 deposition, Bath testified he was the sole director of Skyway Aircraft Leasing Ltd., a Houston company owned by Khaled bin Mahfouz. Bin Mahfouz had been a major shareholder in BCCI, which had been accused of using Mideast oil money to seek ties to political leaders in other countries throughout the 1970s and 1980s.

---

*After President Gerald Ford asked Bush senior to head the CIA in November 1975, he and Barbara called George W. (who had only been in Midland a short time) and requested that he call his siblings in an effort to "very discreetly" gauge their opinions of the appointment.

According to court documents, Bath also swore that in 1977 he represented four prominent and wealthy Saudi Arabians as a trustee and used his name on their investments in the United States. In return, he received a five percent interest in their deals. Federal authorities (the Financial Crimes Enforcement Network and the FBI) later investigated Bath after allegations were made by one of his American business partners that the Saudis were using Bath and their enormous financial sources to influence U.S. policy.

Time reporters Beaty and Gwynne suggest in their book that the $50,000 Bath invested in George W.'s Arbusto Energy drilling company may have belonged to Bath's Saudi clients since the Houston businessman "had no substantial money of his own at the time." Ironically, the money used to underwrite the first business venture of a possible future president of the United States, may have been derived at least in part from the family fortune of Saudi terrorist, Osama bin Laden.*

In 1990, in an attempt to distance himself and his presidential father from the growing BCCI scandal, George W. stated in an interview that neither he nor the elder Bush had ever conducted business with James Bath. Junior went on record at the time as saying that he met the Houston businessman in 1970, when both were fighter pilots at the Air National Guard base at Ellington.

President Bush "knows Bath the way he knows thousands of people," his son told the press, and the two men could not be considered good friends. "I've never done business with him [Bath], and I know the president hasn't either."

A few months later, however, the release of tax documents and personal financial records forced George W. to admit that Bath had indeed been one of Arbusto Energy's original investors. Bush said that to his knowledge, Bath's investment was from personal funds, and no available evidence existed to determine that the money came from Saudi interests.

Numerous questions remain unanswered as to Bath's motives behind his investment in George W.'s first business venture.

---

*U.S. intelligence agencies were concerned that bin Laden might attempt to assassinate George W. or the former president, when both men toured the Middle East and met with Arab and Jewish leaders in November 1998, only four months after the embassy bombings in Kenya and Tanzania.

THE FIRST RACE

In the summer of 1977, with a net worth of more than $500,000 from five gas wells and three oil wells, Junior was "at the top of his game," according to Jimmy Allison, the publisher of the *Midland Reporter-Telegram,* and young Bush's best friend and frequent drinking buddy.

After downing several iced-down Budweisers late one night in Junior's office, Allison suggested that George W. make his first foray into politics by seeking the seat of veteran Democratic U.S. Representative George Mahon, who was retiring after forty-four years in Congress.

Junior's original response was a hearty laugh, and then he realized his longtime friend was "as serious as a heart attack."

Although George W. and Allison had known each other since the Bush family moved to Midland from Connecticut in 1948, Allison was actually closer to the senior Bush, whose successful congressional campaign he managed in 1966. He later joined Bush's staff in Washington, D.C., where he was so revered by coworkers and his boss that he was known simply as "the Aide."

In 1969 and 1970 Allison served as the deputy chairman of the Republican National Committee, but later resigned the post to organize a political consulting firm in the nation's capital. He returned to Midland in the summer of 1974 to rejoin his family's newspaper as executive vice president and then became its president after the death of his father in January 1975.

Junior respected Allison's political savvy and listened intently as his longtime friend, "gifted with a buoyant optimism which he transmitted through sparkling eyes that gleamed excitedly like wet stones," listed all the reasons why George W. should run for Texas' 19th Congressional District, even though Bush had only lived in the area for two years.

Bush agreed to think it over while the two men adjourned to another oilman's house for their weekly poker game. After winning $150, which Junior regarded as a favorable omen, he told Allison he had decided he would "take a shot at the family business." Naturally, George W. asked his father's former campaign director and congressional aide, to manage his own bid for political office. But Allison had to decline. He had been diagnosed with leukemia.

The news that his best friend—a man only forty-five years old—was terminally ill, sent shock waves through Bush, especially in light of the fact that it was the same disease that had taken his baby sister's life. His initial reaction was "fuck politics," although Allison pleaded with him to reconsider. And then Junior crashed, going on a week-long drinking binge.

For seven straight days he stayed on one continuous drunk, waking up each morning with swollen eyes, cobwebbed thoughts, and a parched mouth. After throwing up in the shower, he would mix a bloody Mary to settle his nerves and then start all over again. Finally, on the seventh morning, he stared at himself in the mirror and didn't like "the demon looking back." He drank a pot of black coffee and then made three calls: one to Allison, telling him he was going to stay sober and run for Congress; the second one to his brother, Neil,* asking him to come to Texas and be his campaign manager; and the third to the West Texas media, notifying them of a press conference at which he would declare his Republican candidacy.

"Let's face it, George was not real happy," recalled Midland oilman and Bush friend, Joe O'Neill. "It's the first-son syndrome. You want to live up to the very high expectations set by your father, but at the same time you want to go your own way, so you end up going kicking and screaming down the exact same path your father made."

"THE CALM TO HIS STORM"

A month after announcing his intentions to run for Congress, George W. was reintroduced to a former Midland resident, Austin public school librarian, Laura Welch. The couple fell in love and were married three months later.

Laura grew up in Midland, the only child of Harold and Jenna Welch. Her father was a homebuilder and her mother a homemaker who helped her husband keep his accounting books. She "vaguely" knew George W. in the seventh grade at Midland's San Jacinto Junior High. But Junior and his family moved to Houston when he was in the eighth grade, and Laura spent the remainder of her teenage years easily making A's in school, burying her nose in "tons of books," and hanging out with her friends at Agnes' Drive-In, her favorite place to buy Cokes.

After graduating with a degree in education from Southern Methodist University in Dallas in 1968, Laura traveled briefly in Europe and then relo-

---

*Only weeks earlier, Neil Bush had graduated from Tulane University in New Orleans with a bachelor's degree in international relations. He had intended to immediately pursue a master's degree in business, but elected to take a year off from school to direct his oldest brother's congressional campaign.

Although George W. requested his brother's help as manager of his campaign, he asked his father to "stay at home. I wanted to win or lose on my own."

cated to Houston, where she taught school for three years at John F. Kennedy Elementary. She also worked as a librarian for a year at the Kashmere Gardens branch of the Houston Public Library in the northeast part of the city. Incredibly, she and Bush had lived in the same apartment complex, the Chateaux Dijon, in southwest Houston during the time he was flying for the Texas Air National Guard, but they never met.

When Laura's second-grade class advanced, she moved with them. Years later, she admitted that the kids simply stole her heart. Sharing her love of books, she used to read to them several hours each day. She was so interested in children's literature, in fact, that she relocated to Austin and the University of Texas and earned a master's degree in library science in 1972.

In 1973 and 1974, she returned to Houston to work at the children's desk at the public library, and then later in the year she moved back to Austin to accept a position as the librarian at Dawson Elementary School.

When she was visiting her parents in Midland in 1975, friends tried to set her up with George W., but she declined. "I thought he was someone real political, and I wasn't interested," she later said.

Finally, in 1977, mutual friends matched up the two at a backyard barbecue and he says their blind date "has to be described as love at first sight," admitting that he was attracted to her because he found her to be "a very thoughtful, smart, interested person—one of the great listeners. And since I'm one of the big talkers, it was a great fit."

"We were really ready to get married," Laura recalled. "It just went a lot faster than it would have if we had met when we both lived at the Chateaux Dijon. . . . I think we were both happy to find each other."

"He was struck by lightning when he met her," Barbara Bush said, recalling how he spent a summer at the family's summer home in Maine "calling back to Midland every minute. And then one day he said he was going home. I think he had called [Laura's house] one day and a man answered."

By the time they met, Junior was on the tail end of his "young and irresponsible" years. Although he was still drinking, he had slowed down considerably.* And his "constant bed-hopping with West Texas bimbos," as one of his oilman buddies so aptly described the height of Bush's bachelor days, had come to an end as he prepared himself for the Republican primary battle ahead.

---

*Although generally confined to bed, his body ravaged by disease, Jimmy Allison would telephone Midland liquor stores and bars frequented by his best friend, and request that they not sell Bush any hard liquor, only beer or wine.

"By then I'd lived a lot of life, and I was beginning to settle down," George W. acknowledged. "When we met, I was enthralled."

Bush's parents were also elated that their oldest, and admittedly, wildest son had finally "sowed the last of his wild oats" and was getting married, especially to such a practical and down-to-earth woman. When Junior introduced Laura to his family, his usually serious younger brother, Jeb, bent down on one knee, proposal-style, and flung open his arms and asked George W. what his nervous parents would not: "Brother, did you pop the question, or are we just wasting our time?"

Bush often bristles at comments from his family and friends that Laura transformed him from drunk and reckless to sober and mature. "If I were a totally irresponsible person, she wouldn't have married me," adding that she reminded him that "at some point in time I had to make a decision—whether I wanted to drink or be a productive citizen." He does give her credit, though, for slowing him down. "She brings a lot of stability, a lot of common sense to our relationship." She is more low-key than George W.—"the calm," as one of his aides once put it, "to his storm."

They married three months after the backyard barbecue, at a small, intimate wedding attended by only close friends and family, then dove into his fledgling congressional campaign, which Junior admitted at the time had "really intensified our relationship. We're both running for office. Sure, we have our squabbles. But we are both in this together. We campaigned the whole first year of our marriage."

There were trying times during the Republican primary, however, when his opponents branded him a Northeastern outsider and carpetbagger, and he confessed to Jimmy Allison's Midland newspaper that he was "really tired and I just want Laura and I to hang out by ourselves at home."

One day during the campaign, Junior had to miss a rally in the West Texas town of Levelland and begged his wife to go in his place. Reluctantly, she agreed. When she arrived, she rose and repeated a line she had memorized earlier that day. "My husband told me I'd never have to make a political speech," Laura said to the crowd. "So much for political promises." Then, forgetting the remainder of her speech, she nervously mumbled a few words about George W.'s finer qualities and sat down after only a minute and a half. Although she publicly spoke rarely after that embarrassing incident, whenever she did take the podium, she always began with the same introductory joke, "George promised me I'd never have to make a speech . . . "

The only political advice her famous mother-in-law ever gave her was to never criticize your husband's speeches "because there will be plenty of others who will do that."* Laura adhered to that admonition over the years, with one notable exception.

"What did you think of my speech?" Junior asked his wife as he was turning into their driveway after a long and difficult day of campaigning in Lubbock in 1978. When she honestly replied that it "really wasn't that good," he drove the car into the garage door.

PRACTICE RUN

Bush was considered the dark horse of the congressional race, "a nice guy with no chance to win," as one area newspaper reported. He had only been living and working in Midland for a couple of years and had no recognizable political qualifications. Aided by an amateur campaign staff managed by his brother, Neil, and picked by just about everyone in the district to be "buried alive" in the Republican primary, Junior (with his new wife at his side) ran passionately against former Odessa mayor Jim Reese, who had the support of Ronald Reagan.† Not only was the former California governor and presidential hopeful popular in West Texas, Reese was well-known and opposed the retiring Mahon in the previous congressional race, garnering forty-six percent of the vote.

Bush staked out moderate positions with a pro-entrepreneur, anti–Jimmy Carter platform, but Reese labeled him a liberal East Coast Republican aligned with the "Rockefeller wing" of the party. George W. opposed Reese on term limits for members of Congress, calling the concept "simplistic" and promising to serve "until I'm not effective." He also argued that the Equal Rights Amendment for women was unnecessary and, while he stated he was personally opposed to legalized abortion, he was not in favor of a "pro-life" amendment.

---

*When Barbara Bush once suggested to her then-president husband that his speech was less than satisfactory, he spent the next several weeks attempting to prove to her that the rest of America had loved it.

†Even though Bush knew in reality that Reagan's endorsement of his opponent and financial assistance through his PAC was nothing more than a preemptive political strike against Junior's father, who was expected to challenge Reagan for the GOP presidential nomination in the coming months, Bush was still stunned by the timing of the support.

The elder Bush complained at the time to the *Washington Post:* "I'm not interested in getting into an argument with Reagan. But I'm surprised about what he is doing here, in my state . . . They are making a real effort to defeat George."

But the biggest issue in his 1978 primary race was the elder Bush, who Reese claimed was a member of the Rockefeller-founded Trilateral Commission* and favored a singular and global governing body. Junior shot back that he was averse to "one world government and one monetary system, and if the Trilateral Commission supports those things, I'm sure my father is a dissenting voice."

George W. also said Reese "insulted the voters" by suggesting that much of his support came from people who thought they were voting for his father, George H.W. Bush. "We don't need Dad in this race," he declared, a line he would often repeat during the 2000 presidential election. "We don't need anybody in this race except the people in this district."

Junior may not have been born in Midland as his opponent had repeatedly claimed, but George W. took the oil town overwhelmingly, giving him a 1,407-vote edge over Reese in the runoff election for the Republican nomination, despite the fact that the former Odessa mayor won sixteen of the congressional district's seventeen counties.

In the fall general election campaign, George W.'s opponent, Kent Hance, a conservative Democratic state senator and Lubbock attorney who would later switch political parties, also portrayed Junior as a transplanted Yankee and graduate of the country's most elite Ivy League schools: Andover, Yale, and Harvard. "He had a wonderful education, and we used that against him," remembered Otice Green, Hance's political adviser back then. Political ads highlighted the facts that while Bush was at Yale, Hance was attending Texas Tech, and while Bush was getting his MBA at Harvard Business School, Hance was a "local boy" enrolled at the University of Texas law school. Bush, in turn, denounced Hance as a potential errand boy for the

---

*The controversial Trilateral Commission was organized in 1973 by the Rockefeller family to keep informed of political activities in foreign countries and to foster better relations between the United States and other nations at a time of considerable friction among world governments. The Commission's members believed that the United States was no longer in such a singular leadership position as it had been in earlier post–World War II years, and that a more shared form of leadership—including Europe and Japan in particular—would be needed for the international system to navigate successfully the major challenges of the coming years. The Trilateralists' emphasis on international economics is not entirely disinterested, for the oil crisis forced many developing nations with doubtful repayment abilities to borrow excessively. All told, private multinational banks, particularly Rockefeller's Chase Manhattan, have loaned nearly $52 billion to developing countries.

In his autobiography *With No Apologies,* former senator and Republican presidential candidate Barry Goldwater termed the Trilateral Commission "David Rockefeller's newest international cabal," and said, "It is intended to be the vehicle for multinational consolidation of the commercial and banking interests by seizing control of the political government of the United States."

"tax-and-spend" Democrats President Carter and liberal House Speaker Thomas "Tip" O'Neil.

"Look at their record on oil and gas, on inflation . . . and it goes on and on," George W. claimed. "I feel we need a businesslike attitude in Washington, D.C. The question is who can stem the tide in Washington. Who can be a leader?"

Evidently not his opponent, Hance countered, painting Bush as a carousing, immature, spoiled rich kid who liked to party. Refraining from innuendo and rumors that Junior was "addicted to strong drink and women," Hance, a former university law professor, went straight for the facts and reproached Bush for hosting a recent campaign keg party for Texas Tech University students in Lubbock.

Although Junior largely ignored the controversy surrounding the "Bush Bash," he later told friends that he probably would have won if he had aggressively defended himself against the accusation. "It was cheap politics," Bush later said. "It was smart because it obviously had an effect." When Hance made a campaign issue of it, Junior was faced with a difficult choice: His opponent owned the property on which a Lubbock bar, a Tech student hangout, was located. Should he expose the connection? "I made the decision not to," Bush said. "Just an instinctive move. In retrospect I probably should have counterattacked with, 'How hypocritical is this?' " Instead, he stayed quiet and Hance observed that the incident illustrated "a big difference in our backgrounds."

When the West Texas dust settled and the ballots were counted on the first Tuesday in November 1978, George W. received forty-seven percent of the vote, although he spend a third more money than Hance.*

Publicly, Bush was a gracious loser, congratulating his opponent on an issue-driven and honest campaign. "We ran the good race, we ran hard," he told his disappointed supporters on election night. "I learned a lot about myself. I just was a better person for having run."

---

*Bush was criticized during the campaign when contributions and expenditures reports filed with the Federal Election Commission showed that sixty-four percent of the political donations he received originated outside the congressional district, with much more of his financial support coming from outside the state. Contributors included the vice-chairman of E.F. Hutton, the owner of the Los Angeles Dodgers, the chairman of the Bank of America in San Francisco, the commissioner of major league baseball, the owner of Frito-Lay, Hollywood film producers, the chairman of Pepsico, an executive of RCA Corp., vice-chairman of Ford Motor Company, the general counsel for Eli Lilly and Co., Mrs. Douglas MacArthur, former Secretary of Defense Donald Rumsfeld, and, of course, multitudes of insurance and petroleum companies, PACS, and other influential and wealthy individuals.

Privately, however, George W. was being subjected to his own personal hell. He had sacrificed more than a year of his life to a losing congressional race and, combined with the tragic death of Jimmy Allison (both he and his father were pallbearers) just three months earlier, Bush reasoned that it was way more than one man should bear alone in life.

So, much to his wife's dismay, Junior found solace in another old friend—Jack Daniels.

Seed Money

Laura knew she couldn't change her husband, explaining to friends that no one has the power to change anyone—people have to be motivated to change themselves.

Always a librarian at heart, she left books dealing with alcoholism scattered throughout their Midland home. When Bush finally sobered up after a post-election month of binging on whiskey,* he began reading chapters she had book-marked for his convenience. "Recognizing the Signs of Problem Drinking," "Symptoms of Alcohol Abuse," and "I Can't Be an Alcoholic Because . . . "

Laura never once lectured her husband about his obvious addiction because she knew he would just deny he had a drinking problem, which, in turn, would lead to arguments between the couple. Instead, she read "tons of books," visited with old friends, idled through magazines, worked in her garden, and cooked Junior's favorite comfort food—meatloaf, hamburgers, and tacos.

"Laura's quiet," Barbara Bush once said of her daughter-in-law, "but she accomplishes a great deal with quietness."

The turning point came on January 5, 1979, two months after George W.'s election defeat. His father filed his intention to form a presidential search committee and called his son later that evening to tell him that he planned to officially announce his candidacy for president in May.

Although the elder Bush had served in Congress for two terms and held high-level appointments as U.N. ambassador, GOP national chairman, CIA director, and head of the American liaison staff in China, most people out-

---

*Bush later told Laura that his grandfather and father had taught him that "you must be a politician to be successful" and that he had run for the congressional seat out of a sense of "passing on of tradition, passing on legacy, passing on responsibility."

side of the Washington Beltway had never heard of George Herbert Walker Bush. He said he needed the entire family to help him campaign across the country and asked if he could count on his oldest son's assistance.

Junior promised his support, but on a limited basis. "I've just spent over a year on my own campaign," he reportedly told his father. "I've neglected my business and family responsibilities and now it's time to make some money and give you and Mom some more grandkids."

True to his word, over the course of the next year, George W. made an all-out effort to be a better husband and transform Arbusto Energy (which was mocked by his election opponents as "Ar-bust-o") into a cash-generating drilling company. While his brothers and sister campaigned in primary states, Junior left his wife and business only on rare occasions to fan out across America with his siblings.

Barbara Bush later wrote in her memoir: "One of the real joys of the [1980] campaign was our children. They all put their own lives on hold to campaign for George. George W. was just coming off his run for Congress in West Texas, and although he needed to get on with making a living, he campaigned as much as he could."

Pete Teeley, who was Bush senior's press secretary during the presidential race, noted that Neil Bush was involved "to a considerable" degree and Jeb, Marvin, and Doro to lesser degrees. George W., who would later serve as his father's senior campaign adviser in 1988 and 1992, "didn't do much" in 1980, Teeley acknowledged. "He was trying to make a living at that time."

While the elder Bush went on to be elected vice president on the Republican ticket with Ronald Reagan in the fall of 1980, George W. began raising "seed money" to organize a publicly registered drilling partnership, in hopes of "bagging the elephant"—the oilmen's phrase for making a significant strike.

He had achieved moderate success with Arbusto during the oil boom of the late seventies, when drilling opportunities were abundant. But by 1980, the company's balance sheet was showing the strain of leaner times. Arbusto had less than $50,000 cash in the bank and more than half of its assets was money owed to it by others. The drilling company also was in debt to the tune of almost $300,000 in bank loans and another $120,000 to its creditors.

George W. relied extensively on family ties to pump new capital into Arbusto, drawing on the resources of leading U.S. financiers, industrialists, and corporate executives, who were willing to take a chance on the relatively inexperienced oilman. Midlanders who knew him at the time said that Junior's money-raising skills far exceeded his ability to drill successfully for oil.

"He had no big strikes. His strength was in fund-raising," offered Dennis "Wemus" Grubb, one of Bush's close friends. "He was able to get money with ease because of his name."

David Rosen, an independent Midland geologist, said Junior "put money together through his father's friends. He made no bones about it," adding that young Bush wasn't a very successful oilman. "They accepted him because of who his father was."

"They were mainly friends of my uncle," George W. explained, recalling the financial support network he received from Jonathan Bush, a prominent stockbroker active in New York Republican circles, who introduced him to several clients of his brokerage firm.

"John Bush called me one day and told me about his nephew, George, who was in the oil business," remembered Russell Reynolds, Jr., an old family friend who runs an international executive recruiting company. "He asked me if I would be interested in investing. So George W. came to see me, and I thought he was an absolute star."

More than fifty investors eventually raised almost $5 million worth of revenue for Arbusto's oil and gas drilling endeavors. Some of the largest financiers included: John D. Macomber, CEO of Celanese Corp. and William H. Draper III, a leading venture capital investor. The two executives contributed a combined $172,550 and would later be appointed as presidents of the U.S. Export-Import Bank during the Reagan and Bush administrations. George L. Ball, the chief executive of Prudential-Bache Securities, one of the nation's largest brokerage firms, gave $100,000. Lewis Lehrman, a founder of the Rite-Aid pharmacy chain, invested $47,500, which was pocket change compared to the $7 million of his own money he spent in 1982 in an unsuccessful race for governor of New York.

Bush family members also provided at least $180,000 in investment capital to Arbusto, including $25,000 from George W.'s grandmother, Dorothy Bush, and $80,000 from Fitzgerald Bemiss, godfather of Junior's younger brother, Marvin, and a close childhood friend of Bush senior.

George W. later acknowledged that without his uncle's brokerage firm connections, his chances of raising sufficient funds as a thirty-two-year-old with little experience in the oil business were "not very good."

Jonathan Bush remembered his nephew as a "very hard-working guy, and he had a darned good little company. Everybody liked dealing with him, and it wasn't a hard sale, frankly." Although Junior's family background wasn't part of the sales pitch, "it couldn't have hurt George," his uncle said.

Because Arbusto's seed money was largely generated between 1979 and 1982 during the same time period that George W.'s father ran unsuccessfully for the 1980 Republican nomination for president and his first year as Reagan's vice president, allegations of conflict of interest were directed at both the senior and junior Bush.

"There are many pockets in a politician's coat, and sometimes the more subtle pockets are the ones people prefer," said Larry Makinson, executive director at the Center for Responsive Politics, a nonpartisan research group in Washington. "If you can help out somebody's son in a business venture, [it is a way] people can establish long-term relationships that may prove vastly more fruitful than their original dollar investment in some start-up company."

George W. vehemently disagreed that his company's investors would eventually be paid in political dividends and reap a windfall at the expense of the American public. "These are sophisticated people that weren't interested in losing money," he claimed. "They were interested in making money. . . . I think ideas are a lot more important than my name. People don't like to throw money away."

"No, they don't," agreed a former Texas Republican Party fund-raising consultant. "There is a connection between money and power. The big name backers in Bush's company obviously believed they would one day get a return for their investment."

Business As Usual

In November 1981, George W. was in final negotiations to secure a one million dollar investment when he received a phone call from Laura's doctor. He was going to become a father of twins the next morning at nine.*

Two weeks earlier, Laura had been hospitalized in Dallas at Baylor Medical Center and confined to bed after physicians discovered she was suffering from toxemia, a pregnancy-related form of high blood pressure. When the disease reached the severe stage, Laura's doctor chose to deliver the babies by cesarean section to protect them from the additional stress of labor and in order to normalize Laura's blood pressure and improve her general condi-

*After trying unsuccessfully to have children for three years, the Bushes were in the process of adopting, and had applied for twins, when Laura became pregnant.

tion. Although Jenna and Barbara, named for their grandmothers, were almost two months premature, the twin girls were healthy and free of any lasting side-effects associated with their mother's difficult pregnancy.

After Bush was assured by doctors that his wife was receiving optimum maternal support at the hospital and that intensive neonatal care was being provided for the prematurely born infants, he returned to Midland the next day to continue negotiations with Executive Resources, a Panamanian company owned by New York investor Philip A. Uzielli.

Less than two months later, Executive Resources paid George W. $1 million in exchange for ten percent of Arbusto's stock. Although Bush acknowledged that the drilling company was not worth $10 million (according to financial statements, Arbusto had a book value of just $382,376 at the time), he said Uzielli was "betting on the future" because Arbusto owned oil leases and had plans to develop them when the price of crude was expected to approach or surpass one hundred dollars a barrel.

Bush stated he later discovered that Uzielli had been the college roommate of James A. Baker III, the longtime top political aide, cabinet officer, and adviser to George W.'s father. "I knew it afterward. I didn't know it at the time," he said, although he was first introduced to Uzielli by Jonathan Bush two years earlier, when an Uzielli business partner, George Ohrstrom, and his wife, invested $100,000 in Arbusto.

After Uzielli purchased ten percent of the company, Arbusto was renamed Bush Exploration because company officials believed "Bush" in the title would attract more investors than a Spanish name, but the drilling partnership raised just $1.3 million, less than one-fourth of its goal. Its drilling ventures met with calamitous results, and investors lost more than seventy-five percent of their investment.

As the price of crude continued to drop, Bush once again found himself in the precarious position of trying to save his company. Uzielli's Executive Resources purchased an additional ten percent share, but the price had fallen from $1 million to just $150,000 for the stock.

Uzielli described investment in Bush's oil business as a "losing wicket. It was disastrous—through no fault of George's," he said. "The good Lord didn't put any oil there."

By April 1984, Bush Exploration (and as its previous corporate incarnation, Arbusto Energy) had drilled ninety-five holes; forty-seven yielded oil, three yielded gas, and forty-five were dry. The company had raised a total of $4.7 million from limited partners and distributed $1.5 million back to them, according to securities filings.

Junior was only rescued from bankruptcy when Bush Exploration was purchased by Spectrum 7 Energy Corp., a Texas financial services firm that had already successfully recruited investors for its public drilling programs (limited partnerships). The company's two primary shareholders were William DeWitt, Jr. and Mercer Reynolds III, two staunch Reagan/Bush supporters from Cincinnati, who would later help George W. assemble the group of investors to purchase the Texas Rangers baseball team in 1989.

Paul Rea, a Midland geologist and oil executive and one of Bush's best friends, made the drilling decisions for Spectrum 7 while DeWitt handled the business end of the company from Cincinnati. Rea later stated that by the early 1980s, DeWitt had become so involved with his other interests that he was looking for an executive to manage Spectrum 7.

"He asked me to find someone in Midland who would be able to run the business down in Texas," Rea recalled. "DeWitt had gone to Yale and Harvard, and I thought maybe George might be a good one to invite to lunch. They had mutual friends from the Ivy League."

Over lunch, DeWitt and Bush secured a deal. "We were really interested in George, not his company," Rea later said. "Bush had name recognition. Here's a guy who immediately gets in the door to talk to investors."

As part of the September 1984 deal, Spectrum 7 Energy Corp. merged with Bush's ailing company by swapping more than 1.6 million shares of Spectrum 7 stock for the four thousand outstanding shares of Bush Exploration. George W. became the chief executive officer and in addition to his $75,000 annual salary, was awarded 1.1 million shares in the parent company's stock, which would later prove invaluable. Bush's friend, Rea became president.

Young companies like Spectrum 7, which borrowed heavily to buy high-priced reserves at the height of the oil boom, were considered vulnerable when the world oil prices collapsed in 1986. The company operated more than 180 wells for thirteen drilling funds it managed, all of which provided a modestly positive cash flow. When crude prices plummeted to almost ten dollars a barrel, Bush sought to increase their production in an attempt to keep Spectrum 7 solvent, although the company had lost $400,000 in the previous six months.

Hundreds of other oil companies filed for bankruptcy when unexpectedly low prices erased profits, shrank the value of the oil reserves, and made it all but impossible to raise or borrow money to explore and drill. Independent oilmen like Bush were going under every day, dragging with them six of Midland's banks and its real estate, oil services, and retail industries. Instead of laying off the exploration staff, reducing overhead, and watching Spectrum's assets deplete while hoping and praying the price of oil would come back up, Bush went looking for another merger, this time with a bigger company.

Rescue came in 1986 in the form of Dallas-based Harken Energy Corp., a company that was aggressively taking over troubled oil firms. Harken absorbed Spectrum's $3 million worth of crushing debt, purchased its 180-well operation and in the process Junior received $600,000 worth of Harken stock in return for his 14.9% stake in Spectrum. As a consultant to the company for "investor relations and equity placement," Bush was paid $80,000 to $100,000 a year, and was allowed to buy Harken stock at forty percent below face value as a member of the company's board of directors.

Years later, when he was running for governor of Texas, George W. told voters his efforts to steer his oil companies through the bust of the 1980s taught him how to "empathize" with the struggles of average Texans. "Everybody in the Permian Basin felt the same effect," he said, "and it didn't matter who your daddy was."

BORN AGAIN

Since the birth of Jenna and Barbara five years earlier, George W. had begun what one friend described as his "long, winding road to maturity." He had slowed down on the drinking (usually just an after dinner drink and a couple of beers in the evening while watching TV), stopped smoking cigarettes, and ran three miles to five miles every day at noon at the local YMCA.

"Each step was another exercise in discipline. He likes that," Laura explained. "It makes him feel good to give up bad habits."

Although the impetuosity Bush displayed in his youth was tempered by his marriage and the birth of his twin daughters, it was Reverend Billy Graham, America's evangelical statesman, who ultimately taught Bush to discipline his energies and guided him through his transformation to devoted family man and recovering alcoholic.

For decades, Graham had preached to hundreds of millions of people worldwide, rubbed elbows with kings, and acted as confidant to several American presidents. But to the Bush family, he was more than a spiritual adviser, he was a close and dear friend, who frequently vacationed with them at their summer compound in Kennebunkport, Maine.

During the 1980s, Graham developed a uniquely special bond with the vice president's eldest son. Junior reminded the evangelist of his own son, Franklin, who at the age of twenty-two, after a lengthy period of hell-raising and hard-drinking rebellion, committed his life to Jesus Christ. There were difficult times over the years, Graham told George W., when his son would tell him that he was a lost cause. Graham thought it ironic that he had helped millions of people around the world find a personal relationship with God, but he had seemingly failed in his own household, with his own prodigal son. Finally, after years of one-on-one ministering from his father, Franklin saw the light.

In 1986, during a walk on the beach in Kennebunkport, the evangelist asked Junior if he was "right with God." Bush responded that for the past five years he and his family had regularly attended services at a Midland Methodist church and he had even taught Sunday school class on several occasions.

Graham stopped walking and put a hand on Junior's shoulder. "You didn't answer my question, son," he said sternly. "Do you have the peace and understanding with God that can only come through our Lord Jesus Christ?"

Bush lowered his head and admitted that although he had grown up in the church, he "didn't always walk the walk," and had a nagging feeling that something was missing in his life. Although he had survived the collapse of the oil industry by merging Spectrum 7 with Harken Energy, the buyout had signaled the end of Bush's career as an independent oilman. Bush said he felt like a failure and instead of turning to God for strength, he acknowledged he had been drinking excessively to dull the pain and sense of loss.

"To be without God in this life is to be terribly lonely," Graham noted. "If there is one thing I want you to take back to Texas, it is this: God loves you, George, and God is interested in you. To recommit your life to Jesus Christ, you have to give up that one last demon before you can become a new man. Give it to Him, George, he'll take the burden, and set you free."

Graham's influence on his new disciple was "like planting a mustard seed. It took time to grow," Junior admitted, "and I began to change." Bush's reckoning with his "demon" came a few months later at the Broadmoor Hotel in Colorado Springs, Colorado, where he had gone with Midland friends for a collective 40th birthday celebration. For George W. it was a party to end all parties, after his brother Neil came in from Denver, and the friends stayed up late, laughing and drinking. The evening dinner at the venerable resort was extravagant, complete with a multi-course meal, several bottles of sixty-dollar Silver Oak cabernet and repeated toasts to all the birthday celebrants. Bush and fellow oilman, Don Evans (who would take on the role of his finance chairman in the coming years), both turned forty that month, and their wives would reach the same age in the fall. Also in attendance were the couple who had introduced the Bushes at their backyard barbecue, Joe and Jan O'Neill (she was also nearing forty).

"We weren't *that* loud," remembered Joe O'Neill. "But the next morning, nobody felt great."

Contrary to some accounts of the morning after, Bush didn't make any major proclamation at breakfast. He said nothing at first, not even to his wife, Laura. "It's easy to say, 'I quit,' " he later acknowledged. "But this time I meant it." It wasn't until Bush returned to Midland that he told her he had stopped drinking.

"He just said, 'I'm going to quit,' and he did," Laura recalled. "That was it. We joked about it later, saying he got the bar bill and that's why."

"I didn't get the sense at all that it was anything momentous at the time," said Jan O'Neill. "I think it was a big turning point in his own mind, but these things never take on momentous meaning until you follow through."

So what really happened the morning following the group's all-night party that prompted Bush's sudden vow of sobriety?

Alone in the hotel bathroom, Junior stared at the face in the mirror—a man with disheveled hair, crusted vomit on his chin, and bloodshot eyes that were beginning to tear up. He fell to his knees and sobbed uncontrollably, asking God to save him before he drank himself to death. From that moment on, he swore he'd never touch another drop of alcohol again. And he hasn't, later calling the talk with Graham and the morning he quit drinking "the defining moments" of his life.

"Christ has made a huge difference in my personal life," Bush told an Austin, Texas church congregation years later. "I firmly believe in the power of intercessory prayer."

During his campaign for Texas governor and president, George W. has been repeatedly hounded by the press with scrutinizing questions about his hard-drinking years and why he abruptly stopped one morning. "A lot of people say, 'Well, gosh, what's in his background, that he had to quit drinking?' " Bush often states. "What they ought to say, 'This is a guy that's disciplined enough to quit drinking.' "

Laura Bush said her husband's drinking years ended overnight, but it was not an overnight decision. "I think he had been thinking for probably a couple of years that he was drinking too much and it was interfering with his life."

Bush has frequently acknowledged in interviews that "alcohol began to compete with my energies. . . . I'd lose focus." Although he once said "he couldn't remember a day he hadn't had a drink," he added that he didn't believe he was "clinically alcoholic." Even his father, who had known for years that his son had a serious drinking problem, publicly proclaimed: "He was never an alcoholic. It's just he knows he can't hold his liquor."

Dr. Logan Gray, a specialist in the treatment of alcoholism and substance abuse, offered, "No other progressive and potentially fatal disease is more often denied than alcoholism. Even members of the alcoholic's family, who may suffer as much as the victim, often fail to recognize or refuse to acknowledge the existence of alcohol abuse by their relative," Dr. Gray said.

Bush's wife, who repeatedly begged him to quit, also seems to be in denial regarding her husband's years of alcohol abuse. "George never was a drinker who drank during the day," she once claimed. "He never did. He didn't have a Bloody Mary at lunch—ever."

"It is not *when* a person drinks," countered Dr. Gray, "but whether the amount can be controlled."

"Once he got started he couldn't quit, didn't shut it off," admitted Bush's close friend, Don Evans. "He didn't have the discipline."

More disturbing, however, is the vague hint in the Bushes' comments that George W.'s personality underwent a darker transformation when he was drinking heavily. "I wasn't pleasant to be around. . . . I wasn't so funny when I drank. All you have to do is ask my wife," he has said. "If you're feisty anyway, you don't need any reason to be more feisty."

By his own account, Bush also spent a great deal of time in Midland bars, where his kind of ragged nervous energy turned him into a bully after he drank. "George is pretty impulsive and does pretty much everything to excess," admitted Laura. "Drinking is not one of the good things to do to excess."

Less than three months before the birthday party in Colorado, Bush encountered Al Hunt, then the *Wall Street Journal*'s Washington bureau chief, at a Mexican restaurant in Dallas, where Hunt was dining with his wife, Judy Woodruff, and their four-year-old son. The current edition of *Washingtonian* magazine had just hit newsstands, featuring sixteen pundits who predicted that Jack Kemp would be the 1988 GOP nominee instead of Vice President Bush.

Hunt said an obviously drunken George W. approached his family's table in the restaurant and began loudly cursing at him in front of his young child. "You fucking son of a bitch," Hunt has quoted Bush as saying at the time, "I saw what you wrote. We're not going to forget this."

Charles Younger, a Midland orthopedic surgeon who jogged three or four miles with Bush most every day, allowed that when his close friend, a spree or binge drinker, had one too many "he could say some things that were not reflective of how he really felt when he was not drinking."

George W.'s father knew, however, that his son didn't need alcohol to make the metamorphosis from Dr. Jekyll to Mr. Hyde. Ever since he was a boy he had always been alternately sharp-tongued and funny, combative and consoling, charming and abrasive—just like his mother.

They were personality traits George W. would need as he reentered the hardball arena of politics, not as a candidate, but as his father's "loyalty enforcer" for the 1988 presidential campaign.

★ 4 ★

Home Run

Baseball is unique. It's a game of individual achievement for a cause greater than all. Kind of like politics.

—George W. Bush

Hatchet Man

"I'll be sort of a surrogate for my father," Junior publicly described his role as an unpaid senior adviser on the senior Bush's presidential campaign in the fall of 1986. "When his vice presidential responsibilities won't allow him to perform certain campaign duties, I'll be filling in for him. I'll be making speeches, helping in the fund-raising efforts and taking part in strategy sessions. It's kind of a no-title position."

Although the presidential election was still two years away and George W.

was still living and working in Midland (as an "active Harken Energy board member and consultant"), for all practical purposes he was already giving his new job his full attention, spending most of his day "with the phone growing out of his ear," as one campaign official put it, in an attempt to raise millions of campaign dollars from boot-clad West Texas oilmen for the upcoming primary battle.

"They want to talk to me because I'm the candidate's son," Junior acknowledged. "And, of course, I have access to the candidate."

Practically all nationwide polls showed his father as the front-runner for the GOP nomination, despite the recent Iran-Contra scandal that had mired the Reagan/Bush administration in its most serious controversy since it came to power in 1980. Both the credibility of the president and the political prospects of his vice president had been damaged with the continuing revelations about the administration's covert arms dealings with Iran and the stunning news that money from those transactions was channeled to the Contra rebels fighting communism in Nicaragua.*

After his twin girls finished their school year in May 1987, George W. relocated his family to the nation's capital, moving into a house only a few miles from the vice president's official residence. "When others see how hard we're working, it serves as a good example," Junior told the press. "It's important for people to see that the Bush family is totally committed."

---

*The problem for Vice President Bush went beyond his role as President Reagan's loyal cheerleader and would-be successor. Bush was a former CIA director and a member of the National Security Council; it was the council's staff that carried out the arms deals and the funneling of money to the Contras. The worst case scenario occurred, however, after Reagan told the press that his vice president raised no objections to the administration's arms shipments to Iran, an assertion that was in direct conflict with Bush's contention that he had expressed "certain reservations" about "certain aspects" of the dealings with Iran. In addition, Retired Air Force General Richard Secord testified before the joint congressional committee investigating the Iran-Contra scandal, that he believed Vice President Bush attended a meeting where the secret operation to supply arms to the Nicaraguan Contras was discussed. Secord's testimony contradicted statements by the vice president's office that Bush never attended such a meeting. The congressional report later cited a White House log showing that Bush did indeed attend the August 6, 1985 meeting with President Reagan, Secretary of State George Schultz, Secretary of Defense Casper Weinberger, National Security Adviser Robert C. McFarland, and White House chief of staff Donald T. Regan.

Campaign senior adviser, George W., acknowledged to the press that the Iran-Contra arms deal was creating political problems for his father. "The Iran thing has created enough confusion so it takes away one of our strengths, and that is getting people to see what George Bush is made out of and what his worth is," he said. "What it does, it tends to confuse voters so they don't focus on George Bush's strengths. . . . He is the best qualified guy to run the government."

Considered the most politically savvy of the Bush children, Junior assumed a major role in his father's campaign as an unofficial political adviser and chief troubleshooter, operating directly out of the Washington headquarters.

"He was an assessor of problems," recalled Mary Matalin, Republican strategist and Bush family confidante. "If they were real, he did something. If they weren't, he at least made people feel better. He was a general morale booster."

"He was brought in as the disciplinarian among a staff that was seen as talented but self-promotional," one senior campaign official explained, mentioning ad chief Roger Ailes, campaign manager Lee Atwater, and chairman James A. Baker III. "You had a lot of egos there and Bush's son was the only person there who didn't have another agenda other than what was best for his father. I don't want to overstate his role. It wasn't like he was the brains of the operation, but he was a figure to be reckoned with."

"Political professionals look upon candidates as the baggage they have to carry on their way to being famous," explained Chase Untermeyer, an old family friend who was the director of personnel in the Bush White House. "George W. was there to remind the various prima donnas that their main job was not to make themselves look like geniuses. It was to get George Bush elected."

Doug Wead, a former campaign staffer, noted that "Junior particularly enjoyed putting people who thought they were big shots in their place . . . harassing them with wisecracks and booming it out so everyone could hear it."

As a behind-the-scenes operative who also displayed and demanded unquestioned loyalty to the vice president, George W. earned a reputation as a "hothead who took care of business brusquely and with vivid language."

George W., serving as his father's "loyalty thermometer," threw his weight around from a generic office, where he chewed on an unlit cigar and spat bits of tobacco leaf in a plastic foam coffee cup. "He understood walking the plank," said Samuel K. Skinner, one of three chiefs of staff in the Bush White House. "He believed that if a guy brought you to the dance, you went home with him. You didn't leak to the media, you didn't waver, and you didn't feather your own nest."

"I was a pretty straightforward person," Bush has said in his defense. "Maybe people in Washington are use to double-talk."

One frequent recipient of Junior's tongue-lashing was campaign manager

Lee Atwater,* whose office was across the hall from George W.'s. On one particular occasion, when the valued political strategist appeared in *Esquire* magazine with his pants around his ankles (but gym shorts in place) as part of a celebrity feature called "One Leg at a Time," Junior "chewed on Atwater's ass like a hungry fat man at an all-you-can-eat buffet."

"I reminded Lee he was working for George Bush," Junior said. "I didn't appreciate the picture or the story. My dad didn't appreciate the picture or the story. And worse, my mother didn't appreciate the picture or the story. My dad expected there to be certain conduct during the campaign."

The senior Bush later assessed his son's role as his hatchet man: "Sometimes he did a lot of heavy lifting," he explained. "He could go to people and save me the agony of having to break the bad news to them. He did it. And that seasoned him."

"If the Vice President wasn't happy with any member of his campaign staff," said Janet Mullins, the political director of Bush's presidential campaign. "George W. was the guy he sent in."

Junior also developed a reputation for unflinchingly bullying reporters who he believed were critical of his father. When the *Washington Post* called his father "the Cliff Barnes of American politics," a reference to J.R. Ewing's hapless nemesis on the nighttime soap opera *Dallas,* whom the newspaper found "blustering, opportunistic, craven, and hopelessly ineffective all at once," George W. phoned the *Post*'s publisher, Katherine Graham, and "gave her an earful."

In its infamous October 19, 1987 cover story, "Fighting the Wimp Factor," *Newsweek* described the vice president's "crippling handicap" of being seen as a "wimp." The senior Bush had been a "vassal to Kissinger" at the United Nations and in Beijing, the article alleged, and to avoid appearing as a tele-

---

*Although George W. and Atwater became "great friends" and jogging buddies, Junior was directly recruited to be his father's "eyes and ears" in an effort to keep Atwater, the organizer of Reagan's 1984 campaign, "kind of focused and on track." The senior Bush didn't initially trust the young and brash political strategist, especially when it was learned that two of Atwater's business partners became part of rival Jack Kemp's campaign for the Republican nomination. Ironically, it was Atwater himself, who suggested that George W. be allowed to join him full-time in the campaign to demonstrate his loyalty to the senior Bush and his pursuit of the presidency. "I wasn't a spy," Junior later said, "but I was there to keep a watchful eye on operations."

More alike than either had imagined (both were reformed drinkers), the two men were soon colluding to manipulate the elder Bush. "You'd hear George say, 'I can't ask him to do that,' and then Lee say, 'Goddammit, you have to!' " recalled a White House staffer.

Before Atwater died of brain cancer in 1991, he began a spiritual quest. In his final days, Bush read the Bible at his hospital bedside.

vision wimp, he had "tried for the past 10 years to master the medium, studying it as if it were a foreign language. He has consulted voice and television coaches. He tried changing his glasses and even wearing contact lenses . . . Bush's tight, twangy voice is a common problem. Under stress, experts explain, the vocal chords tighten and the voice is higher than normal and lacks power." According to *Newsweek,* fifty-one percent of Americans found that the perception of being a "wimp" was a "serious problem" for Bush.

Junior was furious over the magazine's cover story, calling it "a cheap shot" and threatening to "take the guy who wrote the headline out on that boat," a reference to the senior Bush's speedboat, *Fidelity,* in which the vice president was depicted on the cover. George W. also called *Newsweek* Washington bureau chief, Evan Thomas, to inform him that the Bush presidential campaign had officially cut off all contact with the magazine and its reporters.

After the "Wimp Factor" story was published, its author Margaret Warner, who was not a "guy" as Bush assumed, phoned him and he "let her have it. I said, 'This is disgraceful. You spent all this time to write a two-page article, and it had the word 'wimp' in it seven times about George Bush?' I was furious," Junior later said. "I wasn't yelling, but I was very firm. She blamed it on her editors, and I said, 'Then you ought to quit. You ought to quit if that's the kind of journalistic integrity you have.' "

Prior to the Iowa caucuses, Atwater and Junior devised a plan to counter the senior Bush's wimp image. As preparation for a live interview with Dan Rather's *CBS Evening News,* the two men advised the vice president to "come out of the blocks aggressively," especially since reports had reached the Bush campaign that the network news anchorman and others at CBS were anticipating an interview that would harm the vice president.

"Some of it was pretty hair-raising," acknowledged Peter Teeley, communications director for the presidential candidate. "It was put to me that Rather was really going to confront Bush, and someone expected one of these two guys to crumble."

Although the vice president initially believed that Rather was a "fair guy" who wouldn't ambush him, Junior convinced him otherwise. "He's going to try to hang your scalp on the wall over Iran-Contra," George W. reportedly told his father. "You've got to come out swinging. And if he gets down and dirty, like we expect him to, then throw the shit right back in his face over the time last year when he was belly-aching that the U.S. Open was delaying his newscast and he stormed off the set, leaving the screen black for seven goddamn minutes."

Although advance promotional spots run by CBS prior to the vice president's interview indicated that the network planned to do more than a mere "political profile" of Bush, the show's five-minute setup piece preceding the interview promised "the questions that keep coming up in his campaign . . . on arms to Iran and money to the Contras."

As expected, Rather immediately began attacking the vice president on his role in the scandal, to which Bush responded, "If this is a political profile for an election, I have a very different opinion as to what one should be . . . I find this to be a rehash and a little bit, if you will excuse me, of misrepresentation on the part of CBS, which said you're doing a political profile of all the candidates, and then you come up with something that has been exhaustively looked into."

Rather brushed the vice president's comment aside. "Let's talk about your record," he said.

Bush countered by saying that the only thing he was hiding was "what I told the president." After admitting to having "erred on the side of trying to get these hostages out of there [Iran]," Bush stared straight ahead at the camera and followed his son's advice. "How would you like it if I judged your whole career by those seven minutes when you walked off the set in New York?"

Rather proceeded to lambaste the vice president, never offering him an opportunity to respond. After Rather's executive producer, Tom Bettag, yelled "Cut! Cut! Cut! You've got to cut!" into the newscaster's earpiece, he did, although many viewers thought he abruptly and rudely terminated the interview.

"The bastard didn't lay a glove on me," Bush later said to his son and other aides.

Although the vice president's performance went a long way in demolishing the wimp factor, Bush still came in a distant third behind Republican challengers Bob Dole and television evangelist Pat Robertson in the Iowa caucuses. Aboard Air Force Two en route to the New Hampshire primary, George W. pulled Atwater aside and said, "If we lose this one, we're dead. Get out a dirty tricks book, Lee, and start reading."

The campaign manager accordingly ordered a mammoth media buy of 1,800 gross ratings points, enough to guarantee that the average New Hampshire TV viewer would see Bob Dole "straddling" the question of whether to raise taxes eighteen times over the final three days before the primary. Once again, the senior Bush, who deplored negative advertising, was reluctant to go on the offensive, but Junior argued, "Dad, you may not win if we don't use this ad."

New Hampshire governor, John Sununu, the vice president's principal supporter in the state also urged Bush to run the Dole "straddling-the-fence" commercial and promised a nine-point victory for his friend in the primary. Oddly enough, the final result was thirty-eight percent for Bush and twenty-nine percent for Dole, securing the governor the post of White House chief of staff after Bush was elected president.

In the South Carolina primary, George W. and Atwater were more concerned about a possible upset by Robertson, who had mounted a major effort in the state. Shortly before Election Day in the state, a scandal was publicized involving another television evangelist, Jimmy Swaggart, a close friend of Robertson and an active supporter of his presidential campaign. The married Swaggart admitted to having had intimate relations with a prostitute in a sleazy motel, which caused a backlash against television ministries such as Robertson's Christian Broadcasting Network.

Robertson accused the Bush campaign of leaking Swaggart's "sins" to the press at a time that would be especially advantageous to the vice president. Meeting the press, the Republican challenger pointed to "the evidence that two weeks before the primary . . . it suddenly comes to light." Robertson added that the vice president's campaign was inclined to "sleazy" tricks, and suggested that his own last place finish in the New Hampshire primary was "quite possibly" the result of "dirty tricks" by Atwater and his staff.

Although Bush responded by dismissing his rival's charges as "crazy" and "absurd," sources close to the 1988 campaign, state that the vice president, who rarely wanted his fingerprints on any political hatchet work, probably gave the "okay" for the scandalous exposure of Swaggart with a "wink and a nod" to his son and Atwater.

The two political strategists boasted that they had built a "fire wall" in the southern Super Tuesday states that would prevent Dole, Robertson, or any other Republican challenger from seizing the party's nomination. True to their word, Atwater and Junior "front-loaded" Bush's effort in the south with money, political operatives, and television. In the March 8 Super Tuesday polling, the vice president won in Florida, Texas, Alabama, Arkansas, Georgia, Louisiana, Mississippi, North Carolina, Oklahoma, Tennessee, Virginia, Missouri, and Maryland, plus Massachusetts and Rhode Island outside of the geographic region. With the across-the-board triumph, Bush captured six hundred of the 803 delegates at stake that day.

The following July, while Bush went fishing in Wyoming and awaited his long-sought coronation at the Republican National Convention in New Orleans, George W. did a slow boil while watching the Democrats' political gathering in Atlanta, where Massachusetts Governor Michael Dukakis was nominated along with Lloyd Bentsen, a U.S. senator from Texas, as his running mate.

Ann Richards, then Texas' state treasurer, roused the convention delegates with her customary verbal firepower. "I am delighted to be here with you this evening because after listening to George Bush all these years, I figured you needed to know what a real Texas accent sounds like," she said, uttering her now famous remarks before a national television audience. "And now that he's after a job he can't get appointed to, he's like Columbus discovering America. He's found child care. He's found education," she continued, leading to the most repeated one-liner of the Democratic convention: "Poor George, he can't help it. He was born with a silver foot in his mouth."

Junior suppressed an urge to throw the bottle of non-alcoholic beer he was drinking at the time through the television screen. Instead, he picked up the telephone and called Atwater, ordering his father's campaign manager to list Dukakis's weak points on a 3-by-5 card. A few days later, Atwater's research director, Jim Pinkerton, provided George W. with seven topics: taxes, defense, drug penalties, the death sentence, pollution in Boston Harbor, the Massachusetts prison-furlough program, and the veto of a bill requiring the Pledge of Allegiance in public schools.

After the Republican convention nominated Bush and his running mate, Indiana Senator J. Danforth Quayle* (more commonly known as "Dan"), the two began attacking Dukakis with those issues as a means of reducing and ultimately reversing their opponents' eighteen-point lead in the polls. Bush repeatedly said on the campaign trail, "I'll never understand, when it came to his desk, why he vetoed a bill that called for the Pledge of Allegiance to be said in the schools of Massachusetts. We are one nation under God. Our kids should say the Pledge of Allegiance."

While the senior Bush waved the flag at one political rally after another between Labor Day and Election Day 1988, his son, Atwater, and ad chief

*Although Atwater approved of Bush's choice of Quayle as "somebody different" and "young and right," the vice president's son (who shouted out Texas' delegate votes at the convention, putting his father over the top and thereby making the nomination official) pushed for the ever-popular Elizabeth Dole, Reagan's former secretary of transportation, pointing out that she would help his father attract both Reagan Democrats and women who had been alienated by the GOP's stringent pro-life stance.

Roger Ailes, quietly went about their business of producing negative, but highly effective, television "attack" ads. One showed filmed footage of Dukakis circling the lot of a General Dynamics plant with a helmet on his head as he waved from the open turret of an M-1 battle tank, with a voiceover pointedly declaring, "And now he wants to be our commander in chief." Another TV spot that attacked the Democratic nominee on a specific issue, panned across the littered and polluted waters of Boston Harbor.

Never before, *Time* magazine later reported, had "attacks on an opponent, rather than promotion of one's own agenda, [become] the primary target of a presidential campaign." But the most controversial Bush ad was a black-and-white "revolving door of justice" that showed a silent procession of men in drab prison uniforms filing through a turning gate, in and out, and right back into society. A narrator's dramatic presentation noted that Governor Dukakis had vetoed the death penalty and given prison furloughs to "first-degree murders not eligible for parole" while "many committed other crimes like kidnapping and rape."*

The ad made no mention of a certain Willie Horton, a black convicted murderer who was released from a Massachusetts jail on his tenth furlough and then absconded to Maryland, where he raped a white woman and stabbed her fiancé. It wasn't necessary because a similar ad produced by "Americans for Bush," which ran on cable TV for twenty-eight days beginning with the second week in September, showed and named Horton.

The impact made by Horton's mug shot fused ideally with the revolving prison door of convicts, leading Bush's critics to complain that the ad was thoroughly racist without being nominally so, much like Nixon's "crime in the streets" shorthand for racist backlash during the 1968 presidential campaign.

Shortly thereafter, another attack ad appeared on television, which featured the fiancé of Horton's Maryland victim, quickly followed by another ad featuring the sister of Horton's teenage murder victim. During each of the ads, paid for by yet another sponsor, this time the pro-Bush National Security Political Action Committee, a voiceover informed viewers that the heinous crimes were caused by Dukakis' "liberal experiments." By that time, the Horton story had been discussed and dissected by the major network news programs, local television and radio stations, and newspapers and magazines throughout the country.

---

*The Bush ad failed to mention that the Massachusetts state prison-furlough program had been instituted by Dukakis' Republican predecessor, Frank Sargent.

Barbara Bush wrote in her diary on October 31, 1988: "Under Governor Dukakis, Massachusetts allowed weekend prison furloughs. One weekend, convicted murderer Willie Horton raped a woman and stabbed a man in Maryland. George used this heinous incident to illustrate that Dukakis was not tough on crime.* Then a pro-George independent committee—not our campaign—decided to turn the example into a campaign ad, using the image of a sinister-looking Willie Horton, who was black, as the focus. We got blamed for dirty politics and racism. Baloney. The ad was not ours, and the truth of the matter is, Willie Horton should not have been out of prison. . . ."

Technically and, more importantly, legally, the Bush/Quayle campaign was not behind the Willie Horton ads. In a successful effort to provide his father with plausible denial, Junior had raised the necessary funds and assisted in establishing the various "sponsors" and political action committees that financed the controversial ads. Although the Bush/Quayle campaign denied having any association with any person or organization that was responsible for the television commercials, the campaign refused to repudiate them.

It was later revealed that the so-called "independent" group, the National Security Political Action Committee, had established ties not only to the Republican Party, but to Bush ad chief, Roger Ailes. At least three production people used for the ad, Larry McCarthy, Floyd Brown, and Jesse T. Raiford, were veterans of Ailes Communications, suggesting possible collusion.

A Federal Elections Commission investigation to determine compliance with their regulations strongly suggested possible cooperation from the Bush/Quayle campaign, but left its official findings inconclusive. As journalist Martin Schram later wrote for the *New Republic,* the Bush campaign staff protested "loudly and publicly with all the anguish of a pro wrestler pounding the mat in feigned pain."

George W.'s inflammatory attack ads against Dukakis had dealt a fatal

---

*Bush, who portrayed his Democratic opponent as soft on crime for granting furloughs to prison inmates, provided key political and financial assistance in the founding of New Directions, a Houston halfway house to which hundreds of felons were admitted each year after receiving parole or early release from the Texas Department of Corrections.

Chartered in 1970, New Directions initially only accepted individuals who had been discharged from prison after completing their sentences. But in 1971, the halfway house began accepting parolees, the numbers of whom had increased due to a federal court order to ease overcrowding in Texas state prisons. New Directions' temporary residents included felons convicted of a wide range of crimes, including murder and other violent acts. In November 1981, Jeffery Allen Barney, on parole from an auto theft conviction and housed at New Directions for two months, raped and strangled Ruby Mae Longworth, the wife of a Pasadena, Texas minister who had befriended and helped the parolee obtain a job. Barney was later convicted and executed by lethal injection in 1986.

blow to the Democrats. With his father and Quayle sitting comfortably on a double-digit lead over their opponents going into the final weeks before the national election, Junior remarked to Atwater and Ailes that the Republicans were "looking at a fifty-three percent popular vote, the equivalent of a Super Bowl rout."

Then the well-oiled campaign was blindsided by rumors of a sex scandal between the senior Bush and Jennifer Fitzgerald, a British woman who worked in his vice presidential office, first as appointments secretary, and later as executive assistant, the "gatekeeper" who effectively controlled who had access to her boss.

The so-called Jennifer problem had been rehashed in every Bush national campaign since 1980, but this time the *Washington Post*'s respectable reporting team of Bob Woodward and Walter Pincus, in a six-part series just before the 1988 election, fueled the rumors of Bush's sexual dalliances with Fitzgerald by noting unexplained absences during the years when he was preparing for the 1980 primaries. Bush's "excuse," the investigative reporters wrote, was having to fly to Washington for top secret meetings of former CIA directors, thus making him incommunicado. Woodward and Pincus quoted Stansfield Turner, Jimmy Carter's director of the intelligence agency, as saying he "never knew former directors had meetings and there were none when I was there."

The gossip became so intense and the political damage so threatening that George W. was dispatched by the Bush campaign staff to ask his father if there was any truth to the rumors that his longtime executive secretary was also his mistress.

"The answer to the 'Big A' [adultery] question is N-O," Junior told Howard Fineman of *Newsweek*. His mother told Kathy Lewis of the *Houston Post* that she had not been pleased that her oldest son's name appeared in connection with the "whispering campaign" waged by her husband's opponents "because he opened the door for other people [to ask questions]. But I understood it. If it had been my mother and father, I would have spoken out, too."*

After the adultery allegations were successfully disposed of, at least until the next presidential campaign, the Bush/Quayle ticket went on to win 53.4 percent of the popular vote in forty-two states. On the negative side, however, half of the Republicans' electoral votes came from states in which they

---

*After the election, Lee Atwater admitted to other Bush campaign staff members that he was responsible for engineering the defusing *Newsweek* denial by George W.

received less than 55.5 percent of the two-party vote, demonstrating that there was certainly no runaway Bush/Quayle landslide.

In addition, the Republican Party actually lost seats in both houses of Congress and the voter turnout hit a new post-World War II low, with just 49.1 percent of eligible voters showing up at the poll. The new president could expect to govern the country with the votes of just 26.8 percent of the eligible voters on his side.

Soon after the 1988 election, a small cadre of fifteen fiercely loyal Bush supporters began to divide the spoils of a hard-fought war. The sole task of the so-called silent committee was to determine who had been politically dedicated enough to the president-elect to merit prestigious positions in the new administration. Heading the committee, of course, was Junior, leading one journalist to christen him "the Nancy Reagan of the Bush White House."

During one session, he proposed that an old family friend, Dallas catalog baron Roger Horchow, be appointed chairman of the National Endowment for the Arts. The other members of the group questioned Bush's choice. "Because he gave money to my father," was George W.'s rather matter-of-fact response.

A quick cross-check of Federal Election Commission (FEC) filing records indicated that Horchow had hedged his bets, however, contributing campaign donations to both Bush and Dukakis.

A red-faced George W. who has been described as being a "lot harder nosed about things than his daddy," slammed his fist on the conference table. "The double-crossing son-of-a-bitch," he said. "Cross his name off the list."

Family and friends agree that Bush's eldest son also has a long, exacting political memory. A classic example was when Craig Fuller, the vice president's chief of staff, was expected to move to the same position in the new administration, but was blocked from making the transition to the powerful job by an influential George W., who believed Fuller, a California Reaganite, was "inattentive" to the Bush family and longtime associates. Junior also had a personal ax to grind.

Pulitzer Prize–winning journalist Richard Ben Cramer, writing in *What It Takes,* his mammoth book on the 1988 presidential race, recounts an incident while Bush was vice president in which Fuller bumped George W. and his wife and two daughters from their reserved seats at a Houston Astros baseball game. While the bulletproof vest-clad senior Bush attempted to throw out the ceremonial first pitch, his oldest son was throwing a tantrum in the stadium's presidential box.

Midland oilman, Bobby Holt, a close family friend who raised tens of millions of dollars for the Bush/Quayle campaign, warned Fuller that he was now "on Junior's bad side" and "never, ever fuck with his family again," according to those in attendance.

George W. never forgot how Fuller embarrassed him in front of his family and political associates that day. During the presidential transition period, Junior made certain that his father rewarded John Sununu for his help in engineering Bush's New Hampshire primary victory, by appointing him chief of staff, effectively replacing Fuller, who had held that title since 1985.

Chairing the "silent committee," George W. "had exactly the right standard," noted one of the group's members. "He has a great ability to see through guff."

"When I had the chance to work during the presidential transition with George W. in Washington, my office was in between his office and Lee Atwater's," recalled Jim Oberwetter, a Republican activist and later director of governmental and public affairs for Dallas-based Hunt Oil Company. "I don't want to make the President mad at me, but having had a chance to work alongside both of them for a period of time, George W. Bush has more political sensitivities, a more political way about him than does the President. . . . He will be much easier to elect when he decides to run for office than his father was."

In the aftermath of the election, even the elder Bush came to appreciate his son's political instincts. "It was a wonderful experience for both of us," he said in later years. "He was very helpful to me, and I think it toughened him for the real world."

George W.'s Midland friend, Joe O'Neill noted that the younger Bush had made the transformation during the campaign from hothead to heir apparent. "George went up there as Sonny Corleone and came back as Michael," he said, using an analogy from *The Godfather.*

Most Washington careerists were surprised that Junior decided against working in his father's administration and planned to return to Texas with his family. "People were shocked when I said I wasn't going to hang around," he said. "The assumption was that I was up there to be a lobbyist or something. I knew from day one I was leaving the minute the campaign was over."

During his stint as his father's senior adviser for the presidential campaign, Junior frequently admitted to the press having future political aspirations. When Texas Governor Bill Clements announced that he wouldn't seek reelection, the handsome, articulate, and personable younger Bush was often touted as a possible gubernatorial candidate in 1990.

George W. stated that he had accepted living temporarily in the shadow of his famous father but admitted that, sooner or later, he would have to branch out and make a name for himself, either in politics or business.

Privately, he constantly complained of being called "Junior" by the press and political colleagues, but publicly he said, "In a presidential campaign two people named George Bush can be really confusing. You just have to swallow your pride a little."

For over a year, campaign literature authorized by his father, touted the key role being played by his son, "George Jr." After the election, however, he informed the press that "enough is enough," declaring it was time to set the record straight. "The head of the family," he explained, "is named George H.W. (Herbert Walker) Bush—that's one more initial than he bestowed on me, his oldest son, George W. Bush." He further explained that he had decided to go along with being called "Junior," in order "to facilitate matters."

After the inauguration, however, George W. was eager to establish his own public identity and lift his profile so high that running for public office would seem like a natural progression.

The telephone call from major league baseball commissioner, Peter Ueberroth, could not have come at a better time.

Play Ball!

When Edward L. Gaylord, a minority owner of the Texas Rangers, exercised his option to purchase the controlling interest in the baseball team from cash-strapped Texas oilman Eddie Chiles, he faced strong opposition from major-league owners because of his involvement in the television industry. The Oklahoman owned station KTVT in Forth Worth, as well as The Nashville Network (TNN) and Houston's KHTV. KTVT, which was carried by several cable systems, had television broadcast rights to the Rangers and the baseball ownership committee feared that the Texas team would become another "superstation" franchise such as the Atlanta Braves and the Chicago Cubs.

After the owners twice rejected Gaylord's bid to buy Chiles' fifty-eight percent majority interest in the Rangers, Commissioner Ueberroth phoned his good friend, George W., the eldest son of the new president of the United States, and asked him to form a syndicate of investors to provide an alternative to Gaylord's offer.

Although other groups had expressed an interest in buying the Rangers, Ueberroth, who had close ties to the Republican Party, assured Bush that his family connection would prove advantageous in his efforts to purchase the team. George Argyros, owner of the Seattle Mariners and one of the strongest opponents to Gaylord, had served as president and remained active in the Young Presidents, a Republican organization. New York Yankees owner George Steinbrenner, a member of the ownership committee, had also long been active in GOP functions.

"I saw a business opportunity and I seized it," Bush later said. "If you want something you have to move and move quickly," which is what he did in his quest for the baseball team. He initially planned to have only one partner in the venture: Roland Betts, a fraternity brother from his days at Yale University and president of a New York company that financed motion pictures.*

"George was going to be the general partner and name figure and I was going to be in the background providing the money," Betts explained. "That was the way it was till mid-February when Commissioner Ueberroth decided he wanted Dallas-based money."

In an effort to win the blessing of Ueberroth, the other team owners, and Chiles, Bush immediately began contacting businessmen he knew and some he did not know to form an expanded partnership. To clinch the deal, he persuaded a competing investment group headed by Forth Worth entrepreneur Richard Rainwater to join with his own, but only after Bush offered assurances that he wasn't going to run for office in the near future.

Bush's $606,000 investment, an amount that he initially refused to disclose to the media, was at least partially a sweat equity, meaning that his 1.8 percent in the team would be increased to 11.8 percent when the Rangers were later sold due to his active involvement in assembling the investors. He was named managing general partner (a job that paid him $200,000 per year) by the other general partner, Dallas financier Edward "Rusty" Rose, and the sixty-nine other investors, more for having put the deal together than for contributing his fair share of the $86 million purchase price (for eighty-seven percent of the sports franchise and Arlington Stadium). In reality, sources

*In the wake of the Littleton, Colorado high school massacre in April 1999, the Texas governor publicly stated that a "society that has romanticized violence" with its movies was largely to blame for the tragedy that left over a dozen students dead. Ironically, from 1983 to 1993, Bush was a paid director of Roland Betts' Silver Screen Management Services, Inc., which raised more than $1 billion through limited partnerships to finance the filming of twenty-one R-rated movies, including violent films such as *Shoot to Kill.*

involved in the sale state that Bush was named managing general partner because his major assets was his "family's name and political influence."

"Look, I don't deny it," Bush told the press, acknowledging that his name and connections played a major role in his success. "But I was also the person that aggressively sought the deal. I was a pit bull on the pant leg of opportunity. I wouldn't let go." He declined, however, to identify the other limited partners in the investment group, arguing that their anonymity wouldn't affect the public's trust in the franchise. Two of his partners were William DeWitt, Jr. (son of the former owner of the Cincinnati Reds) and Mercer Reynolds III, both major contributors to the Bush presidential campaign, and the primary shareholders of Spectrum 7 Energy Corp., the Cincinnati-based financial services firm that had merged with George W.'s troubled oil exploration company in 1984. Others included Connecticut real estate whiz Craig Stapleton, Bush's cousin through marriage; former Marriott Corporation executive Fred Malek, who had been a member of Nixon's inner circle; and two more Cincinnati investors: produce wholesaler Bob Castellini and broadcasting executive Dudley Taft.

At the press conference to announce the change of Rangers ownership, seventy-eight-year-old Chiles, who had known George W. since he was three years old,* told the media: "We think we've found the right people," to buy the sports franchise. "It's very important that the team stays in Texas and Bush has agreed to keep it here in the Metroplex [Dallas-Fort Worth area]."

In attendance at the media gathering was minority owner Edward Gaylord, who had a contract right of first refusal to nix the deal, but chose not to block it, he said, because the general partners were Texas-based. Gaylord also stated that he was so impressed with Bush that he would retain a portion of his thirty-three percent interest in the team. "I may be more enthused about this than Eddie," he added, noting that his soon-to-be former business partner looked despondent.

Chiles, who once described his acquisition of the hapless baseball team almost a decade earlier as the biggest mistake of his business career, told the media that "selling the Rangers was one of the great losses of my life. It was like losing part of my family. It was very traumatic."

"Negotiating with Eddie was like trying to pry a father away from his favorite son. He needed to sell the team, but he didn't really want to let it go,"

*Chiles had been friends with the Bushes since the Midland years in the 1940s and '50s. He used to call George W. a "young pup" and when his sister, Robin, was diagnosed with leukemia, Chiles flew her to hospitals in his private plane.

Bush noted. "When we win the World Series, Eddie deserves to be in the locker room drinking champagne with us."

Promising to retain Chiles as the Rangers' chairman of the board to act as a consultant, Bush added: "To us this is not a takeover. To us this is an infusion of new blood in a very stable franchise."

George W. made a smooth transition of power in the team's ownership exchange, which was in direct contrast to the example set by the Dallas Cowboys only a month earlier. When the professional football franchise was sold to Jerry Jones, he not only fired head coach Tom Landry, practically a Texas legend, but said he would be a "hands-on" owner from "cleats to jocks to socks." His arrogant attitude and abrupt termination of Landry offended most Cowboys fans.

"I'm in charge of hats and bats," Bush joked, then added on a more serious note, "We're not going to tell the baseball people how to play baseball. We won't be meddling. There won't be any changes in the front office and on the field."

Bush, who was reportedly interested in the upcoming Texas governor's race, was asked by the media if his new high profile position as the Rangers' managing general partner would provide him with the necessary public exposure. But he deflected all questions about his political aspirations. "Right now, the only race I'm interested in is the Pennant race," he said.

The First Big Tease

Bush and his family purchased a modest new brick home in the affluent Preston Hollow development in North Dallas, settling into a new life in the Texas metropolis that Laura described to friends as a "hybrid between Midland's simple homespun values and the phoney baloney of Washington."

While Laura involved herself in civic and charitable organizations, gardening, and the PTA (Jenna and Laura had enrolled in a nearby public school), her husband split his time between the Rangers' eleventh floor executive offices a half mile from Arlington Stadium and Harken Energy Corporation's headquarters near the Dallas–Fort Worth International Airport.

Bush, whose salary at Harken was increased to $120,000 a year in 1989, described his role in the oil exploration company as an "active consultant" to chief executive officer Mikel Faulkner on "mergers, acquisitions and special projects." Harken also loaned the president's son $180,375 (at five percent interest)* for the purchase of company stock, which, in 1989, made him the firm's second largest individual shareholder.

Publicly, Bush continued to play coy about his political plans, insisting that he hadn't decided whether to run for governor, "although I'm the right age." He kept busy in 1989, making a series of social rounds, raising his already-high public profile, and leading the media to view him as a "non-declared" gubernatorial candidate, a strategy he would successfully engage in future political campaigns, especially in the 2000 presidential race.

In an effort to generate exposure during baseball's off-season and maintain the rabid speculation over his political prospects, George W. seemed willing to attend any social function that garnered media coverage. While Lee Atwater, the president's campaign manager and Republican Party national chairman-designate, "passed the word to Texas political operatives to pave the way" for young Bush's race for governor, he appeared at numerous community events and receptions.

At the Dallas Civic Garden Center's Flora Awards luncheon, which he emceed at the Grand Kempinski Hotel, George W. was openly discussed not only as a GOP gubernatorial challenger but a future presidential candidate. When he spoke at the St. Valentine's Day Luncheon and Style Show for the Leukemia Society his political stock rose after he publicly displayed his previously unseen humorist side. Noting that one of his "buddies" was excited to attend the luncheon after he heard "that there would be lots of liquid refreshment for the guys," his friend remarked that the event echoed "the great ideas of your father . . . 1,000 pints of light."

Other social functions, including Bush serving as honorary chairman of the Dallas Auxiliary, a volunteer group that aids nonprofit charitable organizations, provided him with significant public exposure and generated support for his anticipated bid for the Texas governorship. At each event, those in attendance consistently urged George W. to run for office, and he always demurred, politely telling them to wait until late summer for him to make a decision.

The forty-two-year-old Bush "is going to have to demonstrate he has something going for him other than who took him home from the nursery," said University of Houston political scientist, Richard Murray. "You're not going to elect a governor because he is somebody's kid."

When NBC-TV interviewed "the new president's eldest son," Bush re-

---

*Harken's 1989 and 1990 SEC filings stated that the board of directors "forgave" $341,000 in loans to unspecified executives.

peated his usual mantra, "I haven't made up my mind if I'm going to run, yet," and attempted to downplay the lingering impression that because he was the Ivy League son of the president and able to buy a baseball team, he was wealthy either through inheritance or oil windfalls. "I'm living in Dallas, trying to make a living," he told a national television audience. Then, in a reference to the celebrated gibe Texas State Treasurer and expected gubernatorial candidate, Ann Richards, made about his father at the 1988 Democratic National Convention, he added: "No silver foots for this Bush."

In other interviews he noted that his Rangers' office was in a corner that did not afford a view of Arlington Stadium, all in keeping with the owner's perceived lack of self-importance. "Who cares about the size of my office or whether it overlooks the ballyard?" George W. asked. "The way I live, I don't drive fancy cars, I don't live in humongous houses. There's no statement in that, it's just my nature. . . . I view cars as utilitarian. Mine [a 1985 black Pontiac] happens to work. My wife drives a seven-year-old Malibu station wagon. When they quit or when the maintenance becomes too expensive, then we'll buy another car."*

During an interview with John McLaughlin, Senator Phil Gramm of Texas, a close friend of George W., stated that he had conferred with the president's son, and there was "a pretty good chance" he would seek the office of governor in 1990. "I do think that George W. has good political tools—in some way, as good or better than his dad's," the senator said. "He's smart and, remarkably, after having gone to Yale and Harvard, he still is a redneck with a good common touch," adding that Texans "will be licking their chops" in anticipation of a race between Bush and Ann Richards, "the lady with the bouffant who gave the mean speech at the convention that started things turning our way."

"Bush is a rich kid playing twiddly-sticks," said Ed Martin, executive director of the Texas Democratic Party. "But he's not going to play twiddly-sticks with the Texas voters. They're going to reject this Prince George son of the president, and rightfully so because he doesn't have the experience or credentials to run the state."

Bush was quick to answer his critics. "I know there are some people saying, 'The boy has never paid his dues,' " he said. "But I went to ninety-four

---

*Bush's well-crafted, down-home style was always on display. At the Rangers office he repeatedly wore a pair of shoes with a large hole in them, prompting his colleague, Rusty Rose, to purchase him a $120 pair of Gucci loafers for his birthday, which Bush returned to Neiman-Marcus and exchanged for cash.

counties in 1988 carrying the banner not only for George Bush but for a lot of people running for the state legislature. . . . If it's important in primary politics to have touched the people, I have done it—a lot. And I'm going to do it again."

In early February 1989, George W. began stumping for himself on a "Lincoln Day" tour of nine key Texas areas, that was touted as a preview of his possible 1990 gubernatorial campaign. In his self-described "Baseball, Apple Pie and First Family" speeches throughout the state, he stressed his belief that the 1988 presidential election proved "principles matter in politics, and if they mattered last year, they're certainly going to matter in 1990."

Bush also repeatedly stated in cities such as Houston and Lubbock that the chief factor in his decision to run for governor would be the feelings of his wife and twin seven-year-old daughters, another ploy of feigned indecision he would use in 2000. "They've just endured the wars of a presidential campaign, and we managed to come back as a stronger family," he claimed. "The question then is whether my wife, a former librarian, is prepared to step out into the public arena one more time."

In reality, Laura Bush was not part of the political equation. The only people actually involved in the decision-making process were her husband and her in-laws. "He trusts my judgment," George W. said of his father. "He said I should follow my own instincts." Barbara Bush's advice, however, was broadcast across the nation: "George is a man on his own," she said, "and I'd rather he ran in eight years, four years, whatever." Privately, she told her son that the "famous father factor" might pose a threat to him if he ran for governor and won. "The timing is not right. If the administration is doing well," she reportedly said, "there is no reason to assume you will get any particular credit for that. But if it's doing poorly, you are more likely to be assessed some blame or responsibility."

By the time baseball season opened,* Ann Richards, the state Treasurer since 1983, and wealthy Midland businessman, Clayton Williams, had officially announced their candidacies for the Democratic and Republican nominations for governor, respectively.

As the Rangers' managing general partner and public face, Bush was a constant presence at Arlington Stadium during the summer of 1989. When

*The Rangers opened the season in Arlington Stadium against the Detroit Tigers. Former Dallas Cowboys coach Tom Landry, whose name, too, had been bandied about concerning a possible run for the governor's seat, had been invited by Bush to throw out the first pitch. When asked what he would do if pitted against the NFL coaching legend in the Republican primary, George W. replied, "I'd punt."

he wasn't sitting in the stands with the fans or standing in line for hot dogs, he was autographing thousands of his own baseball cards or chatting with future Hall of Fame pitcher Nolan Ryan on the pitcher's mound while the flashbulbs popped. As a self-described "baseball nut," George W. was thoroughly enjoying a sport that he loved and admired.

Although the press relentlessly badgered Bush about his political aspirations, he always said he hadn't made a decision, preferring instead to regale reporters with his encyclopedic knowledge of baseball. He could name the starting nine on the 1954 New York Giants. He enjoyed having the names of semi-obscure former ballplayers thrown at him. Offer up a name like Pumpsie Green and Bush could identify him as an early 1960s second baseman for the Boston Red Sox.

If Bush was asked to respond to Democrat Ann Richards' acknowledgment that she was a recovering alcoholic, the former heavy drinker dodged the query and pointed out that the stadium had instituted "alcohol-free zones" for families and other fans who did not want to sit with rowdy beer guzzlers; and if the press wanted to know what he thought about Republican Clayton Williams' "3 D's" ("Don't Do Drugs") youth program, the Rangers owner said that the team players were constantly reminded "as role models to remain clean and drug-free."

During the July Fourth holiday, family and friends state that Bush had privately concluded he "would not be on the political playing field in 1990." Although he wouldn't make his decision official until later in the summer, he was beginning to sound less like an undeclared candidate in remarks to the press.

"In order to become an excellent candidate for governor, you have to have a one hundred percent, all-consuming desire to be governor," Bush explained. "There can be nothing that can divert your attention away from that total commitment to the race. Right now I'm determining the extent to which I have fire in the belly and I will readily confess there are two kinds of extinguishers. One is the Texas Rangers. I'm having a great time with the Texas Rangers and, too, with my little family."

Bush told his good friend and Yale classmate, Roland Betts: "You know, I could run for governor but I'm basically a media creation. I've never done anything. I've worked for my dad. I worked in the oil business. But that's not the kind of profile you have to have to get elected to public office."

Although he desperately wanted to avenge the political slight inflicted by Ann Richards on his family, George W. heeded his mother's advice and decided to sit out the election for four more years. In addition, he had grave reservations about running against Williams, the Midland millionaire who had pledged to spend $5 million, including $3 million of his personal funds, to win the Republican nomination. "My pockets just aren't that deep," Bush told friends.

On the first day of August 1989, with little fanfare or advance notice, he walked into the posh downtown Tower Club and announced in a speech to the lawyers division of the Dallas Jewish Federation: "There's been a lot of speculation about my own plans for next year," Bush said. "I've had time to think and sort things out, and at this time I'm not a candidate for governor in 1990."

Asked what he meant by "at this time," George W. replied that he had learned to "never say never" in politics. Acknowledging that polls indicated he could have swept the field of potential candidates, he cited family and business concerns as the reasons he ruled out a run for the Texas governorship.

"We have seven-year-old daughters—twins—that are just beginning to become little adults," Bush said. "I know that the strains of the campaign are such that fathering, being around and being there when needed would be nearly impossible."

Noting that he also wanted to focus on the Rangers, he admitted that he lacked the time and desire to mount a successful gubernatorial campaign. "I just didn't have that sense that I could look contributors and potential supporters in the eye and say, 'I'm willing to give you all I've got to be governor right now.' "

As he exited the Tower Club, one tenacious reporter followed him to the elevator and asked, "Off the record, Mr. Bush—If you had run for governor and won the Republican nomination, do you think you would have been elected?"

Bush didn't hesitate in responding. "No doubt about it."

"What if the ever-popular Ann Richards would have been your opponent?"

He looked away in the distance for a moment, as if contemplating what might have been a lively, rough-and-tumble governor's race. "I would have kicked her ass from the Gulf Coast to the Panhandle."

As George W. stepped into the elevator, the reporter asked one final question: "Still off the record, sir. If Richards wins and runs for reelection in 1994, will you be a candidate then?"

Just before the doors closed, he hollered back, "You betcha, buddy!"

★ 5 ★

Wins and Losses

I recognize what my talents are and what my weaknesses are.
I don't get hung up on it.
Being George Bush's son has its pluses and minuses in some people's minds.
In my thinking, it's a plus.

—George W. Bush

Exclusive Rights

In 1989, Harken Energy Corporation suffered losses of more than twelve million dollars against revenues of one billion dollars. That same year, Bush received $120,000 for consulting services to the company and stock options worth $131,250. He also was on the company payroll as a director and served on the exploration advisory board.

Although Harken was a small oil company, it paid big dividends to its top brass. In 1989, other executives in the firm drew six-figure salaries and five-figure bonuses. The following year, Harken's board of directors lavishly awarded three more executives with six-figure "incentives and performance" compensation packages, even though the company lost $40 million and shareholder equity plunged to $3 million, down from more than $70 million in 1988.

"It's a lot of jiggery-pokery," Wall Street analyst Barry Sahgal called Harken's tangled web of mounting debt, excessive executive pay, and "unusual" stock swaps.

Harken's largest creditors were threatening to foreclose on the struggling Texas company when suddenly, in January 1990, it acquired the exclusive and potentially lucrative rights to drill for oil and gas in Bahrain, a small Arab island emirate off the east coast of Saudi Arabia, about two hundred miles southeast of Kuwait. Energy analysts marveled at how Harken, a relatively small, unknown company with operations primarily in Texas, Louisiana, and Oklahoma, was able to beat out the more experienced and major international conglomerate, Amoco, especially since Harken had never drilled a single well overseas or offshore.

"This is an incredible deal, unbelievable for this small company," Charles Strain, a Houston-based energy analyst, told *Forbes* magazine. Under the terms of the agreement, Harken was awarded the exclusive right to explore for, develop, produce, transport, and market oil and gas throughout most of Bahrain's offshore territories.

So how did a small independent oil company with no international experience secure a potentially profitable foreign concession?

Favorite Son

In 1987, George W., whose father was vice president at the time, traveled to Little Rock, Arkansas to capitalize on his family's connections with Stephens, Inc., the largest investment banking and brokerage firm outside of New York.

Jackson Stephens, the financial institution's wealthy and influential cofounder, had been a major Reagan/Bush campaign contributor during the 1980 and 1984 elections. (In 1988, Stephens would become a member of the exclusive "Team 100" GOP group comprised of 249 individuals who donated at least $100,000 each to the Bush presidential campaign. Stephens' wife, Mary Anne, an outspoken and longtime nemesis of then-Governor Bill Clinton, would also be appointed Arkansas co-chairman of the 1988 Bush for President campaign at the personal request of senior adviser, George W.)

When Harken Energy needed an infusion of cash in the spring of 1987, the younger Bush personally met with Stephens, who had grown extremely rich over the years after underwriting one third of Wal-Mart's public offering in the early seventies, and requested his brokerage house's financial assistance with a $25 million stock offering.

Stephens, Inc. made arrangements with the London subsidiary of Union Bank of Switzerland (UBS) to provide the needed funds to Harken in return for a stock interest in the Texas-based oil company. As part of the Stephens-brokered deal, Sheikh Abdullah Bakhsh, a Saudi real estate tycoon and financier, who at one time owned nearly ten percent of Little Rock's Worthen Bank, joined Harken's board of directors as a major investor. Stephens, Inc., UBS, and Bakhsh each had ties to the now notorious and scandal-ridden Bank of Credit and Commerce International (BCCI), which at one time had over four hundred branches in seventy-eight countries with assets of over $20 billion, including drug-trafficking and arms-smuggling proceeds, looted savings and loans, and defrauded depositors of legitimate financial institutions. As he had done in 1977, when another BCCI figure, James Bath, invested heavily in Arbusto Energy, Bush was once again doing business with people who had ties to BCCI, commonly referred to by the U.S. Justice Department as the "Bank of Crooks and Criminals."

It was the Little Rock investment firm who handled the brokerage when Middle Eastern front men for BCCI made an early attempt to purchase First American Bank in Washington, D.C. (BCCI later acquired First American's predecessor, Financial General Bankshares.) Stephens, Inc. also played a significant role in introducing the BCCI virus into U.S. banking when it arranged the sale of Bert Lance's National Bank of Georgia to Ghaith Pharoan, identified by the U.S. Federal Reserve Board as a "front man" for BCCI's secret acquisitions of American banks.

At the time of the Harken investment, UBS was a joint-venture partner with BCCI in a bank in Geneva, Switzerland. According to Congressional hearings transcripts, UBS also helped BCCI skirt Panamanian money-laundering laws by flying cash out of the country in private jets, and was involved in Ferdinand Marcos' illegal transportation of 325 tons of gold out of the Philippines.

Sheikh Abdullah Bakhsh, as reported in the *Wall Street Journal* and in the book *False Profits* by Peter Truell and Larry Gurwin, had been an investment partner in Saudi Arabia with BCCI front man Gaith Pharoan. Khalid bin Mahfouz, another BCCI figure and head of the largest bank in the Arabian Peninsula, was Bakhsh's banker.

If any of Harken's shady business associations raised questions in the mind of Bush, the oil company's six figure–salaried consultant, director and second largest individual shareholder, he reportedly never voiced them in board meetings or in private conversations with other executives.

In April 1989, Bahrain's energy minister, Yousuf Shirawi, telephoned his "good friend" of thirty-five years, Houston oil consultant, Michael Ameen, an American-born son of Arab immigrants who had spent twenty-two years with Aramco and another thirteen as head of Mobil's Middle East operations. As a top Aramco official, Ameen "had close-up dealings for years with the Saudi royal family and its advisors," including Kamal Adliam, a BCCI principal and former head of Saudi intelligence. Ameen also was reportedly a close friend and associate of Sheikh Abdullah Bakhsh.

After Bahrain terminated exploration negotiations with Amoco, Shirawi asked Ameen to recommend a small independent American company "with technological know-how" to explore Bahrain's offshore holdings and give the government "its full attention," unlike the major multinational oil conglomerates.

"A smaller organization has less layers of decision makers, so it can move faster," noted Bryon Ratliff, at Price Waterhouse. "That's true worldwide. It's a riskier way to do business, but sometimes the rewards pay off."

"I'd worked with the majors like Mobile," recalled Ameen. "I didn't know a small company." By coincidence, one of the oil consultant's friends, David Edwards, an investment adviser with Stephens, Inc., called ten minutes later on a totally unrelated matter. During the course of their telephone conversation, Ameen mentioned Shirawi's request and, Edwards, in turn, recommended Harken Energy.

During contract talks between Harken and Bahrain, Ameen—simultaneously working as a U.S. State Department consultant—briefed the incoming American ambassador to the Arab nation, Charles Hostler, a San Diego real estate investor and a $100,000 contributor to the Republican Party. Although Hostler later claimed he never discussed Harken Energy with the Bahrainis, sources privy to the negotiations stated that the ambassador opined that the Bush administration would look favorably on any oil deal of which his son was a part.

Ameen, who introduced the Dallas-based oil company to governmental officials in Bahrain, was later paid a $100,000 finder's fee bonus by Harken "for bringing them the deal."

The financially-strapped firm lacked the required capital, however, to finance a large offshore drilling operation on the other side of the world, and was forced to solicit additional investors to underwrite the exploration venture. George W., the consummate fund-raiser, assembled a partnership with Fort Worth's Bass Enterprises Production Company. The billionaire Bass family, who had contributed more than $200,000 to the GOP in the later 1980s, agreed to provide $25 million for seismic data and drilling of the first three exploratory wells in Bahrain in exchange for fifty percent of Harken's profits.

When the *Oil and Gas Journal* reported that Harken had won the exclusive rights to drill in Bahrain, questions were raised by the media as to whether the contract—believed to be possibly quite profitable—was an attempt by the Arab country to curry favor with the Bush administration through the president's oldest son, who sat on the oil company's board of directors.

"It's obvious why they [Harken's board] kept George Bush," said Phil Kendrick, oilman and former owner of Harken Energy. "Just the fact that he's there gives them credibility. He's worth $120,000 a year to them just for that."

"George was very useful to Harken," Stuart Watson, a former director of the company, told the *Dallas Morning News* in 1994. "He could have been more so if he had had funds, but as far as contacts were concerned, he was terrific."

George W. bristled at allegations of undue political influence and the suggestion that he had benefited financially from his famous name. "My father has never lifted a finger to make any business transaction go forward for me," he told members of the press.

"This is not a self-made man," argued Ed Martin, the executive director of the Texas Democratic Party. "Sometimes market forces provide a remarkable string of good luck when your name is George W. Bush."

More controversy regarding the Bahrain deal erupted when the *Dallas Times Herald* reported that a number of people connected to the opprobrious Bank of Credit and Commerce International (BCCI) also had links to certain Harken Energy company officials and to the Arab nation. What made the exclusive drilling concession especially embarrassing for Harken and Bush was the fact that BCCI had used Middle Eastern oil money to seek ties to political leaders in several countries.

George W., of course, insisted that his father's position as president of the United States was coincidental at the time the Bahrain deal was negotiated, and claimed that as a Harken director and member of the oil company's exploration advisory board, he opposed the offshore venture.

"I thought it was a bad idea," Bush later claimed, noting Harken's lack of expertise in overseas drilling. He also added that he "had no idea that BCCI figured into" the Texas company's financial dealings.

"The kid was initially against the project," Michael Ameen said of Bush. "He felt it might be too much for Harken because the company had no international experience and might not be strong enough financially to handle it."

Bush, however, told conflicting stories about his own involvement in the Bahrain deal. He first stated that he was "so scrupulous" he had "recused" himself from company negotiations, alleging that he left the room when Bahrain was being discussed "because we can't even have the appearance of having anything to do with the government." Later, Bush amended his recollection, claiming that he had adamantly opposed the deal as too ambitious for a small firm like Harken.

Company officials have stated, to the contrary, that George W. was ecstatic about the prospect of Harken drilling in the oil-rich Persian Gulf. "Like any member of the board, he was thrilled," one executive asserted. "His attitude was, 'Holy shit, what a great deal!' "

Perhaps the most troubling aspect of the Harken-Bahrain business transaction was a possible conflict of interest regarding one of the oil company's directors and his involvement in U.S. foreign policy discussions concerning the Middle East. When the Saudi tycoon, Sheikh Abdullah Bakhsh, ended up with a ten percent stake in Harken as part of the Stephens-brokered deal to provide the company with a $25 million stock offering in 1987, Bakhsh placed his American representative, Palestinian-born Chicago businessman Talat Othman, on Harken's board of directors. After the Harken-Bahrain contract was signed, Othman was added to the list of fifteen Arabs who met with President George Bush, then-White House chief of staff John Sununu, and National Security Adviser Brent Scowcroft three times in 1990—once just two days after Iraq invaded Kuwait—to discuss Middle East policy. Othman and Bakhsh's attorney claimed that the Chicago investor and Harken board member was invited to the high-level White House meetings because of his "longstanding involvement in Arab-American affairs."

INSIDER INFORMATION

Four months after the Harken-Bahrain deal was sealed, the U.S. State Department sent a top secret report to Scowcroft that warned that Iraqi president Saddam Hussein was threatening his neighbors in the region and oil interests in the Persian Gulf would be jeopardized if Iraq invaded Saudi Arabia.

Initially the promise of a lucrative oil strike in the Middle East kept speculative investors buying stock in Harken Energy and lenders making loans. But when rumors began circulating that American troops might be dispatched to the Gulf to protect vital U.S. interests, Harken's financial advisers at Smith Barney issued a devastating report, voicing alarm over the company's rapidly deteriorating financial standing. The bottom line: Harken owed more than $150 million to banks and other creditors and nearly all of its value was in the Bahrain assets. To make matters worse, the first well wasn't scheduled to be drilled until early 1991.

On June 22, 1990, Bush suddenly unloaded sixty percent of his Harken stock—212,140 shares—for a tidy profit of $848,560, more than 2½ times their original value. The transaction came a week prior to the end of a quarter in which the company lost $23.2 million. A quarterly report, issued in August 1990 only days after Iraq's invasion of Kuwait, documented the loss and company stock plummeted to $2.37 per share. Bush, who sold at $4.12 per share, denied having any inside knowledge at the time, although he sat on Harken's board, its audit committee, and a panel looking at corporate restructuring, which had met in May and worked directly with the Smith Barney financial consultants.*

Bush's June 1990 transaction was an insider stock sale, but Securities and Exchange Commission (SEC) records indicate he did not file the required disclosure form, which was due no later than July 10, until eight months later. Bush later maintained that it was filed on time but the paperwork was lost by the SEC. "I'm very comfortable in looking you in the eye and saying I did nothing wrong on this," he told the press, adding that his stock sale was "entirely legal and proper."

The SEC investigated the president's son in 1991 for possible insider trading, the allegation of selling the stock with an insider's knowledge of nonpublic, market-moving news, such as a poor earnings report, but ended its review in October 1993 without filing charges.

"Please be advised," Bruce A. Hiler, associate director of the U.S. Securi-

---

*Although analysts like Charlie Andrews of 13D Research Inc. of Brewster, New York, had urged investors in March 1990 to buy Harken's stock because "the potential inherent in the Bahrain oil exploration deal is so great," Harken's bankers had clamped down on the company after it violated terms of a $115 million loan package. The renegotiated loan agreement, reached May 21, 1990—only a month before Bush sold the bulk of his stock—featured strict terms, including a high interest rate of twelve percent, less credit for acquisitions, a $750,000 fee, and requirements by some major stockholders to guarantee $22.5 million in debt. The next day, Harken announced plans to raise $40 million, $15 million of which would repay bank debt. The balance would infuse cash into two of its companies and fund acquisitions.

ties and Exchange Commission's enforcement division, said in the letter to Bush's attorney,* "that the investigation has been terminated as to the conduct of Mr. Bush and that, at this time, no enforcement is contemplated with respect to him."

Another passage in the SEC letter stated, however: "It must in no way be construed as indicating that the party has been exonerated or that no action may ultimately result."

Questions remain as to whether it was a real investigation or a whitewash of an insider stock sale by the son of a sitting president of the United States. At best, it was incomplete, and at worst, a possible cover-up.

The investigation was tainted because the SEC chairman at the time was Richard Breeden, a former lawyer with the Houston-based law firm Baker & Botts. Breeden had been deputy counsel to the elder Bush when he was vice president and received his SEC appointment after Bush became president.

In addition, the SEC general counsel was James R. Doty, who, working previously as a private lawyer, assisted George W. in the negotiation of the legal contract for the purchase of the Texas Rangers baseball team in 1989. Bush had acknowledged that he sold the Harken shares to repay $500,000 in loans from the United Bank in Midland which he used to fund his stake in the Rangers partnership.

"The case was handled and all decisions in the case were made by enforcement division attorneys, all of whom are career prosecutors," emphasized William McLucas, the SEC's director of enforcement. "Investigations conducted by the commission and the enforcement division are free of political influence, and this investigation was no different," he added.

After taking eight months to notify the government of his sale of Harken stock, Bush also missed the filing deadline for reporting other insider trades involving the Dallas oil company, according to SEC records.

Bush's November 1, 1986 acquisition of 212,152 shares of Harken stock as a result of the merger of his Spectrum 7 company with Harken was not reported until April 7, 1987. (The filing also disclosed Bush's March 10, 1987 purchase of an additional eighty thousand shares.)

An April 22, 1987 filing listed a December 10, 1986 purchase of eighty thousand shares of Harken stock. Bush's attorney stated that it was the same

*The October 1993 SEC letter, coveted for its political value, was issued at the request of Bush, who planned to run for Texas governor in 1994, and wanted to have "something in writing to show anyone looking into" his sale of Harken stock.

eighty thousand shares reported in the April 7, 1987 filing, but could not explain why it was reported twice or which date was correct.

Bush's June 16, 1989 purchase of twenty-five thousand shares of Harken Energy stock was not reported until a September 7, 1989 filing.

"George W. can thank the good Lord that Clinton and Starr gave the office of the independent counsel such a bad name," said an investigator with the SEC, "because a special prosecutor with limitless authority and a bottomless budget would have his work cut out for him during a second Bush presidency. Consider George W.'s shady business transactions over the years in light of newly established standards for impeachable offenses and suddenly Slick Willie's land deal in Arkansas doesn't look so bad."

Just as Clinton didn't see anything illegal with the Whitewater development deal because he "lost money," Bush said he did "nothing wrong" at Harken Energy, noting instead that all three wells eventually drilled in Bahrain "were dry holes."

The success or failure of the Persian Gulf contract was not an issue to the SEC. Rather, their investigation focused on whether Bush "cashed in" on his family's store of political influence and whether he traded on exclusive, non-public, insider information to amass a great deal of wealth.

Unlike other millionaire Texas oilmen before him, including his father, Bush's fortune was made from stock swaps and bailouts, rather than oil booms and gushers.

"The Most Miserable Year of My Life"

In late 1991, with Harken Energy in deep financial trouble and his father in even worse political distress, Bush took a leave of absence from the board of directors and from his consulting job* with the beleaguered oil company to return to his post as "hatchet man" for the 1992 presidential campaign.

"For the president' son, it was like jumping from the frying pan into the fire," said one former White House aide. "He really didn't want to take the job. He was battle-scarred from allegations of influence peddling with the Bahrain deal and all he wanted to do in the winter of 1991 was get the Rangers ready for Pennant contention and go to his girls' PTA meetings. But his daddy's back was against the wall."

*Bush's compensation as a consultant dropped from $120,000 in 1989 to $44,000 in 1991 as Harken continued its downward spiral and record losses.

During his drive every morning from his Dallas home to the Texas Rangers' office in nearby Arlington, George W. grew increasingly concerned as he listened to his fellow Texans rant and rave on the numerous talk radio stations. Like many voters across the nation, they lacked confidence in the president, particularly in his ability to handle domestic affairs and revive an anemic economy:

". . . Every day you pick up the paper and see another company is laying off workers. But until recently, Bush was saying the country wasn't in a recession . . ."

". . . I think he has his head buried in the sand. He needs to stop going overseas so much and take care of his own people . . ."

". . . I personally feel he is lacking in compassion for the middle class. He's left us behind . . ."

". . . He's lost the respect and support in Texas, the state where he votes and where he got his political start . . ."

The president's son was in almost daily telephone contact with his father and campaign officials in Washington, summarizing the "pulse of the people." At first, he refused to relocate to the nation's capital even on a temporary basis, choosing instead to visit the White House about once a month. But when he did make one of his infrequent appearances, "the shit always hit the fan," as one campaign aide put it.

"I'm not a thousand-pound gorilla," the younger Bush said of his role, "but do I talk to my dad? You bet. Do I bring a different perspective than what he usually hears? You bet. Does he do every thing I suggest? No way. But he can always be totally sure that my agenda is his agenda."

"Nobody blows off anything George says," said a campaign official at the time, noting that he was a "quick study, with astute political instincts. He knows people all over the country. He's got a good sense of what's going on out there. And unlike other political aspirants on the Bush reelection team, George is an effective advocate for his father's best interest."

"He is the number one troubleshooter, the number one political antenna, the number one confidant of his father, the number one problem fixer," explained Mary Matalin, the highly respected Republican political strategist who worked closely with the younger Bush as his father's deputy campaign manager.

Many GOP political analysts said that part of the president's problem was "his big heart and sense of loyalty" and having trouble "doing things a politician has to do," like firing incompetent or politically embarrassing subordinates, which he believed was demeaning of his high office.

The first head on the hatchet man's chopping block was controversial White House Chief of Staff, John Sununu, who had played a key role in getting the elder Bush elected in 1988. The abrasive and outspoken former governor of New Hampshire had been struggling to keep his job for months amid repeated calls for his resignation from Republicans and Democrats alike, many of whom blamed his hard-right views for the White House's slow response on domestic and economic issues.

Widespread press reports earlier in the year revealed Sununu's extensive travel aboard Air Force planes for personal reasons, such as Colorado ski vacations and trips to Boston to see his dentist, costing taxpayers hundreds of thousands of dollars. In a move aimed at defusing the political damage to the president, the White House imposed special restrictions on Sununu's travels. Even after being grounded, the chief of staff persisted in stirring up controversy by using a White House limousine to ferry him to a stamp collectors' show in New York.

Sununu, the butt of late-night talk shows and of political cartoons, was typically combative in trying to counter allegations of impropriety, repeatedly accusing reporters and liberal political foes of orchestrating a smear campaign to force him out of the White House. Then in an unprecedented move for a chief of staff, Sununu criticized his boss in open defiance and asked conservative Republicans to launch a public show of support, urging the president keep him on the job.

"Since it appears that everybody is laying all the problems of the country and the administration on John Sununu's doorstep, some of us that very much want to see him retained . . . need to step up and defend him," Congressman Vin Weber of Minnesota declared at a joint Capitol Hill news conference with U.S. Representative Henry Hyde of Illinois.

Finally, the president, who had to force Ronald Reagan's chief of staff Donald Regan, out of his White House post when he was vice president, requested George W. to do the same to Sununu. "Tell him to take the fall," the elder Bush reportedly said to his son, while publicly remaining supportive of his top aide, calling him "a class act."

George W., long a supporter of Sununu and his confrontational style of management and politics, paid the chief of staff a visit at the White House the day before Thanksgiving. Bush bluntly told him that the president, who had seen his approval ratings plunge after incidents connected to Sununu's tenure, needed him to "fall on the grenade like a good soldier," adding that he had lost the confidence of top Bush loyalists in the administration and in the Republican Party.

The chief of staff cried when Bush told him that he needed to compose a letter of resignation, effective December 15, in which he profusely apologized for the embarrassment he had caused the administration. As a reward, he would continue to hold a cabinet-level slot as a counselor to the president.

Sununu straightened and wiped his swollen eyes. "Is this request coming directly from the president?" he asked, showing a hint of the trademark arrogance.

"Let me put it this way, John," Bush shot back. "I'm not freelancing."

A few days later, while en route to Florida aboard Air Force One, Sununu presented the president with a handwritten five-page letter of resignation. "In politics, especially during the seasons of a political campaign, perceptions that can be effectively dealt with at other times can be—and will be—converted into real political negatives," Sununu wrote. "Until recently, I was convinced that even with the distorted perceptions being created, I could be a strong contributor to your efforts and success."

But the embattled chief of staff later told reporters that Bush "doesn't need an extra political target that folks would be shooting at, and I think it's best for the president that I move on," he said.

In a gracious letter accepting the resignation he had indirectly sought, Bush wrote to Sununu: "You have never wavered in your loyalty to us and more importantly, your loyalty to the principles and goals of this administration. You have indeed helped with the issues and you have intercepted many of the 'arrows' aimed my way."

After successfully "putting Sununu out to pasture," George W. returned to Texas to oversee preparation for his baseball team's spring training and to campaign for his father in his home state. "I think I can bring an added dimension by staying out here and staying in touch with folks like the Athens, Texas Rotary Club," Bush told a Republican gathering, noting that his assignments were "inspirational director, loyalty checker, and troubleshooter."

Once a month, however, he would "storm into Washington," to review the reelection effort at campaign headquarters, where he "hung people out to dry and then just plain hung them" for not reacting properly to fast-moving political developments. When the president became increasingly displeased with the entropy around him, complaining of cliché-ridden and boring speeches and murky campaign themes, that unhappiness was conveyed in rather salty language to senior aides by George W.

"Sometimes the agendas get confused," he said. "I had one agenda, and that was in the best interests of George H.W. Bush. I told some people in the '92 campaign that I didn't appreciate them trying to climb off the good ship

George Bush before it docked. And, yes, I occasionally told a member of the press corps that I didn't like the way they were treating my father."

The national media repeatedly made mention of George W.'s "thin-skinned reputation" for defending his father's honor during the 1992 presidential campaign, referring to him as "the Roman candle of the family . . . and the likeliest to burn the fingers."

A self-described "high-energy person," the younger Bush acknowledged that he understood why the press considered him a "hotheaded, peevish prince" at the time. "I was unhappy about what I was seeing, which was my dad losing the presidency," he later said. "I was unhappy about some of the stories in the press, and I was unhappy about how some in his entourage weren't being as supportive as I think they ought to have been."

"He was a much more humble fellow in 1988," said a longtime GOP activist. "In '92 he had an answer to almost everything." But most of the time, George W.'s political instincts were right on the money, even if his father didn't always heed his "hard truth" advice.

He was the first Bush adviser to focus on the seriousness of Texas billionaire H. Ross Perot's grassroots candidacy,* arguing that he was entering the race largely to fulfill his personal vendetta against the president and was

---

*The bad blood between Bush and Perot, who was once described by *The Economist* as "a short little man, with a yapping drawl, sticking-out ears, and a head like a bottle brush," began in the late seventies as Bush was ending his tenure as CIA director. Perot, who had grown wealthy by obtaining federal contracts to handle Medicare payments via his Electronic Data Processing company, traveled to Maine to offer Bush a job managing one of his new oil companies. Bush politely declined, but the eccentric, temperamental Texan took the refusal personally.

During the Reagan administration Perot traveled to Vietnam in violation of the Logan Act on a personal mission to locate thirty-nine American POWs allegedly performing slave labor in Southeast Asia. When he returned empty-handed, Reagan refused to meet with him and pawned him off on his loyal vice president. Perot suggested that he might offer to buy all of Cam Ranh Bay as a form of ransom, or attempt to pay $1 million for each returned prisoner. Bush rejected both ideas. "Well, George, I go in looking for prisoners, but I spend all my time discovering the government has been moving drugs around the world and is involved in illegal arms deals," Perot alleged. "I can't get at the prisoners because of the corruption among our own covert people." He told the vice president that other officials around him were not corrupt but merely incompetent. As for Bush himself, Perot told him, "The world is full of lions and tigers and rabbits. And you're a rabbit." Bush later acknowledged that he "was then in Perot's crosshairs."

True enough, in the coming years he publicly called Bush "weak" and a "wimp," especially during his presidential term. Privately, he and his lawyer, Tom Luce, contracted a Washington attorney, Berl Bernhard, to investigate a $48 million tax deduction obtained by Pennzoil, whose chairman, J. Hugh Liedtzke, was Bush's former Zapata Petroleum partner. Perot also tried to interest the *Washington Post*'s Bob Woodward in writing a scandalous article about Bush, but the investigative reporter declined, citing lack of incriminating facts.

"trying to steal away" some key states; warned the Bush campaign staff a year before the election that "complacency is the enemy" and the president's high poll numbers were unrealistically "stratospheric" because of the country's euphoria over victory in the Persian Gulf War; along with former president Gerald Ford attempted to persuade his father to dump the seemingly hapless Dan Quayle ("another political liability") from the Republican ticket; urged his father to bring back media adviser Roger Ailes, and "go ballistic" in negative television ads attacking Bill Clinton, the Democratic nominee, like they successfully did against Michael Dukakis in 1988; advised the reelection effort to focus on Perot's opposition to the Gulf War, his support of abortion rights, and the $146,550 he and his family had given to congressional campaigns since 1978; talked the elder Bush into going to Bentonville, Arkansas, "home of Wal-Mart and Clinton's own backyard," to present the company's founder, the revered and terminally ill Sam Walton, with the Presidential Medal of Freedom, the nation's highest civilian award; and implored his father to "green light" the use of GOP private investigators who wanted to track down rumors of young black women Clinton had allegedly impregnated in south Arkansas while he was the state's attorney general.

Unlike Dukakis, Clinton was a skilled practitioner in the art of campaigning and Perot simply had the enormous personal wealth and taste for revenge. Soon enough, George W. found himself the target of attacks by the national media as journalists began scrutinizing his past business dealings, including the exclusive Bahrain drilling contract and the insider sale of Harken stock just before the company's report of declining earnings.

Just as he defended his father against the "chip-on-the-shoulder hostility of the press," George W. was equally sensitive about accusations aimed at himself. When the headline of a front-page story in the *Los Angeles Times* boldly proclaimed "Bush Kin: Trading on the Name? Evidence Suggests the President's Relatives May Be Exploiting Their Relationship," George W. threw a tantrum in his Rangers office. At the Republican National Convention in Houston, he stormed out of an interview with a Salt Lake City TV station when the reporter questioned the elder Bush's commitment to "family values" because "you have three crooks in the family." And after the *Wall Street Journal* ran a six-column article on the business dealings of George W. and two of his brothers,* he vented his anger at *Journal* reporter John Har-

---

*In addition to George W.'s wheeling and dealing, the media was taking a closer look at his younger brothers Neil and Jeb and didn't like what they saw, especially since their father claimed that only a return to traditional "family values" could cure the "poverty spirit" that plagued America.

wood on an airport tarmac during the last days of the campaign even though Harwood hadn't written the article.

"You question a man's integrity," a red-faced Bush said, "you better believe he'll get angry."

On Election Day 1992, however, it was the populace who were mad as hell. After more than three decades of steady decline in voter participation in the election of presidents, 104,423,000 Americans stood up and were counted—posting the largest percentage turnout since John F. Kennedy was put in office. Bill Clinton took forty-three percent of the three-way vote, compared to Bush's thirty-eight percent and Perot's surprising nineteen percent (the best finish by an independent candidate in a presidential election since Teddy Roosevelt in 1912). As *Newsweek* stated, "Americans had grown weary of twelve years of Republican rule, symbolized by a president who seemed insensitive to their bread-and-butter concerns."

It was one of the most unusual campaigns for the White House in the history of the United States, in which an unprecedentedly popular Republican

---

Neil Bush served as a director of Silverado Banking, Savings and Loan in Denver, Colorado, from 1985 until 1988, when the thrift collapsed. During that time, Neil made over $200 million in loans to two developers who were investors in JNB Exploration, Neil's unsuccessful oil company. Federal regulators determined that, while Silverado was granting multimillion dollar loans to Neil's two partners, he was completely dependent on them for his income. The failure of Silverado—its closure delayed until after the 1988 election—cost taxpayers about $1 billion. The developers defaulted on $132 million in loans, contributing to the debacle. Two years later, a court brief by the federal Office of Thrift Supervision stated that Neil's failure to disclose conflicts of interests demonstrated evidence of "personal dishonesty" and of "willful and continuing disregard for the safety or soundness of Silverado." Noting that he suffered from an "ethical disability," regulators demanded that he pay a $50,000 fine for his propitious lapses at Silverado. He closed his oil exploration business and moved to Houston to take a position as director of finance for TransMedia Communications Inc., a sports cable company owned by a longtime Bush family friend.

Jeb Bush and one of his business partners, Cuban-American developer Armando Codina, borrowed money from Broward Federal Savings and Loan in Sunrise, Florida for an office building. When the thrift collapsed in 1988 with $285 million in bad loans, federal regulators discovered the Bush-Codina partnership had defaulted on a $4.6 million loan. According to the negotiated deal with the government, Bush and Codina wrote a check for $505,000 to the Federal Deposit Insurance Corporation (FDIC), and the government agency in turn allowed the two men to retain possession of their office building while taxpayers absorbed the $4 million loss.

In August 1989, President Bush signed a sweeping $159 billion savings and loan rescue package. "I'm proud to sign this monster," he said at a Rose Garden bill-signing ceremony, a "crucial first step" in bringing the embattled industry back from disaster. The $159 billion was the Bush administration's estimate of the rescue cost through 1999 and reflected the government's obligations to save 223 S & Ls in 1988 under the Southwest Plan, plus the cost to close or merge five hundred more weak associations beginning in 1989. The price tag also included the government's share of interest to finance the bailout plan. However it was estimated that the actual cost would balloon in thirty years to $285 billion.

president saw his political fortunes plunge after a victorious war because of a stagnant national economy; a Democratic front-runner was nearly destroyed by allegations of draft dodging, pot smoking, and womanizing—only to recover; and an unorthodox billionaire who began his run for the White House on Larry King's CNN talk show, quit less than a year later, and then re-entered the race only a month before the national election.*

His father's reelection defeat left a lasting mark on George W. "November '91 to November '92 was the most miserable year of my life," he later acknowledged. The experience also changed his relationship with his father, a man only twenty-two years his senior. "It's one thing to know a guy as your dad and another to know him as a warrior, to be in the trenches with him during a tough political fight."

Although the loyal son never criticized his father during the 1992 campaign, George W. was also smart enough to learn from the elder Bush's mistakes. A month after the election, he returned to his eleventh-floor Texas Rangers office and made a "lesson plan," as his former schoolteacher wife, Laura, called it:

- Refuse to take anything for granted in politics. His father's popularity in the polls plunged at breakneck speed after Operation Desert Storm freed Kuwait from invading Iraqi troops.
- Have a message that you believe at gut level so that it can be clearly and strongly enunciated. ("The vision thing matters, and you've got to explain it so people can understand it.")
- Come out of the starting blocks with a competent, rapid-response campaign staff. The White House had drifted into political gridlock and Clinton already had a significant lead by the time he replaced what a number of Republican political strategists called "the worst-managed presidential campaign in GOP history."
- Don't lose your cool. The president ended the 1992 campaign calling Bill Clinton and his running mate, Al Gore, "these two bozos."
- Acknowledge a slight economic downturn early on, look people in the eye, and admit there are problems, but you're going to fix them ("feel their pain"). During an interview with CBS at the Republican National

*Perot alleged in a 1996 interview with David Frost that "highest-level" Bush strategists pleaded with him to stay in the 1992 presidential race so that Clinton wouldn't win by a landslide. "They knew Clinton was going to beat them," Perot said, "and it was just a question of how much."

Convention, George W. stated he wished "that Dad had owned up to the recession earlier on."

- Establish a few simple but tightly focused issues and never quit hammering at them. His father let Clinton decide the talking points the two of them were going to debate during the campaign. "That was a major mistake," he later said.
- Don't make promises you can't keep. And never, ever say, "Read my lips—no new taxes."
- Come out swinging—whether incumbent or challenger. While Clinton and Perot slugged away at Bush, he announced he would not strike back until after he was renominated at the national convention. "It's hard to face two candidates who are out there bashing away at you when you don't bash back," George W. complained at a gathering of Texas Republicans during the campaign. "We've got a lot of people out there ready to go to war but they just can't wait for the general to suit up."

After completing his "lesson plan," Bush left his office and took a walk in the outfield as he often did when he just wanted to be left alone with his thoughts. The election was over and his father seemed depressed after returning to Houston. In a recent telephone call with his oldest son, he had cried and softly said, "It hurts. It really hurts to be rejected." There was another lesson and George W. made a mental note: *Never lose. It hurts too damn much.*

Only a day before, the former presidential adviser had announced at a press conference that he wouldn't be seeking the U.S. Senate seat vacated by Texan Lloyd Bentsen, who had been named by President-elect Clinton to be Secretary of the Treasury in the new administration. After initially indicating he was interested in running in the special election, George W. took himself out of the line-up of would-be Senate candidates, stating: "I appreciate the many folks who asked me to seize that opportunity and run, but winning would have meant uprooting our family, and we want our girls to grow up here," the Dallas resident said. "Besides I love my life in baseball." He did promise, however, to "keep my options for a future race for public office."

The loyal son sat down in his front-row seat on the first-base line and looked around at the aging Arlington Stadium. With his father's forced retirement from politics, it was now time to finally move out of his shadow and forge a distinct and separate identity. By spearheading the financing, construction, and development of the Rangers' new state-of-the-art stadium, he would showcase the business skills he would bring to state government.

"The greatest stadium ever built," as Bush described the $19 million planned arena, would seat tens of thousands of potential voters and every time the veteran Nolan Ryan set another pitching record, he would be there to share the limelight in his Texas-size stadium—a personal symbol of accomplishment for a man who wanted to become the next governor of the state.

Bush Stadium

Arlington Stadium, built in 1964 for a minor league franchise, had been the home of the Texas Rangers since former owner Bob Short moved the Senators from Washington, D.C. in 1972 and renamed the team something more fitting the Lone Star State.

Almost half of the stadium's 43,508 seats were in the less expensive (two to five dollars a ticket) outfield bleachers. The principal complaint among attending fans was that it was nothing more than an expanded Class AA park, which it actually was. At one time, it was ten thousand-seat Turnpike Stadium, where the minor league Spurs played, and had been enlarged three times over the years. But the stadium's current configuration didn't allow it to be adequately augmented.

"The first time I went down there, I was just shocked," said Rangers partner and Bush friend, Roland Betts. "At our first meeting, that was the mantra: To turn this thing around and add value to our investment, we were going to build a new stadium."

When Bush and his partners purchased the Rangers and, consequently, the stadium in 1989, they immediately began talking to officials from Dallas and Fort Worth—two cities equally located almost twenty miles away in opposite directions from the city of Arlington—about the possibility of relocating the team in exchange for a new ballpark.

Although the Rangers had never won their division, the previous owners had steadily raised ticket prices through the years, while attendance at the games had remained well below capacity. If the team was not playing to a full house, then why build a new stadium, critics repeatedly asked the Rangers' managing general partner.

"What'll make them come to the game is a nice stadium," Bush explained, "Where we build is an exciting issue. We don't know, but that stadium will be built and located with our fans in mind because when our fans win, we all win."

Bush strongly hinted that nearby Dallas, which lost the Cowboys professional football franchise to suburban Irving in the early seventies, was the leading contender to build the Rangers' new "monument to the sport," he said, "We're not trying to extort anybody, but I think it's vital to have every potential revenue source to compete."

Fearing the loss of the baseball team, which was part of the entertainment corridor that included the Six Flags amusement park, Arlington Mayor Richard Greene agreed in October 1990 to a deal with Bush and his partners that included increasing the local sales tax by a half-cent to provide them with $135 million to build a new baseball-only stadium.

As the city of 263,000 debated the upcoming referendum on the tax increase, each side pleaded its case to the public. The proponents, led by Mayor Greene, attempted to make the issue appear simple: think about the threat of the Rangers' departure to Dallas and whether Arlington could survive such a blow to its pride and economy or pay a half-cent sales tax hike that would cost each resident an estimated one dollar a month. He also stated that many residents believed that hosting a Major League Baseball team gave Arlington an elite status enjoyed by only twenty-three other cities.

Opponents accused the Arlington mayor of resorting to scare tactics and claimed that he accepted the terms of the Rangers stadium deal without hard bargaining on behalf of the city's residents. Under the terms of the contract between Arlington and Bush and his partners, the city would sell $135 million in bonds to be retired over seventeen years through sales tax revenue and stadium seating. The Rangers would only contribute $30 million toward the project's overall cost of $190 million, generated largely from a one dollar surcharge on each ticket sold during at least the next dozen years. The remaining money would come from interest earnings and previously issued city bonds. The stadium would be operated by the Rangers organization, which would keep the ensuing revenue. In return, Bush and his partners would pay $5 million in annual rents and maintenance fees to the city. After those payments totaled $60 million, the Rangers could take the title to the ballpark complex, an arrangement that sparked charges that the Rangers' owners would be getting the stadium for much less than it cost to build.

"I would love to see the Rangers stay and prosper in Arlington," said Roger King, a real estate appraiser and vocal critic of the project. "But let's face it, Bush and his partners are getting richer at the taxpayers' expense and have used governmental coercion to do so with the hollow threat that the

Rangers would leave town. What am I getting out of it? A percentage of the box office receipts? I don't even think I'm getting a break on the cost of a hot dog and a cold beer at the next game."

Others involved in the sales tax referendum opposition publicly denounced the project as a government-subsidized real estate venture that enriched a group of private investors. They also said it was at odds with Bush's political posturing regarding the capitalistic virtues of free enterprise and nongovernment inference.

Bush rejected the criticism, stating that the Rangers organization was going to develop "the greatest baseball facility and complex ever built as a result of a partnership, a joint venture between some entrepreneurs who think big, who aren't afraid to risk, and the citizens of a city that isn't going to stand pat."

Just before the referendum, Bush recruited his star player on the Rangers to make a pitch for the tax and the new stadium: pitching legend Nolan Ryan. With his aw-shucks demeanor, he made a passionate plea that "Joe Six-Pack" could understand. "I know from a fan's standpoint and a ballpark standpoint and the ballplayers' standpoint we're in need of a new stadium," he said in ads taped at the office of his cattle ranch in Alvin, Texas. "How do you finance? That is a good question and it's a problem. Any time you have any kind of bond issue that pertains to taxes, you're going to have people opposed to it. But I'm a believer in progress, and I don't care what kind of progress you get, you have to pay for it, and it has to be funded somehow."

Ryan concluded by putting himself in the position of the Arlington resident who occasionally attended a Rangers game at the stadium. "Then it would be worth twelve dollars [a year] to me not to have to drive thirty or forty miles somewhere to watch the ballgame. Plus the community pride that you take in having a ball club and the prestige that it brings."

Voters were left to decide whether the proposed stadium deal was the "fair, public-private ownership" claimed by Bush, his partners, and the mayor, or the one-sided giveaway, "good old-fashioned corporate welfare," alleged by opponents.

In January 1991, sixty-five percent of Arlington voters overwhelming approved the sales tax increase—nearly 34,000—more than in any election in the city's history.

In addition to local approval by the City of Arlington, Bush and his partners needed legislative approval to establish a financing authority that could issue bonds. In April of 1991, Bush used his political clout to push through the Texas Legislature a bill written by Arlington State Representative Kent

Grusendorf, which permitted the creation of the Arlington Sports Facility Development Authority (ASFDA), a governmental agency also vested with the power of eminent domain.

Shortly after the bill was signed into law by Governor Anne Richards, an ASFDA appraiser assigned the value of a privately owned 12.7-acre tract of land located adjacent to the ballpark site at $3.16 per square foot, for a total value of $1.515 million. The governmental authority made an offer at that price to the owners of the land, heirs of television manufacture magnate Curtis Mathes, who countered with $2,835,000 ($5.31 per square foot) for the commercially viable acreage.

The ASFDA in turn offered the Mathes family a lowball price of just $817,220, considerably lower than what the agency's appraiser had suggested. The Matheses refused to sell, and the ASFDA used its powers of eminent domain to seize the land and turn the condemned property over to the Rangers for future development use.

The Mathes family sued the Texas Rangers owners, including Bush, and the ball club's law firm, Jackson & Walker, accusing them of violating fair business practices by conspiring to illegally obtain their land. Jackson & Walker was representing both the Rangers and the Matheses when the city of Arlington began proceedings to acquire the property for the Rangers' stadium complex.

Glenn Sodd, the attorney who filed the suit on behalf of the Mathes family, noted, "It was the first time in Texas history that the power of eminent domain had been used to assist a private organization like a baseball team." Local governments, such as cities, were generally authorized to condemn land only for a public purpose.

"The Rangers wanted to have a monopoly on that entire location and the only way for them to get the monopoly," Sodd argued in court, "was to use their political power to change the law in Texas and use their political power to coerce the city to use this new law to condemn all of their competitors in the area."

Evidence in the lawsuit suggested that the Rangers owners were planning to condemn the Mathes property and other tracts of land at least six months before the ASFDA was created. In an October 26, 1990 memo from Mike Reilly, an Arlington real estate broker and part owner of the Rangers, to Tom Schieffer, team president and limited partner, he wrote of the Mathes acreage: "In this particular situation our first offer should be our final offer. . . . If this fails, we will probably have to initiate condemnation proceedings after the bond election passes." Reilly's memo was written nearly three weeks before the Arlington City Council called for a sales tax increase referendum for the stadium, and a full three months before the ASFDA was created by the state legislature.

A jury found that the ASFDA's offer of a mere $817,220 for the Matheses' 12.7-acre (which also sat next to the Six Flags amusement park) was substantially low, and it awarded the family heirs $7.2 million, including accumulated interest.

Bush remained unapologetic about the condemnation of the Mathes property to further his business interests. "This is a case where there is established law, established process, and established procedures," he said, "so I see no problem with that."*

Ironically, in the coming months, the gubernatorial candidate would staunchly and strongly advocate less government intrusion into the property rights of Texans when he ran against incumbent Ann Richards, declaring: "I understand full well the value of private property and its importance not only in our state but in capitalism in general, and I will do everything I can to defend the power of private property and private property rights when I am the governor of the state."

Just days before making his official announcement that he would run for the Republican nomination, Bush beamed with the pride of a new father as he showed off the final stages of construction on the Rangers' new stadium, The Ballpark at Arlington (a generic name personally chosen by Bush).†

He delighted in pointing out its towering walls of red brick and pink granite that gave the stadium a neoclassical look on the exterior, similar to the state Capitol Building. Lone stars, Texas longhorns, and light-fixture baseballs decorated the entryways. The interior of The Ballpark included a symmetrical design with no columns, much like Arrowhead Stadium in Kansas City; a white façade on the upper deck roof faintly reminiscent of Yankee Stadium; and a manual scoreboard to please the fans yearning for a taste of yesteryear. The seating capacity was fifty-two thousand and would

---

*After Bush became governor of Texas, he signed a bill in 1999 that limited the Harris County-Houston Sports Authority's eminent domain powers to condemn land.

†Although Bush assured fans that they'd grow accustomed to the simplicity and understated charm of the stadium's new name, listeners of talk radio stations in the Dallas-Fort Worth area continued to call in and complain about The Ballpark at Arlington: ". . . Sounds like a Little League field . . ." ". . . I guess every ice cream store has to have a plain vanilla . . ." and ". . . Did George W. Bush name his children The Daughter followed by his address?"

include a picnic area in center field adorned with an enormous "T" made of bluebonnets, the state flower.

"Here is visible evidence that I can think big thoughts, dream big dreams, and get something done" Bush told reporters. "Politically, it means I was able to dream a dream . . . and build something that will last a long period of time." Then sweeping his hand through the stadium arches to point to a field where a manmade lake would soon be built, he added, "And when all those people in Austin say, 'He ain't never done anything,' well, this is it."

Stopping the tour in the front row seats, behind the Rangers dugout, he patted the back of his personalized dark green seat which offered an expansive view of The Ballpark. "You've really got to want to be governor to leave a seat like this," he said. "But I'm ready for a new game."

★ 6 ★

THE FAMILY BUSINESS

It's in the blood. Once your family's in politics, you see how it works and you move in that direction.

—Doug Hannah, longtime friend of George W. Bush

Now hatred is by far the lasting pleasure.

—Byron

A CASE OF MISTAKEN IDENTITY

DESPITE HER LIBERAL IMAGE, ANN RICHARDS WON THE GOVERNOR'S OFFICE IN A CONSERVATIVE STATE IN 1990 LARGELY BECAUSE HER REPUBLICAN OPPONENT, MIDLAND MILLIONaire Clayton Williams, self-destructed, alienating thousands of voters with crude remarks about rape and other gaffes in the final days of the campaign that raised questions about his political qualifications.*

*During the campaign, Williams, who once led Richards by as much as 20 percentage points, made jokes about rape and recovering alcoholics, refused to shake Richards's hand in public,

With her silver bouffant, business suits of cobalt blue, and wisecracking homespun charm, Governor Richards had become the chief saleswoman for Texas, a highly visible and colorful presence in a state known for producing colorful politicians. She had been featured in *Vogue, Vanity Fair, Glamour, Cosmopolitan, Ladies Home Journal,* and the *New York Times Magazine.* She had traded one-liners with Leno and Letterman and was profiled on *60 Minutes.*

According to the polls in 1993, Richards was the most popular Texas governor in thirty years, although her approval ratings had dropped from seventy-three percent to sixty-three percent since 1992. Bush, who saw his father's popularity plummet after the Gulf War, believed she was politically vulnerable, especially after surveys showed that her record was long on style and short on substance.

During her first term, Richards had delivered a statewide lottery to Texans and with it the dreams of unlimited wealth, initiated programs to provide immunizations for poor children, and presided over the most massive prison construction agenda in state history to keep violent criminals behind bars longer. In an attempt to diversify Texas government, she appointed more women, blacks, Hispanics, and openly gay people to sit on policy-making state boards and commissions than her predecessors.

The governor's record also showed that she signed a $2.7 billion tax increase during her first year in office—after making a campaign promise that it wouldn't be necessary to raise taxes—and had overseen a thirty percent increase in the state budget. She briefly favored a statewide property tax for schools but abruptly withdrew her support in the face of opposition from school superintendents and school boards, and she backed a constitutional amendment for school finance that was soundly rejected by voters. She also failed to follow through on a promise to bring teachers' pay to the national average.

"Ann hasn't been defined very much," Bush told the press. "She's gotten a free ride. I haven't read too many editorials on her failure to lead on the education issue. She's kind of ducked. So it may require a campaign to define her."

"You know, Sam Rayburn used to say that any jackass can kick down a barn, but it takes a carpenter to build one," Richards responded, quoting the powerful and legendary former U.S. House speaker from Texas.

---

acknowledged he wasn't familiar with a ballot proposition that dealt with gubernatorial appointment powers, and admitted he hadn't paid any federal income taxes in 1986.

Bush stated that when he decided to run for governor, he "didn't take a poll. I didn't sit around with focus groups or travel around the state. . . ." But in reality that's exactly what he did in the summer of 1993 before he made his official announcement. Encouraged by surveys indicating that forty-two percent of Texans would consider voting for another candidate in the next gubernatorial election, Bush devoted three months "consulting with a wide variety of political allies and personal friends," who advised him to run a near-flawless campaign tightly focused on four popular issues: limited government, local control of schools, family values, and individual responsibility.

Bush's confidants also politely but firmly reminded him of the longstanding charge that his father seemed to want to be president more than actually wanting to promote an agenda and counseled George W. to counter that same suspicion by aggressively promoting a gubernatorial agenda.

While Texans speculated that Bush would challenge Richards for governor, he would only say, "I've got a lot of neat things to do right now. If politics comes along and there's an opening, that'd be great, but I don't have a game plan."

By Labor Day, however, he had certainly created an opening in the race, after he met privately with two other well-known potential Republican candidates, GOP activist and Houston oilman Rob Mosbacher, and Tom Luce, a former associate of Ross Perot who ran unsuccessfully for governor in 1990. Both men told reporters that they balked at the idea of running a "tough, expensive race against their longtime good friend." Mosbacher, whose father served as President Bush's commerce secretary and chaired the elder Bush's campaign organization in 1992, pronounced the Republican gubernatorial contest "pretty much ended" because serious potential candidates realized that George W. started "with a huge advantage in terms of name ID," years of service to the GOP, and a network of potential financial supporters.

Against the advice of his wife Laura—who preferred a quiet life of tending to her garden, reading books, and taking care of their daughters—Bush took his first formal step toward becoming a candidate for governor in mid-September when he filed the appropriate forms with the Texas Ethics Commission establishing a campaign committee that could raise money for the race.

"I will run because of my commitment to Texas and my concern for its future," Bush proclaimed. "Texans want an expanding economy that creates jobs and opportunity, less government, safer communities, and better schools for their children.* I am committed to reaching those goals."

Responding to Democrats who lambasted his lack of political experience, Bush noted that he was a former oilman and the current managing general partner of the Texas Rangers, a multimillion-dollar-a-year business that enabled him "to provide the strong, independent leadership our state needs for its governor." He also asked if anyone ever told businessman Ross Sterling, who as governor saved the Texas oil fields from plunder in the 1930s, that he was not qualified to run. Or did anyone tell lawyer-businessman John Connally, who arguably was the state's most visionary governor in the sixties, that he was unfit because he had not previously held elective office?

Bush's critics immediately fired back, asserting that being a minority owner of a professional baseball team was not grounds for getting elected. Running a business that was a monopoly in a large metropolitan area was not exactly the most demanding job in the world, they alleged.

In the autumn of 1993, nobody actually believed Bush could unseat the wildly popular Richards as governor. The political pundits and many in his own family, placed their money on Jeb, the quieter, more cerebral brother, who had announced that he was running in the gubernatorial race in Florida against the folksy and formidable incumbent, Lawton Chiles.†

Only days before his formal announcement, however, George W. was confident that he could "win and do it convincingly," especially after the latest poll showed Richards' campaign with a lead of only eight points over Bush, which was almost identical to the edge a similar survey gave Republican Clayton Williams over Richards in 1990. Richards went on to win the 1990 election with 49.6 percent of the vote.

"Ann made a name for herself and her tongue in 1988 by ridiculing my fa-

---

*Dissatisfied with the public school system, Bush had recently transferred his eleven-year-old daughters to Hockaday, one of the city's most prestigious private schools, where he admitted he would be paying about $8,000 a year for each girl's education.

†Jeb, like Bill Clinton, always wanted to be president. Unlike his brothers, he did not follow their father into the oil business. He also went to the University of Texas, not Yale, married a young Mexican woman he met in a high school exchange program, and converted to Roman Catholicism. Jeb arrived in the Sunshine State in 1979 to help organize his father's campaign for the Republican presidential nomination and decided to stay, achieving a certain visibility as the state's secretary of commerce in 1987–88. Like his brother, George W., his political platform in the 1994 governor's race contained much that was Republican standard issue: antiabortion, anticrime, antigovernment, and antitaxes.

ther," the younger Bush told his advisers. "She built on that attention to mount a successful campaign for governor in 1990. But if she wants a second four-year term, her biggest roadblock is going to be another George Bush."

On November 8, 1993, exactly one year from Election Day, the forty-seven-year-old Bush formally began his campaign in front of an enthusiastic crowd of about three hundred supporters in the ballroom of a Houston hotel only a mile from the home of his parents, who were noticeably absent. (Although the former president was in Puerto Rico and Barbara Bush had a "previous commitment" to do radio interviews for a program in which she read stories to children, the couple had been "requested" earlier by their son to refrain from attending his formal announcement so that "they wouldn't steal the spotlight.")

"I am not running for governor because I am George Bush's son," he declared at the first stop on a five-day, twenty-seven-city tour that would launch his candidacy for the Republican nomination. "I am running because I am Jenna and Barbara's father. . . . People ask me why I would give up baseball, why I would put my wife and two girls through the ruthless scrutiny of a campaign. Those people ask me if I have any concern for what this will do to my family. My answer is that my concern for them is why I am here. Our education system is not providing our children with what they need, our justice system is not keeping criminals in jail, we have a property tax that keeps growing and we have the fastest-growing government in the nation," he continued, reciting a speech he wrote months earlier. "I want to do something about that. What I offer the people of Texas is a modern-day revolution. It's a revolution of hope, change, and ideas. It can only be launched by a new generation of leadership taking responsibility, and it can only succeed with your support."

Noting that it would it be tough to run against "a well-liked person," Bush nevertheless said, "Our leaders should be judged by results, not by entertaining personalities or clever sound bites." At stops in San Antonio and Austin, he readily admitted that "the question becomes can I run Texas and can I take Texas where I want to take it. The answer to that is, 'Absolutely.' I've run businesses. . . . I've lived all over the state, urban as well as rural. I understand the state. I've risked capital. I've provided jobs for folks. I've been through good times and bad as a small businessman."

Throughout his twenty-seven–city Texas tour, however, Bush continually suffered mistaken identity problems. One metropolitan radio station announcer informed her listening audience: "Former President George Bush kicked off his gubernatorial campaign . . ." One man interviewed outside the hotel where Bush had just given a speech, shrugged and opined, "Well, he's sure got a record to run on." Even the *Houston Chronicle* published a photograph of the father with an accompanying article about the son."

The younger Bush shrugged off the confusion good-naturedly, noting that his similarly named father did carry Texas twice in his presidential campaigns. Then turning serious, he would add, "What I want to do is focus on the issues I want to discuss in the election and not spend all the time hung up on whether I'm George Bush or his son."

Richards, displaying a willingness to immediately engage her expected Republican challenger, and eager to remind voters about the familial connection at every opportunity, argued that most of the federal tax burdens "that have cost Texans so much money were enacted under the Republican administrations in the White House."

With the battle lines clearly drawn, obviously the challenge for George W. was defining the difference between himself and former President George Bush. As one campaign adviser put it, "He was extremely proud of who his father was and what his father stood for, but if he was going to beat Ann Richards then he had to let voters know who he was, besides just being the son of former President George Bush, and what he would do if elected governor."

THE PRE-GAME SHOW

Although it was widely accepted as fact that Richards and Bush, would be, respectively, the Democratic and Republican candidates for governor in the general election, the two did not actually receive their party's nominations until the March 8, 1994 primaries. Richards easily defeated political unknown, Gary Espinosa, a retired sandblaster, and Bush's victory came as no surprise when he razed his nominal opposition, Ray Hollis, a building demolition expert.

With the barely-noticed primaries* out of the way, the voters and the media had hoped the two candidates would conduct a clean, major-issue-oriented campaign rather than one based on emotional sound bites and character assassination. But with the "main event" showdown between a famous face and a famous name only eight months away, Richards and

*Of the state's nine million registered voters, 17.5 percent participated in the primaries, a record low turnout.

Bush came out swinging, making it difficult for Texans to make an intelligent choice of who should lead the state for the next four years.

"We have moved from an economy that rose and fell with every price fluctuation in West Texas crude into an economy that is diversified, that is strong, that is leading this nation into recovery," Richards claimed, noting that 456,000 more Texans "are working today than on the day we took office."

Bush's campaign fired back with a fax entitled "Setting the Record Straight: Comparing Gov. Richards' Rhetoric with Her Real Record," which painted a picture of Texas in despair. "More Texans are out of work today than when Richards became governor," the release stated, noting there were 539,400 out-of-work Texans in January 1991 and 624,000 at the end of 1992.

On the voters' number-one issue regarding crime, Richards boasted, "We placed our support and concern with the victims, and we passed an anti-stalking bill, revised the penal code, doubled the maximum sentence for violent criminals, doubled prison capacity and cut the parole rate by two-thirds. And as a consequence," she boasted, "we are seeing a decline for the first time in the state of Texas in ten years."

The Bush campaign staff responded with Department of Public Safety statistics that showed the overall crime rate was indeed down, but violent crime was up by 5.8 percent since she took office. A Bush spokesperson posed the question: "Ask Texans do they feel safer walking around the malls, in the streets, and the answer is no."

Many nervous and influential Republicans were questioning why Bush (still six to ten percentage points behind in the polls) rarely attempted to engage Richards directly, using surrogate speakers or news releases in political campaign attacks on his opponent.

"The advantage of speaking through a surrogate," claimed one Bush campaign staff insider, "was that we could say sulfurous things about our opponent and put that on record without our candidate taking personal responsibility for it." In addition, a private poll conducted by the Bush campaign showed that the Republican was in a statistical dead heat with Richards and all he needed to do to win the governorship was avoid mistakes, stick to the issues, and retrieve the conservative female voters who abandoned GOP nominee Clayton Williams for Richards in 1990.

In an attempt to provoke her opponent into direct confrontation, Richards sarcastically referred to him as "young George" and "shrub"—as in a little bush—and continued to label him a "phantom candidate" who hid behind press releases issued by handlers and refused to come forward to speak for himself.

"When you try to get him into a posture of actually defending a position, the next thing you know he sort of evaporates and gets back to the kind of pat speech that he's got," Richards told reporters. "I'm going to tell you seriously that I think he means well. I really think he wants the best for all of us. I just don't think he is quite prepared for this level of operation. . . .I think he is saying whatever they tell him before he goes to see you all. Somebody in the back rooms says, 'OK, this is the pitch of the day or of the week or whatever it is' and then he goes out and says it."

Speaking to the Texas Press Association, Richards portrayed herself as one of the "common folk" while portraying her opponent as a privileged elitist who had no understanding of most Texans. After claiming that she had the "background of understanding what the lives are like of ordinary working people," Bush countered the following day when he addressed the media organization.

"She said a lot of bad things about me," he complained. "My attitude about it is let's just debate philosophy. Results matter. I'm not out of touch. I've worked with working people everyday at my ballpark. I'm campaigning, and I listen. This should not be a campaign of insinuation, a few funny sound bites. This ought to be a good and honest debate about what's best for Texas' future. Let me put it to you this way," Bush continued, "if people are happy with the schools then I'm not the right person [for governor]. I'm going to deregulate the school districts so that local parents and teachers and administrators can develop programs that best fit their kids. If people think, as the governor does, that violent crime is down and everything is safe on the streets, then don't vote for me. I don't think that way. I hear from too many about how dangerous their lives are. And I want to protect the innocent."

"It's easy for George W. Bush—a man who's never had to balance a multibillion-dollar state budget or negotiate with a legislature full of contrary politicians—to 'talk tough' on crime," the governor retorted, noting his lack of political experience, a theme she repeatedly hammered in her attacks on Bush. "I tell you, he is just like your brother-in-law, who was supposed to help with the moving . . . they show up after it's all done and tell you that the furniture is not in the right place."

Richards also successfully linked the Texas Republican Party's ultraconservative platform with her opponent as she attempted to drive a wedge between Bush and the mainstream voters. In campaign speeches throughout Texas she noted that the GOP agenda called for a repeal of the minimum wage, opposed bilingual education, supported legislation permitting citizens to carry concealed weapons, and opposed the kind of public financing that Bush received to help build The Ballpark in Arlington for his Texas Rangers baseball team. When Richards criticized him for having refused to take a firm stand on specific issues in the GOP platform, Bush grudgingly had to acknowledge that he had not read the party's agenda but that he endorsed it in principle.

"If you're afraid to take a stand on something as simple as party rhetoric," Richards argued, "how are you going to make a decision on the tough issues that come to the governor's desk every day."

After a closed-door meeting with Republican strategists and heavy contributors to the political party—who complained that Bush was engaged in foolish delay of a full-force campaign against Richards—the gubernatorial candidate abruptly changed course three weeks before Labor Day, the traditional start of the fall campaign season, in a last-ditch effort to capture the hearts, minds, and votes of Texans.

"This was all a pregame show," said Republican political consultant, Matt Broyles. "When the real game started, it *really* got ugly."

"MR. DOOM AND GLOOM"

Although Bush claimed his campaign's first television ad would focus on issues of importance to Texans, and not on mudslinging, the graphic images of a woman being grabbed at gunpoint in a parking garage and police draping a sheet over a young boy's body, were aired statewide while Bush declared in a voiceover that Texas was considered "the third most dangerous state in the nation. No wonder, because in the last three years, 7,700 criminals have been released early from prison." Bush promised, "I will end early release of criminals and end parole altogether for rapists and child molesters."

Richards' staff quickly attacked the sixty-second commercial as "scare tactics" that distorted the governor's war against crime, noting that the 7,700 criminals released early from prison during her administration included three thousand nonviolent offenders and 4,700 who had to be released because they were sentenced prior to 1987 and 1991 changes in the mandatory supervision law that bypassed the parole process. Her aides also noted that thirty-eight thousand inmates received early release in 1990, during her Republican predecessor's tenure in office, and that the state added seventy-five thousand prison beds during her administration.

The Bush commercial began a week after Richards first went on airwaves in Houston and Dallas with a commercial promising to get tough on juvenile crime and calling for a statewide teen curfew. "Bush decided to reach back into his old bag of dirty tricks and pull out a Willie Horton," said one Republican campaign strategist, recalling George W.'s and Lee Atwater's infamous 1988 ad, which was used successfully against Governor Michael Dukakis in the elder Bush's bid for the White House.

In addition to touting his crime-fighting package and calling for "able-bodied" welfare recipients to "get work or more education or lose their benefits," the Republican candidate used the one-minute commercial to introduce himself as "a successful businessman with deep roots in Texas." The short biography noted that he "ran an oil business" and was now "managing partner of the Texas Rangers." The ad neglected to mention, however, that Bush was the son of a former president.

"George Bush's wealth was produced via stock swaps and bailouts. His so-called oil business was a tax shelter for wealthy friends of his father," claimed Chuck McDonald, Richards' campaign spokesman, who also called the use of shock pictures and scare tactics in the crime segment of the ad "irresponsible."

If Bush intended to send a message to his opponent that he would no longer be mistaken for just another nice guy, the new aggressive strategy worked. "If this is the game they want to play, then we'll play it," a furious Richards told her campaign staff, "but it is not my choice." She promptly added that she learned a life-long lesson from the battering that Democrat Dukakis took in his unsuccessful presidential race against her opponent's father. "You cannot stand by and leave unfair charges unanswered—and we won't. I wanted to set the tone with our issue-oriented television ad—to say how strongly we felt about juvenile crime and what we were going to do about it. Voters don't want to hear all that negative, trashy stuff," she continued. "But I want to make it clear that I'm not one of those shy violets who's going to sit back and be taking it across the head and not respond."

The day after the negative Bush ad ran on television stations throughout the state, the relentless candidate continued his attack on his Democratic rival, accusing her administration and the Texas Education Agency of lowering standards for performance of public schools "to make them look better in the election year."

At a Northeast Texas rally packed with close to a thousand supporters, mostly teachers, Richards responded to Bush's criticism. "A lot of people in this room are more qualified to be governor. Of course, you don't have as famous a name," said Richards, who was a school teacher herself before she entered politics. "You just work like a dog, do well, the test scores are up, the kids are looking better, the dropout rate is down, and all of a sudden you've got some jerk who's running for public office telling everybody it's all a sham and it isn't real and he doesn't give you credit for doing your job," she continued, drawing cheers from the crowd. "So far as he is concerned, everything in Texas is terrible. This election is the same old stuff. It's a bunch of people who come in after the fact . . . always finding fault, never able to even thank a teacher for the good job they do. . . . He has never expressed an opinion or idea on the subjects that were critical to the future of Texas in his life until he went into the public relations room and brought it out and presented it because now he wants to be governor."

Although she never actually mentioned Bush by name in her speech, reporters asked her afterwards if she was calling her Republican opponent "some jerk," to which she replied, "Give me a break. This campaign is going to come. Don't rush it."

After the speech, Bush spokesperson Reggie Bashur, decried the change in Richards' campaign tone. "Today apparently marks a significant departure for Governor Richards as she and her advisers have decided that negative campaigning is their lone hope to attempt to reverse her political troubles," Bashur said. "George W. Bush has run his campaign on the issues and has offered reforms for fundamental change and meaningful policies and programs."

However, while Richards was currently running positive, issue-oriented campaign commercials in East Texas highlighting the fact that her administration had benefited the area's economy and a new ad in Houston and Dallas that promoted her record on fighting crime, Bush in a prepared statement denounced the governor as a "liberal" who had lowered herself to "derogatory name calling."

At a campaign stop, Richards admitted to calling Bush "some jerk" but said it was intended as a "generic comment" about anyone who questions her administration's progress in fighting crime and improving public schools. "Our teachers and our law enforcement officers work hard," she said. "I'm not going to stand back and let people put down the progress they've made. I'm part of a team with them, and when people put them down, put down the improvements they've made, I'm going to fight for them."

Much of Governor Richards' personal and political charm was, and always had been, attributable to her way with the rhetorical knife. Her reputation for being quick with the lips was well-deserved and went back for many years, well beyond her most famous "born with a silver foot in his mouth" remark, directed at the elder Bush in 1988. But calling George W. "some jerk" was lacking in wit and humor, according to public opinion polls, and contributed to an impression that the governor was desperately overreacting.

While the "jerk" comment dominated news coverage of the gubernatorial campaign for the next several days, Bush happily played the role of the scorned opponent. The last time he was called a "jerk," the Republican candidate recalled after a speech to a Houston PTA group, was in "fourth grade at Sam Houston Elementary School. I didn't think that fellow knew what he was talking about then and I don't think she knows what she's talking about now," he said, referring to his political opponent. "She can call me anything she wants, but in eighty-three days, she's going to call me 'governor.'"

Energized by surveys that noted "jerk" was too harsh and demeaning for a man whose wit and sensitivity Texas voters were beginning to appreciate, Bush quickly launched the next aggressive media blitz. "While she was still explaining the 'jerk' comment to the press and voters," said one Bush campaign official, "we decided to go for a one-two punch while she was wobbling around wondering what hit her."

First came a new television commercial questioning the governor's statements that she was winning the war against crime during her tenure as governor. Against a backdrop of three acts of criminal violence, Bush claimed in the ad, "We have a serious crime problem in Texas because we don't keep violent criminals behind bars. There should be no parole for rapists or child molesters. We need to end the mandatory early release of prisoners."

Calling Bush "Mr. Doom and Gloom," Richards cried foul and asked Texas television stations to pull the ads off the air because they were inaccurate attacks on her record as governor. "He's not going to win by running a campaign of lies," she argued. "You have to draw a line somewhere between political rhetoric, scare tactics, and a lie."*

---

*In truth, the overall crime rate had dropped in the previous two years, and violent crimes declined by 2.3 percent in 1992 and 3.5 percent in 1993. However, in 1991, during Richards' first year in office, violent crimes rose a dramatic 12.7 percent when the criminal justice policies of her Republican predecessor were still in place. Since she had been in office, the penal code had been rewritten to require that capital murderers spend at least forty years in prison and other violent criminals—such as rapists and child molesters—would have to serve at least half of their actual sentence before being eligible for parole. Richards sought to end all parole for capital killers but was turned down by the legislature.

The very next day, Bush launched his second wave of media attacks against Richards with a series of radio commercials accusing her of being soft on landowner rights in environmental fights. In one ad, he noted that the governor "didn't even raise a fuss" over federal proposals to declare parts of thirty-three counties a critical habitat for the golden-cheeked warbler, a native Texas bird that was on the endangered species list. The designation meant that the land could not be developed, and farmers complained it affected their use of the acreage as well. "If Richards had her way, you couldn't build a house, school, hospital, road, or new business unless some Washington bureaucrat first gave the okay," an announcer alleged in the Bush radio ad, which suggested that the governor was against private property rights.

By Labor Day a new Texas poll indicated Richards' reelection campaign had remained stagnant for the past ten months, while Bush took the momentum with continuous, hard-hitting television and radio advertising. The governor was leading her Republican challenger forty-seven percent to forty-three percent among likely voters, with ten percent undecided and one percent favoring another fringe candidate. The margin of error was plus or minus four percentage points, essentially showing a virtual tie between the two candidates.

"The Bush campaign was very happy that the race was so close with only two months remaining before the elections," said Republican political consultant, Matt Broyles. "Earlier in the year, internal Bush polls showed that many Texas voters believed it was the former president who was opposing Richards. In an effort to distinguish the father and the son, George W. was prominently featured in his campaign commercials."

Voters may have finally realized that the ousted president wasn't attempting to regain the political limelight in a bid for Texas governor, but Richards' campaign strategists encouraged her to keep the one-term president and his politically inexperienced son in "the same breath" during the campaign's final weeks.

On the heels of his ads attacking her record in office on environmental issues and property rights, Richards aired new radio commercials in rural Texas featuring two men debating her Republican challenger's family connection and his abysmal reputation as a businessman:

Man #1: "That young Bush boy, you know the former president's son, he talks a good game, but has ever done anything?"

Man #2: "He makes a big deal about running a baseball team. Fact is, he only owns a little more than one percent of the Texas Rangers."

Man #1: "Every business he's ever been involved with had to be bailed out by his daddy's friends. Seems like he always gets to start at the top. Now he expects to do the same thing in state government."

Another Richards commercial directly challenged Bush's attack on her position on private property rights. The ad noted that his baseball team and the City of Arlington had condemned property around the new stadium to build restaurants and offices to benefit the sports franchise and its owners, including Bush, who had portrayed himself as a devoted protector of private property rights.

"Well, tell it to the private property owners of Arlington, Texas," said the Richards ad. "The ones who had the misfortune to get between George W. Bush and a fast buck."

When Bush complained that the ads were false and Richards was trying "to demean me personally" by referring to him as "that young Bush boy" the governor told the press, "I expect my campaign to respond strongly any time my opponent engages in negative campaigning. To do anything less would allow the Bush campaign to distort the positive strides that have been made in Texas."

According to Richards campaign officials, the governor resented being forced to run a hard race by "someone obviously out to settle a personal score" with lots of money, name identification, and no public record of his own. Perhaps it was that resentment that explained the contempt she seemingly had for Bush as she and her campaign, in a decided twist on 1994's prevailing political wisdom, regularly denounced him as a nonpolitician and "greenhorn" who couldn't begin to come close to her in the areas on which she primarily was campaigning—her multiyear experience in politics and government offices.

In the waning weeks of the gubernatorial campaign, she continued to pound like a jackhammer on her opponent, taking dead aim at Bush's effort to pitch himself as a successful businessman, a core issue in his attempt to unseat the governor. In her most aggressive ad of the campaign, Richards claimed firms he was affiliated with had lost hundreds of millions of dollars since 1979.

"He says that he is a successful businessman," said an announcer on the commercial. "But official records show that every other Bush business venture has lost money, big money, net losses of $371 million. . . . Texas is on the comeback trail. But can we afford the business experience of George W. Bush?"

Using supporting documents filed with the Securities and Exchange Commission, the Richards campaign claimed Bush earned $1.38 million in compensation while serving on the board of directors of four financially struggling firms, including Harken Energy Corporation; Tom Brown Inc.,* a Midland energy company; and Caterair International, a Maryland airline food concern.

In the ad, Richards referred to records filed with the SEC, which showed that Tom Brown posted losses of $18.6 million since 1989. Caterair had lost $285 million since 1990 and was facing possible bankruptcy when Bush resigned from the board of directors in May 1994. Bush "says he's a successful businessman, but when his company is facing bankruptcy he jumps ship and lets his partners sink," noted the Richards campaign.

Bush immediately issued a new commercial featuring the Republican challenger wearing a suit and speaking directly into the camera. "For whatever reasons, the governor has chosen to attack me personally," he said. "Now that's her right to do so, but personal attacks will not solve our crime problem in Texas. Personal attacks will not improve our schools. And personal attacks will not reform the welfare system. The governor and I have honest disagreements on the issues and that should be the focus of the campaign, not personal attacks."

Campaigning for her son during the gubernatorial contest's waning days, former first lady, Barbara Bush, told supporters that Richards' aggressive criticism of George W.'s business career was the motivating reason that she decided publicly to help her son in his pursuit of the Texas governorship. "The things Richards is accusing of him are dishonest and twisted, and they're ugly," she told cheering crowds. "Why doesn't she talk about schools and taxes and the things people are interested in? Crime is a major issue. Why doesn't she talk about those things?"

At campaign rallies and scheduled appearances in Fort Worth, Dallas, and San Antonio, Bush called the Richards ad "mudslinging at its worst," but was

*Nine days after the 1994 election, Bush resigned from the board of Tom Brown Inc. and reaped more than $300,000 by cashing options in the Midland oil and natural gas exploration company.

evasive when reporters asked how accountable he should be for the losses at companies where he had drawn a salary as a board of director.

"It was sanctimonious for the Bush campaign to run six weeks of television commercials attacking the governor's record in office and then get outraged when she examined his business background," said GOP political strategist, Matt Broyles. "Which should have raised a fair question. Was Bush involved in decision making for all the companies he listed on his business resumé and, in the process, gaining valuable leadership experience, or was he primarily a figurehead? He tried to have it both ways. One day he was traveling around the state telling Texans that they should vote for him because of his experience in the corporate world and then the next day playing dumb when asked about the activities of his business associates."

Though all public polls and campaign internal survey data showed that the governor's attacks on Bush's career were failing to register with voters, the governor remained relentless, almost as if she were the underdog challenger in the race. A television ad that premiered on October 19, the first day of absentee voting, opened with a photo of Bush, followed by newspaper headlines about his sale of more than $800,000 of Harken Energy stock and Richards' contention that records of a Securities and Exchange Commission investigation of insider trading were not being made public.

Bush also refused to release 1989 and 1990 income tax returns that could have shed light on the Harken deal and the transaction that made him part owner of the Texas Rangers baseball team. The Republican candidate opted to release only his returns for the years Richards had been in office—1991, 1992, and 1993. "He's doing more than just about any other gubernatorial candidate has done," said Reggie Bashur, a spokesperson for the Bush campaign, referring to Richards' 1990 opponent, oilman-rancher Clayton Williams, who declined to make public any of his income tax returns.

"If you're going to run for office," Richards told the press, "everybody needs to know where your money comes from, where your money is invested, who your associates are, for all the obvious reasons: to make sure you don't have a conflict in your service."

Bush ignored the request for the earlier tax returns and instead focused the voters' attention on one of Richards' longtime associates, Bill Clinton, who was so unpopular in Texas in 1994* that even state Democrats were try-

*Clinton ran second in Texas behind President George Bush in the 1992 election and became the first Democrat since 1845 to win the White House without carrying Texas. A poll conducted by First Market Research in 1994 showed only twenty-three percent of Texans held a favorable view of the president, while forty percent regarded him unfavorably.

ing quietly to distance themselves from the president and avoid a repeat of 1978, when Jimmy Carter's unpopularity cost the party the Governor's Mansion for the first time since Reconstruction.

For the next several days, leading up to their only statewide debate, Bush reminded Texans at every campaign stop that Richards headed the national convention that nominated Clinton for the presidency. "Clinton represented an antigovernment sentiment among voters that we thought we might be able to exploit," explained a former Bush campaign strategist. "We believed that voter unhappiness with Clinton would drive Republicans to the polls who normally only voted in presidential election years. Even though it was a midterm election, Clinton had essentially nationalized the governor's race because he had alienated so many Texans."

During the candidates' only face-to-face confrontation—a televised sixty-minute debate held in Dallas three weeks before Election Day—Richards and Bush recycled their familiar campaign themes in front of four journalists, twenty-one citizen panel members, and a full auditorium of spectators.

Richards once again tried to portray her Republican challenger as a business failure and too inexperienced to run state government; and Bush, who remained on the defensive against allegations of insider trading, draft dodging, and influence peddling, pointedly mentioned Richards' loyalty to the president.

Speaking last, Bush underlined the "big differences" between himself and the incumbent governor, "I am the conservative candidate, she is the liberal candidate," he said, noting that Richards would "work hard to see" Bill Clinton reelected president in 1996. "I, of course, will not."

After the televised debate, talk radio stations throughout Texas were inundated with irate callers incensed that Bush seemed to be constantly "trashing Ann or trashing the state." One listener to WBAP in Dallas noted: "Finally, the real reason that George W. Bush is seeking election came to light in the debate last night. It has nothing to do with Bush wanting what is right and good for the people he will be elected to govern. It has to do with the 1996 elections. In his closing statement of the debate, Bush did not express his concerns about leading the state in preparing for a future in a global economy, instead he indicated his intentions to campaign against President Clinton in the 1996 elections. Is Bush in the governor's race for no other reason than to seek revenge for the defeat of his father in the last presidential election?"

With less than a month before the voters cast their ballots, however, another vengeance-seeking ghost from Election Past made an appearance: Ross Perot.

Bloodied and Bruised

During an appearance on CNN's *Larry King Live,* Perot, the former 1992 independent presidential candidate, urged Americans to give the Republican Party a chance at the congressional helm in the midterm elections, but said Texans should stick with Democratic Governor Ann Richards, whom he described as the "best horse in the race."

Richards, a top campaigner for Clinton in 1992 who worked diligently to keep Texans from voting for Perot, said the following day: "I have been one of those who always thought that Ross Perot raised questions that no one else was raising. And for all of the fun that is poked at his poster boards and his depiction of how to solve problems, I've really always admired it."

Bush, who possessed inside information that Perot had made a standing offer to help the governor's reelection campaign months earlier, was nevertheless cautious and equally diplomatic in his own comments following Perot's appearance on the Larry King show. "He is an interesting historical figure," said Bush, whose father's 1992 presidential reelection bid was damaged by the nineteen percent vote garnered by Perot. "He is a man who is obviously a successful businessman who decided he wanted to get in politics and changed the dynamics of the 1992 election in a big way."

Both gubernatorial contenders knew that in a close election, Perot and legions of his United We Stand America (UWSA) grassroots organization of unannounced membership totals and untested political clout, could make a difference in the outcome.

"It is something that is real," UWSA executive director B.B. Corn said when asked if there was an identifiable Perot vote in the electorate. "We know we've got this pool of folks out there that are at least leaning in our direction and are going to listen to what we say and, at least, have some portion of their opinion made up by what we do."

Corn believed UWSA influenced the outcome of interim special elections in Kentucky, Georgia, Arkansas, and New Jersey. Now he was ready to see the level of influence UWSA could have in a major election cycle.

In Texas, UWSA state director Bill Walker believed the Perot vote was pivotal in the governor's race, which, all polls showed, was statistically even.

"There are a lot of people out there who are not members of our organization but look toward Mr. Perot for his judgment and his leadership," Walker claimed.

Exactly one week before Election Day, Perot formally endorsed Richards for reelection at a joint news conference. "She is one of the greatest governors in the history of our state," he proclaimed. "Never forget that running this state is a big business, not a sport," a reference to Bush's background as managing general partner of the Texas Rangers baseball team.

Perot also used the opportunity to help Richards distance herself from President Clinton, who was constantly being linked to the Texas governor in current Bush TV commercials. "She doesn't belong to anybody but the people of Texas. That includes the president of the United States," he said. "If they disagree, they disagree. If she and the Democrats disagree, they disagree."

The billionaire politician/radio talk show host described himself as a longtime Richards fan and stated he voted for her in the 1990 gubernatorial election over Republican Clayton Williams. (Perot at that time was still associated with the GOP.) He said he supported her in the current election because she had competently managed the state's budget and diligently worked to bring new businesses and jobs to the state in the past four years.

"Political campaigns are nothing but talk, but whoever wins has got to get results," Perot said. "Look at the record," which, he added, "speaks of itself."

Although he never mentioned him by name, Perot said Bush was not qualified to be governor. "Let's assume you and I are neighbors and the plumbing's broken, and I come over and I say, 'You want me to fix it for you?' Your first question to me would be, 'Ross, do you know how to fix a pipe?' I'd say, 'No, but I'd like to fool with it.'" Perot also said voting for Bush would be like hiring an inexperienced person to "fly your plane" or "treat your sick child."

During the press conference, Perot strongly denied that his endorsement of Richards had anything to do with the 1992 election, specifically President Bush's campaign staff (and senior adviser, George W.), which publicly raised questions about his qualifications and mental stability.

"No sour grapes," Perot snapped back. "No basis for that conjecture."

Richards, in turn, noted that her new benefactor had offered his support a few months earlier, but she said she did not want to solicit his help unless she believed she could be reelected to another term of office. "I called Ross yesterday and said, 'I'm doing very well and I think we can win this race and now I'd like you to be in there and put the cap on for me.'" Claiming that his support added to "the momentum" for her reelection bid, the governor said,

"I'd like to tell you frankly I did not come to him and ask him to help until I felt we had turned a corner. The truth is, I didn't want to put him on the spot."

"I do not care who endorses my opponent," Bush told about one thousand supporters at a Houston rally. "That's not going to change the fact that the status quo is not acceptable to most of Texas." He added that he didn't know if Perot was motivated by a dislike for his father, but dismissed Richards and the erstwhile presidential candidate as "interesting characters," claiming that "the people of Texas are not going to vote for governor based on personality or endorsements. Ross Perot and I disagreed in 1992, and I'm not surprised we disagree in 1994."

In addition to the formal endorsement, Perot wrote a letter on Richards' behalf that ran as a full-page political ad in state newspapers. He also taped several thirty-second radio commercials, including one in which the Dallas-based billionaire said in his familiar twang: "There's an old Texas saying, 'When you see a snake, kill it.' When Ann Richards became governor, her office was full of snakes. She had to balance the budget. We now have a $2.2 billion surplus."

"What really angered George was Perot's hypocrisy," said a close confidant and Bush campaign official. "He had the gall to run for president in 1992 with no political experience and wanted people to vote for him simply because he said he would bring a professed common sense business approach to government. When George decided to run for governor, Perot belittled him for doing the same thing."

Standing on the tailgates of pickup trucks in Texas towns with names like Nacagdoches, Waxahachie, and Hillsboro, Bush spent the final days of the hard-fought campaign eating chicken-fried steaks, downing nonalcoholic beer, and bemoaning Richards and Perot, who were touring together as they swept across the state in "a final push for the Bubba vote."

"I'm not concerned about Mr. Perot," Bush claimed as he scoured the state in search of a tightening number of undecided votes. "My attitude is that when you go to vote, you will realize that Mr. Perot's endorsement will not make the schools any better or the welfare system any better or will not change the juvenile justice systems that needs to be changed," he said, adding, "I don't care if you're a Ross Perot fan or an independent. I want your vote."

Bush was telling the crowds the truth when he maintained he wasn't "concerned about Mr. Perot." The latest internal data and private polls showed Perot's personal endorsement in the gubernatorial race would make less than ten percent of the respondents more likely to support the governor. Furthermore, only 27.1 percent of those surveyed said they had a favorable opinion of the former presidential candidate.

Although Perot was very unpopular in the state, Clinton was held in even less esteem, mostly due to his longtime friendship with Richards and, more importantly, because Clinton defeated the elder Bush in 1992, a man many Texans still held in high regard. When the long, acrimonious gubernatorial race came to an end on election night, Bush won handily and rode into office on a Republican trend that resounded across the nation. A volatile electorate coupled with anti-Clinton sentiment helped the GOP take control of both Houses of the U.S. Congress for the first time in forty years and score major gubernatorial triumphs, taking statehouse races from the Democrats in New Mexico, New York, and Texas.

In the Lone Star State, Bush became only the second Republican to be elected Texas governor since Reconstruction when he defeated Richards 53.5 percent to 45.9 percent. "What Texans can dream, Texans can do," Bush told cheering supporters after he stepped onto the podium of his election night party at the Capitol Marriott in Austin shortly after 10 P.M. Standing by his side were his wife, Laura,* and his two daughters. "This victory tonight is a great honor. The vote carries with it an awesome responsibility. Texas is ready for a new generation of leadership," he continued, adding that he would "reach out" to those who had not supported him in an effort to "lead, not divide."

Richards said she wished her Republican successor well in the next four years. "He deserves Godspeed," she told the crowd of loyalists gathered in the Texas Ballroom of Austin's Hyatt Regency hotel moments after phoning her congratulations to Bush. "I don't want anyone here to feel like they have lost a thing. I don't want any of us to go home with nothing but pride in our hearts," she said. "We had a great four years; we worked hard; we ran a good race. It is not the end of the world; it is the end of a campaign."

Most political analysts believed that an important element of Bush's winning strategy during the race was his success in forcing Richards to defend

---

*When Bush decided to run for governor against his wife's wishes, she made it clear that she wasn't going to be a stereotypical politician's wife, who would always be at her husband's side during the campaign. True to her word, she seldom left their home in Dallas for over a year, preferring instead to be a full-time parent to their daughters while her husband traversed the state in pursuit of the governorship. When she did hit the campaign trail, she spoke mostly to GOP women's clubs and usually shared personal reflections and humorous anecdotes about her family. She often declined to discuss political issues.

herself against the charge that she was close to an unpopular president. But exit poll results indicated the governor's troubles ran deeper than voter anger with Bill Clinton, with Texans turned off by her negative campaigning and her perceived failure to adequately address key issues.

Voters claimed that Richards seemed to have missed the lesson that Bush's father learned in the 1992 presidential election—that personal attacks don't work when the constituency is riveted to issues. In 1992, it was the economy, and in 1994 it was crime and education, two reform messages constantly preached by Bush for over a year. So did Richards—when she had time left over from criticizing her opponent's business record and lack of political experience. One-third of those interviewed outside precincts around the state thought her negative attacks on Bush were unfair.

"You could argue her campaign was a reflection of her," said Bush's chief political strategist, Karl Rove. "No central message, chaos, dissension in the campaign, preoccupation with her opponent. She both simultaneously underestimated him and treated him with contempt."

Bush won because he set the agenda from the beginning, while she ran on experience in office rather than on her ideas for the future. "Step one was to be as issue-specific as we could possibly be," the governor-elect explained. "We white-papered the world right off the bat."

Though the rate for all violent crimes dropped during the Richards administration, Bush managed to make his get-tough-on-crime message a major issue. And though Texas schoolchildren's test scores were up and the dropout rate down, Bush successfully focused the voters' attention on education reform.

"In 1992, my good dad was unable to get a message out that he cared about domestic policy," Bush later recalled. "I learned a lesson, that message matters. He got defined by the opposition."

Exit polls also showed that about fifty-six percent of the state's male population voted for Bush because men had become more sympathetic to hardline Republican positions on issues such as crime and taxes. The religious right also flexed its muscle on Election Day in Texas, with evangelical voters casting almost three-fourths of their votes for Bush. Richards also didn't benefit much from Ross Perot's last-minute endorsement, which was announced with great fanfare a week before Election Day. Texans who had voted for him in the 1992 presidential election, split 2-to-1 against the governor and in favor of Bush.

After finishing his victory speech, the new governor-elect and his family went back upstairs to their hotel room to watch election results on television, leaving a ballroom filled with hundreds of exuberant supporters eager to celebrate the return of the GOP to the Governor's Mansion.

Alone for seemingly the first time in over a year, George W. closed the door to the suite's master bedroom and called his parents in Houston.* It was one of those classic bitter-sweet moments in life that he would remember for many years to come. He had pulled an upset in defeating Richards, but his brother, Jeb, the first son to take an interest in a political life, had narrowly lost to the incumbent governor, Lawton Chiles, in Florida. The Bush brothers' hopes and dreams of presiding over two of the largest states in the country had evaporated in the span of a few hours.

"It's a great night for Texas," the former president said, congratulating the new governor-elect.

"I'm a little bloodied and bruised, though," George W. admitted.

"It was a tough race, but we admire you for the way you kept the campaign focus on a positive, forward-looking message," the senior Bush said. "You fought the good fight and stayed on the issues and made your mother and me very, very proud."

About that time, Barbara Bush picked up an extension and reiterated what her husband had already said. Her voice was breaking and she kept the conversation short.

"She's pretty crushed about Jeb losing," his father said, sounding apologetic. "She knows he'll take it hard."

"He would have been a great governor," George W. remarked, "but you of all people, dad, know such is life in the political world. You can't go into politics fearing failure."

The father and son discussed other statewide elections and the scope of the GOP's national triumph for another minute or two and then George W. hung up the phone.

With the passing of the family's political leadership from one generation to another now out of the way, Bush ordered a peanut butter and raspberry jelly sandwich from room service.

---

*The younger Bush had waited until the campaign's final day to involve his father, who attended a rally with his son in Houston. "I did not want to confuse the electorate nor give my opponent the chance to blast my dad," George W. later explained.

★ 7 ★

"Ann Doesn't Work Here Anymore"

Hate the evil and love the good and establish judgment in the gate.

—Amos 5:15, a marked passage in the Bible that Ann Richards left in the governor's office for her successor, George W. Bush

Necessarily, legislation is a matter of compromise.

—President Warren G. Harding

"What Texans Can Dream, Texans Can Do"

Under an overcast but rainless sky, George W. Bush took the oath of office as Texas' forty-sixth governor shortly after noon on the Capitol's south steps, heralding the Bush name into major-league politics for a third generation, a record acknowledged by the Reverend Billy Graham in his inaugural invocation.

"We thank you for the great heritage the new governor brings to his office," the frail evangelist prayed. "We thank you for the life of his grandfather

[Prescott] in the U.S. Senate and his father as president of the United States. We thank you for the moral and spiritual example his father and mother have set for us all."

Bush's parents joined him on the dais, along with his wife, Laura, thirteen-year-old Barbara and Jenna, and the new governor's four siblings, including his brother, Jeb, "looking happy and proud, but also something else, maybe a little sad, too."

The former president and first lady tried gamely to keep public attention focused on their son and they largely succeeded until Democratic Lieutenant Governor, Bob Bullock, the powerful leader of the state Senate, saluted the elder Bush in his second-term inaugural remarks.

"As a father, I know the immense pride you have," the renowned Texas politician said. "As an American I thank you for your service to the state and to the country and for helping to bring world peace. And as a Texan, welcome home. We're glad you're here."

The former first family accepted the adulation with gentle nods. It was a far cry from the last time the Bushes were on public view at an inauguration. Two years earlier, they had sat stone-faced at the Capitol in Washington as Bill Clinton was sworn into office.

As the former president wiped tears from his eyes and hugged one of his granddaughters, some of his former enemies made their presence known on the perimeter of the inaugural crowd. Protesters identifying themselves as members of Earth First! and Greenpeace carried banners proclaiming, S&L, CIA, FOR BUSH'S CRIMES WE PAY and GEORGE BUSH IS A MURDERER.

Having his family present also brought an emotional response from the new governor. His voice nearly cracking, George W. improvised from his prepared speech to add "Mom and Dad" to the list of those he thanked for attending, while his parents basked in the moment. The sustained applause from the crowd seemed to warm the chill, moist air that enveloped the swearing-in ceremony.

Governor Bush started his speech by pledging bipartisan cooperation with Texas House Speaker J.E. "Pete" Laney, Lieutenant Governor Bullock, and the state's Democratic-controlled Legislature in an effort to improve schools, reform the welfare system, crack down on juvenile crime, and overhaul the state civil lawsuit system.

The Republican, who defeated Richards in a campaign designed to portray her administration as inadequate in addressing the state's problems, graciously praised the Democratic governor. "My predecessor served our state well," Bush said. "The example she set gives heart to those who battle adversity and hope to those who wonder if opportunity is limited. Today, as Governor Richards leaves office, Texas owes her a debt of gratitude." (The outgoing governor adhering to Lone Star tradition, did not attend the inauguration.)

The inaugural crowd was less than half the number that turned out four years earlier for Richards' swearing-in. And while Republican partisans were overjoyed at witnessing the GOP occupation of the governor's office for only the third time in the twentieth century, the crowds seemed somewhat reserved. Richards, only the second woman elected Texas governor, had energized her followers by inviting them to join her in a march up Congress Avenue to the inauguration.

Borrowing heavily from his campaign stump speech, Bush focused on "restoring government to its proper role," noting that the Tenth Amendment of the Constitution gave states all power not specifically granted to the federal government. "The spirit of that amendment has been forgotten in recent decades. I pledge to you, it will be forgotten no more," Bush promised, to the audience's applause. "As governor, I will use every resource at my disposal to make the federal government in Washington heed this simple truth: Texans can run Texas."

Local citizens, he said, also should have a greater say in what is best for their schools and communities. "By trusting Texans, the state is more likely to focus on its principal responsibilities: good and safe streets, excellent schools, help for those who cannot help themselves, and respect for private property."

The governor said he recognized that by giving greater freedom from government to individuals, "we run the risk that sometimes, some of them will fail. But mistakes made closest to the people are those most easily corrected."

For this vision to succeed, Bush claimed, Texans were going to have to return to pre-1960s values. "For the last thirty years our culture has steadily replaced personal responsibility with collective guilt. This must end," he declared. "The new freedom Texas seeks must be matched with personal responsibility. The very future of our society depends on it."

Concluding his inaugural address, he uttered the slogan for the day's events, "The history of our special land tells us this: What Texans can dream, Texans can do."

Afterward at one of the many corporate-sponsored inaugural festivities,* Jack Allen, a oilman from Dallas, commented on the new governor's promises in typical Texas fashion: "For the moment, Bush's speech sounds like the beginning of a new era in our state," he said between bites of sliced brisket at a picnic on the west lawn of the Capitol, where blue-jeaned visitors mingled with suit-clad lawmakers. "But like the old cowboys used to say in West Texas, 'If the doin' is as easy as the talkin', we'll be happy in the bunkhouse by sundown.'"

The Art of Personal Politics

The nineteenth-century framers of the Texas constitution—under which the state government still operates today—were strongly motivated to create one of the weakest governor's offices in the country. Reconstruction was just ending, and Texans were still suffering from the Radical Republican record of Governor Edmund J. Davis, who had officiated over one of the most abusive and oppressive state administrations in U.S. history.

At Davis's request, a Radical majority in the legislature had approved a series of authoritarian laws that, in many cases, even violated the Reconstruction constitution and granted the governor the power to declare martial law; appoint mayors, district attorneys, and hundreds of other officials; and create a repressive state police force to persecute citizens.

After Texans finally voted Davis out of office in an election that made the Richards and Bush slugfest look like two kids playing in a schoolyard, Davis refused to leave office until a heavily-armed Texas militia marched on the state Capitol.

The cautious authors of the 1876 constitution explicitly gave the office of governor few opportunities for strong leadership,† and instead invested the lieutenant governor's office with considerably more influence over legislation and government operations. The main powers of the state's chief exec-

*The $1.5 million tab for the celebrations surrounding the oath-taking ceremony (including a ninety-minute parade, a concert, a barbecue lunch on the Capitol grounds, and three formal gala balls) were subsidized by Anheuser-Busch, Coke, Pennzoil, and thirty-five other corporate sponsors. Bush denied that the donors were buying influence, but did acknowledge that CEOs of some of the companies were on his campaign donor list. Critics complained that the corporations received "access" to the governor in exchange for their generosity, citing a reception for sponsors preceding the inauguration ceremony and an exclusive brunch on the governor's first full day in office.

†*Congressional Quarterly* ranks Texas' governor as the nation's second weakest.

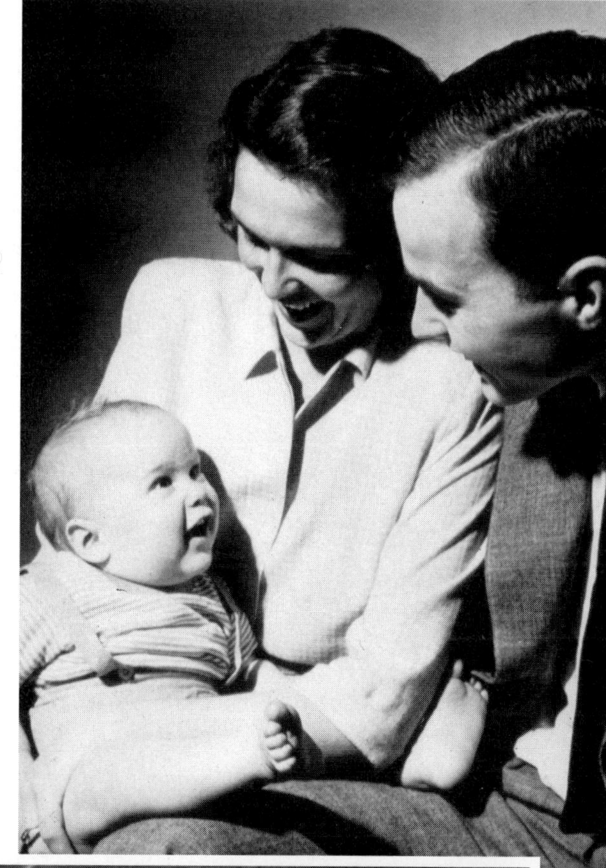

Baby makes three. The future president and first lady pose with their first-born son, George W., in their small apartment in New Haven, Connecticut where the elder Bush was a student at Yale University, ca. 1947.

(Photo courtesy of the George Bush Presidential Library)

The Bushes pose with their cowboy boots–clad son and his paternal grandparents, future senator Prescott Bush and his wife, Dorothy, after relocating to Odessa, Texas, a blue-collar town at the heart of the post–World War II oil boom.

(Photo courtesy of the George Bush Presidential Library)

Although he concedes he was "never a great intellectual" during his Ivy League years at Yale University, George W. was nevertheless quite popular on campus, and was elected president of Delta Kappa Epsilon fraternity. When the *New York Times* accused the Greek letter society of using a hot coat hanger to brand pledges, Bush defended the practice to the press, claiming that "there's no scarring mark, physically or mentally."

(Photo courtesy of the George Bush Presidential Library)

On January 1, 1967, the *Houston Chronicle* announced the engagement of Congressman Bush's twenty-year-old son to a Rice University coed, Cathryn Lee Wolfman. After the engagement was called off, sources close to the couple say, "They were good friends and they both took it hard...losing the woman he loved, combined with the fear of going to Vietnam, kind of pushed him over the edge."

(Photo courtesy of the Houston Chronicle*)*

On September 4, 1968, Congressman Bush ceremonially pins the officer's bar on his son, a new second lieutenant in the Texas Air National Guard. Questions remain over thirty years later as to whether the elder Bush used his political influence to obtain a coveted slot in the military reserve for his son, which allowed him to remain stateside during the Vietnam War.

(Photo courtesy of the George Bush Presidential Library)

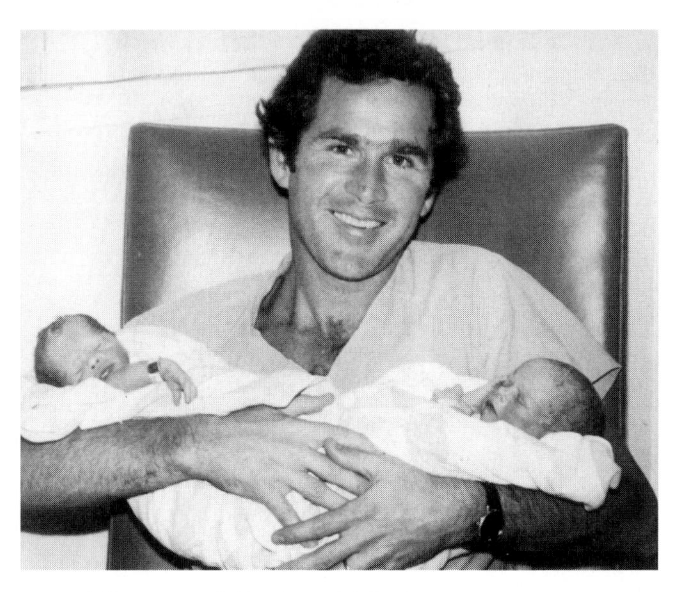

In November 1981, following a difficult and life-threatening pregnancy, Bush's wife, Laura, gave birth to premature twin girls, Jenna and Barbara, named for their grandmothers.

(Photo courtesy of the George Bush Presidential Library)

Bush poses with his wife, Laura, and their two daughters at the family compound overlooking the Atlantic Ocean in Kennebunkport, Maine. In 1977, a month after announcing his intentions to run for Congress, Bush was reintroduced to a former Midland resident, Austin public school librarian Laura Welch. The couple fell in love "at first sight" and were married ninety days later.

(Photo courtesy of the George Bush Presidential Library)

(top)
"I'll be sort of a surrogate for my father," George W. described his role as an unpaid advisor on the elder Bush's 1988 presidential campaign. "When his vice presidential responsibilities won't allow him to perform certain campaign duties, I'll be filling in for him. I'll be making speeches, helping in the fund-raising efforts and taking part in strategy sessions." As his father's chief troubleshooter and "loyalty enforcer," he earned a reputation as a "hothead who took care of business brusquely and with vivid language."
(Photo courtesy of the Midland Reporter-Telegram; *photo: Jerry Mennenga and Diane King,* MRT *librarian)*

With his father in political distress in 1992, George W. returned to his post for the reelection campaign against Bill Clinton and Ross Perot.
(Photo courtesy of the George Bush Presidential Library)

This family photo of the Bush clan vacationing together at Kennebunkport, Maine, hung on the wall of the governor's office until George W.—reading that his father had resigned his membership from the NRA at the same time that the governor was advocating the passage of a right-to-carry-concealed-handgun law—threw his reading glasses across the office, striking the wall and shattering the glass on the framed family portrait.

(Photo courtesy of the George Bush Presidential Library)

Hanging on the wall in Bush's office is a ludicrous portrait of legendary Texas governor Sam Houston, a painting that Houston commissioned himself. "The lesson that picture tells you," the governor often tells school-age visitors, "is there's a fine line between being the governor of Texas and making a fool of yourself."

(Courtesy of the Sam Houston Memorial Museum)

(opposite)

Predicting that his first legislative session would be remembered as "the most substantive in Texas history," Governor Bush signed 217 bills into law in 1995, fulfilling the lion's share of his 1994 campaign promises. Several state lawmakers complained the new governor benefited from the fact that several of the priority issues had been topics of discussion in the Legislature before he was elected.

(Photo courtesy of the Midland Reporter-Telegram; *photo: Jerry Mennenga and Diane King,* MRT *librarian)*

On December 3, 1997, less than a year from Election Day, Bush, accompanied by his wife, Laura, formally announced his campaign for a second term as governor of Texas at Sam Houston Elementary, his boyhood school in Midland.

(Photo courtesy of the Midland Reporter-Telegram; *photo: Jerry Mennenga and Diane King,* MRT *librarian)*

On a Sunday afternoon in early March 1999, four months after he was reelected to a second term as governor and an even longer period of political theater, Bush officially unveiled the multicultural and diverse group of high-profile Republicans who would comprise his presidential exploratory committee.

(Photo courtesy of the George Bush Presidential Library)

utive are the ability to veto legislation, call and set the agenda of special legislative sessions, and, with the consent of the Senate, appoint hundreds of members of policy-setting boards and commissions. But, even with the appointment power, much of the state bureaucracy is still under control of several other independently elected officeholders who often don't share the governor's goals or political views.

His or her most important leadership opportunities, however, are not detailed in the constitution. They are made possible by the stature of the office, its high visibility, and the fact that, to many Texans, state government is personified by the governor. This gives the chief executive an invaluable public forum, a bully pulpit, from which to propose ideas, define and sell his or her vision of the future to the electorate, and bring public pressure to bear on the legislature to enact the governor's agenda.

When the Seventy-fourth Texas Legislature convened in January 1995 for its 140-day session, Governor Bush told lawmakers he was voted into office by an electorate that thought schools weren't good enough, crime was too high, lawyers made too much money, and welfare was too cushy. Not coincidentally, the conservative-leaning Legislature, led by Lieutenant Governor Bullock and House Speaker Laney, had already been working on overhauling state laws governing all four.

By presenting himself as an eager and respectful pupil, Bush managed to bond with the two powerful Democrats, in an effort to ensure that his priority programs won legislative approval. At their first meeting, the House Speaker pointedly told the new governor, "Mr. Bush, we can make you a good governor—if you let us."

During the legislative session, George W. would occasionally drop by their offices to discuss policy—as opposed to them having to visit him at the Governor's Mansion—a minor loosening of protocol that won Bush points. In addition, every Wednesday morning Bush, Bullock, and Laney would breakfast together.

"We disagree, but you'll never read about it," the governor said of his meetings with the two lawmakers. "The way to forge good public policy amongst the leadership of the legislative branch and executive branch is to air our differences in private meetings that happen all the time," Bush explained. "The way to ruin a relationship is to leak things and to be disrespectful of meeting in private."

Not only did the new governor establish a close working relationship with Bullock and Laney, he also aggressively courted and supported other key Democrats whom he needed for his reform package. As payback to those legislators, Bush refused to campaign for their Republican opponents in the next election.

The governor's official calendar through his first three months of office showed that he had met one-on-one with at least fifty House members, including twenty-one Democrats, and with almost half the Senate. He often roamed the halls of the underground Capitol extension in late afternoon, dropping in on lawmakers unexpectedly. Additionally, Bush held private breakfasts and luncheons at the Governor's Mansion with legislators to air differences and cut deals out of the voting public's eye.

His name and title commanded respect, but when Governor Bush walked into the room his demeanor was that of "just one of the guys." He was casual, friendly, sincere, and uncomplicated. "A roll-up-your-sleeves-and-get-the-job-done" kind of governor who didn't categorize legislators as Republican or Democrat. He saw them only as Texans.

Lawmakers from both parties said they liked this new-style governor, adding that he was more personally accessible than his predecessor. And Democrats who opposed Bush on public policy issues praised him for showing a willingness to listen.

"Even if you disagree with him, if you are able to convince him your position is right, he is willing to change his mind," said state Representative Hugo Berlanga, chairman of the Mexican-American Caucus. "At least he listens, and it doesn't appear that he is set in concrete."

Although the governor tried to keep a low profile and work behind the scenes with lawmakers during his first legislative session, the first bill that he signed in 1995 created such a firestorm of controversy he even considered calling it quits from politics after his first term ended.

LOCK, STOCK, AND THE NRA

Noted sixteenth-century Italian political figure and historian, Niccolo Machiavelli, once remarked of the Swiss that they were ". . . the most armed and most free people in Europe," citing the fact that it was no accident that liberty and private arms coexisted in the same country. Former President James Madison, in refuting a European friend's pessimistic view of America, boasted that "unlike your governments, we are not afraid for our citizens to have arms." George W., a self-described student of history, is fond of quoting both historical figures when debating whether private citizens have the right to keep and bear arms.

This was especially true during the 1994 gubernatorial race, when the Republican candidate endorsed a concealed handgun proposal. In 1993, Texas legislators approved a measure that would have established a nonbinding referendum on whether the state's residents should be allowed to carry concealed weapons. Then-Governor Richards vetoed the bill in a ceremony that included dozens of uniformed officers. Bush later stated, however, that he would have signed it into law had he'd been the state's chief executive at the time and promised to strongly support another similar bill even "without the referendum" if elected, which outraged many Texas police officers.

"Arming the public is not the answer," said Mark Clark, spokesman for the Combined Law Enforcement Association of Texas (CLEAT), a statewide organization with a membership of almost twenty thousand rank-and-file police officers. "The level of violence on our streets right now is unacceptable. It makes no sense whatsoever for me as a police officer or for me as just a citizen to say, 'Let's put more guns out there to try and solve the violence issue.'" Clark added that he believed widespread public attention to carjackings and other high-profile crimes made support for the proposal particularly strong in the metropolitan areas such as Dallas and Houston.

"Such a law would have a profound effect on the justice system," argued John Thomas, a veteran of the Dallas County Sheriff's Department. "It will make it difficult to determine the guilty party when there is a street shootout. I can just imagine the lawyers asking witnesses who drew first."

Not only were Thomas and thousands of other Texas law enforcement officers adamantly opposed to a law allowing citizens in the state to carry concealed weapons, they also strongly believed that any proposed right-to-carry law should be put to a statewide referendum so as to minimize the effect of the National Rifle Association and other special interest groups.

Police groups who were influential in killing the 1993 concealed handgun proposal, fired some of the first shots when the bill was reintroduced in the Texas Legislature after George W.'s election as governor. CLEAT publicly announced that a survey sponsored by the organization showed seventy-nine percent of Texans wanted to vote on any proposed gun law in a statewide referendum. The survey of eight hundred registered voters also showed sixty-four percent strongly supported a requirement of gun carriers to have liability insurance and sixty-one percent believed in mandatory psychological testing of private citizens considered for permits to carry pistols.

"It's such an issue of importance to the state that it cannot be decided here in the legislature in 140 days," said CLEAT President Ron DeLord. "It needs the battle back and forth in the public arena and should be left to the voters to decide if they want this type of statute."

Former Texas Speaker of the House, Gib Lewis, who later became a highly paid state lobbyist for the National Rifle Association, told the press that the influential organization opposed a referendum and the proposals for liability insurance and psychological testing. "It would certainly make the cost of a gun permit prohibitive for anyone of medium or moderate income," Lewis claimed.

Privately, Governor Bush "put the squeeze" on key members of the Legislature to oppose any insurance and testing requirements, and especially putting the handgun issue to a public vote. "We had a referendum on November 8," the governor repeatedly told them during late night strategy meetings, referring to his defeat of Richards and the election of other state officials who supported a concealed weapons proposal.

The new governor also said a referendum was unjustified because, he believed, the ban on handguns at the time was unconstitutional. During planning sessions with Lieutenant Governor Bullock and State Senator Jerry Patterson, one of the legislative sponsors of the handgun bill, George W. "made it just as clear as the rear end of a goat going up the side of a mountain" that the right to keep and bear arms was the torch of American liberty.

"No movement in America should so alarm Americans as the gun control movement," the governor's aides have quoted him as saying at the time, "because its true aim has nothing to do with crime, but everything to do with disarming honest and decent Americans in an attempt plainly intended to take away their freedom."

Although numerous police officer organizations; concerned citizen groups; and Mayors United on Safety, Crime and Law Enforcement (MUSCLE), a crime-fighting alliance formed by the Lone Star State's big-city mayors,* regarded the concealed weapons proposal as a threat to public safety, the so-called right-to-carry bill shot from the Senate Criminal Justice Committee with little opposition and was approved almost immediately by the full Senate during the first few weeks of the 1995 Texas legislative session.

*Bruce Todd, Mary Rhodes, Richard Greene, Nelson Wolf, and Bob Lanier, mayors of Austin, Corpus Christi, Arlington, San Antonio, and Houston, respectively, saw the handgun bill as adding to the crime problem, not helping it. Houston Mayor Lanier, for many years an outspoken opponent of concealed weapon legislation, said the nation had "just gone too far in that direction." Mayor Rhodes of Corpus Christi, predicted traffic altercations that involved hand gestures would escalate into gunplay if more people carried weapons. After a closed-door session with MUSCLE, Governor Bush told the press that the mayors did not understand "that it is going to make for a more peaceful world."

While supporters of the concealed handgun law argued that the police could not sufficiently protect the citizenry, and Texans should be given a fighting chance to defend themselves, opponents were asking legislators why the proposed bill established so many places off limits to weapons. For obvious reasons, they understood the proposal's provisions against bringing pistols into schools, bars, prisons, and the passenger areas of airports. But some Texans questioned the decision to allow business owners to selectively prohibit the carrying of firearms onto their premises. Why should a law-abiding Texan with a concealed weapon permit be forced leave his handgun in his pickup, parked two or three blocks away, and risk having it stolen if his truck were broken into? How much protection, these same concerned citizens asked, would a license holder find in a pistol locked up in her automobile if attacked by an assailant and raped in a dimly-lit parking lot or garage?

R.T. Castleberry, writing in the *Houston Chronicle,* complained: "Legally, I can carry a gun, but I'm not allowed anywhere to carry it. It's Catch-22 lawmaking at it's finest," he said. "As a gun owner, I was genuinely interested in acquiring a carry license. But, having seen the list of places in which guns are prohibited, I've decided to save my time and money."

Each side in the concealed handgun debate was given to constantly citing statistics, but most numbers were inconclusive. The murder rate in Florida had dropped since that state enacted a right-to-carry law in 1987, but other violent crimes had increased. Florida, a state of thirteen million people in 1995, had issued only 266,710 handgun licenses since the bill became law, and approximately 150,000 were still valid at the time of the Texas handgun debate. Florida law allows anyone over twenty-one to seek a concealed weapon permit unless they have a felony conviction or a history of drug abuse or mental illness. The three-year renewable license is granted after a background check, completion of a gun safety course, and payment of a $137 fee.

Joe Besaraba, formerly of Hollywood, Florida, was one of the Sunshine State's 150,000 residents licensed to carry a concealed weapon. In May 1990, Besaraba, a forty-four-year-old street person known as "Crazy Joe," gunned down Hollywood bus driver Sydney Granger, who had tossed Besaraba off for drinking beer. A passenger was killed and a bystander was paralyzed. Besaraba, who was sentenced to two death sentences, had a record that included out-of-state arrests for assaulting a policeman and drunken driving. He listed a soup kitchen as an address and helped support himself by volunteering to take experimental drugs.

Nothing on his record disqualified Besaraba from getting a permit, according to John Russi, director of the Division of Licensing in the Florida Department of State. "I don't know that any system could be one hundred percent safe," he acknowledged, noting the concerns of some Texans who questioned the reliability of background checks of those seeking a license to carry a concealed weapon.

Despite the heavily-financed and well-organized public campaign by the minority opponents of the right-to-carry bill in Texas, frequent polls conducted by statewide newspapers and television stations continued to indicate strong support for the concealed handgun proposal. But the slaying of six people during a shooting spree in the coastal city of Corpus Christi on April 3, 1995, sparked new controversy, intense legislative debate, and ultimately constructive changes to the right-to-carry bill.

Half a dozen people were killed when a former employee of a Corpus Christi refinery inspection business walked into the office and shot five people, then turned the gun on himself. Within hours, the city's police chief, Henry Garrett, spoke out against the handgun proposal, along with several Corpus Christi lawmakers, who vowed to toughen licensing requirements in the bill. Representative Vilma Luna told the press that she would attempt to amend it to increase training requirements from a ten-hour minimum to a forty-hour minimum.

"My intention is to make sure we're very careful and that this is a well thought-out bill," Luna said, "and that we put requirements in the bill that are reasonable and make sense and will help promote the ultimate goal of making sure that the people who are getting these permits are carefully screened."

"We've lost six people here in less than a week from handguns," a distraught Chief Garrett emotionally stated at a press conference. "I think that ought to send some type of really strong message to the people in the Legislature who so strongly support this ridiculous bill." Attempting to regain his composure, the police chief continued, "This whole city's in shock. We're walking around in a daze. How much of this type of violence do we have to put up with? Do we correct it by putting more guns out there?"

Representative Hugo Berlanga, another state lawmaker from the coastal city, said like Luna, he would also seek to increase training hours but would first try to amend the bill to make it contingent upon voter approval, a measure Governor Bush was adamantly against. "More than ever I think the people deserve a right to vote on this issue in a binding referendum," Berlanga told to the media. "Any doubts I had about the bill have been solidified by the tragic events that have occurred in my hometown."

Less than a week earlier, Grammy Award–winner and reigning queen of the world of Tejano music, Selena Quintanilla Perez, had been murdered with a five-shot .38 caliber handgun in a Corpus Christi motel room by Yolanda Saldivar, the founder and onetime president of the Selena fan club. The shooting came after a bitter falling out over the singer's financial affairs, including a clothing boutique managed by Ms. Saldivar. Mark Skurka, a prosecutor in the case, said in closing arguments that the defendant "took the gun, cocked the hammer, pulled the trigger, and killed her [Selena]. What could be a worse way to die than to be shot in the back in a cowardly way?"

After the six slayings at the refinery inspection business, Abraham Quintanilla, the slain singer's father and a Corpus Christi resident, made a public request to Selena's fans: "Though it's hard to find any positive aspects to this tragedy, we would urge the community to oppose the present bill before the House and Senate," Quintanilla said.

In light of the Corpus Christi murders, a new poll showing that Texans were split 50-50 on the handgun bill, and strong support for a statewide voter referendum on concealed weapons, Senator Carlos Truan publicly challenged Governor Bush to change his mind and oppose the right-to-carry proposal before the Legislature. "In view of Selena and the other tragedies, I would hope the governor would change his position," Truan stated at a press conference.

Although the governor did not personally respond to the senator's request, his press secretary, Karen Hughes, issued an evasive, but revealing, one-line response: "Governor Bush continues to support allowing Texans to carry handguns for self-protection."

The governor's seeming lack of sympathy for the Corpus Christi tragedies and his single-mindedness in aggressively pushing the concealed handgun law through the state legislature, forced many Texans to question if his strong support of the bill was a political payoff to the National Rifle Association.

Susan Gates publicly chastised the governor and the Legislature in the op-ed section of the *Houston Chronicle*: "Shame on Gov. George W. Bush. Shame on the Texas Legislature. With all the serious problems in our state—education, drugs, poverty and the continuing fight to bring our state up to a standard that lets us compete with other states for high-paying jobs—which is one of the first bills they bring to a vote? A bill to allow Texans to carry concealed handguns. If this is an example of their priorities, heaven help us for the next four years. I know that these guys owe favors to the National Rifle Association for big campaign bucks, but they could have shown a little old-fashioned discretion before they repaid their benefactors. . . . I guess we've been sold to the highest bidder. I honestly don't know how they sleep at night."

Ironically, only a few days before the final passage of the concealed handgun bill in the House of Representatives, the governor's father resigned his lifetime membership in the National Rifle Association over the group's reference to federal agents as a collection of "jackbooted government thugs." In a May 3, 1995 letter to the NRA's president, the former president protested the comments made by Executive Vice President Wayne LaPierre in a NRA mass-mailing to its membership seeking funds and support for its efforts to defeat a ban on semiautomatic weapons.

In the solicitation letter, La Pierre wrote, "If you have a badge, you have the government's go-ahead to harass, intimidate, even murder law-abiding citizens." He also referred to the Bureau of Alcohol, Tobacco and Firearms (ATF) raids on the Branch Davidian compound near Waco, Texas, and Randy Weaver's home in Ruby Ridge, Idaho, as evidence of the federal government's willingness to attack innocent civilians. "Not long ago, it was unthinkable for federal agents wearing Nazi bucket helmets and black storm trooper uniforms to attack law-abiding citizens," LaPierre boldly claimed in his fund-raising letter.

"Your broadside against federal agents deeply offends my own sense of decency and honor, and it offends my concept of service to country," wrote an uncharacteristically angry Bush, who as president and political candidate, frequently had praised the NRA. "I am outraged," he protested in the letter, which was released publicly by his office in Houston. "Please remove my name from your membership list."

In a brief statement, LaPierre refused to apologize. "Our words and actions will be completely vindicated" during congressional hearings on the ATF bureau, he said. The NRA then criticized Bush for going public with his decision to cancel his membership in the organization. "Surely, a private exchange between us might persuade you to at least reserve a final opinion until all the facts are examined," Thomas L. Washington, NRA president, stated in correspondence to Bush. Washington also complained that the group, with its membership of 3.4 million, had unfairly come under attack after the Oklahoma City bombing for inciting antigovernment hate groups with its rhetoric against gun control. Washington said the organization had been forced to defend itself against the "NRA bashing frenzy."

Gib Lewis, the NRA lobbyist in the Texas state capital, read a carefully worded statement to the press, saying that he understood why the former president responded angrily to LaPierre's comments and how the NRA had been made vulnerable by its antigun stance in the wake of the bombing of the Alfred P. Murrah Federal Building in Oklahoma, which took the lives of 168 people, including nineteen children.

Acknowledging that the loss of Bush's membership in the group would tarnish their public image, the former House Speaker-turned-lobbyist, told reporters, "There's always been a very close relationship between President Bush and the NRA. The bottom line is he's at odds with one person. I hope it's not blamed on the NRA as a whole."

Neal Knox, second vice president of the NRA and one of the organization's most fervent anti–gun control voices, further inflamed the controversy when he claimed that "a lot of NRA members would be delighted that Bush has resigned from the group."

In a prepared statement, the governor declined to comment directly about his father's *very* public resignation from the National Rifle Association, saying only that the former president "has strong feelings and has every right to express those feelings." Privately, the younger Bush was furious that "the old man had aired this dirty laundry in public," especially in light of the governor's ongoing public battle to win final passage of the concealed handguns law in the state legislature.

Adding insult to injury was the fact that George W. first learned of the elder Bush's announcement when he saw the headlines "Former President Bush Angrily Resigns From NRA" on the front page of the May 11, 1995 morning edition of the *Houston Chronicle*. According to aides, the red-faced governor threw his reading glasses across his office, striking the furthest wall and shattering the glass on a framed photo of the Bush family at the Kennebunkport compound on the coast of Maine.

"The governor was cussing so loud when he called his father that his mother threatened to hang up the phone," a Bush assistant revealed. "For days afterwards, he kept hinting to his staff and even to the press that he might voluntarily be a one-term governor. He would sit in his office, chewing alternately on Super Bubble and the stub of a cigar, and repeatedly say, 'This job doesn't pay me enough to put up with all this shit, especially when my old man is stabbing me in the back in front of the whole damn state.'"

In an attempt at public damage control, Ray Sullivan, one of the governor's spokespersons, stated to the press that the younger Bush, who was not a member of the NRA, knew Alan Whicher, the Secret Service agent his father mentioned in his resignation from the NRA. Sullivan said the governor had been with Whicher's widow at the April 23 memorial service for victims of the Oklahoma City bombing a month earlier. "I know the governor was moved by the meeting," Sullivan said.

"Laura and I were sitting there, and a secret service agent I remembered from the White House days came up and said there's a family here that was very close to your dad," the governor later recalled. "They had just come from seeing President Clinton, and the agent said, would I talk to the wife, and I said sure, and we had a big tearful embrace right there. . . . It was a tough moment."

In his letter to the NRA, former President Bush said Whicher "was no Nazi. He was a kind man, a loving parent, a man dedicated to serving his country—and serve it well he did."

Although George W. was not particularly close to the forty-year-old Whicher, who guarded the elder Bush during his terms as vice president and president, the governor considered Secret Service Agent Mickey Maroney, who was part of the younger Bush's security detail while he lived in Dallas, one of his "best buds." The fifty-year-old Maroney, a Texas native, was also killed in the bombing of the federal building in Oklahoma City.

"He went to the University of Arkansas," the governor said. "I used to needle him all the time about that, and he was a football player, a big guy who was a fun and decent man."

Opponents of the concealed handgun legislation were quick to point out that Timothy McVeigh, who had no criminal record before he was arrested and later sentenced to death for masterminding the bombing massacre, would have qualified for a gun license, under the new right-to-carry weapons bill.

"I wouldn't be signing it if I thought it made Texas a more dangerous place," the governor responded. Indeed, a little more than a week after the House passed the concealed weapons proposal, the governor signed the bill into law, tossing out a ban on carrying weapons that was adopted by another Republican governor, E.J. Davis, 125 years earlier during a meeting of the post-Civil War Legislature.

"Today we signed a bill that gives Texans who feel the need to carry a weapon to protect themselves the right to do so," the governor announced at the signing ceremony, "assuming they are properly licensed and trained to do so."

The law required citizens who were twenty-one or older, with no criminal histories, mental illness, or substance abuse problems to undergo ten to fifteen hours of training and pass a proficiency exam before receiving a four-year permit (which cost $140) from the Texas Department of Public Safety to carry a concealed handgun. Instructors were to be trained in several elements of certification, including laws relating to weapons and the use of deadly force, handgun proficiency and safety, nonviolent dispute resolution, and proper storage practices for weapons. State officials estimated that about one percent of Texans, or approximately 180,000 residents, would apply for licenses.

Representative Ron Wilson of Houston, another sponsor of the right-to-carry bill, noted he began fighting for the law almost a decade earlier after a man attacked his wife. He told the press at the signing ceremony that Texans would now be able to protect themselves.

Representative Kevin Brady, one of only two Republicans to oppose the bill's passage in the House, pulled his horn-rimmed glasses from his face to wipe away tears when Bush signed the handgun bill into law. In September 1967, when he was only twelve-years-old, Brady was pulled out of a huddle during football practice to learn his father had been fatally shot in Rapid City, South Dakota, by a man licensed to carry a concealed weapon. The man, who his attorney father was representing in a divorce, pulled out a pistol during the trial and killed Brady's dad, the estranged wife, and the court clerk. The judge was shot, but lived. The murderer was sentenced to life in prison, where he eventually died.

Openly weeping at the memory of his mother having to raise five children on her own, Brady remarked, "I couldn't look Mom in the eye and vote for this." Considered a champion for victims' rights, the state lawmaker acknowledged that Governor Bush, other Republican officials in Texas, lobbyists for the NRA, and constituents in his conservative county north of Houston, pressured him to vote for the handgun legislation.

"I really do believe in the Second Amendment, but there ought to be limitations," Brady told members of the press. "The ones we have today are pretty sound—you can protect your home. But we don't need a law to let us carry guns everywhere we go. . . . When human beings get emotional, when things get out of control, I'm convinced that fifteen hours of training isn't going to be worth the certificate it's printed on."*

The fact that the right-to-carry law wasn't first approved by Texas voters in a referendum, which Governor Bush adamantly opposed, particularly an-

*In early 1999, a study by the Washington, D.C.-based Violence Policy Center documented 2,080 arrests by concealed-handgun holders in Texas since the law authorizing the permits took effect in 1996.

gered Brady. "I trust people to make the right decision in the long haul," he said. "But when it comes down to my vote, it's an awfully personal issue."

Only days after the governor signed the concealed handgun bill into law, the National Rifle Association, in a full-page newspaper advertisement thanked the Legislature for passing the measure. Governor Bush was also saluted by the gun owners' lobby.

The ad, published in the morning and evening editions of the capital city newspaper, the *Austin American-Statesman,* boldly proclaimed that "a bond of trust deserves a word of gratitude" in recognizing the governor's personal efforts in securing the bill's passage through the Senate and House. The NRA also praised the legislature "for recognizing and codifying the fundamental right of self-protection."

State lawmakers who opposed the bill's passage during the legislative session argued that the new law would put more guns in circulation and increase the likelihood of law-abiding citizens, often innocent bystanders, becoming gunshot victims. The legislators also pointed out in various sound bites on the Capitol steps that the new law sent a disturbing message to children, who were already barraged with depictions of violence in movies and on television, that you could somehow solve your problems by strapping on a pistol.

Representative Paul Moreno of El Paso complained that the right-to-carry law would contradict adults who told their teenage children not to take guns to school for protection. "We are creating a monster," he said. "We are sending the youngsters the wrong signal."

"More guns, more bullets being fired," predicted Senator Royce West of Dallas. "More projectiles of steel and lead hurtling randomly through the walls of homes and classrooms."

Ironically, during the same week that the state lawmakers sent the governor the concealed handgun bill for signature, his office announced that he had signed another measure, which was designed to encourage parents to keep guns out of the hands of children.

The second bill imposed a $500 fine on an adult who left a loaded gun unsecured so that a child could handle it. The penalty would be increased to a year in jail or a $4,000 fine if the child fired the weapon and killed or seriously wounded himself or another person.*

*In 1997, the public interest group, Texans For Gun Safety, conducted a survey among all Texas county/district attorneys and discovered that only four percent of them had charged an adult under the law during the two-year period following enactment, and only two percent of those adults charged were actually prosecuted. During this same two-year period, however, there had been shootings by children in fifteen percent of the counties in Texas.

Governor Bush's critics complained that the penalty was a mere slap on the wrist and found it suspicious that the governor and certain state lawmakers chose to pass both laws in the same legislative session.

"Maybe the child protection law will save some young lives," Senator West privately told other legislators, "but I think in reality it may also soothe the consciences of Governor Bush and some of my fellow legislators who are probably having trouble sleeping at night."

Hijacking the Issues

Whether Governor Bush was a persuasive leader or just a lucky politician in the right place at the right time, the Seventy-fourth Legislature's biennial session adjourned at the end of May 1995, fulfilling the lion's share of Bush's 1994 conservative campaign promises, even though none of the reforms went as far to the right as he wanted them to go.

During the gubernatorial race, candidate Bush repeatedly said, "We must change a welfare system that has created dependency on government. I know full well, like most Texans know, that dependency upon government saps the soul and drains the spirit."* His original welfare reform plan called for capping benefits to women who bore additional children while receiving government assistance, testing recipients for drugs, limiting the number of times a person could be on welfare to one, and ending government assistance after two years. Much to his disappointment, none of Bush's proposals made it into the final bill.

"The original legislation that was filed—the 'Bush welfare reform proposal'—was quite punitive," said state Representative Elliot Naishtat, vice chairman of the House Human Services Committee. "What we ended up with was an approach to moving people from welfare to self-sufficiency that minimizes the harm caused to recipients and their families."

The "more balanced" welfare reform bill passed by the Seventy-fourth Legislature required recipients to spend at least thirty hours per week at

---

*During Governor Richards' administration, Texas ranked forty-eighth out of fifty states in the amount of money given to welfare mothers under the Aid to Families with Dependent Children program. According to a report by the Texas department of human services, the average welfare family had only two children and the typical monthly cash assistance was only $188, a government entitlement that Bush considered to be "a princely sum." State welfare officials also estimated that sixty-nine percent of recipients were on welfare rolls for less than two years.

work or at least twenty hours per week in a job training program during any one-month period for which they received benefits; imposed time limits for welfare assistance to one to three years, depending on the recipient's education and work experience; and required recipients to sign a "responsibility agreement," promising to cooperate in the establishment of paternity, immunize and screen their children for health problems, and maintain a drug-free lifestyle.

Another of Bush's "big four" reform proposals involved the criminal justice system, primarily the end of automatic parole for prisoners. Bush defeated Governor Richards in 1994 in part by promising to end "mandatory supervision," a system that required prison inmates to be released once their "good time" and actual time served equaled the number of years of their sentence. Bush also pledged to voters that he would make the abolishment of mandatory supervision releases retroactive to include those already behind bars, even though legal experts on his staff argued that such a move would violate state and federal constitutions.*

"George Bush looked the people of Texas straight in the eye and promised to end early release of all prisoners, knowing full well he couldn't do it," said one state senator, who was member of the legislature's criminal justice committee. "Anticrime laws—no matter how popular—cannot be applied retroactively to those already serving time in prison. It's very central to our idea of justice in this country that you can only be punished for the law you broke, and the length of punishment is part and parcel of that."

The bill that the Seventy-fourth Legislature passed and the governor signed in 1995 eliminated mandatory supervision release only for those convicted of any crime after September 1, 1996, the day the law went into effect. Although Bush condemned Governor Richards during the campaign as being soft on crime when 5,622 inmates were released courtesy of mandatory supervision, prison officials estimated about seventy thousand convicted felons already in prison and not covered by the new law would be returned to society over the next several years.

The Legislature also supported the governor's agenda on strengthening juvenile justice laws. Lawmakers passed bills lowering from fifteen to fourteen the age at which a juvenile could be tried as an adult for capital murder and first-degree felonies; required one-year minimum sentences for juve-

---

*The governor initially said he would challenge the legality repealing the mandatory supervision law, but later declined, claiming that he didn't want to embroil the state of Texas in a possibly lengthy and costly court battle.

niles sent to the Texas Youth Commission, and increased the juvenile detention system's capacity by 2,360 prison beds (although the governor had sought 3,500); established a statewide database of juvenile records accessible to all law enforcement agencies; and required that certain repeat offenders for lower level felonies serve their sentences in prison instead of state jails. Bush did not, however, win passage of a bill prohibiting anyone under eighteen from having a firearm, except for hunting and other special situations.

Another key plank in Bush's bid for election in 1994 was the promise to overhaul the state's education systems and grant greater freedom to local school boards. "To encourage innovation, to seek excellence," he said, "we must free local teachers, parents, and administrators to design schools which fit their communities' needs."

Although the legislature decontrolled schools, created the first "home rule school districts" in the nation, granted educators more authority to remove disruptive or violent students from the classroom, made excellence in the core subjects the goal of public education, and increased the minimum pay for teachers, Governor Bush did not get his wish to increase the state share of public school funding from forty-four to sixty percent.

The last of Bush's four major legislative reform proposals, civil court procedures, which he said during the gubernatorial race would probably be his most significant project if elected, was basically passed without a compromise effort on the part of the governor. The probusiness legislative body passed seven bills to address the mounting perception that the court system was unfair to companies being sued. The new laws, which were quickly signed by the governor, limited punitive damages, overhauled the state's deceptive trade practices, made it more difficult to sue doctors for malpractice, protected government employees acting in their official capacity, limited the liability of companies when more than one was to blame, and allowed judges to sanction lawyers for filing frivolous lawsuits.* The governor claimed that tort reform was "good for business" in Texas, and that everyone benefited because insurance premiums would fall. However, in the following years, rates did not decline and the insurance industry recorded profits at a forty-year high.

---

*A 1995 study by Public Citizen, a watchdog group founded by Ralph Nader, later released a report to the Associated Press that showed three-fourths of the companies in which Bush owned stock, were defendant corporations and could be drastically affected by lawsuit reforms, including Baxter International Inc. and Baxter Trevanol Labs, two companies at the center of more than three thousand breast implant suits.

Boasting that his first legislative session in office would be remembered as "the most substantive in Texas history," Governor Bush signed 217 bills, including the right-to-carry concealed handgun law and the four key issues of his 1994 campaign platform.

"I won by 352,000 votes," Bush told the press, alleging a conservative "mandate" after the election. "And when you stand up in front of the Legislature and outline a legislative agenda that was endorsed by the will of the people, that helps remind people that this is what Texans want. . . . I had confidence that we could collectively score big legislative victories, because these were conservative notions, endorsed by a conservative electorate, with conservative bodies—the House and Senate."

State Representative Sylvester Turner of Houston claimed that the package of bills the governor pushed through the Legislature were "a shell" without substance. Turner said the juvenile justice bill would just put more youth in jail without rehabilitation, and he said the welfare bill would do little to get mothers off government assistance and into jobs.

"If the question is whether or not he has had action on the items he identified in the campaign, the answer would be yes," Turner acknowledged. "If you're asking whether those laws were good at achieving the objectives that were stated, the answer would be no."

In any normal year, however, passage of any one of those major pieces of legislation would have been considered a noteworthy accomplishment. Yet those measures—and much more—took place in the limited time frame of the 140-day legislative session.

Much of the credit had to go to the new governor, who freely admitted that he learned valuable lessons watching his father in 1990 assemble a coalition of thirty-seven nations in opposition to Iraq's invasion of Kuwait. That alliance eventually led to the defeat of Iraq in the Persian Gulf War. On a smaller scale, the younger Bush accomplished a similarly impressive feat during the Seventy-fourth Legislature, especially during the session's final month when he privately told lawmakers, "This is my bottom line."

"Part of the process in the legislative process is to push and shove and maybe twist an arm or two, regardless of the party," Bush later admitted.

Critics complained, however, that the new governor benefited from the fact that state lawmakers had been working toward welfare reform, "home rule" school districts, and juvenile justice reform before Bush raised the issues in the 1994 gubernatorial campaign.

State Senator Gonzalo Barrientos said that the governor was getting undue credit for the work of the Legislature. "We have an old Mexican saying, 'Just because the rooster crowed when the sun came up doesn't mean the rooster made the sun come up,'" the lawmaker said. "I think you'll find some comparison there."

"Basically, he got on board a train that was already leaving the station," said Ed Martin, Texas Democratic Party Executive Director. "He walked up and down the aisles meeting the conductors and the passengers, and then he moved up to the engine and waved at the people of Texas as the train went by."

But even Martin gave Bush credit for the successful "personal politics" of his private meetings with lawmakers, something his predecessor, Ann Richards, never did. Martin said it allowed Bush to be an effective persuader in the Seventy-fourth Legislature's final days.

"He had those issues, the big four, and he had some clear vision about what he was going to do," said Tony Proffitt, a longtime and trusted political aide to Lieutenant Governor Bullock. "He was intelligent enough to know they were important issues that were already being worked on, and that working on those, he would accomplish something other than a stalemate."

Although the governor later acknowledged that his four primary campaign issues had been topics of discussion before he was elected, he took offense at any suggestion that he had been given too much of the credit by Texans for the 1995 reforms.

"I think they might have been addressed," the governor said of the issues he stood accused of hijacking, "but I think they might have come out differently."

Bush argued that civil-justice reforms, for example, might not have passed at all if Richards were still governor, because she was supported by the plaintiffs' lawyers who vigorously opposed them.* Simultaneously, he did not discount the fact that his respectful and close working relationship with Bullock and Laney had helped him win passage of his key legislative package.

"The point was, they shared credit with me, and I shared credit with them," Bush said. "I think that's an important part of the process."

Consequently, the new governor received high job performance ratings, but they were almost entirely a measure of his personal popularity, not his

---

*Bush alleged during the bitter 1994 gubernatorial campaign that Richards had received more than $2.7 million in political contributions from personal injury lawyers since 1990.

executive ability. As preordained in the state constitution, the most powerful person in Texas was Lieutenant Governor Bullock,* who controlled the Texas Senate—and thereby, state government—by determining what legislation would pass and what wouldn't. Bush certainly owed his early success to Bullock's willingness to cooperate. Had the lieutenant governor chosen to be partisan and obstructionist, he could have made Bush look inept and ineffectual.

"[He] could have sabotaged me," the governor later admitted, "and I'm grateful he didn't." The key to his success as a governor, or at least the perception to voters that he was a "can-do" chief executive, would be his relationship with Bullock.

Aides and assistants to both men say that Bush made an all-out effort to "soften up" the powerful lieutenant governor, who had a reputation for being crusty and ornery. Bush went to Bullock's ranch in Llano, a two-hour drive from the state capital, for the sole purpose of personally delivering Christmas presents. When Bullock was later hospitalized for a week with a mild case of pneumonia, the governor visited him almost every day "just to hang out," Bush claimed.

"I think I was realistic and practical enough to know Bullock was a strong man in the Senate," the governor later acknowledged. "I was a wise enough person to see if I could befriend him. If it was impossible to befriend him, I was prepared to go on my own. But the better course of action any time is to try to make alliances if they can lead to a common purpose."

"Bush needed to appear as a hands-on, see-what-I've-done governor if he was going to use the office as a stepping stone to the presidency," said one of Bush's top aides, "and the key to that success was Bullock. Using political skills that were more akin to Clinton than his father, Bush personally bonded with the lieutenant governor."

To hear Bush describe it, their relationship was like an arranged marriage in which genuine affection grew. But the one time the governor ventured out on a political mission alone and pursued the most significant policy endeavor of his tenure—tax reform—without first consulting Bullock, he quickly learned how dependent he was on the powerful politician's goodwill.

---

*Bullock was first elected lieutenant governor in 1991. Prior to that, he served as state comptroller from 1975 to 1990, as secretary of state from 1971 to 1972 and state representative from 1957 to 1959. He also worked as a gubernatorial aide from 1969 to 1971, as an assistant attorney general from 1967 to 1968 and for the Texas Historical Commission from 1963 to 1965.

★ 8 ★

The Measure of the Man

I've got a vision for a better tomorrow for my state, and I know how to bring people together to achieve common objectives. I know how to sell the case.

–George W. Bush

He doesn't know much, and he hasn't done much, but everybody likes him.

—Syndicated columnist and author, Molly Ivins

Shades of Clinton

After his first legislative session had ended, Bush was enjoying some of the highest approval ratings ever recorded for a Texas governor. One poll showed that fifty-nine percent of those who were surveyed thought it would be "fun to have him over for dinner." Fashioning himself as an affable and informal governor, he has said his greatest asset may be his striking Clintonian ability to get along and understand ordinary people, to remember names and faces.

An often repeated comment from Texans was "the governor's nothing like his daddy," noting that the younger Bush was more conservative, and more politically astute, more wily, more witty, more quick-tempered, and more charming than the former president ever was.

No introvert, the governor relished meeting people, and actually became invigorated by the endless public exposure that being the state's chief executive demanded. Although he kept such a packed schedule that associates called him "the Energizer Bunny," he somehow always found the time to horn in on tourists' photo-taking sessions at the Governor's Mansion, and occasionally would invite school groups to the inner sanctum of his private office,* where he would point to a ludicrous portrait of Sam Houston on a far wall. The legendary Texas governor, cast out of office because he refused to swear allegiance to the Confederacy, was standing in a toga among the ruins of Carthage, a painting that Houston commissioned himself.

"The lesson that picture tells you," he would say to young people visiting his office, "is there's a fine line between being the governor of Texas and making a fool of yourself." Bush would also note that his favorite hero overcame humiliating defeats and alcoholism to become a political legend. "He wrestled with self-doubt, he wandered for years looking for direction," the governor would continue. "The turning point in his life came when he looked in the mirror and saw the reflection of a man he no longer respected. And that very day he vowed to turn his life around, and he did."

The next leg of the office tour included the governor's collection of autographed baseballs and he was always most enthusiastic about one ball signed by members of the raucous Texas band ZZ Top. Acting mischievously, he would show the young visitors a photo of himself, neat and businesslike in his suit and tie, standing between two long-bearded, black-attired, sunglasses-wearing members of the band.

Bush would gesture to another wall, where the words to his favorite hymn were framed. "Not a morning goes by," he said, "that I don't stop and think about what they mean to me personally, 'A charge to keep I have . . . To serve the present age, my calling to fulfill.'"

Finally, completing his impromptu tour, he would lean back in his executive chair, and passing a hand through his wiry locks, would conduct a short question-and-answer session with the school kids.

---

*When Bush came into office in January 1995, Texas taxpayers had just finished spending $187 million to have the 107-year-old state Capitol enlarged, refurbished and restored to its turn-of-the-century architectural splendor. Not satisfied with the way his predecessor had the nine hundred-square-foot, second-floor governor's private office reconfigured during the restoration, Bush had the State Preservation Board enlarge the office to the tune of $60,000, which was funded by corporations, PACs, and GOP contributors.

"Where do you and your family live?"

"A quarter of the Governor's Mansion is sealed off from public view. That's where my wife, Laura, the first lady of Texas, our teenage twin daughters, Jenna and Barbara, our dog, Spot, and India and Cowboy, our cats, live."

"Where do your daughters go to school?"

"They go to the private St. Andrews Episcopal School. Bushie—that's what the first lady and I call each other—who is a former teacher and librarian, felt strongly, and so did I, that a private school would give the girls a nurturing environment and take some of the pressure off them from living in a new city with a father who is governor. They study real hard and occasionally win awards. Jenna was recently elected president of the student body at St. Andrews. She just moved right in and ran. Kind of sounds like her dad."

"Do you help them with their homework?"

"My wife and I like to go to bed at nine P.M., earlier than our daughters, where we read and watch the news for awhile. But sometimes I stay up late and type the girls' theme papers for them if they need help."

"Do you all take vacations together like other families?"

"We have a lake house in East Texas and sometimes we get away for the weekend, where I go bass fishing, my wife reads one book after another, and the girls just hang out. But now that they're older, the girls don't like to go to the camp house like they used to. They'd rather stay back here in Austin and watch TV and talk forever on the telephone with their friends."

"Does the first lady work at a real job?"

"She has a windowless office in the basement of the Capitol across the street. Like my mother, who was America's first lady, Laura promotes reading, libraries, and early childhood education.* But her main devotion in life is our two daughters. Jenna and Barbara couldn't ask for a better mother in life, or me a better wife. She truly is my best friend."

"Has your life changed much since you were elected governor?"

---

*Although unassuming and reserved, Laura Bush has transformed herself into one of the most effective first ladies in Texas history, even occasionally outdistancing her husband in popularity polls. While traveling Texas to promote a statewide reading initiative, she is often hounded by overflow crowds clamoring for her autograph. "She has a wonderful presence," said one woman who attended the first-ever Texas Book Festival, a three-day event, which raised more that $600,000 for statewide public libraries. "She seems to be genuine, and that is such a rarity these days." Just as some people are curious to see if George W. will become as prominent as his father, others wonder if Laura Bush will turn out to be as popular as her mother-in-law, one of this century's best-loved political wives.

"No, Laura and I still go out to dinner to eat Mexican food with friends, watch videos, and I love to sit in a lawn chair on summer nights listening to Rangers baseball games on a boombox. Every morning, while Laura drinks coffee and reads the newspaper, I get up at dawn for a three- to six-mile jog."

In addition to being widely accessible to young people ("I think he's fake," said one departing high school teen. "He laid it on too thick.") and other tourists visiting the Governor's Mansion, Bush also nurtured a buddy-buddy relationship with Texas reporters. Unlike many Republican politicians who view the media as the ideological enemy, he often bearhugs some of his favorite male reporters, addresses them by nicknames, plays speed golf with them (finishing eighteen holes in an hour and thirty seven minutes), and engages in wisecracking banter.

"I've come to the realization that some of the simple tenets of life matter in the political world," Bush has said. "Like . . . as we say in West Texas, 'visiting with each other' and spending time listening to the other person."

It was one of his impromptu meetings with the Texas media that got him into trouble midway through his first term as governor.

Dead on Arrival

On a November afternoon in 1996, two months before the seventy-fifth legislative session began, Bush called reporters together on the front lawn of the Governor's Mansion and announced that he was requesting Texas lawmakers to use state budget savings to reduce local school property taxes by $1 billion over two years. The governor called it a "down payment" on his promise to provide Texans with relief from the "choking" effect of $10 billion a year in property taxes, on which public schools had become increasingly more reliant.*

Although Lieutenant Governor Bullock and House Speaker Laney had said in a joint press conference after the conclusion of the 1995 legislative session that they would "look to the governor at this time to lay out a plan" to take the "burden off property taxes," Bush might have surprised them

*At the time, approximately fifty-five percent of the cost of operating school districts in Texas was funded with local property taxes. A 1996 study by Citizens for Tax Justice, a labor-funded advocacy group in Washington, ranked Texas among the "Terrible Ten" states for poor and middle-income taxpayers, who paid proportionately more of their income in state and local taxes than the wealthy. The property taxes paid by a Texas homeowner with a $10,000 annual income were sixty-three percent higher than for a homeowner with a $100,000 a year income.

when he exerted his gubernatorial power in late 1996 by staking his claim on a function that in Texas is reserved for the legislature—formulating the state budget.

Claiming that he was "willing to make bold decisions and be a bold leader," Bush proposed using state budgetary savings and economic growth to reduce local school taxes by $1 billion over the next two years, but he provided no details on how many taxpayers would benefit or how the state would carry out the plan. "We don't have it fully fleshed out," he told reporters gathered on the lawn of the Governor's Mansion.

By making his announcement the way he did, Bush jeopardized his bipartisan relationship with Bullock and Laney, who first heard about his tax reform plan when he held his press conference, and that didn't sit well with the lieutenant governor, who hated surprises. Pressed for a response to the governor's comments, Bullock coldly replied that he didn't want to "get the cart before the horse," cautiously noting that he didn't know if Bush's proposal was feasible until he had seen the details of his plan.

Bush said he didn't advise the two powerful Texas political leaders beforehand because "I didn't feel like they were going to be supportive of it. It wasn't personal. I think they were trying to protect the legislative prerogative of how to spend the state's money," he said. "And I was the executive branch, laying claim to part of it. I think I semistrained the relationship—strained is too strong a word—I think I disappointed them by announcing my plan the way I did. I immediately marched over and told them about it after I did it."

By the time he made his State of the State address to lawmakers in January 1997, two weeks after the legislative session began, Bush's "down payment" called for in November had evolved into a detailed plan to drastically reform the state's tax code so that the Texas public education system would rely more on financing from state taxes and less on local property taxes. He no longer was content in going after a $1 billion tax cut, but a complete overhaul of the state's tax structure—the most widespread changes in almost four decades—that would ultimately result in almost $3 billion in cuts.

Though a thirty percent drop in property taxes sounded politically appealing to lawmakers, the devil was in the details of Bush's proposal, which was essentially nothing more than a tax redistribution plan. Calling the reform package "fair and reasonable," Bush claimed it would slash school taxes on the "average home in Texas—a home valued at $61,500—by as much as forty percent." However, he sought to help replace the lost education revenue with a one-half cent increase in the sales tax from 6.25 cents per dollar to 6.75 cents, making Texas' rate the second highest in the country. He also asked the Legislature to set aside $1 billion of the state's surplus in the next two-year budget and enact a new 1.25 percent business activity tax to more "uniformly spread the tax burden among companies operating in Texas."

Bush's proposal posed major financial consequences for millions of Texans and, of course, represented huge political stakes for the governor, especially after he told lawmakers in his State of the State speech that he intended to use all his "political capital" to win passage of the tax reform plan. The proposal immediately received a hostile reaction from the press, voters, powerful lobbying interests, and a majority of the legislators of both parties.

Bush's new, broad-based "Texas Business Tax," which would have replaced the state corporate franchise tax, drew fire from restaurant owners, retailers, auto dealers, attorneys, architects, engineers, and other service professionals who didn't pay the franchise tax because they were organized as partnerships, rather than corporations. But the Coalition for Property Tax Reform, which included oil refineries and other large industries with large amounts of taxable property, applauded the governor and his efforts to force small business owners to accept more of a tax burden.

Critics also asked if it was fair to lower property taxes for homeowners and landlords (who included tax costs in their rents) without attempting to make some provision to share the tax savings with renters, particularly low-income families. According to the U.S. Census Bureau, renters lived in almost forty percent of Texas housing units in early 1997. Under the governor's plan, there was no assurance that apartment owners would lower apartment dwellers' rents, but they would certainly have to pay a higher sales tax and higher prices for consumer goods that businesses would charge to cover the new Texas Business Tax.

Dick Lavine, a tax analyst for the Center for Public Policy Priorities, which analyzes the impact of government policies on low- and middle-income people, noted that about sixty percent of Texans earning $19,000 or less a year were renters, compounding the problem. "The renters get almost nothing from Bush's tax plan," Lavine complained. "They just have to hope that their landlord will share the bounty." Most apartment owners acknowledged, however, that they wouldn't be able to share any savings they might have realized on their property taxes because, under Bush's tax reform proposal, they would have to begin paying the business activity tax.

State Representative Kevin Bailey of Houston, claimed that "the reality is that Governor Bush is catering to the affluent residents in the affluent school districts and affluent businesses. The people who need the tax breaks most will not get them." Many Texans agreed, complaining in letters to statewide newspaper editors and call-ins to talk radio stations, that they believed the governor was primarily interested in getting a tax break for wealthy business owners who had high property taxes.

"It's hypocritical of Bush, who built a new baseball stadium for the Texas Rangers through the condemnation of private property by the city of Arlington and a taxpayer subsidy of $135 million, now preaches the salience of private property ownership and holding the line on taxes," one listener lambasted the governor on a radio station in Dallas. "I guess it depends upon whose property and whose taxes."*

Critics of Bush's tax plan also asked if it was fair to keep raising the sales tax, already one of the highest in the country and regressive because it hit the poor the hardest. And for those who itemized their federal income tax deductions, many of them asked if it was fair to reduce a major deduction—the property taxes on their house—and replace it with a higher sales tax, which they couldn't deduct.

"The governor came up with a poor plan," stated state Representative John Hirschi. "I don't think he had any constituency supporting him on the plan he came up with. He had a popular issue, tax reform and lowering property taxes, but a very weak vehicle for accomplishing a popular idea."

State Representative Paul Sadler, the chairman of a special House committee that would deliberate Bush's tax plan, also was highly critical of the proposal, calling the new business activity tax "essentially an income tax" on service professionals. Sadler also questioned whether the governor's plan would adequately fund public education, commenting that he didn't want to go through the "gyrations" of passing a new tax law "if we don't create a tax that helps the schools, and I'm not convinced this tax helps the schools."

---

*Under a seldom-used tax law, Governor Bush and more than a dozen friends qualified for substantial property tax exemptions on their East Texas lakeside retreat. A 1977 measure allowed a club to designate property as "recreational, park, and scenic land" and reduce its taxes. The property had to be at least five acres and be covered by a deed restriction for at least ten years. The loophole had allowed Bush and seventeen other residents of the exclusive Rainbo Club development, about ninety miles southeast of Dallas, to cut nearly half of their tax liability.

Bush, whose only taxable property was the weekend getaway house, wrote a $343 check to the club, which owned 1,187 acres and paid the taxes. Members leased the land (three acres in Bush's case) and owned their homes. County appraisal district records showed that the 1,187 acre development would have been valued at $652,850 if assessed at fair market value. Under the special conditions of the 1977 law, the assessment fell to $258,400. The total property tax bill was $6,174. At fair market value, the annual property tax bill would have been $13,534. Bush and the other owners resorted to the recreational and scenic land provision in 1992 after county officials stripped the property of an agricultural-use exemption that had lowered the tax levy.

Lieutenant Governor Bullock and House Speaker Laney were also skeptical of the Bush's plan, citing a business tax similar to the governor's had failed considerably in other states. After the two legislative leaders warned him that his tax reform initiative would probably not be endorsed by lawmakers in the new session, Bush hit the road for two months, traveling all over the state in an attempt to seek public support for his proposal and hopefully persuade voters to put pressure on their elected officials.

"A Dallas policeman told me he is worried he can no longer afford his home, because his property taxes have increased much faster than his salary has," the governor declared in his oft-repeated stump speech. "A state senator from El Paso told me working Texans are moving across the border to New Mexico, driven out of Texas by high property taxes.

"Too many senior citizens are strapped by property taxes that are higher than their original mortgage payments," he continued. "Too many young Texans cannot afford to buy homes because property taxes price them out of the market. Too many working families cannot save for their retirement or their children's college education because property taxes devour their income. Rents keep rising as landlords pass on their property tax increases."

Bush claimed that his proposed Property Tax Cut Act of 1997 would not only provide significant property tax relief for Texans, but also would fundamentally change the way the state funded the education system. "This is a plan that is capable of growing to meet our schools' growing needs. It will carry us, year after year, into the next century," the governor said from Corpus Christi to El Paso and several cities in between. "We must act boldly now or face a crisis later. Change is never easy. But I believe the people of Texas elected me to take on the tough challenges. I hope you will join me. Contact your state legislators. Make your voices heard for lower taxes and a fairer way to fund schools."

While the governor was campaigning for his tax reform plan throughout the state, House Speaker Laney seized the property tax issue from Bush without the governor even knowing what hit him. Bush expected his proposal to be hammered out in the House Ways and Means Committee, chaired by Representative Tom Craddick, a fellow Republican and close Bush friend from his hometown of Midland. Instead, Laney formed a special House committee chaired by Representative Paul Sadler, a Democrat he could trust more than Craddick. Sadler's committee, which Laney formed without first consulting Bush, deliberated the tax plan and grilled Albert Hawkins, the governor's budget director.

Simultaneously, Lieutenant Governor Bullock told the press that two key elements of the Bush plan—a new business activity tax and an increase in sales—would be opposed in the Senate if they survived the House. "There doesn't appear to be any open support . . . among Democratic or Republican senators," Bullock stated matter-of-factly. "And I think there is genuine concern on the part of senators of both parties about a sales tax increase. It's got a real bite to it. I cannot find a lot of support for the governor's proposal over here as a total package," the lieutenant governor added, acknowledging that he had not discussed the tax reform plan for "quite a while" with Bush.

Painfully realizing that his plan would probably be scrapped, the governor, in typical fashion when controversy began to swirl, distanced himself from the fray, saying the tax reform proposal was intended merely as an outline on which legislators should work their will. "It would be a heck of a lot easier to be a dictator than work in a democracy," he joked during a speech to a business group. "But this is the process. There are a lot of smart people in the Legislature who have good ideas, and I look forward to hearing what they are."

"It's a bad bill—it's a tax hike, not a tax cut," said Tom Pauken, a staunch conservative who chaired the Texas Republican Party. "It seems to be what you would expect from a liberal Democrat," noting that the right flank of the GOP assailed the plan as a complicated tax shift—instead of a cut—and urged that killing the Bush bill was necessary because it had no prayer of surviving the House.

"While property tax reform is an admirable goal that people from all walks of life and all political persuasions support," said state Representative Kevin Bailey, "the governor's plan would achieve that goal at the expense of Texas' working families and small-business owners. In fact, those individuals and businesses who would benefit the most under the Bush plan need tax relief the least. Although the governor claims his plan would provide a $262 tax break to Texas families, a hard look at the numbers tell us the Bush plan would give . . . two-thirds of Texas families who earn less than $50,000 only a fraction of what the governor has claimed in his public statements. The average family would receive no more that $7.50 a month—the cost of one small pizza."

The tax reform bill that ultimately passed the House bore little resemblance to the governor's original plan. Bush's proposed new business activity tax was discarded as expected, while the House bill would expand the existing corporate franchise tax to include business partnerships such as doctors, lawyers, accountants, and other professionals. The House plan would have also paid for property tax cuts by imposing new or higher state taxes on dozens of items and services (haircuts, aviation fuel, cigarettes, alcoholic beverages, commercial leases, etc.).

Disappointed that his own tax reform proposal went down in flames in the House, the governor nevertheless publicly endorsed their version, as it would have cut property taxes by almost $4 billion, or forty percent. It would also have drastically shifted the burden of public education financing from local school districts to the state. Under the House plan, the state would have been responsible for eighty percent of the funding compared to the current forty-seven percent. It wasn't his own ambitious proposal, the one he bet all his "political capital" on getting passed in the Legislature, but the House bill met several of Bush's objectives, including the elimination of the so-called Robin Hood school-finance system that took tax revenue from property-rich school districts and redistributed it to property-poor ones.

During the Seventy-fourth Legislature, Bush was a masterful politician, working tirelessly with lawmakers to ensure that his four reform proposals were passed during the session. But in 1997, the governor kept an uncharacteristically low profile during the tax reform debate in the House. When the bill appeared headed for defeat in the now Republican-controlled Senate, Bush reentered the negotiations, meeting senators individually in the governor's conference room adjacent to his office on the second floor of the Capitol. With a silent Lieutenant Governor Bullock at his side, Bush attempted to use his personal charm to persuade the reluctant lawmakers, most of whom were members of his own party, to support a compromise tax reform bill. But the governor seriously miscalculated their loyalty.

Nine days before the Seventy-fifth Legislature concluded, the tax overhaul bill was declared dead. When combined with the defeat of the governor's major push for utilities deregulation to "bring lower electric rates to Texans" and a law requiring minors to have parental consent before obtaining an abortion, the property tax reform plan's failure left Bush facing the prospects of having little to show for his second legislative session.

While many political analysts noted that the tax bill's demise showed a lack of leadership by the governor because he couldn't forge a compromise with the Republican-controlled Senate, others claimed its failure would help Bush politically in the long run because it likely would have had the unpopular result of raising taxes.

"What started out as an idea with good intentions turned out to be a very messy tax bill," said GOP Chairman Tom Pauken. "He will be better off without this."

John Weaver, a Republican consultant, also stated that the governor should be relieved at its fate. "In crass political terms he ought to be thankful that the two sides could not get together," he said, adding the bill's passage with its major tax increases could have hurt a possible Bush Republican presidential nomination bid in the year 2000. "He'd have to be explaining the tax increases in places like Iowa and New Hampshire, and you don't want to be explaining instead of advocating."*

Weaver said Bush should have been applauded, however, for instigating a major property tax relief plan. Bullock, Laney, and other legislators agreed that the governor was "courageous" for taking up the fight of tax reform, rather than a failure for losing it, and as a concession for his "noble attempt," offered him a "save-face" plan: a proposed constitutional amendment that would allow the use of $1 billion in state budget savings to increase homestead exemptions from $5,000 to $15,000. If voters approved the measure in a state referendum, homeowners would be able to deduct an additional $10,000 on their primary home's appraised value, which was used to calculate property taxes. As a result, the slim break would save the average homeowner about $140 a year—or twelve dollars a month—in school taxes.

Opponents of the bill questioned whether it amounted to meaningful tax relief, noting that it would put little cash into homeowners' pockets and, once again, offered no alleviation to the millions of Texans who were renters. More disturbing, critics complained, was the fact that funding for public health, education, and welfare programs were reduced to save $1 billion from the state budget to reimburse local school districts for tax revenue losses triggered by the increased homestead exemption.

"The biggest tax cut in state history will be viewed positively" the governor responded. "People will say, 'We appreciate the leadership style of George Bush, and we appreciate the successes that were achieved," he said, adding that because of the new local tax break, the state would increase its share of funding the public school system from about forty-six percent to almost fifty percent.

In one of the lowest turnouts in Texas history, voters by a margin of 9-to-1 approved the constitutional amendment designed to give homeowners a tax break by raising the state-mandated school property tax homestead exemption. "Any time any vote is over ninety percent, I am pleased and sur-

*Sure enough, in 1999 Republican challenger Steve Forbes seized on the issue to attack his rival. Comparing Bush to his father, who reneged on his pledge not to raise taxes as president, Forbes said: "This is the kind of shell games a lot of politicians like to play, but when you look at the details they were tax increases."

prised," the governor told the media. "It's clearly a signal the people of Texas appreciate a property tax break."

Two years later, Bush would promote himself to the American people as the Texas governor responsible for the largest single tax cut in state history, but most residents of the Lone Star State never saw any tax savings. Within weeks of the voter referendum, twenty-two of the thirty-five largest school districts in Texas raised their tax rates, effectively negating whatever relief a homeowner would have experienced through the higher homestead deduction.

Bush failed both substantively and tactically in his attempt to achieve real tax reform as governor, but the Texan who might have been the most disappointed with the defeat of Bush's original property tax-cut initiative was Fort Worth billionaire, Richard Rainwater, a major financial backer of the governor's political career and a partner in the ownership of the Texas Rangers.

If the Bush-sponsored tax cut bill had passed as it was originally proposed, Rainwater would have saved $2.5 million in school property taxes for his Crescent Real Estate Equities investment company. The bill would have also capped business real estate taxes, saving Rainwater millions on valuable commercial property his company owned in Houston, Austin, Dallas, and Fort Worth.

Although Bush wasn't able to provide his wealthy benefactor with a substantial tax break, the governor made certain that Rainwater and the companies he controlled, received millions of dollars through business dealings with the state of Texas.

The Man Behind the Throne

Richard Rainwater has been described in business magazines as "one of the financial greats of the age," "a deal-making legend," and "one of the nation's most astute investors." The billionaire speculator, ranked among the wealthiest 100 Americans, has made his money by buying or obtaining controlling interest in corporations that are faltering in what appear to be intrinsically unstable industries. He hires experts in the field to restructure those companies and then sits back and waits for economic cycles to change and bring them back to profitability. Along the way he has assembled the world's largest hospital chain and one of the world's largest drilling companies.

According to financial disclosure reports he filed as a gubernatorial candidate in 1994, Bush had profited handsomely from his ties with Rainwater in four business ventures, including the Texas Rangers baseball team. Rainwater Management Partners and Continental Plaza Ventures had contributed to Bush's personal wealth, but G.F.W. Energy, which Rainwater formed in 1988 by bringing together a top natural gas financier and major investors, had paid Bush sizable dividends several times since his initial investment in 1993.

During the 1994 governor's race, Ann Richards contended that Rainwater "owned" the Republican candidate. "Mr. Rainwater is responsible for giving George W. Bush the job he has today as president of the Texas Rangers. It's not just the $100,000 he invested in the Bush candidacy, but Bush is completely beholden to Mr. Rainwater for his paycheck," alleged Richards spokesperson Chuck McDonald.

Jim Hightower, author, radio talk-show host, and former populist Agriculture Commissioner in Texas, claimed, "For more than a decade, George W. Bush has not made a move without consulting The Man—and I don't mean his father," Hightower said of Rainwater, adding that he had "done very nicely while his pal has been governor."

Bush has adamantly denied that his business partners, especially Rainwater, have profited since his election. "I swear I didn't get into politics to feather my nest or feather my friends' nest," he told the press after the *Houston Chronicle* published an extensive look at his business dealings and alleged collusion and conflicts of interest. "Any insinuation that I have used my office to help my friends is simply not true."

An examination of business transactions raises numerous questions about certain state government actions and proposals that have provided considerable benefits, actual or potential, to Rainwater and other Bush business partners.

In 1997, the state-run Teacher Retirement System of Texas (TRS) pension fund sold two office buildings and a mortgage on a third building to Rainwater's Crescent Real Estate Equities corporation, which the governor became an investor in when Rainwater rolled Continental Plaza into Crescent's real estate portfolio.* All three sales were conducted without engaging in the usual open-bid process because TRS Chairman Ronald Steinhart believed "the very generous price that we are receiving [from Crescent] eliminates the need."

*The vice-chairman of Crescent, John C. Goff, and the corporation's president, Gerald Haddock, were limited partners in the Texas Rangers with Rainwater and Bush. Crescent's vice president for administration was William D. Miller, the attorney who assembled the financial package for The Ballpark at Arlington.

The teacher retirement system lost $44 million when it sold the first property, an Austin office building known as Frost Bank Plaza, to Crescent for $35 million after the pension fund invested more than $90 million in the complex over the years. The second deal, however, proved quite profitable when Rainwater's company purchased a downtown Dallas office building for $238 million, exceeding TRS's original investment of $65 million. But the third property transaction between TRS and Crescent, the purchase of the mortgage to the Trammel Crow Center for $162 million, forced the teacher retirement system to write off $7 million in principle and $19.4 million in interest. (The Trammel Crow Center was owned by a partnership headed by the influential Trammel Crow family of Texas, which had contributed more than $100,000 to President Bush's 1988 campaign and also $27,000 to George W.'s 1994 gubernatorial campaign, even when the family's real estate business was in dire financial straits.)

"I don't talk to my business associates about doing business with state government one way or the other," the governor claimed.* Officials in his office and TRS also stated there was no record that Bush or his aides were involved in the Crescent deals with the state-run teacher retirement system.

However, a 1995 letter from TRS acting executive director, John R. Mercer, to the governor demonstrated the Bush administration's interest in TRS activities, noting that the pension fund's board, at the governor's request, had delayed selecting a new executive director until Bush could make appointments to the TRS governing board. Ronald Steinhart was later appointed chairman and urged the other members to accept Crescent's "very generous" offers for the office buildings without accepting other bids. (Steinhart became one of Texas' leading financiers in the late 1980s and early 1990s through Team Bank, which experienced accelerated growth by purchasing the assets of failed financial institutions from the Federal Deposit Insurance Corp. during President Bush's administration.)

Another transaction that resulted in Rainwater profiting during his business partner's tenure as governor occurred when Bush signed a sports facility financing bill into law during the Seventy-fifth Legislature. The bill

*After Bush proposed in his January 1997 State of the State address to the Legislature that lawmakers consider privatizing Texas mental institutions, Rainwater struck a $400 million deal the very next day to buy ninety-five psychiatric hospitals, including eight in Texas, from Magellan Health Services, Inc. Although the Legislature eventually failed to pass the privatization initiative, Rainwater was well positioned to prosper enormously if the Bush proposal had become law.

allowed Texas cities to levy new taxes on rental cars and other items to finance the construction of new professional sports stadiums.

While the Bush-supported legislation was being debated by lawmakers, Crescent had purchased a $400 million real estate portfolio from a Dallas businessman that included a twelve percent stake in the Dallas Mavericks NBA team and a pledge that Ross Perot, Jr., the sport franchise's majority owner, would pay Crescent a $10 million bonus once a new arena was built within seventy-five miles of Dallas.

The governor signed the bill at the close of the Legislature in June 1997, prompting final negotiations on an arena deal between the city, the Mavericks, and the Stars, a National Hockey League team. A few months later, Dallas voters approved construction of a $230 million indoor sports facility, the completion of which would trigger the $10 million bonus payment to Crescent.

Bush's biggest cash windfall due to his association with Rainwater came in 1998 when media mogul Tom Hicks,* the owner of the Dallas Stars, agreed to purchase the Texas Rangers for $250 million, the second-highest franchise fee paid in baseball history.

"When it is all said and done, I will have made more money than I ever dreamed I would make," Bush told reporters the day after the sale to Hicks was announced. In 1986, the West Texas oilman had claimed he was "all name and no money," but a dozen years later George W. was all of both.

Since Bush, Rainwater, and the other partners had purchased the Rangers in 1989, the value of the team had surged, in large part because of the lucrative arrangement the Rangers organization made for the state-of-the-art Ballpark at Arlington. After the stadium was completed in September 1993, the team's value escalated from $106 million to $132 million, according to the annual assessment of major league sports franchises by *Financial World* magazine, and increased considerably in the next five years.

When Hicks offered $250 million for the Rangers, he was not only paying for the team, but also the stadium—which the Rangers owned but taxpayers paid for through a half-cent sales-tax levy—and three hundred acres of prime development land next to the sports facility and the Six Flags amuse-

*As chairman of the University of Texas Investment Management Company, a little-known, quasi-state agency chaired by Hicks, the nonprofit corporation managed the state's $9 billion higher education trust, known as the Permanent University Fund. Since Bush had been governor, the PUF had investments in Rainwater's Crescent Equities exceeding $8.9 million.

ment park. (*Financial World* named The Ballpark at Arlington in 1997 the most profitable venue in major league baseball.)

"Taxpayers put up the money that increased the value of this franchise, and Governor Bush is the beneficiary," claimed one state legislator who questioned the ethics of the deal and unsuccessfully pushed his colleagues for an investigation.

With Hicks' purchase of the Rangers for $250 million, Bush became an instant multimillionaire, receiving almost $15 million on an initial investment in 1989 that totaled a mere $606,000—a profit of more than 2,300 percent.* Rangers President Tom Schieffer, who became the team's managing general partner when Bush became governor in 1995, explained that Bush earned a return of $2.7 million on his 1.8 percent ownership interest and another $12.2 million "promote fee" bonus for having put together the original team of investors of Rainwater and others in 1989. As part of the original contract, Schieffer said, once his partners recouped their investment with interest, Bush's share of the team would jump from less than 2 percent to more than 11 percent.

The most troubling aspect of the Rangers sale was the fact that Bush never placed his financial interest in the team in a blind trust when he became governor, fomenting conflict-of-interest allegations. According to financial disclosure filings at the Texas Ethics Commission, Bush voluntarily transferred his stock portfolio and other assets into a blind trust in January 1995, but neglected to do so with his general partnership interest in the Rangers because it would have amounted to a change in team ownership. The measure "would have required a vote of the baseball owners," Bush explained at a press conference. "We just didn't think it was necessary to get

*In April 1999, Bush and his wife Laura paid $3.77 million in federal income taxes on 1998 income of $18.4 million, the bulk of the amount coming from his share of the Rangers' sale. The tax return marked a dramatic increase over Bush's 1997 income, when he paid $77,084 in taxes on $258,375 in earnings, including his $88,008 salary as governor.

Bush's 1998 income tax return also disclosed that he had two money market accounts with a total value of between $600,000 and $1.25 million, three checking accounts with a total value of between $30,000 and $45,000, and no debts. The governor also earned capital-gains income of between $100,000 and $1 million from the sale of real estate investments, capital-gains income of $100,000 to $1 million from Advance Paradigm stock and capital-gains income of between $50,000 and $100,000 from the sale of investments in oil and gas. Bush reported his largest asset was his investment in U.S. Treasury notes, which he valued at between $7.2 million and $14 million. He claimed on his income tax return that those notes earned him between $351,000 and $1.2 million in 1998. Additionally, he received the first half of a $250,000 advance from William Morrow & Co. for his presidential campaign biography *A Charge to Keep*. Bush's share, after commission, was $106,250, which he donated to four youth charities.

that vote," because it would have forced the governor to essentially abandon control of the team.

But what if, instead of baseball, Bush were involved in a lucrative oil deal in which he ultimately was paid almost $15 million cash by a wealthy Dallas businessman, and the entire amount went straight to the governor's bank account and not his blind trust? How long would it take before the media demanded an investigation?

Although Bush said there was nothing wrong with the Rangers sale, and claimed that his success in making money should be seen as plus, not a liability, it could be argued that Hicks—who normally could only contribute to Bush's campaign account—was influence peddling with the governor when he purchased the Rangers and paid Bush several millions of dollars.

Bush's ties to wealthy entrepreneurs affected by state government action and the millions in profit he reaped from the sale of the Rangers should have raised eyebrows in 1998, but press coverage generally overlooked the controversy, and his approval rating with the voters hovered close to seventy percent.

More intense scrutiny by the media outside of Texas would come later, when he decided to make a run for the presidency. After all, the home-state business dealings of a Southern governor occupying the White House at the time had been under investigation by a special prosecutor for years.

"He's the darling of the press," Jim Hightower said of the governor. "Everybody says, 'Well, you've got to like George Bush.' Well, I don't like him—just another rich son-of-a-Bush. He's a do-nothing governor. He's completely tied to corporate money and to the corporate wish list."

★ 9 ★

Crime and Punishment

We're tough on criminals in our state.
If you make your criminal bed in Texas,
we've got one for you to lie in.

—George W. Bush

Bush describes himself as a "compassionate conservative," which in Texas means he asks you how you like your Jell-O just before he flips the switch.

—Craig Kilborn, *The Daily Show*

Money in the Bank

The governor was enthusiastically applauded by a national audience of crime victims and their advocates when he addressed more than 1,500 delegates attending the 23rd annual conference of the National Organization of Victims Assistance (NOVA) in Houston.

As Bush recited his administration's crime-fighting measures, the crowd—warmed up by a color guard trooping dozens of flags and the national anthem sung to indoor fireworks—showed hearty approval of a governor who said he made it clear to other politicians around the country that "justice is about victims."

To illustrate that point, Bush told the audience:

"We have the highest incarceration in the nation . . ." "Parole approvals are down to their lowest in years . . ." "We do not have endless delays" in carrying out the death penalty, and in the Lone Star State, victims' families were allowed to witness executions . . .

The governor also bragged that Texas law now gave death row inmates "one bite of the apple" on appeals. (Legal scholars complained, however, that the law barred courts from considering evidence of innocence that turned up after trial, and could result in the execution of people not guilty of the crime.)

Bush failed to inform the appreciative NOVA members, however, that a recently released annual report showed that the state had awarded $32.6 million to 8,565 crime victims in the previous year to assist them in recovering from violent crimes, but left $182 million sitting in the bank.

The report prompted crime victim groups to insist on better efforts to let victims know there was financial assistance available, and lower restrictions on the funds so that a greater number of people could access the state aid. Critics noted that money for counseling was limited to $3,000, which wasn't enough help in child sexual assault cases, and cited a need for victims services in rural communities.

"I have worked and scratched and crawled and bled for that fund, and I'm beginning to have a lot of concerns," complained Nell Myers, a founder of People Against Violent Crime.

The fund, administered by the Texas attorney general's office, is collected through court fines and charges levied against those convicted of crimes. It is designated for the cost of funerals, medical needs, counseling, and other expenses incurred by violent crime victims and their families.

The attorney general's office, in defense of the unused funds, said the court fees supporting the financial assistance program had been increased during a time violent crime had decreased. According to the Texas Department of Public Safety, however, the crime rate had increased in the state during the governor's first term, reversing a four-year trend, which proved troubling to Bush and his conservative law-and-order platform.*

---

*During the governor's tenure, the Lone Star State trailed only California in the number of gun deaths among the young. In addition, more Texans were killed by guns than automobiles, a dubious achievement shared by only seven other states.

REVOLVING DOOR

The governor suffered even more political embarrassment when it was announced that Larry Don McQuay, who claimed to have molested 240 children and swore he would do it again, would be released from Texas prison after serving six years of an eight-year sentence.

McQuay, a former San Antonio bus driver, was convicted in 1990 of indecency with a child. He was charged with aggravated assault after confessing that he and a six-year-old boy had engaged in oral sex for a period of months. The charge, however, was dropped to indecency with a child in a plea bargain agreement with prosecutors.

While in prison, McQuay wrote several startling letters to Andy Kahan, head of Houston's victim-assistance office, which could only be interpreted as a terroristic threat. "I believe that without adequate treatment, I am doomed to eventually rape and then murder my poor little victims to keep them from telling on me," McQuay said in one letter, adding that he frequently fantasized about brutally raping kidnapped children.*

Although the governor urged the Board of Pardons and Paroles to reexamine McQuay's case and "to seek any possible means to keep this convicted child molester behind bars," his release was inevitable under the system's old mandatory supervision release program, in which good-time credits could be earned and added to the real time served. With his credits, McQuay had completed his eight-year sentence, and the law required his release from prison, no matter how significant the public outcry.

During his 1994 gubernatorial campaign, Bush promised voters that a situation like McQuay's release would never happen in his administration, when, in reality, his criminal justice advisers had told him differently. Like countless other political candidates before him, Bush made crime a major issue during the campaign. He used it effectively against then-Governor Richards, even though the crime rate had been dropping consistently during her tenure; the state was completing a massive prison construction program; she had mandated a sizeable reduction in paroles; and had signed a law doubling the minimum prison time for the most violent offenders.

---

*After taking office in 1995, Bush cancelled government grants that funded two correctional system sex offender and child abuse treatment programs: the Council on Sex Offender Treatment and the Parents Anonymous Prison Project and Aftercare (PAPA). Also, as part of the $1 billion savings in the state budget to provide for property tax relief in 1997, Governor Bush requested lawmakers to drastically cut spending for specialized treatment for sex offenders before they were returned to their communities.

Bush's TV commercials and campaign sound bites, however, portrayed a state plagued by armed criminals that walked the streets, looking for new prey to assault, rape, and murder. Most crime victims' advocates, who preferred his promises to Richards's accomplishments, warmly embraced the Republican candidate.

"I will end early release of criminals and end parole altogether for rapists and child molesters," Bush promised in one commercial, and called for an end to mandatory supervision releases for all convicts, even those already serving time, despite long-standing prohibitions in both state and federal constitutions against such retroactive laws.

In 1995, the Legislature effectively ended mandatory supervision releases for inmates by giving the Texas parole board the power to veto the early release of any prisoner board members believed was a threat to society. But the law applied only to inmates convicted after the law's effective date in September 1996. Lawmakers didn't attempt to apply the new law retroactively, and even the governor's own advisers advised him against it in light of the constitutional obstacles.

Most law-abiding citizens didn't pay much attention to that distinction until it came time to open the prison doors early for McQuay, who was convicted before the law went into effect. The Texas-size furor over his eventual release to a San Antonio halfway house once again stirred up the longstanding debate about mandatory release and public cries of "Bush broke his promise."

In a major exercise in damage control to keep the McQuay case from becoming a future political liability, the governor urged the Legislature in 1997 to quickly pass a bill to ban all automatic early releases from prison and repeal the controversial mandatory supervision law.

"The parole board, not some mathematical formula, should decide whether a prisoner should remain behind bars," Bush declared, citing another recent and highly-publicized prison release—wife murderer Steven Foster Lorke.

The former pharmaceutical salesman was convicted of strangling his wife in 1982 for refusing to engage in sexual intercourse with him. Lorke dumped her body in a field, where it remained until he confessed three months later. He was initially sentenced to life in prison, but his conviction was reversed on appeal and he eventually accepted a plea bargain of thirty-five years. After fourteen years in prison, he was automatically released on mandatory supervision to his parents' home in Houston when his actual time served, plus "good-time" credits equaled the thirty-five year sentence.

State Representative Peggy Hamric, who pre-filed a bill to close the gaping prison release loophole, said recent court rulings had indicated the courts may find it legal to apply the ban on mandatory supervision retroactively. "We are not changing the length of the sentence," she claimed. "We are only changing the conditions under which the inmate is released."

The governor agreed, saying he would declare the bill an emergency to clear the way for prompt passage by the Legislature. "I do not believe our constitution gives criminals any right to get out of jail early, and this will be a priority issue for my administration during the session."

Embarrassed by McQuay and Lorke, prodded by angry crime victims' advocates and encouraged by more lenient interpretations of constitutional restrictions, the governor urged lawmakers to vote quickly on the fast-track bipartisan bill. But after the U.S. Supreme Court ruled a similar law in Florida was unconstitutional, the governor just as abruptly dropped the effort to repeal mandatory supervision releases from prison. Many legal experts and legislators openly questioned Bush's "lack of courage and leadership," wondering why he didn't push for the bill to be passed and then allow it to be challenged in the courts at a later time.

"The governor just threw in the towel early," complained one state senator. "We would have easily passed the bill in the Legislature and he could have signed it into law. It would have taken years for it to get to the Supreme Court and the odds would have been fifty-fifty that the justices would have agreed that the State of Texas was not changing the length of an inmate's sentence," he argued. "When the U.S. Constitution was written, there was no such thing as parole and it is not constitutionally addressed. But because the governor decided to quit without a fight, thousands of heinous criminals are going to be automatically released from prison and there's not a damn thing anybody can do about it."

Victims' rights groups immediately responded with a media blitz highlighting two "poster boys" of crime who would be released in the coming years because Bush didn't have the "moral fiber" to challenge the mandatory supervision law in the courts:

When Coral Eugene Watts was apprehended in 1982 while trying to kill a Houston woman, homicide investigators knew he had murdered several others but had no proof. After agreeing to provide details of his crimes in exchange for a burglary conviction and sixty-year sentence, Watts confessed to killing thirteen women, and alluded to murdering several others. Law enforcement officers believe he was responsible for at least fifty deaths. He will be fifty years old when he is automatically released from Texas prison in 2004, the only confessed serial killer in the nation scheduled to be set free.

David Port was seventeen in 1984 when he confronted mail carrier Debora Sue Schatz in front of his father and stepmother's affluent west Houston home and ordered her into his upstairs bedroom at gunpoint, shooting her to death when she attempted to flee. Convicted and sentenced to seventy-five years in 1985, Port would be released from prison on mandatory supervision in 2012 at the age of forty-five.

But neither Watts nor Port magnified the governor's broken pledge to halt prisoners' mandatory release from prison as dramatically as Lawrence Russell Brewer Jr., a lifelong criminal and white extremist who exited a Texas prison in September 1997, only to stand accused nine months later of involvement in the torture and slaying of a black man.

"Three Robed Riders Coming Straight Out of Hell"

Just after midnight on June 7, 1998, John William "Bill" King, Shawn Allen Berry, and Lawrence Russell Brewer Jr., three young ex-cons who shared an apartment together in the small logging town of Jasper, Texas, left in Berry's pickup truck to "score with some women" after a night of beer drinking.

Shortly afterward they discovered James Byrd Jr., a forty-nine-year-old disabled black man too poor to own a car, walking drunkenly along the street after attending a niece's bridal shower and a party at a friend's house. Berry offered Byrd a ride, which infuriated Brewer and King, who served two years together in a Texas penitentiary and were members of a white supremacist prison gang known as the Confederate Knights of America. Racist tattoos that blanketed their upper bodies reinforced their hatred for other races.

Instead of taking Byrd home, the trio drove him to a deserted country road where he was beaten, stripped, bound by his ankles to the back of Berry's pickup with a 24-½ foot logging chain, and dragged through almost three miles of rural roads, dismembering his body. Marks on his corpse indicated that Byrd was alive and conscious when the torture began as he tried to use his elbows to keep his head above the pavement while his chained body swung behind the truck "like a boat pulling a skier behind it." He died when his head, shoulder and right arm were severed by a roadside culvert. (Police later used seventy-five red spray-painted circles to mark the spots where they found Byrds's keys, dentures, and parts of his body.) The three killers left Byrd's decapitated head in a roadside ditch about a mile from his naked torso which they dumped at the gates of one of the country's oldest black cemeteries.

"Three robed riders coming straight out of hell. That's exactly what it was out there that night," said Assistant County District Attorney Pat Hardy, noting that Brewer and King, masterminded the "dramatic" act to draw attention to a new racist group they were organizing. "Instead of a rope, they used a chain, and instead of horses, they used a pickup truck. After they dragged this poor man and tore his body to pieces, they dropped him right in front of a church and cemetery to show their defiance of God, to show their defiance of Christianity and everything that most people in this country stand for."

Brewer and the other two murderers were linked to the crime by evidence ranging from Byrd's blood on their shoes to DNA taken from saliva on cigarette butts and beer bottles at the crime scene. Berry gave an affidavit when he was arrested that led to the arrests of Brewer and King.

One of the nation's most vicious hate crimes since the civil rights era brought the world's attention to Jasper, an East Texas timber town of only eight thousand residents just west of the Louisiana border. Reporters and television crews from Germany, Denmark, England, Japan, and Australia, among others, trolled the local population for comments.

"Lawrence Brewer was the ringleader of that bunch of rednecks who dragged Byrd to his death. No man deserves to die like that," remarked James Smith, a Jasper resident. "If Governor Bush had kept his promise to end automatic prison releases, Brewer would still be sitting behind bars where he belonged and Byrd would still be alive."

To add insult to injury, when legislators called upon Bush to support an effort to revise the vaguely-worded state law targeting hate crimes in the aftermath of the senseless Byrd slaughter, the governor declined. The current law, passed in 1993, increased penalties if a crime was proved to be "motivated by bias or prejudice." The new bill would use constitutionally accepted language upheld by the U.S. Supreme Court so that offenses motivated by race, color, disability, religion, national origin or ancestry, or sexual orientation would be prosecuted as hate crimes.

"Governor Bush calls himself a compassionate conservative. Indeed, he called the James Byrd family to offer his condolences," said state Representative Senfronia Thompson, the co-author of the legislation. "Now is the time for more than condolences . . . I called upon Governor Bush to show me his compassion by supporting the James Byrd Act."

Forty states and the District of Columbia had already enacted similar hate crime laws. Besides clarifying the definition of a hate crime, the new bill would provide aid to small counties prosecuting hate murders; specify that a victim could sue for civil and exemplary damages; assign a prosecutor in the attorney general's office as a hate crimes director; and require law enforcement officers to receive training in investigating and documenting hate crimes. (In 1997, the Texas Department of Public Safety documented 331 hate crimes in the state. Between 1992 and 1997, nearly 2,300 incidents were reported.)

Bush, who ran for governor in 1994 to be "a catalyst for cultural change," responded that he would prefer to "enforce the laws we have on the books. I think that all crime is hate, particularly the crime that went on there [in Jasper]," he stated. "I think the way to get rid of hate in people's hearts, the best course I know is religion. The truth of the matter is hate and evil exist, and something much larger than government will help heal the hearts of man."

But when Bush was faced with one criminal's miracle of rehabilitation and dedication to teaching other prisoners through her own example to forsake drugs and violence, the governor insisted that she die for her sins rather than continue her internationally acclaimed prison ministry.

No Mercy

During the early hours of June 13, 1983, Karla Faye Tucker, a twenty-three-year-old prostitute and her boyfriend Daniel Ryan Garrett, broke into the Northwest Houston apartment of Jerry Lynn Dean, to steal motorcycle parts. Garrett was surprised to find Dean home, asleep in his bed, and proceeded to bludgeon him to death with a hammer. Tucker, who was angry because Dean once parked his oil-leaking motorcycle in her living room, then struck him with a three-foot pickaxe over twenty times to stop the gurgling he was making. Discovering Dean's companion, Deborah Ruth Thornton, cowering beneath bed sheets in a corner of the room, Tucker then turned the pickaxe on her to eliminate a witness.

When the police arrested Garrett and Tucker five weeks later, she admitted her guilt in one of the grisliest double murders in Texas history. In fact, she confessed that she was surprised at how long it took them to bludgeon Dean to death and boasted to homicide officers that she experienced an orgasm each time she plunged the pickaxe into her victims, even after they were dead. At the crime scene, investigators found the murder weapon still embedded in Thornton's chest.

Tucker's defense attorney argued during her trial that she had been on a three-day drug and alcohol binge and was temporarily insane at the time of the gruesome crime. The jury disagreed and after only seventy minutes of deliberation, found her guilty of first degree murder. Tucker, who admitted during the punishment phase of the court proceeding that even being pick-axed would not be sufficient to atone for her crime, was sentenced to the death penalty. (Tucker's accomplice, who she testified against during this trial, was also scheduled for a state execution for his part in the murders, but died in prison of liver disease in 1994 while awaiting a new trial).

During the next several years, Tucker, who became a born-again Christian in a Houston jail before her trial, ministered to other prisoners and troubled youth, married a prison chaplain, and received several stays of execution while exhausting all legal appeals to overturn her death sentence. In various pleas to save her life, Tucker's lawyer, David Botsford, and supporters—including the district attorney who prosecuted her, the detective who arrested her, a pro–death penalty former U.S. attorney, and relatives of her victims—claimed that she was not the same woman who committed the double murder. Because of Tucker's conversion to Christianity, prison ministry, apparent rehabilitation, and virtually spotless disciplinary record while incarcerated, her numerous defenders believed that her death sentence should be commuted to life in prison.

On December 8, 1997, the U.S. Supreme Court rejected Tucker's request to review her case and ten days later a state district judge set her execution date for February 3. Tucker's case brought unprecedented scrutiny on the Lone Star State—the state with the most active execution chamber in the nation—and its governor, who had the ultimate power in deciding her fate.

As death penalty opponents, religious leaders, and thousands of other people mounted an intense campaign in an attempt to persuade Bush to commute Tucker's sentence, newspaper columnist Bob Herbert wrote of "Texas' bloodthirsty criminal justice officials," in the *New York Times.* "It's a state that has shown itself perfectly willing to execute the retarded and railroad the innocent . . .* Texas is by far the most backward state in the nation

---

*When a bill outlawing executions of the mentally impaired was proposed during the legislative session in 1999, Bush publicly expressed his opposition, saying he liked the law "the way it is right now."

The governor also vetoed a measure that was passed without dissent by the same Legisla-

when it comes to capital punishment . . . As for Texas, the best thing about the Tucker case is the spotlight it is throwing on the state's fetish for capital punishment."

At a rally on the steps of the state Capitol, and only two blocks from the Governor's Mansion, hundreds of death penalty abolitionists pleaded for Tucker's life. Speaker after speaker called on Bush and members of the Texas Board of Pardons and Paroles to show compassion and mercy for the woman whose religious conversion and rehabilitation, supporters insisted, was nothing short of miraculous.

"Executive clemency in this state doesn't exist," said Tucker's lawyer, David Botsford. "This [parole] board doesn't even meet," noting that the eighteen-member panel, which did not convene when voting on death row commutation requests, simply reviewed the paperwork individually in each inmate's file and then faxed, mailed, or phoned in their votes. "They won't even give Karla a chance to plead her case personally," Botsford added. "I submit to you that's un-American."

Although Tucker's attorney had not yet asked the board to commute her sentence, Botsford said he would file a voluminous challenge to Texas' commutation process, arguing among other points that no governor had ever granted a death sentence commutation for humanitarian reasons.

"Governor Bush, this is your moment of truth," claimed Bianca Jagger, the former wife of rock star Mick Jagger and now a leader in Amnesty International. Calling the Texas commutation process "a sham," she said, "There's not even a guidance, there's not even a criteria . . . which serves to determine whether a person definitely deserves a commutation. I think the moment has come for a review of the judicial system in Texas." Jagger, who was allowed to meet with Tucker, called the thirty-eight-year-old inmate "a remarkable woman . . . fully rehabilitated" and one "whose life could mean so much more to this state than her death."

Also speaking at the three-hour rally was Sister Helen Prejean, whose

---

ture, requiring indigent defendants to be assigned a lawyer within twenty days after an arrest. In most jurisdictions in the U.S., an attorney is assigned within seventy-two hours, but in Texas it is quite common for poor detainees to spend a month in jail before being appointed a court representative.

"The harsh reality is that poor defendants get a poor defense in our current system—they have no lobbyists or natural constituency," said Senator Rodney Ellis, sponsor of the bill, after the governor claimed that the measure inappropriately took too much power away from judges. "If we are going to lead the world in incarcerations and executions," the lawmaker said in response to Bush's veto, "then we should at least make sure that defendants are guaranteed effective legal representation."

book, *Dead Man Walking,* the story of a man executed in Louisiana, was made into a movie starring Susan Sarandon and Sean Penn. Calling Tucker a "gentle beautiful, Christian woman," the Catholic nun said that her case "will raise up the death penalty in a dimension we have never looked at before."

On January 20, Tucker's attorneys filed a petition to the Texas Court of Criminal Appeals and state district court in Houston to postpone her scheduled execution so that they could have more time to challenge the constitutionality of Texas' clemency procedure. In the 155-page court document, Tucker's lawyers argued that she had reformed herself during her fourteen-year imprisonment and—while the right to incarcerate her was not in question—that she was no longer deserving of capital punishment.

Her attorney's also claimed that the court needed to review her sentence because "the Texas death penalty system as it presently operates (not as it is constituted) will not prevent the unconscionable and unconstitutional denial of her right to life." The state board of pardons and paroles, Tucker's attorneys argued, did not take rehabilitation into account and therefore had no ability to prevent Tucker from being put to death. Her legal representatives did not claim she was not guilty, only that she was a changed woman and did not deserve to die.

The petition to the appeals court was also accompanied by approximately 200 pages of exhibits supporting her plea of mercy, including a letter Tucker penned to Governor Bush and members of the Texas Board of Pardons and Paroles.

"It was in October, three months after I had been locked up, when a ministry came to the jail and I went to the services, that night accepting Jesus into my heart," she wrote. "When I did this, the full and overwhelming weight and reality of what I had done hit me . . . I began crying that night for the first time in many years, and to this day, tears are a part of my life."

Tucker admitted in her letter that she didn't really understand the guidelines for commutation of death sentences, "but I can promise you this: If you commute my sentence to life, I will continue for the rest of my life in this earth to reach out to others to make a positive difference in their lives," she promised, adding, "I see people in here in the prison where I am who are here for horrible crimes, and for lesser crimes, who to this day are still acting out in violence and hurting others with no concern for another life or for their own life. I can reach out to these girls and try and help them change before they walk out of this place and hurt someone else."

The death row inmate concluded by asking the governor and the board to commute her sentence to life in prison so she could be allowed to pay society back by helping others. "I can't bring back the lives I took. But I can, if I am allowed, help save lives. That is the only real restitution I can give."

Three days later, her attorneys officially asked the board in a clemency petition on her behalf to lessen her punishment to life. The panel, comprised of appointees by the governor, could deny her request or, on a vote of at least ten members, forward a recommendation for commutation to Bush. The Texas Constitution did not allow the governor to act independently to grant clemency or a pardon, and if they did recommend either one, he could still reject their proposal.

Bush had already stated that in evaluating Tucker's case, he would only consider whether there was any doubt she committed the crime and whether she had a fair trial, effectively sending a public message to the pardons and parole board that he did not want them to recommend clemency for humanitarian reasons based on her religious conversion.

The growing international furor increased in the final weeks before Tucker's scheduled execution by lethal injection. Bush declined to meet with a delegation of European leaders who wanted to personally urge the governor to commute Tucker's sentence. He also turned down requests by representatives of the European Parliament who hoped to visit with Tucker in prison. (The 518-member body that advised the European Community, adopted a resolution condemning her execution.) In addition, Pope John Paul II, an official of the United Nations, and the Italian Parliament asked the governor to grant Tucker clemency.

While her petition for commutation was pending before the board of pardons and paroles and her writ of habeus corpus was being reviewed by the Texas Court of Criminal Appeals, the attractive and smiling Tucker pressed her case in an international media blitz campaign that included appearances on CNN's *Larry King Live, Sixty Minutes, Nightline,* the *Today* morning program, *60 minutes,* and the cable documentary *A Question of Mercy: The Karla Faye Tucker Story* on Court TV. She repeatedly told the story of her sordid life before she became a Christian: marijuana usage at age eight, heroin at ten, a groupie at thirteen, married at seventeen, and prostitution to support her drug habit. She maintained that if her pleas were rejected, she would go into the death chamber "speaking out for the love of God."

When the appeals court dismissed Tucker's claims that she was a born-again Christian who no longer represented a threat to society and that the state's commutation process was unconstitutional, her case seemed to have placed the governor in a no-win situation.

If Bush sanctioned the execution, the Christian conservatives—among his biggest backers—would be outraged. If he commuted it, the pro-death penalty constituency would accuse him of being soft on crime. Either way, his political future would be affected by his decision.

Pat Robertson, the televangelist, former presidential candidate, and founder of the powerful Christian Coalition political lobby, had called and personally appealed to the governor for Tucker's reprieve. The death row inmate's apparent repentance and conversion to Christianity had gained the support of the religious right, which was usually in favor of capital punishment.

Robertson told Leslie Stahl in the *60 Minutes* segment on Tucker that if Governor Bush "lets this sweet woman of God die, he's a man who shows no mercy."

In a public plea to the governor, the Reverend Paul H. Sherry, the Cleveland-based president of the 1.5 million-member United Church of Christ; the Reverend Richard Hamm, president of the 900,000-member Christian Church (Disciples of Christ); and the Reverend Joan Brown Campbell, general secretary of the New York-based National Council of Churches, argued that Tucker had been "transformed" while in prison and should have her sentence commuted to a life term.

"Do we believe only in punishment, an eye for an eye?" the religious leaders asked in their statement. "Do we reward transformation with death? Do we want a criminal justice system that does not want repentance and rehabilitation and will not accept it when it happens?"

A majority of Texans strongly supported the death penalty, however. Statewide polls showed that they believed Tucker should be executed, despite her professed religious conversion, and feared that clemency would send out a message that women received special treatment. (Although Texas led the nation in executions, a woman had not been put to death in the state since the Civil War.)

Death penalty proponents argued that the state should abandon the gender bias that had protected so many female perpetrators of heinous crimes and put Tucker to death. "If she was Karl Tucker, a burly black man, instead of Karla Tucker, the petite, attractive white woman, there would be no debate regarding her execution," was a remark often repeated in e-mail to the governor, the op-ed pages of the state's newspapers and on talk radio stations.*

---

*Tucker herself berated those who wanted her life spared because she was a woman. She told the media, "Either you believe in the death penalty for everybody or you don't believe in it for anybody."

According to Richard Dieter, Director of the Death Penalty Information Center, the Tucker resolution represented a serious political dilemma for the governor, who many believed would seek the presidency in 2000. "Whatever his decision, it is a reflection of his personality. It will create an image," he said. "Bush runs the risk of seeming too harsh. And there are a lot of people outside of Texas who might not respond to that kind of image."

Bush pledged not to be swayed by political pressure or issues of gender. "I feel my job is to uphold the laws of the state of Texas, and we should treat this case like any other case," he said, noting that he planned to follow the parole board's recommendation. Several gubernatorial aides claimed, however, that in reality it was just the opposite: Bush had privately told his political appointees on the panel to overwhelmingly deny Tucker clemency, which would take him out of the decision-making process.

On February 2, the day before her scheduled execution, state parole officials, citing the heinousness of Tucker's crime, soundly rejected her plea for mercy. "The board has voted to deny Karla Faye Tucker's request for commutation, and the board has voted to deny her request for reprieve," announced Victor Rodriguez, chairman of the Texas Board of Pardons and Paroles.

Tucker's attorneys immediately turned to a scattershot legal tactic, filing a federal civil-rights lawsuit in U.S. district court, raising essentially the same claim of an unconstitutional commutation process that provided the basis of her petition already pending before the U.S. Supreme Court. Her lawyers also asked the 5th U.S. Circuit Court of Appeals for permission to file another round of challenges to her death sentence in the federal courts. In state district court, they filed a lawsuit alleging that the parole board violated the Texas Open Meetings Act by not meeting publicly to vote on Tucker's case.

"In the years down the road, Texans will look back and say it was a sad moment in Texas history," David Botsford said. "It was a black moment when a young lady who committed a horrible crime but who proved that jury wrong for another fourteen and a half years by not committing any further acts of danger inside the penitentiary, doesn't receive a single vote, not one single vote, from the eighteen members of the board."

The parole panel's decision effectively removed Bush from the emotional issue because, under the Texas Constitution, the governor could not grant clemency unless the board recommended such action. He did, however, have the independent authority to issue a one-time, thirty-day delay in execution, but a spokesperson for the governor's office said that would not be decided until sometime late the next day, after the courts had ruled.

At 6:12 p.m. (CST)* on the evening of February 3, 1998, shortly after all of Tucker's legal appeals failed, Governor Bush held an internationally televised news conference to announce his expected decision. "Karla Faye Tucker has acknowledged she is guilty of a horrible crime. She was convicted and sentenced by a jury of her peers," he said, reading a prepared statement. "The role of the state is to enforce our laws and to make sure all individuals are treated fairly under those laws. The courts, including the United States Supreme Court, have reviewed the legal issues in this case, and therefore, I will not grant a thirty-day delay," he continued, speaking sternly of a law that required enforcement "without preference or special treatment. Like many touched by this case, I have sought guidance through prayer. I have concluded judgments about the heart and soul of an individual on death row are best left to a higher authority. May God bless Karla Faye Tucker and may God bless her victims and their families," Bush concluded, retreating to his office without taking questions.

A few minutes later, strapped to a gurney in Texas' execution chamber, her dark, shoulder-length curls splayed across the antiseptic white sheet that covered the hard, cold deathbed, Tucker made her final statements. She apologized to the relatives of the man and woman she hacked to death with a pickaxe in 1983, told her family she loved them, and thanked prison officials for being "so good to me."

"I'm going to be face to face with Jesus now," she said, displaying the coquettish smile that had charmed television audiences worldwide in the past few months. "I love all of you very much. I will see you all when you get there. I will wait for you."

She then closed her eyes and licked her lips. Twenty seconds after the lethal drugs began flowing through her veins, Tucker gasped twice slightly and uttered a slight groan.

At 6:45 p.m., approximately eight minutes later, Tucker was pronounced dead. Outside the prison, in a dramatic scene that paralleled the worldwide attention on Tucker's case in the preceding weeks, a circus was under way. When word came that Tucker was dead, a loud cheer arose from the crowd of more than 250 demonstrators, while some of her supporters sobbed openly. Some began singing "Amazing Grace" as others shouted "Kill Karla, Kill Karla" and "She sliced, she diced, and now she's got to pay the price."

---

*Tucker's expected execution was the lead story on all of the networks' newscasts. The Fox News Channel was criticized for airing a series of extremely graphic crime scene photos of her victims about an hour before she died from a lethal injection.

"The issues here were not religious conversion or gender but rather culpability and accountability," claimed Allan Polunsky, chairman of the Texas criminal justice board, who stood with other prison officials in an adjacent holding cell while the execution was under way in the death chamber. "Although I believe she finally found God, her religious awakening could in no way excuse or mitigate her actions in the world she just left."

While the controversial issues raised in Tucker's case over the death penalty and Texas' secretive clemency process remained, the state prepared for another high-profile execution: notorious serial killer, Henry Lee Lucas, whose request for clemency from the governor would be, as the *Washington Post* editorialized, "a real test of whether George Bush is made of presidential timber."

A Question of Guilt

Lucas began his life of crime in 1960, when he was convicted of stabbing his mother to death and raping her corpse in Michigan, and sentenced to twenty to forty years in prison. A year later, he was transferred from a state prison to a mental institution, where he was diagnosed as a suicidal psychopath, sadist, and sexual deviant. Discharged in 1975, the drifter teamed up with cannibal and necrophile Ottis Toole* and together they allegedly engaged in an eight-year binge of murder while crisscrossing the country by car. The joyride ended in 1983 after Lucas was arrested for carrying a gun.

When the one-eyed drifter confessed to literally hundreds of killings in twenty-seven states, it opened one of the most incredible cases in the annals of justice. After providing details of crimes nationwide and even leading investigators to gravesites, Lucas later recanted most of the murders, claiming that he only wanted to prove that law enforcement officers "don't do their job." Evidently, investigators were so eager to close several unsolved cases,

---

*Toole was eventually diagnosed as a paranoid schizophrenic and his Florida death sentence was commuted to six consecutive life terms. In prison, the convicted serial killer confessed and later recanted killing six-year-old Adam Walsh, whose 1981 disappearance outside a Hollywood, Florida, mall set off a nationwide manhunt and launched the TV career of his father, John Walsh, as the creator and host of the long-running Fox series *America's Most Wanted.*

On September 15, 1996, Ottis died in a prison hospital of liver failure. Walsh, who repeatedly criticized the police handling of his son's case, questioned why investigators did not attempt to interview Toole on his deathbed or try for another confession. Speaking from a Texas penitentiary after Ottis' death, Henry Lee Lucas said Toole killed Adam and later showed him the remains of the boy in a shallow grave.

they fed the fifth-grade dropout with an IQ of eighty-four details about crimes and let him read investigative reports that allowed him to give explicit confessions.

Lucas eventually received prison terms ranging from sixty years to life for ten slayings, however, and a death sentence for the 1979 rape and strangulation of an unidentified hitchhiker who was clothed only in a pair of orange socks when her body was discovered near Georgetown, Texas.

Over the years, twenty-three appellate judges upheld Lucas' death sentence, but just days before his scheduled June 30, 1998 execution, Governor Bush requested the Texas Board of Pardons and Paroles review Lucas' case and consider clemency based upon a 1986 report compiled by then-Attorney General Jim Mattox.

Numerous pieces of evidence, such as labor records showing Lucas working as a roofer in Florida at the time of the "Orange Socks" murder, interviews with neighbors, and a cashed check, all led the Texas attorney general to the conclusion that it was "highly unlikely" that he committed the crime in question.

"Lucas is a cold-blooded monster who killed many people," claimed Ken Anderson, who assisted in the prosecution's death penalty case against Lucas. "A jury of twelve citizens heard all the evidence relating to the confession and heard all the alibi evidence cited by Mattox," he argued, noting that the trial evidence disputed claims that Lucas cashed a check in Florida the day after the Orange Socks murder and was hundreds of miles away at the time of the killing.

The check was prepared in advance and cashed "at least two and probably three" days after the murder, the prosecutor stated, and serious questions arose about payroll records backing Lucas' assertion that he had been working on a Jacksonville, Florida roofing crew.

"Both Lucas and another employee acknowledged that the foreman frequently marked employees present when they weren't in exchange for a kickback of half the employees' earned pay," Anderson said, adding that the Orange Socks case received closer scrutiny than Lucas' other convictions because it was a death sentence case. "The conviction has been reviewed and upheld for fourteen years by twenty-three different judges."

In an unprecedented move, state parole officials voted 17-1 to recommend that the governor spare Lucas's life. "It is important to note that this person remains convicted of this offense and should remain incarcerated for the rest of his life," board Chairman Victor Rodriguez wrote in a letter to

Bush, noting that the attorney general's investigative report carried significant weight in swaying the eighteen-member panel.

The vote was the first time in the modern era of the death penalty that the Texas Board of Pardons and Paroles had recommended a commutation of a death sentence on its own initiative. Previous commutations had been granted only after major changes in law or, in a few instances, after prosecutors recommended the action because of trial errors.

This was also the same parole board that voted overwhelmingly four months earlier to deny the clemency petition of Karla Faye Tucker. One of her appeals attorneys, George Secrest, called the board a politically-motivated "pawn" of the governor and predicted Bush would rubber stamp the panel's decision. I'm sure they've already had the conversation. It's appropriate they don't kill him [Lucas] for something they didn't prove, but it's awfully ironic that they recommend commuting someone who otherwise is a predator, who has a ghastly record," Secrest said, adding, "They didn't in Karla Faye's case, notwithstanding the good people who supported her, including some from law enforcement. They let her perish."

Within hours of the parole board's recommendation, the governor did indeed commute Lucas' death sentence to life in prison, basing his decision on the possibility that the killer was innocent of the particular murder for which he received the death sentence. "I take every death penalty case very seriously," the governor explained. "The first question I have in each death penalty case is whether there is any doubt about whether the individual is guilty of the crime. While Henry Lee Lucas is guilty of committing a number of horrible crimes, serious concerns have been raised about his guilt in the case."

The prosecutors who sent Lucas to death row expressed outrage; Texas Supreme Court Judge John Cornyn, a Republican who would later be elected state attorney general, said he also believed Bush was wrong to commute Lucas' sentence, noting that the case had undergone sufficient judicial review; and Rosanna Fuentes, the sister of one of Lucas's other victims (and for whose murder he received a life sentence), complained publicly, "I'm very angry. I'm very disappointed in George Bush, and very disappointed in our court system," she said, adding that the convicted murderer should have received the death sentence for murdering her sixteen-year-old sibling, Laura. "I'm completely convinced that he killed my sister. He took the Montgomery County sheriff's deputies where he left her. They made a wrong turn, and he corrected them. He laid down on the spot where he left her body, in the position how he left her there."

A month after commuting Lucas' death sentence to a life term, Bush gave his standard tough-on-crime stump speech to the Sheriffs' Association of Texas and explained how he decided to spare Lucas' life. "It's important to have a governor who understands that you must enforce the law. The role of the state is not to determine the heart. We must leave determination of heart and soul and conscience to a much higher authority than the state," he said, noting that he received over 2,400 letters asking for Tucker's clemency, and 9,002 phone calls to his office, which were almost evenly split in their opinions of mercy or death.

The difference between Tucker and Lucas, he asserted, was the fact that she admitted her guilt and Lucas claimed he was innocent. "I will tell you that for all the death penalties we've had in our state, I am confident that those who have been put to death have been guilty under the eyes of the law," he told the law enforcement organization, adding that Lucas, although perhaps not guilty of the crime that sent him to death row, was still an "evil" murderer. "He will serve until he is dead. There is no chance he will ever walk free. And he should not walk free. He's a very bad man."

Phil Ryan, the Texas Ranger who arrested Lucas for the Orange Socks' murder and puts the serial killer's actual tally of victims at fifteen, argued for his execution. "If anybody deserves to die for something he didn't do, I've never met a better candidate than Henry Lee Lucas."

Secret Meetings

The governor and the Texas clemency process once again came under international attack in the months following the dual death-row dramas when Joseph Stanley Faulder, a sixty-one-year-old Canadian national, had his plea for mercy rejected by the same parole board.

Faulder was convicted of the 1975 murder of the matriarch of a prominent and wealthy Texas oil family during a botched robbery attempt. His defense, like that of so many others facing execution in America, was a travesty. His court-appointed lawyer called no witnesses and presented no mitigating evidence at his trial, and failed to tell the jury that Faulder had permanent brain damage from a massive head injury he suffered during childhood, according to federal and state court documents. Had the jury heard that his mental impairment made him less than fully responsible for the crime (neurologists who examined him concluded he was unable to distinguish right from wrong), his sentence could have been life imprisonment, rather than death.

Faulder languished on Texas death row for twenty-one years before the Canadian government and his family, who believed he was dead, learned of his whereabouts from Faulder's latest appeals attorney from the Texas Resource Center. As his December 1998 execution date rapidly approached, the U.S. State Department joined the Canadian government and the U.N. Human Rights Commissioner in trying to persuade Governor Bush to set aside Faulder's death sentence because state authorities never informed the former mechanic from Alberta that he had the right to contact Canadian consular officials, thus violating an international agreement.

The Canadian foreign minister, Lloyd Axworthy, filed a friend-of-the-court brief in support of Faulder's final plea to have his case heard before the U.S. Supreme Court. "The Vienna Convention requires the 'competent authorities' to give prompt notice to detained foreign nationals of their right to see a consular officer of their own government," the petition stated. "It is undisputed that the state of Texas denied Mr. Faulder's rights of consular notification and access."

Texas officials had maintained that Faulder had a U.S. driver's license when he was arrested and, therefore, officers may not have known he was Canadian. But court documents later released clearly showed that his nationality was known to Texas investigators.

"The consular-notification issues in this case are sufficiently troublesome that they may provide sufficient grounds for according discretionary clemency relief," Secretary of State Madeleine Albright said in a letter to Bush in which she requested a thirty-day stay of execution and offered to send State Department officials to Texas to brief the governor on the implications of the Vienna accord.*

Responding with his own letter, Bush said he was waiting for the State Board of Pardons and Parole to make a recommendation and added that both state and federal appeals courts had upheld Faulder's conviction. "I can understand her concerns and desires," he said of Albright's request at a news

---

*Afterwards, Albright issued a directive to the Department of Justice detailing the obligation to make the right to contact the nearest consulate known to foreign nationals detained for alleged crimes committed in the United States. When suspected railway serial killer Angel Maturino Resendez walked across the Mexican border and turned himself in to Texas Rangers in the summer of 1999, law enforcement officials went out of their way to ensure Resendez was well-informed of his rights under international law.

conference. "In general, I will uphold the laws of the state of Texas regardless of the nationality of the person involved. People can't just come in our state and cold-blood murder somebody. That's unacceptable behavior."

The secretary of state's appeal carried no legal weight, but Canadian officials were hoping it would be persuasive, especially since Bush was expected to run for president in two years. They hoped her correspondence was a reminder that the United States also depended on other countries to respect the Vienna Convention.

As international human rights groups weighed in with fax campaigns, e-mail messages, news conferences, and threatened economic and tourism boycotts against the Lone Star State, an angry Bush told reporters, "No one is going to threaten the governor of the state of Texas, no matter how subtly" and promised that he'd be "fair" in handling the Canadian's clemency case.

A few days before his scheduled execution, state parole officials refused to commute Faulder's death sentence to a lesser penalty and denied his petition for a ninety-day reprieve in a vote of 17-1, with one abstention.

"I have seen no new evidence that questions the jury's verdict that he's guilty of this crime," the governor announced after the Texas Board of Pardons and Paroles issued its decision. "In fact, his request for commutation was not based on any claim of innocence."

In response, the American Bar Association urged Bush to grant a reprieve to consider clemency and called it "troubling" that Faulder's execution was scheduled on the fiftieth anniversary of the United Nations Universal Declaration of Human Rights. "I call upon you to utilize this sober occasion to demonstrate your commitment to the international rule of law and grant a reprieve from execution," the ABA's president, Philip S. Anderson, wrote the Texas governor.

In a last-minute effort to delay his execution, Faulder's attorneys did not challenge his conviction in federal court, but the state commutation process itself. In a request for a hearing, they contended the parole board violated due process because inmates had no way of knowing why the board voted the way it did.

"All the court knows for certain is that the condemned filed a petition for clemency, and the board voted against clemency," said U.S. District Judge Sam Sparks, who moved to temporarily halt Faulder's death, saying he wanted to know more about the secretive way in which Texas decided who received mercy, and who didn't.

In addition, state Representative Elliot Naishtat filed a bill that would require the Board of Pardons and Paroles to meet in open session to consider clemency requests. In a separate bill, Naishtat called for a list of specific issues to be considered in clemency review, including mental state at the time of the offense, whether drinking or drug usage was involved, and whether the inmate was truly rehabilitated.

Under the current law, members of the parole board, in preparing a recommendation to the governor, vote by fax and do not hold meetings in person to discuss cases. They also do not issue reasons for their decisions, which were made by majority vote. The eighteen representatives, all appointed by the governor, argue that they are not a government body and do not have to conduct their business openly.

"It's going to have to take an awfully compelling argument for me to support the change," the governor declared, adding that a more open version of the board's clemency process could be flawed. "There may be a case made that having it in public is going to end up being another trial or . . . a chance for people to rant and rail, a chance for people to emotionalize the process beyond the questions that need to be asked."

Dan Morales, the outgoing state attorney general in late 1998, disagreed with the governor, publicly acknowledging that he had reservations about whether the Texas system was fair and impartial. "There's no question in certain cases that the process does not appear to be an absolutely fair and equitable system," said Morales, who had successfully defended the clemency process before the U.S. Supreme Court several times over the years. "OK, we pass constitutional muster, but can we do better? The answer is yes."

After presiding over a sometimes contentious hearing between state proponents of Texas' clemency process and Faulder's attorneys, U.S. District Judge Sparks ruled that the system satisfied the constitution, but criticized the process as needlessly secretive and marginally fair, but beyond his power to change.

"Administratively, the goal [of the clemency process] is more to protect the secrecy and autonomy of the system rather than carrying out an efficient, legally sound system," the federal judge wrote in his opinion, while also lifting his earlier stay on Faulder's execution. "The board would not have to sacrifice its conservative ideology to carry out its duties in a more fair and accurate fashion."

In ruling against the Canadian, the judge suggested that state officials or the Texas Legislature could head off an onslaught of similar challenges by agreeing to a few simple changes that they had fought in the courts. He advised the parole board, like its counterparts in all other death penalty states, to hold public hearings in clemency cases or, at a minimum, to require members to provide a written summary of the reasons for their votes.*

Thirty minutes before Faulder was scheduled to die by lethal injection, the U.S. Supreme Court granted a stay of execution while it determined whether it wanted to hold formal arguments on claims that the Canadian's rights had been violated under international law; prosecutors suppressed evidence at his trial; and whether the process used by the Texas Board of Pardons and Paroles to review death-penalty cases was unconstitutional.

At a press conference afterward, Bush stated that he hoped the high court's justices would review and resolve the legal matter as quickly as possible. "I've said all along that the courts are the proper place to address the legal issues in this case."

One reporter noted that after Karla Faye Tucker was executed, the Supreme Court ruled in the case of an Ohio prisoner who challenged that state's parole procedures. In that case, five of the justices agreed that "some minimal procedural safeguards apply to clemency proceedings."

Finally, a Canadian journalist cited Canada's abolishment of the death penalty in 1976 and asked Bush what he would say to Canadians "who seem to think that your state is running kind of a Wild West show down here."

The governor maintained his cool, prompting some observers to note that if he were in training for a presidential race, he passed an early, minor test. "If you're a Canadian and you come to our state," he replied, "don't murder anybody."

After the high court later refused to grant Faulder a hearing, the temporary stay of execution was lifted. The Board of Pardons and Paroles, which could have recommended that the governor commute the sentence to life in prison, instead voted 18-0 to allow the execution to proceed. Bush could have delayed Faulder's death thirty days but declined to do so, saying he was convinced that Faulder was guilty and that he received a fair trial.

At 6:18 P.M. on June 17, 1999, six minutes after Texas prison officials began injecting chemicals into his arms, Faulder became the first Canadian executed in the United States since 1952.

---

*In 1999, the state Legislature introduced a measure that limited exceptions to Texas's open government law, but at Bush's request, retained the secrecy surrounding the closed-door meetings of the Texas Board of Pardons and Paroles.

★ 10 ★

New Dog, Old Tricks

Somehow the Republican label means to some folks you can't be compassionate. I've worked hard to show people that the conservative philosophy is a compassionate philosophy, not only in word but deed as well.

—George W. Bush

George W. Bush says he's a "compassionate conservative." Isn't that like a "vegetarian cannibal"?

—Joy Behar, a co-host of ABC's *The View*

"Compassionate Conservatism"

During the Great Depression and World War II, Franklin Roosevelt offered America a New Deal. In the turbulent sixties, under John F. Kennedy, the country embarked on a New Frontier, and his successor, Lyndon Johnson built a Great Society before Richard Nixon and Ronald Reagan dismantled it during the seventies and eighties. Before Bill Clinton sent him packing back to Texas, George Bush advocated a "kinder, gentler" America. In the infancy of the twenty-first century, his son is now eagerly embracing a sound-bite slogan that he hopes will appeal to a wide mainstream of voters and carry him to the White House into the twenty-first century: "compassionate conservatism."

"Conservatism is a philosophy that puts government in its proper perspective, that says government ought to do a few things well, that there is a role for government," the Texas governor has explained. "Compassion says that the policies will lead to a better tomorrow, but there is an activist plan, there is a strategy."

Curiously, the catch-all phrase "compassionate conservatism" now championed by Bush, was first uttered by Bob Dole in the months before he lost the 1988 Republican presidential nomination to the governor's father. As he moved toward a surprisingly strong New Hampshire finish that served as a wake-up call to then-President Bush, Pat Buchanan talked about crafting "a more compassionate conservatism" that, in his version, included public school prayer, congressional term limits, a two-year freeze on spending, and a ban on abortion. Pete Wilson won the governorship of California in 1990, campaigning as a "compassionate conservative," and then, a few years later, adopted a hard line against impoverished immigrants seeking a better life in his state. And even former speaker of the House, Newt Gingrich, tried to lay claim to the label while simultaneously promoting the "take-no-prisoners" social conservative agenda of the Republican Party during the mid-nineties.

In a country where voters are increasingly identifying themselves as either moderates or conservatives, "compassionate conservatism" is the sort of buzz phrase that everyone can embrace, appealing to all stripes of Republicans, independents, and even some Democrats who prefer a blend of Clintonian pragmatism on fiscal matters with tough-love conservatism on social issues. In reality, "compassionate conservatism" is merely another way of packaging the right-wing agenda, a smiley-face version of deregulation, limited government, privatization, and old-fashioned intolerance.

As governor of Texas, Bush has boasted that his brand of conservatism has been more positive than punitive, but his record in office has made it difficult to reconcile "compassionate" with the other half of his self-proclaimed label. And as he continues to define a governing philosophy for the nation, he has made it clear that it is the far right that he is indeed courting while studiously avoiding the seemingly harsh and exclusionary rhetoric often associated with Republicans like Buchanan and former Vice President Dan Quayle.

Many conservative hard-liners, who still blame Bush's father for dismantling Reagan's legacy, are worried that the son is "genetically flawed philosophically." But they need not worry. Bush, who has claimed he is "an activist governor with a conservative agenda," is more in the mold of Reagan than his one-term successor who surrendered the presidency to Bill Clinton.*

POVERTY STATE

During Governor Bush's first four years in office, a robust economy left many Texans feeling prosperous, but millions remained mired in poverty, faring worse than the national average in nearly every way. "Texas is not a rich state. It's Mississippi with good roads," syndicated columnist and author Molly Ivins has said of the Lone Star State since Bush became governor.

According to comprehensive and separate studies conducted by the Urban Institute in Washington, the Center for Public Policy Priorities, and the *Dallas Morning News,* the governor's "compassionate conservative" agenda had actually created two societies in the Lone Star State—one that believed in the American dream and one that was without such hope:

- Texas ranked fiftieth in per capita spending on government programs.
- Almost one in three lower-income† children did not have health insurance while the national average was closer to one in five. (Texas, with 1.5 million, led the nation in the overall number of uninsured children.)
- About thirty-nine percent of low-income children and nonelderly adults reported being in fair or poor health, compared to thirty-one percent nationally.
- Sixty-one percent of low-income families in Texas said they worried about or had difficulty affording food, while this was true for fifty-four percent of low-income families nationally.
- 16.9 percent of Texans (one out of every six state residents) lived below the poverty line, compared to a national average of 13.6 percent.

---

*At the 1997 convention of the California Republican Assembly, one of the nation's premier conservative groups, Bush was awarded its Ronald Reagan Freedom Fighter Award because "we feel that he's been out there" on conservative issues, according to CRA president, Jon Fleischman. Previous recipients include political commentator and presidential candidate Pat Buchanan, noted Iran-Contra figure Oliver North, televangelist Pat Robertson, Senator John Ashcroft of Missouri, and former South Carolina Governor Carroll Campbell.

†The studies defined low-income as families falling under a $32,900 annual income for a family of four.

- Child poverty stood at twenty-nine percent—four percentage points higher than the national average—ranking Texas among the seven worst states in the country, with children under the age of six being the greatest victims. More than seventy percent of Texas' black and Hispanic children six years old or younger lived in poverty or extreme poverty.
- Texas ranked fourth among states in teenage pregnancy rates.
- Poverty-stricken parents who were employed worked an average of more than forty-four weeks, or more than ten months, a year.
- More than seventy percent of poor families with children received most of their income from wages, while only eleven percent relied on welfare for most of their income.
- Only twenty-two percent of out-of-work Texans received unemployment benefits, compared to a national average of thirty-five percent.
- Texas had a higher than average rate of deaths due to child abuse or neglect, with 1.8 deaths per thousand children each year, compared to the national average of 1.4. Texas also ranked below the national average both in investigations of child abuse per capita and removal of children because of child abuse. Nearly three of every four killed were age three or younger and more than two-thirds were minorities. (The studies determined that the upward spike in child deaths was partly because some parents were overwhelmed by the stress of their responsibilities.)

"I think it's fair to say that low-income families in Texas are definitely under real strains and tend to be under greater strain than low-income families in the rest of the country," noted Alan Weil, project director of the Urban Institute's study. "Because there are more of them in Texas, that makes the challenge of meeting those families' needs particularly tough."

It is especially difficult to assist the state's poor if the agency entrusted with half a billion dollars annually to provide better housing for poverty-stricken and working-class Texans seldom relinquishes the funds. In late 1998, a Department of Housing and Urban and Development report noted that the state of Texas had failed to spend more than $100 million in aid intended to help poor families find homes. According to the HUD study, the Texas Department of Housing and Community Affairs had utilized only half of the $184 million it received from the federal Home Investment Partnership program.

State Representative Harryette Ehrhardt of Dallas, said the state's inaction "means human misery for families throughout Texas. There is a housing crisis in this state, and yet the Texas Department of Housing and Community

Affairs is not spending money meant to help poor people get decent housing," said Ehrhardt, who sat on the House panel that oversees the housing department.

Beatrice Lacey, an eighty-nine-year-old widow who had lived in the same home for half a century, should have been a qualified recipient of some of the state housing funds. When she was forced to move because she couldn't afford the costly repairs to her home, she remarked, "This house means so much to me. It's the first thing that my husband and I bought. It's the place where we raised our kids and now I've lost it. I voted for George Bush for governor because I thought he was a decent and compassionate man, but now I see his true colors. Poor people like me lose their homes while his rich real estate buddies get the breaks with property tax cuts. There's something wrong with that."

"In the Same Hospital Bed with the Giant HMOs"

At the end of Governor Bush's first legislative session in 1995, the Patient Protection Act received overwhelmingly bipartisan support with only one state senator and seven members of the Texas House of Representatives voting against the bill.

The legislation, which would have given Texans a laundry list of rights against corporate medicine, proposed standards of plain-language disclosure about covered services, fair and prompt appeal processes for questions related to denial of care and coverage, and a provision requiring HMOs to allow their members to choose doctors outside their insurance networks if they were willing to pay more for the care.

The Patient Protection Act would have also mandated that HMOs cover treatment at M.D. Anderson Cancer Hospital, a government-affiliated medical facility in Houston, if the treatment was not available within their networks, essentially providing quality cancer care to all Texans who needed it.* Only four of twenty-five health maintenance organizations that filed with the Texas Department of Insurance paid for treatment at a comprehensive cancer center such as M.D. Anderson.

Although public opinion polls showed that eighty-four percent of the state's voters were in favor of the bill, Bush vetoed it, stating that the pro-

*At the time, M.D. Anderson was the only medical facility in Texas certified by the National Cancer Institute as a Comprehensive Cancer Care Center.

posed legislation would have been prohibitively expensive for managed-care programs and would have raised the cost of health care for all Texans.

"It was the right thing to do," Bush argued, "because it was a flawed bill that treated one group of HMOs one way and another group of HMOs another way."

The governor's critics, however, were suspicious of his motives, claiming that he vetoed the bill because he was "in the same hospital bed with the giant HMOs." Others alleged that the bill would have drastically affected the profits of a major hospital chain controlled by Richard Rainwater, the governor's frequent business associate and then-partner in the Texas Rangers baseball team ownership.

Since the time of the governor's veto, other states and many medical organizations—even large managed-care conglomerates such as Kaiser Permanente—have joined with physician organizations to embrace key provisions of patient protections.

The "compassionate conservative" health care governor has also publicly stated that families of nursing home residents who qualify for Medicaid should be asked to help defray some of the health care costs for those beneficiaries, a controversial idea that was first raised and then immediately rejected by the Reagan administration.

Race Relations

On March 3, 1999, the *New York Times* wrote in its lead editorial that Bush "could bring a great deal to his party if he stands up for inclusiveness and defends some form of affirmative action."* But when it comes to the issues of minorities, Bush has always found it much easier to talk about "inclusion" than to demonstrate it.

The day before the *Times* published its opinion, Texas state Senator Royce West of Dallas, was voting against three of the governor's appointees to the board of Texas' largest public university system. The well-respected lawmaker didn't have anything against the nominees personally, he was simply

---

*During an interview with the *Washington Post* in April 1999, the governor was asked three times whether he agreed with California's Proposition 209, the anti-affirmative initiative approved in 1996, and all three times he avoided answering the question directly.

Bush has stated repeatedly, however, that racial preferences (or what he calls "affirmative access") are not just wrong, but also unconstitutional.

lodging a public protest statement against the governor for not appointing a single black to the University of Texas System Board of Regents.

Senator West was joined by several other legislators in criticizing Bush because the UT board—which has had only one African-American member in its history—has struggled to increase minority enrollment and faculty at the university, a state institution with a century-long history of segregation.

"African-Americans should be able to sit at the table and give their perspective," Senator West told the press. "From a principle standpoint, when are we going to move Texas to the twenty-first century?"

Mario Gallegos, a state lawmaker from Houston agreed with his colleague. "Whether he's the governor of Texas or president of the United States, we're looking for diversity of these boards."

Bush, who vowed to make significant strides in increasing the number of minority appointments to state boards and commissions as governor, actually decreased minority choices by 15 percent, compared to his predecessor's tenure in office. Nearly 60 percent of Bush's appointments have resembled him in many respects: white, male, with an average age of fifty. Although he promised the minority community that his appointees would accurately reflect the state's population, his record in office indicates otherwise.

A day after Lieutenant Governor Bob Bullock announced a complex plan aimed at getting more minorities elected to district judgeships, Bush offered a simpler solution to reporters, claiming that blacks and Hispanics would have better opportunities at becoming judges if they would dump their traditional allegiance to the Democratic Party.

"To those who worry about the mix of minority judges in the state, they ought to encourage people to switch parties," he said. "One way to solve the problem is for Hispanics and African-Americans to run as Republicans. If you want to be a judge, if you want to get elected in the big counties, the message ought to be switch parties and run."

"I think that it is very short-sighted for anyone to think that African-Americans and Hispanics in Texas don't have the right to choose political parties that white people in Texas have," responded state Senator Rodney Ellis, noting that there was a "very simple reason why minorities choose not to be Republicans in Texas. There are deep philosophical differences between the two political parties in Texas."

The current countywide system of elected district judges had made it difficult for minority candidates, typically Democrats, to win in a state that was predominantly Republican and conservative. The GOP sweep in the November 1994 election left Houston's Harris County with no black district judges, a situation state Attorney General Dan Morales said "looks more like the Texas of 1940 or 1950, not the Texas of 1995."

The plan pushed by the lieutenant governor's bipartisan panel of judges, senators and private citizens, called for gubernatorial appointment of all members of the Texas Supreme Court, Court of Criminal Appeals, and the fourteen regional courts of appeals. In the state's four most populous counties, the judges would be elected by county commissioner precincts and would face subsequent countywide "retention elections" in which voters could oust the judge. Appellate judges would also face retention elections after being appointed. Proponents of the plan claimed that it would boost election chances for minorities and end allegations of campaign finance corruption of judges who ran for office on political party tickets.

To counter Bullock's proposal, Bush publicly reaffirmed his support of the current system of partisan election of judges at all levels in Texas. "I believe we ought to stay the way we are," noting once again that more minorities could become judges in the state if they ran as Republicans rather than Democrats.

Thackeray Barrett, writing for the op-ed page of the *Houston Chronicle* complained that Bush's remark "ranks right up there in sheer arrogance with Marie Antoinette's statement: 'Let them eat cake.' Thank goodness the real elected power in the state of Texas is the lieutenant governor and it is under the competent leadership of Bob Bullock."

Allegations of racial prejudice by the governor were raised at the end of his first term in office when a report was issued noting that of the fourteen pardons he granted, all but one (a Hispanic convicted in 1961 of burglary) had been given to white males.

"I take offense when people accuse me or intone that I make decisions based on race," a seemingly offended Bush protested at a press conference. "I have no idea about the race of the people. I've pardoned fourteen people based on recommendations from my staff and criterion."

"That's pure horseshit," claimed one of the governor's chief advisers on the state's criminal justice system. "Bush reviews an inmate's entire criminal file before making a decision to grant a pardon. It contains everything from his rap sheet to initial arresting officers' reports, from prison psychologists' evaluations to their disciplinary record since they've been locked up. Of course, right on top of the file is their mug shot."

Asked about his decision not to pardon Kevin Byrd, a black carpenter who spent twelve years in prison before DNA tests and all forensic evidence proved that he could not have raped a Houston housewife in 1985, the governor contended that he preferred a judicial course to determine Byrd's guilt or innocence in the crime.

State District Judge Doug Shaver, the controversial eighteen-member Texas Board of Pardons and Paroles, and Harris County District Attorney Johnny B. Holmes, all urged the governor to pardon Byrd based upon evidence that showed that his semen did not match the genetic material taken from the victim. But fearing that Byrd might become his own political Willie Horton nightmare, the governor declined to grant a pardon until "all other legal remedies have been exhausted." Even Byrd's lawyer suggested the governor might have been afraid that Byrd, if pardoned, might get in serious trouble and bring politically damaging publicity onto Bush during a possible future presidential bid.*

State Representative Ruth Jones McClendon also cited the Byrd case as an example of how the governor's pardon process worked against African-Americans in Texas. "The Board of Pardons and Paroles wants him to get a pardon. The district attorney wants him to get a pardon. The judge who heard his trial wants him to get a pardon," the legislator claimed. "So what's the problem?"

Bush replied that McClendon perhaps should take the time to discuss the case with the rape victim in Houston, who remained adamant that Byrd was the black man who attacked her in 1985. Later, however, a court ruled in favor of Byrd, dismissing the charges that had kept an innocent man behind bars for twelve years.

The governor, realizing he needed public relations assistance with the African-American community, reached out to paid consultants Willie and Gwen Richardson, the black owners of *Headway*, a politically conservative magazine with an African-American focus. Willie Richardson likened his role to that of a "matchmaker," setting up a "courtship" between Bush and Texas black voters to make sure they understood the governor was not intolerant to anyone based upon the color of their skin.

As the Richardsons attempted to "help make sure" the Bush support of the black community was heard on African-American talk radio stations and other minority owned and operated media outlets, Bush's consultants

---

*The governor's pardons have not been free of post-release controversy. Steve Raney, who was convicted in 1988 for possessing a marijuana plant and was pardoned in 1995 by Bush, was arrested only four months later on charges of stealing cocaine from a police drug bust while working as a county deputy constable.

found themselves defending their boss against charges of racial exclusion as an owner of the Texas Rangers baseball team.

When Bush and his partners tried to build the taxpayer-subsidized Ballpark at Arlington stadium complex, the presidents of three Dallas-Fort Worth area chapters of the NAACP accused them of failing to award a sufficient portion of work on the multimillion dollar facility to companies owned by minorities or women.

"If you compared minority participation in this stadium to Chicago, Baltimore, and Cleveland, the Rangers show five percent and the others have twenty to twenty-five percent or better," noted Harry Gudger, president of the Arlington branch of the NAACP.

The civil rights leaders demanded that Bush and the other team owners award all of the remaining thirty percent of the stadium construction to minority- and woman-owned companies. If they refused, Gudger threatened to "make Arlington the Arizona of Texas," a less than subtle reference to the boycotts that resulted from Arizona's refusal to grant a state holiday on Martin Luther King's birthday.

In defense, Bush asserted he brought the first black to own part of a major-league baseball team into his Rangers organization: Comer Cottrell,* president of Proline, a company that specialized in African-American health and beauty supplies. The governor stumbled, however when asked by reporters to name the minorities who worked in the Rangers' executive offices.

"You want our center fielder or our left fielder?" Bush joked before naming Norman Lyons, a vice president with the sports franchise. He failed to mention that Lyons was hired in 1993 specifically to coordinate the award of minority contracts after the Rangers organization was criticized by the NAACP. The team's managing general partner also had trouble naming other minority executives. Bush's staff later cited Omar Minaya, a Hispanic who was director of the Rangers' international scouting.

To bolster their claims that Bush had frequently "preached inclusion, but practiced exclusion," state black leaders referred to the resignation of his press secretary Deborah Burstion-Wade, the only African-American on his campaign staff in 1994; his failure to hire minority businesses to run concessions at The Ballpark in Arlington; and his withdrawal from the board

*Ironically, Cottrell publicly chastised Bush and the other Rangers owners for failing to fire three companies that had been awarded contracts for stadium work but were later identified by a regional certification agency as having fraudulently misrepresented their minority ownership status.

of directors of Paul Quinn College, the historically black university in Dallas.

"You know, I say I'm not a divider; I'm a uniter," Bush has claimed in response to allegations of racial intolerance. "I try not to put people into categories and lump people into groups." In explaining the difference between a "compassionate conservative" and the rest of the GOP, Bush continued, "One problem that our party has had is that we've been pretty articulate about what we're against. We need to do better about what we're for."

Bush, the businessman and governor, seemingly has been against inclusion and for exclusion of minorities. Is that the record of a "compassionate conservative" or is it merely benign neglect?*

Environmental Impact

As a senior campaign adviser to his father's successful presidential run in 1988, Bush was instrumental in helping to devise the negative television ad that attacked Massachusetts Governor Michael Dukakis' environmental record. Using Boston Harbor as a backdrop, the elder Bush decried the "five

---

*In July 1999, presidential candidate Bush made campaign appearances in Seattle, but had no plans to address a conference of six thousand minority journalists meeting at the same time to assess the progress of minorities in newsroom hiring and promotion. Organizers of Unity '99 stated that although they had invited Bush months earlier, he told them that his one-day trip to the Pacific Northwest city was so overbooked he could not schedule a speech to delegates representing the nation's four leading minority journalism organizations.

"It may not be racially motivated, but his refusal to show up here and to be in town at the same time will have racial significance," Charles Ogletree, a professor at Harvard Law School, told the *Los Angeles Times.* "In light of his expressed interest in diversity, he has missed a great opportunity to meet and greet the people who will define him to minority communities for the year to come."

Mid-morning on the second day of the Unity conference, a Bush aide telephoned one of the event's organizers and said the governor was at the convention center's loading dock. Once at the conference, however, Bush declined to participate in a Q & A session with journalists, and instead, walked through an exhibition area in fifteen minutes. He admitted he had read the *Times* article that morning in which delegates were critical of his decision not to attend. "That," he said, "made me realize it was an important issue."

Many of the journalists attending Unity said they were even more annoyed by the Texas governor's quick walk-through than by his initial turndown. The conference, they said, was not intended to be a campaign stop for candidates, but rather a way of fostering serious dialogue about race issues. At a news conference later in the afternoon, Unity President Catalina Camina, complained, "Unity: Journalists of Color wishes to express its extreme disappointment over Governor George Bush's inadequate visit to the Unity '99 convention," she said. "As a serious presidential contender, we believe Governor Bush missed a tremendous opportunity to share his plans for the country's future with nearly six thousand journalists representing media outlets of every type, size and place in America."

hundred million gallons of barely treated sewage and seventy tons of sludge" that entered the waterway daily. "My opponent's solution to this pollution: delay, fight, anything but clean up," he fulminated.

Along with the Willie Horton "scare tactic" ad, it was a defining moment of the 1988 campaign. Exposing the Democratic nominee's hypocrisy on environmental matters and contrasting it with his own passion for the environment helped to make Bush president.

Less than a decade later, his son was being accused of "environmental racism" as the governor of Texas, exposing himself to the same vulnerability as his father's opponent. Most certainly Al Gore, the presumed Democratic nominee for president in 2000 and the author of the 1992 best-seller *Earth in the Balance*, is bound to exploit Bush's abysmal environmental record, especially in regards to the dumping of nuclear waste.

Since 1980, states have grappled with the difficult and controversial questions of how and where to dispose of their low-level radioactive waste generated mainly from nuclear reactors and industrial users. Under orders from the U.S. Congress to develop regional solutions, forty-one states banded together in nine separate alliances. Then in 1997, Maine, Vermont, and Texas sought to become the tenth compact ratified by lawmakers in Washington.

Under their tri-state alliance, which the House ultimately approved, Maine and Vermont would pay Texas $25 million each in exchange for being allowed to house their waste at a proposed West Texas dump. But as the trio of partners forged ahead, other compact states began to question their participation in similar alliances, wondering why there needed to be nine or ten disposal sites as envisioned by Congress almost twenty years earlier.

Governor Bush strongly supported congressional endorsement of the Texas Low-Level Radioactive Waste Compact with Maine and Vermont, arguing that without such an agreement, Texas could be forced to take waste from several other states rather than just two.

Many Texas legal advisers and politicians disagreed, claiming that it was "not possible for the federal government to force a state to build a dump, but once it was built, it might be possible to force a state to take nuclear waste from all over the country." U.S. Representative Lloyd Doggett, concerned that Texas could become "the pay toilet for the country," attached an amendment to the compact authorization bill while it was being debated in the House. Under his measure, Texas would only accept waste from Maine and Vermont.

While Congress resumed final negotiations on the pact, state officials chose the desolate Faskin Ranch desert site five miles from the West Texas community of Sierra Blanca as a suitable home for the $34 million burial site, a project passionately opposed by the area's residents and environmental groups in nearby Mexico.

Governor Bush, acknowledging that it was "a very emotional issue for some people," remained convinced that the windswept area was ideal for a nuclear waste dump. "Disposal plans are state-of-the-art," he told the press, and the compact guaranteed that only Texas, Vermont, and Maine would use the site. "If the question is, 'Am I concerned about spent nuclear rods?' Yes, I am. But they won't be going there. It's low-level radioactive waste and only low-level radioactive waste," he claimed, adding that the items that would be stored in concrete canisters were mainly "medical materials" such as rubber boots, gloves, and syringes.

The governor neglected to mention the more potent types of waste that officials in Maine hoped to dispatch to West Texas: "oversize" reactor components too large to place in concrete canisters and other plutonium-drenched refuse from the decommissioned Maine Yankee nuclear power plant.

Bush also did not address the geological instability in the Sierra Blanca area with its frequent occurrence of earthquakes, or the facility's impact on water supplies. With the site about eighteen miles from the Rio Grande and ringed by mountains, scientists had registered differing opinions on how water might be affected downstream, both in Texas and Mexico.

Several residents of Sierra Blanca, called the governor "a traitor to Texas" and contended "environmental racism" was part of the motivation for selecting the small, impoverished town near the Mexican border, especially in light of the fact that the area was already a disposal site for sewage sludge from New York City. Of 3,600 residents, there were only 1,600 registered voters, and seventy percent of the population was Hispanic. The governor angrily denied that Sierra Blanca had been chosen for political reasons, adding that construction of the nuclear waste facility would add one hundred jobs in a county where the average weekly wage was $298.

But as the project came ever closer to reality, more and more businesses displayed a sign in their windows, evidence of the deep-seated opposition to the nuclear waste dump: ATTENTION: TO ANY COMPANY INTENDING TO DUMP HAZARDOUS OR TOXIC WASTE ON OUR HOME, HUDSPETH COUNTY: WE WILL NOT ALLOW YOU TO USE US AS A DUMP SITE. OUR HEALTH, CHILDREN, WATER AND LAND ARE MOST PRECIOUS TO US.

In a rare show of unanimity, all five political parties in the Mexican Congress approved a resolution demanding that the United States and Texas honor a 1983 treaty between then-Presidents Reagan and Miguel de la Madrid. The La Paz Agreement, one of a series of pacts that helped pave the way for passage of the North American Free Trade Agreement (NAFTA), prohibited environmentally dicey projects within a 100-kilometer strip, or sixty-six miles, on each side of the border without both countries' sanction.

A delegation comprised of Mexico's highest-ranking leaders, traveled to the Texas Capitol to meet with Bush, but the governor snubbed the bipartisan group by specifically asking his Secretary of State, Al Gonzalez, to meet with them on his behalf.

"To be very frank, we did feel a little bit put out," Mexican Senator Norberto Corella Gil Samangiego admitted in a press conference. "But we also felt that knowing the purpose of our visit, it stood to reason that Mr. Bush did not want to listen to us because he did not want to tell us that he was the one responsible for the project," the Mexican senator stated, adding that "it is an absolute violation of an agreement that was promoted by the United States."

Texas state Representative Norma Chavez of El Paso, a Texas city only seventy miles from the proposed dump site, noted, "There are ten low-level nuclear dump sites in the country, and every one has leaked." Chavez, along with the Mexican delegation, accused dump supporters of practicing environmental racism. "Why aren't they putting something on the Canadian border? To put it on the Mexican border, we set a precedent if we allow them to build this facility," she said.

Although Texas Congressman Lloyd Doggett previously attached an amendment to the House version of the tri-state compact bill in an effort to ensure that Texas would be restricted from accepting nuclear waste from any states other than Maine and Vermont, the conference committee stripped Doggett's supplemental legislation before sending to the Senate what increasingly looked more like the authorization of a national nuclear waste dump.

The congressman called particular attention to the duplicity of Governor Bush, who in public claimed support of Doggett's amendment, but privately lobbied the conference committee to strip the bill of the restrictive attachment. In letters to the other congressmen, Bush complained that the amendment would cost time and money and infringe on "state sovereignty" by not allowing Texas to negotiate new disposal deals with other states. The governor later claimed that they would only be allowed to use the facility on an emergency, short-term basis.

After brushing aside complaints of environmental racism from Texas'

Mexican-American Legislative Caucus, twenty counties and thirteen cities in the state, two cities in Mexico, and the Mexican Congress, the U.S. Senate passed the controversial compact bill by a vote of 78-to-15.

Senator Paul Wellstone of Minnesota, an outspoken critic of the nuclear waste project, noted that dump sites like Sierra Blanca were "almost always located in a community of color," noting they were never constructed "where any senators live."

Bush, who announced that he was "pleased" with the compact bill's passage, was rebuked by Olive Hershey in the *Houston Chronicle,* noting that a few weeks earlier the governor had flown to the Texas border city of Del Rio to show his humanitarian concern for flood victims, but ignored health and safety risks if the proposed nuclear waste dump in Sierra Blanca leaked dangerous radioisotopes into ground water and the Rio Grande, which flowed a thousand miles between Texas and Mexico.

"Millions of people use the river water for human and animal consumption," Hershey wrote. "Are these people by the governor's reckoning, expendable, like the citizens of [Sierra Blanca's] Hudspeth County?"

The last hurdle for approval of the congressionally authorized nuclear waste site was the issuance of an operating license by the Texas Natural Resource Conservation Commission (TNRCC), a three-member panel comprised of Bush appointees. Only days before the decisive vote by state regulators, however, two administrative law judges recommended the TNRCC not issue an operations permit for the Sierra Blanca project, citing the potential for "unreasonable risk to the health and safety of the public" and "detrimental impact on the environment."*

"I am troubled that two administrative law judges, who spent a great deal of time reviewing the facts and listening to the arguments in this case, do not feel the applicants have proven the safety of the Sierra Blanca site," the governor told the media. He was certain, though, that his political appointees would reject the judges' nonbinding "proposal for decision."

Much to the governor's surprise, the TNRCC determined that the license applicant, the Low-Level Radioactive Waste Disposal Authority, failed to "adequately characterize the fault directly beneath the site" and did not sufficiently "address potential negative socioeconomic impacts from the pro-

---

*The ruling resulted from a series of hearings spanning ten weeks that pitted the state disposal authority and nongovernmental supporters, including nuclear utility companies and medical facilities that generated low-level radioactive wastes, against residents of Sierra Blanca, religious leaders, environmental groups, scientists, elected Mexican officials, politicians, and even antinuclear celebrities.

posed facility." Agreeing with the judges' recommendation, the commission forced the state to abandon its proposed dump in Sierra Blanca.

Within weeks, a Bush-sponsored bill was introduced in the Seventy-sixth Legislature to revise the law to allow private industry to become actively involved in the potentially lucrative nuclear waste-disposal business. Officials in Andrews County, northwest of Bush's former home in Midland, immediately offered an alternative site to Sierra Blanca, which was seen as a big boost for an area that had been hard hit economically by falling oil and gas prices.

Waste Control Specialists, LLC, a Houston-based company that already operated a hazardous and toxic waste dump on a 1,338-acre site in Andrews County, was considered the most likely beneficiary of privatization. Dallas billionaire Howard Simmons, a longtime Bush friend and substantial contributor to his political campaigns, bought controlling interest in the company in 1995.*

In early 1999, according to reports filed with the state, Simmons assembled a team of two dozen lobbyists, including former aides to the governor on federal-state relations and environmental affairs, to assist him in securing a contract from the state to dispose of growing stockpiles of low-level nuclear waste, a prize experts said could eventually produce big profits.

Across the board on environmental issues, the "compassionate conservative" governor has consistently placed corporate profits first before the health and safety of his Texas constituency. According to a 1999 study by the tri-national North American Commission on Environmental Cooperation, Texas pollutes more than any state or Canadian province.

Industrial facilities accounting for more than a third of the state's plant emissions don't have to comply with antipollution requirements because of a loophole in the 1971's Texas Clean Air Act requiring that "the best available control technologies" be used. Facilities built or being constructed before the law went into effect were exempted, or "grandfathered," from the more stringent antipollution regulations and state permits that applied to newer plants.†

Although the governor promised in his January 1999 State of the State

---

*Simmons gave $35,000 to the governor's reelection campaign in 1998. He is also a major contributor to the national Republican Party committees, giving $465,000 during the 1996 and 1998 elections.

†Business leaders defeated legislative efforts in the 1980s to require permits at "grandfathered" industries, arguing that their air pollution would eventually decline as they were shut down or modified.

speech "to make our Texas air cleaner by significantly reducing emissions from older, grandfathered plants," Bush has consistently resisted pressure from environmentalists and citizens groups to force the excluded plants to obtain emission permits and meet modern, more tougher pollution limits or face mandatory shutdown. Citing the enormous costs of installing pollution control equipment and the possible loss of "tens of thousands of jobs across Texas," the governor has favored a program that has allowed the owners of the grandfathered industrial facilities to voluntarily reduce polluting emissions.

In news conferences toward the end of his first term, the governor praised thirty-six grandfathered facilities (out of eight hundred) and their voluntary efforts, which had "already resulted in dozens of plants reducing emissions" by about twenty-five thousand tons a year. Environmental impact studies contradicted Bush's claims, revealing that only three of the thirty-six companies had actually made cuts in pollution, totaling about one-sixth of the twenty-five thousand tons. In addition, only ten other companies had promised future reductions in their older manufacturing plants.

As Bush unwaveringly allowed exempted plants to legally defile the Texas atmosphere, believing that the companies should be given the "chance to do the right thing" voluntarily, further environmental reports revealed:

- The state ranked forty-ninth in spending on the environment.
- Grandfathered facilities in the Houston/Galveston region emitted as much smog-causing nitrogen oxide as over three million automobiles.
- Texas led the nation as the state with the largest volume of air pollution.
- The state's more than 1,600 major industrial sources produced 2.5 million tons of air emissions in 1997 with the grandfathered plants responsible for thirty-six percent—a total of nine hundred thousand tons of nitrogen oxides, sulfer dioxide, carbon monoxide, and other pollutants.
- Houston recorded the nation's highest individual ozone measurement in 1997, exceeding Los Angeles' peak reading and violating the national health standard for ground-level ozone smog. (Other Texas cities, including Dallas-Fort Worth, Austin, and San Antonio, were also very close to violating the standard.)
- Health problems, aggravated by air pollution, like older people's emphysema and children's asthma, were increasing at alarming rates.
- Nearly 230,000 children in seven urban counties were at risk because their schools were within two miles of older, exempted plants that emitted dangerous pollutants.

"Children are especially vulnerable to grandfathered emissions because they are more sensitive to air pollution than adults are," claimed Peter Altman, director of the Sustainable Energy and Environmental Development Coalition. "Children tend to exercise more, are outside more often, and breathe lower to the ground where pollution tends to settle, while their bodies and biological defense systems are still developing and vulnerable," Altman said, adding that if Governor Bush was unwilling to close the loophole in the state's clean air act governing exempted industries, "we must wonder whether his compassion lies with the children of Texas whose health may be at risk from grandfathered pollution."

A coalition of environmentalists, public health campaigners and consumer advocates have claimed that the governor's voluntary plan was a "giveaway" to some of the state's largest, wealthiest companies—mostly electric utilities and oil and gas firms—at the expense of Texans' health. No doubt, the companies have saved millions of dollars by delaying emissions improvements for nearly three decades.

Political action committees and lobbyists representing industries seeking to remain exempt from environmental regulations have contributed more than $10 million to state political campaigns between 1993 and 1998, including more than $560,000 to support Governor Bush, according to a report by the nonprofit Public Research Works environmental group.*

"The report traces the dirty air to the dirty money," asserted Tom "Smitty" Smith of the consumer advocate organization, Public Citizen. "This is a foretaste of what would happen if Bush were to become president. Would our federal environmental protections become voluntary or would he require our biggest polluters to make reductions? He'll face the same issues at the federal level."

During Bush's tenure as governor, a third of the state's rivers and streams also violated federal water quality standards; the Natural Resources Defense Council named Texas one of six "beach bum" states for the second year in a row in 1999 because it lacked a statewide beach water quality monitoring system specifically designed to notify swimmers of potential health risks

---

*As part of their report, "Follow the Money . . . Grandfathered Air Polluters & Campaign Contributions," Public Research Works released a memo that showed oil industry lobbyists thanking "the governor's office and John Howard," Bush's environment policy director, for coming up with the notion of "voluntary compliance" for grandfathered polluters.

Bush also received $169,400 from polluters in the first twenty-eight days of his presidential fund-raising, plus $138,900 from the Houston law firm of Vinson & Elkins. The attorneys' clients included Aluminum Co. of America, whose grandfathered site led the state in air emissions.

from pollution; the Environmental Protection Agency threatened sanctions against Texas, including restrictions on business development and the denial of highway funds, because the governor submitted an incomplete plan on how to clean up Dallas-Fort Worth's excessive pollution; and when the governor successfully fought against centralized vehicle emissions tests—on the grounds that it was inconvenient for motorists—the company that ran the program sued and won $140 million, ninety percent of which was paid from money that had been set aside to clean Texas' air and water.

Although Governor Bush has repeatedly expressed pride in his environmental record ("The air's cleaner since I became governor.") and bristles at suggestions that it needs improving, it is painfully obvious that he is more conservative on issues concerning the environment than his father, who put the first "green" language in any free-trade agreement, signed the Clean Air Act of 1990 and the first treaty against global warming.

Driving on the Right

Catering to the Christian fundamentalist right and its hardcore social agenda has shaped much of Bush's "compassionate conservative" policy since he has been governor of Texas. "I am convinced to fundamentally and permanently change our culture, we need a spiritual renewal in America," the governor has often declared.

With the guidance of Republican strategist and consultant Ralph Reed, the former executive director of the Christian Coalition, and the financial support of multimillionaire Dr. James Leininger,* known as the "Daddy

*Leininger, who has been called "God's Sugar Daddy" by the *San Antonio Current,* is a former physician turned wealthy hospital bed magnate. His business interests include part ownership of the San Antonio Spurs basketball team; Promised Land Dairy, which sells glass-bottled milk stamped with Bible verses to Texas grocery store chains; Kinetic Concepts International, the medical bed and supply company that originated his fortune; Mission City Properties, which manages thirteen office buildings; Focus Direct, a direct-mail company that has produced political materials for candidates he supports; and the Texas Network, TXN, which reaches an estimated ten million Texans a day with television news programs in seventeen of the state's nineteen media markets.

Worth an estimated $300 million, Dr. Leininger contributed $1.9 million to Texas political candidates during the 1996 and 1998 elections through his PACs and foundations in an effort to promulgate his socially conservative causes such as school vouchers, home schooling, antiabortion, tort reform, gay rights opposition, anti-unionism, anti-environmental efforts, a right-wing think tank called the Texas Public Policy Foundation, and the Justice Foundation, which he founded as "a response to the American Civil Liberties Union."

Warbucks of Texas social conservatism," Governor Bush has successfully appeared moderate, while quietly maintaining more extreme views.

On the subject of abortion—the core issue of religious conservatives—he has declared his support for a constitutional amendment to ban legal abortions, but has said that Americans' "hearts are not right" on the issue of overturning Roe v. Wade, suggesting that Republicans should fight for incremental steps, such as banning late-term abortions and requiring parental consent for abortions conducted on teenagers. (Additionally, he has promoted his "Right Choices" youth initiatives that emphasize "abstinence until heterosexual marriage" and laws that would expedite the adoptions of infants born to teenage girls.)

Although he has been lauded by gay-rights groups for admonishing his fellow Republicans to treat homosexuals "with respect and dignity," he fought against a repeal of Texas' antisodomy law and supported a bill in the state Legislature that barred gay couples from becoming foster parents or adopting children in the custody of the state's Child Protective Services agency.

"I look at each person based upon their heart and soul," the governor contended, adding that he strongly believed "what's best for children is a married man or a married woman as their parents. That has nothing to do with whether or not I don't respect somebody. The question is whether I'm for gay adoption and the answer is, I'm not."*

In another attempt to appeal to the religious right of his party and opponents of gay rights, Bush announced that he was against including sexual orientation in a bill to clarify Texas' hate-crimes law, which increased penalties in cases where the victim was targeted for a specific reason such as race or gender.

"I've always said all crime is hate crime," the governor stated. "People, when they commit a crime, have hate in their heart. And it's hard to distinguish between one degree of hate and another."

Bush was harshly criticized by not only gay rights groups but members of the press, including Mark Davis, a host on the talk radio station WBAP in Dallas, who said that the governor's exclusion of gays from the James Byrd Jr. Hate Crimes Act made "him look as if he is being led around the nose by

---

*Nationally, between three million and four million children live in households with at least one gay parent. Researchers have cited no evidence that a parent's sexual orientation affects the ability to raise children, or leads them to have more emotional problems.

extremists in his party," Davis said. "Inclusion in the hate crime statute should hinge on a single criterion: Do the victims become victims because of a characteristic despised by the criminal?"

Sympathetic relatives of hate-crime victims also weighed in on the matter of Bush's ambivalence. Daryl Verrett, the nephew of James Byrd Jr., the black man from Jasper who was violently dragged to his death, stated he was "disappointed" at the governor's position and said that any hate crimes bill approved by the state Legislature should include sexual orientation. Judy Shepard, the mother of Matthew Shepard, a young gay man who was tortured and left to die on a Wyoming fence post, said that Bush's "stand is indefensible."*

"Apparently being a compassionate conservative does not include protecting the victims of hate crimes or their families," noted Elizabeth Birch, the executive director of the Human Rights Campaign, a national gay rights organization.

"Compassionate conservatism—whatever that means—has evaporated like a mirage in the desert," the *Texas Triangle,* a gay-advocacy magazine editorialized. Shown on its cover was the governor with an angel whispering in one ear and a devil in the other.

As Senate negotiations on the bill intensified in the Legislature in 1999, the Reverend James Mayfield, pastor of the Methodist Church Bush attended in Austin, issued a statement: "The James Byrd Jr. Memorial Hate Crimes Act would protect all Texans from the tragedy of hate-based crimes," the minister stated. "As religious leaders, we must send the message that Texas is not a hate state."

On the controversial issue of school prayer, Bush has tried to placate the religious conservatives by proclaiming his support of a constitutional amendment, but added that he preferred prayers said in educational institutions to be silent. The governor has also advocated voluntary prayer before public high school football games, yet he is careful to say that the choice should be left to the students.

---

*According to a Scripps Howard Texas Poll taken during the legislative session, most of the state's citizens disagreed with the governor's opposition to the revised hate-crimes bill. Seventy-two percent of the respondents said they favored laws that provided harsher penalties for crimes motivated by hate. Asked which of four groups should be covered if a new law was enacted, eighty-one percent said racial minorities should be included, eighty percent said women, seventy-six percent said homosexuals, and seventy-eight percent named religious groups.

"Why do I think prayer is important?" he asked the press. "I believe there's an almighty loving God, and I think if students so choose to do so, it's an important principle."

Bush also won support from religious conservatives with his adamant support of the Texas Legislature's Religious Freedom Restoration Act, a bill that prohibited a government agency from restricting a person's free exercise of religion except when there was a compelling government interest and the agency used the least restrictive means of enforcing it. The governor called the RFRA a "signature piece" of legislation that would be the centerpiece for his push to national office.

Noting that courts and government had eroded religious freedom, Bush told the press, "Court decisions have made it easier for government to encroach on people's rights, one small action at a time: one bureaucratic rule, one regulatory decision, one threatened lawsuit," he said. "This is unacceptable in Texas."

Legal scholars claimed that by giving religion leverage against every law, the state would be hindered from stepping in to prevent child abuse and neglect at religious schools and homes, antidiscrimination laws would be undermined, the state would be caught in a morass of court fights in attempts to define religion, and local governments would be left powerless to prevent employees from proselytizing on the job. Opponents of the RFRA also noted that it was almost identical to a federal religious liberty law rejected by the U.S. Supreme Court because it "violated the separation of powers, threatened the federal-state balance, and bypassed the Constitution's amendment ratification procedures."

Professor of Law, Marci Hamilton, claimed that the governor "remains oblivious to the underbelly of the religious freedoms acts and their direct assault on the rule of law," she said. "Some believe his staff has failed to warn him of the real consequences of giving all religions this extreme legal tool. He simply does not seem to understand what such a bill portends."

The governor seemed to make this apparent at his press conference to announce the RFRA when he could not answer specific questions about the bill's impact on state government institutions.

Professor Hamilton added, "No serious candidate for national office can afford to back such legislation. Despite their surface appeal, the religious freedom acts alter the careful judgments reached in every arena just because the one who intends to break the law can claim a religious connection," she asserted. "If Bush does know this, but simply does not care, woe to us all."

"The Texas Religious Freedom Restoration Act says loud and clear: Texas will not stand for government interference with the free exercise of religion," the governor stated when he signed the bill into law in 1999.

By most accounts, Bush has been devoutly religious since his close family friend, evangelist Billy Graham, helped him recommit his life to Christianity in 1986. "I view religion, Christianity, as a continual walk," he has said. Friends say he reads the Bible from "cover to cover every year or two" and always offers a prayer of thanks before meals, holding hands with whoever is eating at his table, whether it's his father or a legislator whose vote he is trying to influence.

Bush has acknowledged that his political philosophy has been shaped by his strong Methodist faith (he once called the Bible a "pretty good political handbook"), and has never shown a reluctance to impose his religious beliefs on the public arena.

"He talks about how he looks to faith for guidance," said the Reverend Tony Evans, a Dallas minister and a prominent speaker in Promise Keepers, a national evangelical men's group. "One of the impetuses for his considering running for president was the biblical teaching he's been hearing," Evans, a confidant of the governor, asserted. "He feels God is talking to him."

The core of the governor's "faith-based legislative agenda" has included proposals to dismantle state-run entitlement programs and allow religious institutions to provide welfare services, tax-paid vouchers to send children to private schools, and church organizations to provide drug treatment programs. The governor has also encouraged state prisons to offer Bible-based counseling and rehabilitation programs that could lead to conversions to Christianity and advocated programs which would permit social service providers to be licensed by "alternative accrediting groups" such as religious organizations, rather than medical and other health care associations.

Speaking in churches and appearing on religious talk shows in an effort to engage religious conservatives who comprise nearly a third of GOP primary voters, Bush has detailed his proposals to give faith-based programs a larger role in attacking society's ills. He has promised that he would rally the "armies of compassion" and set aside $8 billion from the federal budget surplus during the first year as president for new tax credits and grants. They would be used, Bush said, to encourage Americans to give more to charity and boost the role of religious groups in the fight to reduce poverty, welfare rolls, crime and other urban problems.

"In every instance where my administration sees a responsibility to help people, we will look first to the faith-based organizations, to charities and community groups that have shown their ability to save and change lives," the governor has repeatedly stated. "Government cannot be replaced by charities. I know that, you know that. But it can welcome them as partners, not resent them as rivals."

Carole Shields, president of People for the American Way, a civil liberties advocacy group in Washington, countered that Bush's ideas might force religion on people seeking assistance. "It's bad for religion and bad for the clients," she said. "For the clients, they have to take the religion in order to get the service. For religion, the church has to be accountable for that money, and that basically invades the integrity of that religion. Religion shouldn't be responsible for the government."

Peri Arnold, a professor of public policy at the University of Notre Dame, agreed, saying many charities have noteworthy ideas that deserve government support, but suddenly infusing the organizations with a windfall of funding could backfire. "You can understand why a well-intentioned politician says, 'Look at all those people out there so good at holding church suppers—they'd be good at coordinating and organizing relief to the poor.' Well, that's a big leap of faith."

Bush "needs to be aware that it's a very complicated task. It's way more than, 'You guys run our welfare program in the state of Texas,'" said Oliver Thomas, a Baptist minister and civil rights lawyer who is special counsel to the National Council of Churches. "If we take that kind of simplistic approach, there will be widespread abuses, lawsuits and eventually federal judges will step in and shut down these programs."

Stephen Goldsmith, the Indianapolis mayor and Bush's chief domestic policy adviser on his religious-based organizations initiatives, said that the governor wanted "to figure out how we can use government more effectively to make the market work for individuals so it respects individuals and their choices on their own lives," stated Goldsmith, who published the concepts in his book, *The Twenty-First Century City.* "It respects federalism and states rights, and understands that big-government bureaucracies are often counterproductive, but also understands that there is a place for government in helping those who aren't succeeding."

"We must apply our conservative and free-market ideas to the job of helping real human beings," Bush has often said, claiming he had a "message" for Republicans who had given the party an image of being callous and mean-spirited toward the less fortunate. "There must be kindness in our justice. There must be mercy in our judgment. There must be a love behind our zeal."

Satisfied with Bush's "compassionate conservative" governing philosophy and mindful of his front-runner status, the more realistic members of his party's religious right have decided that the former president's son is much more electable than Dan Quayle, Pat Buchanan, or any of the other Y2K Republican candidates.

Bush has already won the support of influential televangelists Jerry Falwell; James Robinson;* and Pat Robertson, the founder of the Christian Coalition, who, promised Bush during "a very frank discussion" that he would raise $21 million, hire one hundred thousand field organizers and distribute seventy-five million "voter guides" to influence the 2000 presidential election for a man who "loves the Lord." Although Robertson unsuccessfully urged Bush to spare born-again Christian Karla Faye Tucker's life, he has repeatedly praised the Texas governor in public forums.

"I never thought conservatism had to have a hard edge," Robertson, a former Republican candidate for president, told reporters at a banquet in politically crucial New Hampshire, where Bush was campaigning. "I believe the Republican Party must show a compassionate face. We can't always be talking about bottom lines and budgets and hard, cold business logic," he said. "We have to have some appeal to the families, to the mothers, to the women, to those less fortunate."

Bush also received a show of confidence from two native Texans who led the nation's largest Protestant denomination. "The Republican nomination is his to lose," the Reverend Paige Patterson, president of the Southern Baptist Convention told the press at an annual religious conference, noting that he was comfortable that a second Bush presidency would favor the conservative Christian agenda. The Reverend Richard Land, president of the commission that furthers the denomination's position on public policy issues, added, "I would say that most of the pro-life, conservative evangelical Christians I know are very excited about some of the things George W. Bush is saying and doing."

Although neither Patterson nor Land could endorse a presidential candidate because of their high-profile positions in the denomination, the public votes of confidence in Bush from the leaders of the almost 16-million mem-

---

*During an appearance on Robinson's nationally syndicated Christian TV show, Bush asked viewers to "pray that God will enter the hearts of fellow Americans, to have everyone help their neighbor" and laid out the basics of his "armies of compassion" concept, a direct descendant of his father's "thousand points of lights."

The televangelist, who had previously warned other conservative Christian leaders "may God forgive them" if they didn't support Bush, ended his joint TV appearance with the governor with a prayer, asking for an end to "the politics of personal destruction."

ber Southern Baptist Convention would certainly influence Christian conservatives who were concerned that the governor might be too moderate.

"Bush's 'compassionate conservatism' slogan is getting across to Americans what evangelical Christians had been advocating for years," Land claimed. "The governor is able to package the message in a way that shows the conservative agenda is not a mean-spirited critique of people's lives, but a way for the country to care for its people and reclaim its values."

The religious leader's evaluation of Bush's "compassionate conservatism" underscored the difficulty facing Bush as he tried to step through the quagmire of tricky social issues in his preparation for a White House bid. He could not win the Republican primaries without support from religious conservatives and to compete in a general election, he had to win the support of moderates as well.

But first Bush had to win reelection as governor of Texas.

★ 11 ★

Walk, Don't Run

If you had to bet your house, and you wouldn't want to, but if you had to bet your house today, you'd bet that in 24 months we will be sitting here worrying about Mr. Bush's cabinet.

—ABC political commentator George F. Will
in the wake of Governor Bush's 1998 landslide reelection

There's something a bit scary about the idea that someone is thinking about running, not because he burns to shape the nation, but because he seems to be in the right place, at the right time with the right name and right friends.

—CBS correspondent Rita Braver

The Dance Begins

Several months before Bush made his official announcement that he was seeking reelection as governor of Texas, there were intermittent news stories, both in Texas and nationally, speculating about his prospects of running for president in 2000 and headlines that he invariably tried to dismiss.

"Forget Washington!" he said repeatedly, noting that his focus was on winning another term in the state's highest office. "I don't think in terms of national or Republican. I think in terms of what is best for the state of Texas. I'm serious. I've got my hands full. It's a big state."

Even while protesting that his mind was strictly on Texas, however, the first term governor had been making several carefully chosen out-of-state trips, to party fund-raisers in South Carolina, Virginia, Ohio, and California, capitalizing on the national recognition he received the previous summer as cochairperson of the 1996 Republican National Convention with the popular New Jersey Governor Christine Todd Whitman.

At an Ohio fund-raiser for gubernatorial candidate Bob Taft, Bush was the center of attention. "People who normally write a check but not attend the event attended the event," said Brian Hicks, the manager of Taft's campaign. "And those who normally do both but don't care about pictures got a picture. Bush was a huge draw."

"He goes to gatherings where you could probably rightly say he's doing some fishing," said George Christian, political consultant and former press secretary to President Lyndon Johnson. "But he's pretty well kept that under wraps. The best politics is easygoing politics. Some of these fellas overdo it when they decide they want to run for something."

Back home in Texas, meanwhile, the governor continued to downplay any presidential ambitions, while privately relishing the sight of his photo on the front page of an out-of-state newspaper trumpeting him as a possible contender for the White House in 2000.

Despite his strong personal popularity among his constituents, Bush didn't want to offend voters who believed he viewed the governor's office as nothing more than a stepping-stone to the presidency. Although he publicly stated he never "took stock in polls," he was well aware of the fact that the latest survey of Texans showed that they were divided on whether he should run for president.

"I know there's a lot of speculation, but my head and my heart is right here at home," Bush told reporters, adding that he intended to put his "heart and soul into the job for four more years." Did that mean he was promising to serve a full four-year term if reelected? "No," he replied when he held a formal campaign kickoff for governor. "But we'll address that later."

Reelection to the Governor's Mansion was, in truth, the first step in a detailed plan designed to move him and his family to the White House in January 2001. Any presidential hopes that Bush coveted would certainly evaporate if he didn't win a second term by a respectable margin. A governor who barely squeezed back into office would be viewed as too weak to carry a national ticket.

Although Bush's primary political focus was to win reelection in a landslide, he couldn't ignore his national audience either. The challenge facing him in the coming months would be the pursuit of two political offices at the same time.

"THE RIGHT STUFF"

On December 3, 1997, less than a year from Election Day, Bush formally announced his campaign for a second term as governor of Texas at Sam Houston Elementary, his boyhood school in Midland.

"Today we face new challenges and choices," Bush told a large audience that had packed into the school's gymnasium. "The times are important. They call for a forward-thinking leader who will make the bold call, who will challenge the status quo, who will stand up and say, 'Follow me.' I am that leader."

With his wife, Laura, smiling at his side, Bush reflected on his first term record, noting that there was more local control of schools, welfare had been changed to put an emphasis on getting people back to work, lawsuit reform created greater fairness in the courts, and parole rates for criminals were the lowest in recorded state history.

"We have laid the foundation for a better tomorrow, and now it is time to build," the governor proclaimed, outlining his plans for a second term in office, based on issues of education, job creation, more law enforcement officials, and even more welfare reform.

The rhetoric of Bush's speech also drew on those by his father and former President Reagan, who won reelection in 1984 by declaring that it was "Morning in America." The governor borrowed a line from El Paso artist Tom Lea to say he wanted to live on the side of the mountain that saw the day dawning, not ending.

"I see the day that is coming," he said, "the day when every single child can read, the day when every single Texan who wants a job can find one, the day when every welfare mom finds the hope and the help she needs to change her life."

While reelection was the theme, Bush's announcement had an undertone that winning a second term as governor was simply the first step toward a run for the White House in 2000, especially after the publication of a recent poll showing the governor ahead of a likely field of Republican candidates in New Hampshire, the site of the first presidential primary.

Although he had promised for months that he would discuss any presidential aspirations when he formally announced his gubernatorial reelection campaign, Bush reneged on his vow in a press conference afterward, "I do not know today whether I will or will not run for president of the United States. I intend to get reelected governor."

Armed with a $13 million war chest of campaign funds, the Bushes left Midland for a six-day, twenty-four city tour designed to highlight the difference between himself and his Democratic challenger, Garry Mauro, the Texas Land Commissioner, who was trailing the popular governor by fifty percentage points in the polls.

Months before the hapless Mauro entered the race, Democratic powerbrokers in the state attempted to dissuade him from running, fearing that his lack of significant funds, name recognition, and traditional party base of support, would be a recipe for disaster for the entire Democratic ballot. Party leaders believed that the best strategy for maintaining control of the House and most statewide offices was to surrender the governorship to Bush and "take a pass" on running their own candidate against the charismatic incumbent.

Although several Texas Democrats dismissed the "surrender theory" variously as "ludicrous," "insane," or "pathetic," Mauro himself acknowledged that "the powerbrokers and the Austin insiders, a number of them, don't want me to run. Their argument is that if we leave Bush alone, somehow or other it will help the rest of the ticket."

Democratic Lieutenant Governor Bob Bullock, who was secretly battling lung cancer* and had decided against running for reelection, predicted that no candidate from his party would be able to unseat Bush and likened Mauro to a "kamikaze" if he persisted in running for governor. Interestingly, the powerful state official was the godfather of Mauro's daughter and his longtime political mentor. Mauro worked for Bullock from 1975 to 1977 when Bullock was state comptroller and he backed Mauro during his tenure as land commissioner, a post he had been elected to four times since 1982.

"He's a fine man, but he can't win that race. He can't do it," Bullock claimed, recalling that Republicans ran a token candidate against then-U.S. Senator Lloyd Bentsen in 1982, prompting Bentsen to raise and spend mil-

---

*When Bullock died in June 1999, only five months after leaving office, Bush interrupted his presidential campaign to return to Texas and eulogize the late Democratic leader as "a friend" who reached out to a "green governor across parties and generations." During a funeral service attended by legislators, former legislators, members of Congress, Lady Bird Johnson, and every living former Texas governor, Bush declared, "What a man! Can you imagine Bob Bullock and St. Peter?" he asked the hundreds of mourners. "Bob's got him locked in a conference room, and he won't let him out until he is happy with his plan for eternity."

lions of dollars to help the entire Democratic ticket. "The Democrats swept the ticket," Bullock said. "The same thing will happen this time" for the Republicans if Bush had a Democratic challenger. "I've often thought, 'Why doesn't Mauro go to Washington and get one of those jobs up there if he doesn't want to be land commissioner?' After all, he's close to Hillary and the President," Bullock noted.

Ironically, it was a sense of loyalty to the Clintons, close friends of Mauro for over two decades, that resulted in his political suicide run against Bush. According to several of Mauro's campaign aides, the gubernatorial candidate—who worked with Clinton on George McGovern's presidential campaign in 1972 and twenty years later coordinated the Texas support for Clinton's own race for the White House—was personally requested by the First Couple to run against Bush in an attempt to inflict damage against one of Al Gore's potential opponents for president in 2000.

Although the governor had managed to parlay a winning personality, a famous name and general public contentment with the state of the state, Mauro, a former football player on Texas A&M University's state championship team, continued to pound away at his Republican opponent, often claiming that his "good friend President Clinton" was responsible for Texas' strong, resurgent economy.

As the gap widened between Bush and Mauro in the polls, the Democratic candidate was subjected to unprecedented political humiliation as over a hundred statewide officeholders in his own party publicly deserted him and endorsed his Republican opponent,* including the state's top-ranking Democrat, Lieutenant Governor Bullock, despite his longtime friendship with Mauro.

"During my public career, I've served under seven governors, and Governor Bush is the best I've served under," Bullock announced to the press. "He has a personal and professional manner, as well as a work ethic and a proven record, that is outstanding. It just does not make good sense to retire a responsive and proven leader," Bullock asserted, adding that he thought Bush would also make a good president because the governor had made it a policy to work in a bipartisan way to ensure that his agenda passed the Legislature.

As Bush crisscrossed the state campaigning to become the first Texas governor to win back-to-back four-year terms, he was asked at virtually every

*Several Democratic candidates' TV ads even carried the slogan "Endorsed by Governor Bush."

stop if he was going to run for the Republican nomination for president in 2000, especially after a new CNN/*USA Today*/Gallup Poll showed Bush beating likely Democratic nominee, Vice President Al Gore, by several percentage points. Hounded by international TV news crews and reporters from the *Washington Post* to *GQ* magazine, Bush always repeated the same well-worn mantra, "I don't know at this point in time whether I will or will not seek the presidency," but intimations of a White House bid were everywhere.

The governor's well-funded, tightly controlled organization had the familiar feel of a professional presidential campaign—the handlers, the throngs of adoring crowds, the waving American flags, and, of course, the always present "Bush for President" signs.

At several campaign appearances he told cheering partisans, "I promise my fellow Texans I will bring honor and dignity to the great office of governor," a thinly veiled comparison to the White House and Clinton's sex scandal with Monica Lewinsky. The GOP frontrunner for the presidential nomination also did little to dampen speculation by claiming he had "the right stuff" to inherit his father's old job and noting that his wife "knows she can be a great first lady of America."

Several political analysts complained that Bush's Hamlet routine ("I haven't made up my mind one way or another") was wearing thin, particularly when he recited a litany of reasons why he would make a great president. Mauro, noting that several polls indicated Texas voters wanted the governor to end the speculation, began driving the point home in his campaign stump speeches around the state.

"I respect Governor Bush's indecision, but when you're running for governor of the second-largest state in the Union and when you have such a unique opportunity in history, I really think Governor Bush ought to speed up his decision-making process and tell the people of Texas," the Democratic candidate said. "Generally, I think it's good for Texas when a Texan decides to run for national office. But if George Bush is going to run for governor, he ought to focus on the challenges facing this state."

According to *Washington Post* columnist David Broder, Bush flatly stated during his campaign in 1998, "I'm interested in being president or I would have said 'no' to the possibility before this. I really made the decision to be in the hunt when I announced for reelection."

However, Bush did not expect his popularity to skyrocket so quickly on the national scene, occurring at least six months ahead of the plan he and his key strategists had painstakingly choreographed. Now the incessant speculation of whether he was running for president had overshadowed his bid for reelection and accelerated the process of media scrutiny, or as he described it, "life in the bubble" for him and his family.

Determined not to allow the increased attention to interfere with the preordained timetable to announce his presidential ambitions after the 1999 legislative session concluded in mid-year, Bush, his Texas advisers, and Washington consultants, recommitted themselves to The Bush Plan, their blueprint for the governor's accession to the presidency.

Step 1: Win Reelection in a Landslide

Republicans and Democrats around the country would be looking at the size of his victory margin and the length of his political coattails in other statewide elections. Although Bush held a fifty-point lead over Mauro almost from the first day of his reelection campaign, his aim was to keep the race from tightening and set sixty percent of the vote as his goal.

To build that margin, he campaigned throughout the state, beginning with his twenty-four city swing in six days following his formal reelection announcement ("Got to show them I want the job"). Over the course of the next eleven months, he mastered hand-to-hand politics, managing to become as much a Lone Star celebrity as Ann Richards at the height of her popularity. Wading into crowds at rallies, he shook hands, clutched arms, patted shoulders, and gave hugs, "pressing the flesh" as another legendary Texas politician, Lyndon Johnson, used to say.

Looser and more accessible than his father ever was, Bush posed for photographs with women with thick manes of freshly lacquered snow-white hair like his famous mother and signed autographs for young, giggly girls who reacted as if they were face to face with a rock star.

Bush's campaign speeches were funny, self-deprecating, and mercifully short. Dressed in jeans and cowboy boots, his West Texas accent was thicker and folksier in the rural parts of the state than when he addressed well-scrubbed, thick-walleted business leaders in Dallas while attired in a pin-striped suit.

"His strengths are his ability to read the political environment and sense the best way to articulate a vision so that it comes across," revealed Karl Rove, the governor's chief political consultant.

"I am a political animal," the governor admitted, "but I don't think campaigns are terribly profound. The issues are profound. The debate should be profound. But campaigning is really just a matter of getting the message out to the voters and getting the voters to the polls. It's not complicated."

A much better campaigner than he was four years earlier, the youthful and personable Bush had mastered the Clintonesque ability of talking with people from all walks of life about a variety of topics. In 1994, he was an untested Republican challenger who had to persuade voters he was more than just a brash businessman with a famous father who wanted to lead Texas. Now he was a formidable candidate for reelection, telling voters on the campaign trail, "I want to win and I want to win big."

STEP 2: CAPTURE THE MAJORITY OF THE HISPANIC VOTE

In the early years of the twentieth century, Democrats were the first to meet boatloads of immigrants to America, offering help, sometimes giving them a silver dollar and earning their loyalty at election time. But increasingly over the years, Hispanics, who have typically voted Democratic, have become more fundamentally conservative in outlook, fiscally and socially, and moved to the GOP side of the ballot.

Around forty million persons of Hispanic origin, nearly 14 percent of the population lived in the U.S. at the time of the 1998 elections. Hispanics constituted the largest single ethnic and cultural minority in the U.S., and would account for a majority of the population in Texas and California by 2020. More importantly, Hispanic voters were predicted to account for 5 percent of the national turnout in the 1998, the highest ever. And for the first time, they were the swing vote in at least seven key races across the country.*

Bush, who received 24 percent of the Hispanic vote in his first gubernatorial race in 1994, set a goal of capturing 40 percent of their votes in his reelection bid in 1998 in an effort to increase his margin of victory over his Democratic opponent. In addition, setting a record for Hispanic votes gar-

---

*According to Al Gore's aides in 1999, the vice president was so eager to court the growing number of Hispanic voters, he was considering one of their own as a potential candidate for the number two spot on a Gore 2000 presidential ticket. Topping the list of possibilities, at least until the Chinese spy scandal involving U.S. nuclear weapons facilities generated adverse publicity, was Energy Secretary Bill Richardson, the popular former congressman from New Mexico who previously served as Bill Clinton's ambassador to the United Nations. Others included California's Lieutenant Governor Cruz Bustamante and Assembly speaker Antonio Villaraigosa, Los Angeles County Supervisor Gloria Molina, and Miami-Dade Mayor Alex Penelas.

nered by a statewide Republican candidate in Texas, would expand his appeal to the minority group nationally. Bush's aides advised him that "we have within our reach the ability to influence" the outcome in ten states, which accounted for 214 of the 270 electoral votes needed to win the presidency.

"I think it's very important for me to show, if I can do well, to show that there's a way to attract votes," the governor acknowledged. "The Hispanic vote is essentially a conservative vote. It is pro-family, it is pro–free enterprise, it historically has been a pro-military vote, it is a very Catholic vote, and, therefore, it's a vote that should be garnered by people of my philosophy."

Recognizing the potential of the Hispanic vote, Bush poured close to a fourth of his high-dollar ad campaign in 1998 into luring their allegiance, including Spanish and English radio and television commercials as well as outdoor billboards. The bilingual governor also stormed across the state, meeting with community leaders; appearing side-by-side at festive rallies with Tejano music star, Emilio; and actively lobbying the Republican National Committee to choose San Antonio, the nation's largest majority Hispanic city, as the site of the party's national convention in 2000. If the Lone Star State's governor was selected as the Republican nominee for president, the resulting Texas drama would make the kind of political statement that could prove invaluable to a party emphasizing its message of an inclusive "big tent."*

"I hope to show that Republicans do have a heart, but I also want to send a message to people from around the country as to how to pick up the Hispanic vote," Bush told the press. "I know what the future's going to look like here [in the Southwest] and we'd better make sure Hispanic children are educated, that Hispanic entrepreneurs and parents are given encouragement, the same as anyone else gets. And yet the language of the Ross Perots and the Pat Buchanans and the AFL-CIO basically says, 'Forget Mexico! Wall them off!' While the language of English-only basically says, from the Hispanic perspective, 'Me, not you. We don't care about you.' When in fact we do. Or at least I do."†

---

*Two days after the 1998 election, the Republican National Committee announced it had chosen Philadelphia as the host city for the GOP convention in 2000.

†The president of the Washington-based National Council of La Raza, the country's largest Hispanic civil rights advocacy group, criticized the Texas governor and presidential front-runner in July 1999, for not addressing its national convention in Houston. "We are disap-

Bush's record proved otherwise and some Hispanics complained that the Texas governor was practicing what they called in California, "Sombrero Politics," where politicians eager to cater to the Hispanic vote, paid a visit to their neighborhood, wore a Mexican sombrero, spoke a few words in Spanish, ate a burrito, took a few photographs for political ads, and then left.

While on the campaign trail in 1998, Bush said "It's very important for the Republican Party not to be seen as anti-Hispanic," but during his first term he had aggressively supported the construction of the Sierra Blanca radioactive waste dump in West Texas; proposed the installation of additional steel fencing ("a Berlin Wall") between Texas and Mexico to help control illegal immigration; opposed any concession of water rights to drought-stricken northern Mexico from Rio Grande reservoirs in Texas; and remained silent on the GOP platform that endorsed a constitutional amendment ending automatic citizenship of illegals born in the U.S.

The *Texas Observer*'s investigative reporter, Nate Blakeslee, claimed that the governor's attempt to develop a "special relationship" with Hispanics during the 1998 campaign was "unprecedented in its scope and ambition," but marked by a significant "lack of substance." One in every three Hispanic children in Texas was without health insurance of any kind and "life along the border has not improved under the Bush administration," Blakeslee wrote, noting the lack of running water, streets without signs and lights, and some of the most deplorable housing conditions in the developed world, where disease rates soared above state and national averages. "The border remains underdeveloped because of a lack of public investment in education, hospitals, and general infrastructure," Blakeslee concluded.*

Barbara Renaud Gonzalez, writing for the *Houston Chronicle,* claimed that the bilingual governor had "used the magic of Spanish to seduce Lati-

---

pointed," said Raul Yzaguirre. "Some of our people are a little angry he didn't show up. If he's taking us for granted, he is misreading our community."

Although GOP challenger, Senator John McCain, and Vice President Al Gore addressed the conference and its 12,000 participants, Mindy Tucker, a Bush spokesperson, said the governor was with his family in Maine, but he had visited with Hispanic groups while campaigning in Michigan, California, and Iowa.

Yzaguirre stated he also found it "troublesome" that Bush did not attend other Latino events, skipping a recent gathering of the League of the United Latin American Citizens, which was also held in the governor's home state, and the National Association of Latino Elected and Appointed Officials in Philadelphia.

*Before leaving Texas to begin his presidential campaign in June 1999, the governor signed a new law bringing basic services to more border residents and preventing the spread of substandard developments.

nos who are desperate to be part of a Texas that is ours to begin with," she wrote, noting that Hispanics in the state had higher rates of infant and maternal mortality, cardiovascular diseases, cancer fatality, HIV infections, and lower life expectancy when compared to the white population. "Bush has mastered the illusion of indifference, while everything remains exactly the same," Gonzalez claimed. "And we gladly fall on our knees because we have been hungry so long."

STEP 3: ELECT A REPUBLICAN LIEUTENANT GOVERNOR

Texas is a state in which the governor and the lieutenant governor run separately and are occasionally from different parties, as was the case with Bush and Bob Bullock. Equally important and politically portentous, Texas is also a state in which the lieutenant governor is not just an understudy waiting in the wings for the chief executive officer to die or become incapacitated—or get elected president—but instead has genuine political clout, since the official presides over the state Senate, chairs the state budget board, and appoints Senate committees. The Texas lieutenant governor essentially has the power but not the glory.

With only the size of Bush's margin over Mauro in doubt, the most important statewide race on the ballot in 1998 was for lieutenant governor, between John Sharp, the Democratic state comptroller, and Rick Perry, the Republican commissioner of agriculture. If Bush traded the Governor's Mansion for the White House, the lieutenant governor would succeed him in Texas. If Sharp won, Texas Republicans would not be pleased with the idea of turning over the governorship of the second-largest state to a Democrat, and Bush's potential presidential rivals would criticize him for putting his own political ambitions ahead of the good of the Republican Party.

As part of The Bush Plan to ensure that Perry became the first Republican lieutenant governor in Texas history, Bush's political strategists orchestrated a massive and expensive voter registration and turnout campaign, targeted to fast-growing suburban counties, which the governor hoped would provide a coattail boost for Perry and other statewide GOP candidates.

Although Sharp and Perry were statistically tied in the polls throughout most of the campaign, Bush's advisers developed a game plan for Perry that resembled a frontrunner's. Based on their confident projections, if the voter turnout was 4.5 million—one hundred thousand more than voted in 1994—and Bush received 60 percent, Perry would secure a nine hundred thousand vote margin. To defeat his Republican opponent, Sharp would have to persuade 450,000 voters to abandon the GOP. If either the turnout or the governor's margin of victory on Election Day was higher, Sharp would have to reverse more than five hundred thousand votes. Bush's political consultants and strategists calculated the only way Sharp could be elected lieutenant governor was a low voter turnout among Republicans due to overconfidence in the ticket, which, they believed, was a very remote possibility.

Bush, acknowledging publicly that the outcome of the lieutenant governor's race would be "a factor" in his decision whether to seek the presidency, solicited his father's help in securing Perry's election. The former president committed himself to only two fund-raisers during the entire 1998 campaign and they both were for Perry. In addition, the elder Bush taped several television ads in which he lavished praise on the Republican candidate. "You have an opportunity here to elect a man to perhaps the most powerful position in the state of Texas," he said. "Everyone in our family strongly supports him. You have a good man. My heart is where Barbara's is, where George's is, in the Perry corner."

STEP 4: ELECT HIS BROTHER AS FLORIDA GOVERNOR

In 1994, Jeb Bush led incumbent Florida governor, Lawton Chiles, by several percentage points in the polls going into the final weeks of the campaign. The legendary Chiles, who never lost an election in almost forty years, closed the gap with a last-minute deluge of Democratic cash, attack ads, and a folksy performance in several televised debates. Bush lost by sixty thousand votes out of 3.5 million cast, the closest election in modern Florida history.

In 1998, he faced Buddy MacKay, a longtime congressman and Chiles' lieutenant governor for the past eight years, but Bush was leading by seventeen points in the polls, mainly because he had moved from conservative ideologue to consensus-building problem solver. During the 1994 race, Bush chose an outspoken born-again Christian legislator as his running mate and raised his opposition to abortion as a campaign issue. He also largely ignored black voters, who traditionally voted Democratic in Florida, even going so far as to candidly tell an African-American woman he'd do "probably nothing" for her community if elected.

Four years later, the more personable and inclusive candidate actively courted blacks, and made much of the charter school he cofounded in a deeply impoverished, mostly black Miami neighborhood. He also downplayed his conservative principles, not side-stepping the abortion issue, but not raising it either. And his running mate was a middle-of-the-road, nononsense Republican star in Florida politics.

Ironically, political analysts predicted Jeb would win the Florida governor's race in 1994, and his brother, George W., would be unlikely to unseat the popular Ann Richards in Texas. Four years later, the oldest brother tore a page out of his playbook and advised Jeb how to win an election: temper your arrogance, admit you were wrong, reach out to new audiences, and stay focused on a short list of priorities. No less important, Jeb's Hispanic wife gave him a direct line to the largest minority in Florida, and soon to be the largest in the country.

How strategically important to The Bush Plan was Jeb's election as governor of Florida? The Sunshine State was the nation's third most populous state with twenty-five electoral votes, which combined with Texas' thirty-two, Bush would lock up fifty-seven of the 270 votes needed to win the presidency. In addition, with the brothers in the statehouse in both Texas and Florida, one in eight Americans would be governed by a Bush. Joining the Roosevelts, Rockefellers, and Kennedys as political dynasties would also have a "snowball effect," according to George W.'s political strategists. Political lineages brought name recognition, experience, and even gave voters a sense of stability, they reasoned.

To ensure an Election Day double victory, the Bush clan turned out in force in Florida, including former first lady Barbara, who sat directly in front of MacKay at the fourth and final debate between the Democrat and her son. Her mission: cheer up Jeb, charm the media and the audience and, most importantly, with her infamous icy stare, shame MacKay into backing down from his strident attacks on her son's business dealings and associates, his judgment and his lack of elective experience.

The Texas governor also dispatched his political strategists to organize Jeb's campaign effort and develop negative television ads that branded Buddy MacKay as a tax-and-spend progeny of big government. Particularly effective were commercials taglined, "He's Not My Buddy!" which nearly doubled Jeb's lead in the polls when they were aired.

More importantly, George W.'s political-financial network garnered more than a $1 million in Texas for his brother's campaign in Florida, which raised concerns among the press, who noted that one-fifth of the Sunshine State political donations came from oil interests. Reporters, state Democratic Party officials and environmentalists loudly voiced their suspicions that the contributions were from oil companies eager to drill offshore in Florida waters, particularly in the Keys.

"If the Democrats in Florida don't understand brotherly love then they better reassess their emotions," responded the Texas governor. "I help my brother because he is my brother. If he asked for help, I'm more than willing to help him."

Florida Democratic Party Chairman Mitch Caesar suspected many of the Texas political contributions to Jeb's gubernatorial campaign were actually intended to help his older brother carry the densely populated state in a bid for the presidency in 2000. "Why would anyone in Texas want to give money to Florida?" he asked. "Obviously, it's his brother. They're playing politics with Florida's future."

William March, a reporter for the *Tampa Tribune* agreed the sudden surge of political donations to Jeb's gubernatorial campaign from well-heeled Texans had more to do with George W. "His supporters back home know that if he runs for president, it would help him greatly to have a Republican in the Florida Governor's Mansion—especially if it's his brother."

Election Day

Texas Governor Bush achieved the first step of his blueprint for his election to the presidency when he celebrated a massive Lone Star landslide of historic proportions on November 3, 1998, winning 69 percent of the vote against his Democratic rival, Garry Mauro, whom he outspent 4-to-1.* Bush received the largest percentage of the vote ever won by a Republican statewide candidate in Texas, and in the process carried every region of the state and 240 of its 254 counties. He won nearly two of three votes in the state's two most populous counties, carrying Harris County (Houston), the state's largest, with 65 percent, and Dallas, the second largest, with almost 66 percent. Bush also became the first Republican gubernatorial candidate ever to carry heavily Hispanic El Paso County, despite a campaign appearance for Mauro by Vice President Al Gore, and historically Democrat Travis County, the seat of state government in Austin, with 60 percent.

*Mauro struggled to raise about $5 million even with the help of campaign appearances by President Clinton, the First Lady, and Vice President Al Gore. Bush topped $17 million, with contributions from every state in the Union.

The governor garnered 65 percent of the women's vote (up from 50 percent four years earlier), and 49 percent of the Hispanic vote, easily surpassing his goal of 40 percent as outlined in step two of The Bush Plan to capture the presidency. Additionally, he made strong inroads among African-American voters with 27 percent (an increase of 15 percent since 1994),* nearly one out of every three Democrats (31 percent), and nearly three of every four Independents, while securing 98 percent of the Republican vote.

The governor's commanding victory was not a solitary one as he carried all fourteen statewide Republican candidates, including the lieutenant governor-elect Rick Perry, into office on his momentum and long political coattails. In Florida, Jeb Bush triumphed as governor, handily beating his Democratic opponent, Buddy MacKay, marking the first time since the Civil War that Republicans controlled both the Governor's Mansion and the Florida Legislature. Jeb's victory made the Bush brothers the first siblings to occupy state governorships simultaneously since 1967, when Nelson Rockefeller served as chief executive of New York and his brother Winthrop presided over Arkansas.

The Texas governor also demonstrated in his reelection bid that he was a compelling campaigner and that he could raise a great deal of money—skills that were essential in a national race. Bush and the Texas first lady helped collect $10,426,861 for Republican candidates and GOP organizations across the country by appearing separately and jointly at seventy-two fund-raising events in 1998. Fifty-four of the appearances were for Texas office-seekers and Republican Party groups. (In addition, the couple raised almost $4 million at thirty political events in 1997 as preparation for the 1998 election.)

Logistically, Bush's well-oiled campaign machine had the feel of a presidential bid, or at least the final tune-up for the big event to come. "Mauro was outspent and outmaneuvered, but he fought the good fight in every way possible,"† remarked Allan Saxe, political scientist at the University of Texas at Arlington and a columnist for the *Fort Worth Star-Telegram.*

---

*After the election, two other exit polls conducted by the nonpartisan Southwest Voter Registration Education Project, and Dallas political analyst Dr. Dan Weiser, contested the surveys of the Associated Press and television news organizations, alleging that the media didn't poll enough voters in heavily Hispanic and black precincts. The new studies indicated that the governor drew 37 percent of the Hispanic vote, instead of 49, and received only 6 percent of the African-American vote, compared to the previously reported 27 percent.

†During their one televised debate two weeks before the election, political analysts praised Mauro as being well-informed, better prepared, and more knowledgeable about state government than the governor on several points. With Bush leading his Democratic opponent by

Even Bush's election night speech to a packed ballroom of loyalists sounded very much like a stump speech for the presidency. "Tonight's resounding victory says my compassionate, conservative philosophy is making Texas a better place," the governor proclaimed, with his wife and one of his twin daughters at his side. "But today's election says something more. It says that a leader who is compassionate and conservative can erase the gender gap, can open the doors of the Republican Party to new faces and new voices."

Bush was sending a clear message to his political party on an election night when the GOP lost five House seats, failed to make gains in the Senate and saw their control of state governorships slip from thirty-two to thirty-one, including the loss of California. It was the first time since 1934 that the party of the president gained seats during a midterm election.

In post-election damage assessment, Republicans agreed that their message had somehow gotten lost in the year-long anti-Clinton rhetoric of the Monica Lewinsky affair and impending impeachment hearings. Before voters had gone to the polls, House Speaker Newt Gingrich and his GOP cohorts in Congress had anticipated that an electorate sickened by Clinton's sexgate scandal would swing to the right and increase the Republican majority in the House by a dozen seats. The voters instead awarded Democrats with more seats in the lower chamber.

"I totally underestimated the degree with which people just get sick of twenty-four-hour-a-day talk television and talk radio, the degree to which this whole scandal just became sort of disgusting by sheer repetition," admitted Gingrich, who vowed only a few months earlier that he would mention "Monica" in every speech. "We probably should have almost maniacally focused on cutting taxes, reforming government, working on saving Social Security."

"If you make it a referendum on a president with a sixty-seven percent approval rating, you shouldn't be surprised if the election goes against you," Bush told his inner circle, noting that the GOP leadership, in a last-minute campaign personally approved by Gingrich, began pummeling the Democrats in targeted congressional districts with $10 million worth of TV ads concentrating on Clinton's affair with the young White House intern.

---

almost fifty points, why did the governor provide Mauro with the opportunity to potentially score a late-round knockout punch? "It was dress rehearsal for a national campaign," explained one of Bush's political strategists. "The governor needed to go one-on-one with an opponent, sort of like a sparring partner, as practice for upcoming debates against Quayle or Buchanan or, even Al Gore, who surprisingly kicked Perot's ass during a debate about NAFTA on Larry King's CNN show."

1998 ELECTION RESULTS

	Bush (percent)	Mauro (percent)	Bush Improvement Over 1994 (percent)
All	69	30	16
Male	72	27	14
Female	65	34	16
White	78	21	16
Black	27	71	12
Hispanic	49	50	21
18–29	67	33	9
30–44	68	32	14
45–59	66	31	14
60+	71	29	23
$15,000–30,000 income	59	41	8
$30,000–50,000 income	67	32	12
$50,000–75,000 income	76	23	23
$75,000–100,000 income	68	32	8
Over $100,000 income	74	22	11
High school graduate	65	35	15
Some college	75	25	17
College graduate	68	31	10
Post-graduate	65	32	17
Democrat	31	69	21
Republican	98	2	11
Independent/other	73	24	16
Liberal	28	72	10
Moderate	60	40	21
Conservative	90	10	11

Overall turnout for the 1998 election was the worst in at least two decades of gubernatorial races in Texas. Only 32.5 of the state's registered voters cast ballots.

Bush, whose landslide victory and voter-friendly "compassionate conservative" agenda enhanced his position as the front-runner for the Republican presidential nomination in 2000, urged GOP leaders around the country to push for Gingrich's resignation from Congress immediately following the election. Bush stated that a different style of leadership was needed now, more collegial, more detail-oriented, and less confrontational. Quoting GOP consultant Mike Murphy, he declared, "We have to stop wrapping our cookies in barbed wire."

In a telephone conversation with one Republican congressman, the Texas governor said, "Look, I'm probably going to run for president. I think I can get the nomination. If I lose the presidency to Al Gore, I want it to be because of my own mistakes, not because of Newt Gingrich," who had been demonized in Democratic attack ads during the 1998 election as the mastermind behind GOP extremism and callousness.

Under siege from members of his own party, abandoned by his protégés and admirers, and forced with ultimatums from Republican leaders across the country, Gingrich announced only seventy-two hours after the election that he was not only going to surrender the speakership but would resign from Congress. "I'm not willing to preside over people that are cannibals," he angrily and bitterly complained to his fellow Republicans.

For the Texas governor, the nation's biggest GOP winner in the party's otherwise disastrous midterm elections, the House Speaker's abrupt departure was sweet revenge. In the early 1990s, then-Minority Whip Gingrich earned a reputation as a nonconformist by sabotaging President Bush's budget compromise by claiming that the White House made concessions to congressional Democrats. Gingrich also attacked the president during his 1992 reelection campaign for maintaining the status quo and failing to promote a more strident, right-wing agenda.

Six years later, Gingrich had been run out of office and another Bush was being hailed as the future leader of the divided and dispirited Grand Old Party.

The Texas Two-Step

A major part of The Bush Plan to win the presidency was to delay his official announcement as long as he could without sacrificing his front-runner status in the polls. As one of his top political strategists put it, "It's kind of like the woman who plays hard to get. The more you are merely fantasizing and not meeting the real woman, the higher your expectations get."

On the morning after the 1998 election, with polls showing him beating Vice President Gore by twelve percentage points, Bush faced a phalanx of TV cameras and a host of international media representatives and claimed that he had not decided whether he would run for president in 2000. "There's a time for politics. That ended last night," he said. "Now it's time for policy. The only thing I can tell you about all this speculation is that it's just that, and I won't make up my mind until after the legislative session gets started. The only future I'm thinking about is how I will get what I campaigned on into law."

During his reelection campaign, the governor promised voters another property tax cut, more welfare reform, and a crackdown on juvenile crime. He also pledged to end "social promotions" of students and to ensure that every child learned to read.

The governor's success in filling his campaign promises could be the first indication of how he would fare as a national candidate. "He needs to set a direction for the national Republican Party based on issues and forget about the expectations game," said Scott Reed, who managed Bob Dole's 1996 presidential campaign. "Focus on issues and everything will take care of itself."

As predetermined in The Bush Plan, the governor would announce a presidential exploratory committee (which would allow him to raise money) in March, after he'd presented his proposals to the state Legislature, and then declare his candidacy later in the summer, when the biennial session concluded. If he made his anticipated announcement before the governing body's conclusion, his advisers believed he would be lambasted mercilessly for not paying enough attention to the state's business. In the intervening four months, the seemingly coy Bush had to bide his time by being as notoriously elusive as the Texas Two-Step–dancing Lone Star governor in the hit Broadway play and movie, *The Best Little Whorehouse in Texas.*

Immediately following the election, Bush engaged in one of the most time-honored and delicate rituals of American politics: claiming that he was not running for president while walking in the right direction at a pace he hoped would be of his own choosing. Journalists repeatedly reported that one could not spend much time talking to the governor without sensing a real reluctance.

"I'm not sure that I want to spend the rest of my life living in the bubble," he often said, claiming that he was having the time of his life being governor of Texas, where he could go to a Rangers baseball game or drop in for a Sunday service at a black church. "I would never be able to go into a fishing store by myself and buy fishing lures and get out on a lake by myself," he contended.

After he exhausted the ploy of personal reluctance towards losing his privacy, Bush claimed he had reservations about putting his family, especially his teenage daughters, "through the meat grinder of national politics." In a joint press conference with his wife, Laura, the governor said he was interested in running for president, but would weigh his family's concerns.*

"I don't know many seventeen-year-old girls who'd say, 'Dad, gosh, I can't wait for you to drive me into the national spotlight,' particularly given the way the atmosphere is these days," their father said, noting that he and his wife shared the Clintons' "profound sadness" over *People* magazine's decision to do a cover story on their daughter, Chelsea. Adding that his two girls, Jenna and Barbara, would be entering college in 2000, the same year of the presidential race, the governor said he was "mindful of their sentiments," but claimed the ultimate decision of whether he would make a White House bid would be his. "I would lie down and die for 'em," he drawled. "But they don't have a veto on this."

While the Texas governor maintained he was still officially undecided, though "thinking about it a lot," political observers noted that he was carefully laying the groundwork for a national campaign. "Bush is running," CBS's Dan Rather said matter-of-factly of the governor's feigned indecision. "He may get knocked out along the way, or he may yet decide to pull out. But his campaign is already formed, well-financed, and moving forward."

Bush held a series of private meetings at the Governor's Mansion with small groups of prominent and wealthy Republicans, whose support he sought to help raise the $25 million typically needed for a presidential campaign. "He said, 'Obviously I'm considering this and you guys would be important if I elect to go forward,'" said Brad Freeman, an acquisition specialist and longtime Bush friend from Los Angeles. Another California attendee

*In 1991, Bush, his wife, and their young daughters, received round-the-clock Secret Service protection after Iraqi dictator Saddam Hussein threatened their lives in retaliation for the elder Bush's presidential role in the Persian Gulf War.

was Howard Leach, one of the nation's largest contributors to Republican candidates and a national finance chairman of the GOP.*

Bush met several times with a group of public policy experts who discussed foreign relations, Social Security, and tax reforms as issues he would pursue in a presidential contest. Present at the briefings were former U.S. Secretary of State George Shultz, former U.S. Secretary of Defense Dick Cheney, former White House Council of Economic Affairs chief Michael Boskin, economist Martin Anderson, former arms control negotiator Paul Wolfowitz, and others, such as Condoleezza Rice, an expert on the Soviet Union in the Bush administration.

Indianapolis Mayor Stephen Goldsmith, a free-market advocate and proponent of privatization, headed a group that advised Bush on domestic policy. Larry Lindsey, a former Federal Reserve governor and Harvard professor who authored a book defending the Reagan tax cuts discussed economic matters with the governor, noting his concerns about the declining national savings rate, increasing U.S. indebtedness to foreigners, and the possibility of a global meltdown. Martin S. Feldstein, professor of economics at Harvard and a sharp critic of President Clinton's Social Security plan, flew from Boston to Texas to brief Bush, but claimed before he could gain entry into the governor's inner circle of advisers, he had to promise support for Bush's unannounced presidential bid.

The governor also sought to bolster an international image during "listen and learn" meetings with Israeli and Egyptian leaders in the Middle East, although he claimed the "nonpolitical" trip was merely a vacation with his wife. Welcomed in Israel as a full-fledged foreign dignitary, Bush encountered a firestorm of controversy, however, when Jewish leaders asked him to clarify previous remarks he had made on religion.

In a 1993 interview in his Dallas office before the formal kickoff of his first gubernatorial campaign, George W. told the *Houston Chronicle* of asking evangelist and family friend, Billy Graham, to referee a family discussion

---

*Bill Clinton, who won California in 1992 and 1996, was the first Democratic presidential candidate to carry the Golden State since 1964, and Republicans were anxious to stage a comeback. Wealthy donors committed to Bush include the CEOs of Cisco Systems and National Semiconductor Corp., two Silicon Valley giants; Stockton developer Alex Spanos, owner of the San Diego Chargers football team; media magnate Rupert Murdoch; developer Donald Bren of Newport Beach; and Costa Mesa investor George Argyros, former owner of the Seattle Mariners baseball team.

A private Democratic poll put Bush in front of Gore in California, a state the vice president had courted assiduously. Whoever wins California in 2000, will almost certainly move to the White House, especially if he has Texas's and Florida's electoral votes in hand.

by telephone. Bush, a Methodist, said he had told his mother, an Episcopalian, that he believed there was no place in heaven for anyone who did not accept Jesus Christ as personal savior. His mother called Graham, who agreed with Bush's "interpretation of the New Testament," but warned mother and son to "never play God" and "don't be harshly judgmental of others." Bush's comments to the press caused a brief stir at the time, particularly in the Jewish press, but were never a major campaign issue.

After his overwhelming reelection and his front-runner status as a potential presidential candidate in late 1998, the *New York Times* revived the controversial remarks in a major profile. Just before departing for his "family vacation" to the Middle East, Bush briefed reporters on his international agenda while attending a Republican Governors Association meeting in New Orleans. Although clearly going for a laugh at his own expense, he said the first thing he was going to say to his Israeli hosts was that they were all "going to hell."

Jews, who already questioned Bush's 1993 religious intolerance comment, called the New Orleans quip "inappropriate." Walking the tightrope of a probable presidential candidate, the governor couldn't afford to offend the Christian right-wing whose political involvement was guided by their religious beliefs, nor could the governor alienate influential Jewish voters.

At a press conference in Texas upon his return from the Middle East, reporters asked him how he explained his earlier remarks to Jewish leaders in Israel. "My faith tells me that acceptance of Jesus Christ as my savior is my salvation," Bush responded. "And I believe that. I also, though, made it very clear that it's not the governor's role to decide who goes to heaven. . . . That's God's role."

In another attempt at expanding his foreign policy credentials Bush played golf with Argentine President Carlos Menem, who was on a state visit to the U.S. that included meetings with President Clinton and other Washington officials. He hosted a meeting at the Governor's Mansion with William Hague, the head of Britain's Conservative Party, who wanted to discuss Bush's "compassionate conservatism" themes. The Tory leader said afterward that he believed he could gain valuable insights from the governor in the same way that Prime Minister Tony Blair learned from President Clinton.

As the Texas Capitol took on the look of a mini-United Nations, Bush also conducted meetings with former Canadian Prime Minister Brain Mulroney, whose tenure was viewed as a disaster for his Conservative Party, and two dignitaries from the Persian Gulf nation of Qatar. The governor told the press the presidential "speculation has seemed to have caused more governments to send their ambassadors my way."

In preparation for the early primaries, Bush sent letters to veteran campaign organizers in New Hampshire, asking them to "keep their powder dry" and delay taking positions with other presidential candidates. He also called Steve Grubbs, past chairman of the Iowa GOP, to congratulate him on the birth of his fourth child and talk politics. "The fact that I'm calling you shows that I'm interested in Iowa," Grubbs quoted Bush as saying, noting that the state held its presidential caucus just before the New Hampshire primary.

In the governor's second-term inaugural address, he fleshed out themes that transcended the borders of Texas and sounded like the elements of a likely presidential campaign. Using the same trio of ideas that had powered almost all of President Clinton's major addresses, Bush spoke of the need to expand opportunity, demand individual responsibility, and nurture a sense of community across racial lines.

In an appeal to minority voters, the governor appointed Michael Williams, an African-American and former assistant secretary of education for civil rights in the Bush White House, to a vacancy on the three-member Texas Railroad Commission, the powerful agency which regulated the state's oil and gas production. Williams noted to the media it "would be inappropriate to suggest that race played no role" in his appointment. Bush also named a Hispanic, Al Gonzales, to the Texas Supreme Court.

The governor included in his expanding national network of advisers, Ron Pacheco, who in 1996 became the first Hispanic Republican elected to the California Legislature in 115 years. In the 1998 elections, he rose to minority leader of the Assembly, and Bush called soon afterwards with congratulations and an invitation to come to Texas for a meeting. "It's logical" politically, Pacheco noted, given the strategically important role California and Hispanic voters would play in the 2000 election. "But I didn't get a call from anybody else that's running for president. That tells me that he knows what he's doing, and he's paying attention," Pacheco told *USA Today.*

Pledging not to travel out of Texas on political trips while the state Legislature was in session during the first five months of 1999, Bush sent videos detailing his accomplishments to key campaign donors, to elected Republicans in state and national offices, and GOP activists throughout the country. The tapes contained speeches, campaign ads, interviews and television news footage, including multiple references to Bush's possible entry into the 2000 presidential race. Using a combination of heroic music, slow motion, and a variety of film formats, the tapes' longer tribute pieces had an unmistakable documentary feel.

In response, a majority of the Republicans in the California state Legislature sent Bush a letter urging him to run for president. "We ask for your favorable consideration to lead America as our president, and we commit to you our support," the petition said, which was signed by twenty-two of thirty-two Republicans in the state Assembly and three of fifteen GOP senators, including all four Hispanic Republicans.

The Draft Bush 2000 Committee, comprised of almost a hundred current and former Republican members of Congress, also signed a letter of support urging the governor to run for president. The group was spearheaded by retired Representative Gerald Solomon* and Staten Island borough president and former congressman Guy Molinari, who served as the elder Bush's New York presidential campaign chairman in 1988. The committee announced its formation after a new poll among Republicans in New Hampshire showed Elizabeth Dole, the former cabinet secretary and wife of the GOP's 1996 presidential nominee, in a virtual tie with Bush in the New England state.

A delegation of North Carolina lawmakers delivered yet another letter from fifteen Republican state senators and thirty-eight of the state's fifty-four GOP House members promising their support if Bush ran for president. After their meeting at the Governor's Mansion, the legislators told the press that they hoped he named North Carolina native Dole as his running mate. They noted that the governor should head the ticket because he had a proven record of winning elections in Texas, but Dole had held only appointed positions in the Reagan and Bush administrations.

At the urging of the governor's father, former president Gerald Ford also publicly endorsed Bush as the GOP's best hope to regain the White House and suggested that Mrs. Dole should be a vice presidential candidate.

Arriving in two private airplanes, a delegation of about fifteen Iowa lawmakers met with Bush at the Governor's Mansion and presented him with letters of endorsement signed by sixty-six House and Senate members, more than seventy percent of the Republicans in the Iowa Legislature. "Should I decide to run, they'll take an active role in my campaign," Bush told the press afterwards.

---

*In 1979, by contrast, then-U.S. Representatives Gerald Solomon and Trent Lott attempted to secure congressional endorsements for Ronald Reagan, but they were only able to garner fifteen supporters.

A few days later, he had lunch with five Republican leaders of the New Jersey Legislature who gave Bush "some encouragement as to why he should run," said Bill Palatucci, who arranged and attended the meeting. After the lawmakers left, the governor offered his strongest statement to date on a possible presidential bid, telling reporters, "I'm warming to the task" of seeking the White House. "I'm seriously thinking about running for the president."

Governor Bush's long and tentative presidential prospecting harkened back to the noncampaigns of Ronald Reagan and former New York Governor Mario Cuomo.

In November 1975, Reagan ended what *Newsweek* called "a year's suspenseless deliberation" by announcing he would challenge President Ford for the Republican presidential nomination. Reagan lost, but it set the stage for his landslide 1980 presidential victory over Jimmy Carter.

By contrast, Cuomo considered a presidential run in 1991 by announcing he was "without any plans to make plans." Draft committees formed and political advisers made the requisite pilgrimage to Albany. "You don't get drafted for the presidency," the governor said at the time. The perceived front-runner for the Democratic nomination, Cuomo eventually announced he wouldn't be a candidate. Three years later, he lost his bid for reelection as governor.

The hallmark of Bush's deliberations was keeping his promise to stay in Texas while the Legislature was in session, except for a few trips such as the national governors' conference in Washington. "There's an advantage to being a little coy, in that it frees you from some of the rugged scrutiny that the already-declared come under," noted University of Texas political science Professor Bruce Buchanan. "It also highlights the fact, especially if you are someone who can get people to come hat in hand to beg you to run, it highlights the fact that you are a desirable and an attractive commodity."

Without having to leave home, Bush had methodically assembled an impressive national network of advisers, collected commitments from deep-pocketed contributors,* and hosted delegations from several key states, all urging him to run for president in 2000.

In some ways, it was a latter day version of the "front porch" campaign that former Ohio governor William McKinley conducted in his successful White House race more than one hundred years earlier. Instead of the front

*Meetings between Bush and major GOP campaign donors were never listed on the governor's daily schedule that was made public.

porch, Bush used the backyard of the Texas Governor's Mansion as the setting for meetings with academics and evangelicals, state legislators and U.S. congressmen, captains of industry, policy experts, foreign leaders, and the grassroots operatives who would comprise his campaign team.

After a lunch with Colorado officials, Bush stepped out on the lawn of his official residence to meet with the press corps, flanked by the Rocky Mountain State's Governor Bill Owens, who grew up in Texas, and Congressman Scott McInnis, also of Colorado. Both elected officials urged Bush to join the White House race and predicted he'd win if he did.

"He's got appeal that crosses party lines," claimed McInnis. "Mark my words, if he makes the decision, he will be the next president," Governor Owen agreed, saying that Bush could unite "not just the Republican Party, but also . . . the country."

Bush and his two out-of-state supporters suddenly found themselves on the defensive, however, when reporters suggested that the Texas governor had been orchestrating the "Draft Bush" movement that had gained ground among Republicans in Congress and in a growing number of statehouses.

"The request is not coming from Texas. The request is coming from the other direction," McInnis claimed. Owens added: "He didn't call us. We made the call."

In truth, the seeds of the "grassroots" movement to get Bush into the presidential race were carefully planted some time earlier, largely by Karl Rove, the chief architect of the governor's political strategy and organization, who has often been described as "the one indispensable component" in Bush's gubernatorial campaigns.

Rove, who never graduated from college but later taught at the LBJ School of Public Affairs at the University of Texas, honed his aggressive campaign style as a colleague of the late Lee Atwater, a former chairman of the Republican National Committee and perhaps the GOP's best-known exponent of negative campaign politics.

A Bush family insider since 1973, when he was chairman of the College Republicans National Committee (and taught party youth "dirty tricks" according to the *Washington Post*), Rove worked for the elder Bush's political fund-raising committee, then for the 1980 Reagan/Bush campaign. In 1981, he started his own political consulting firm, Karl Rove & Co., and engineered the younger Bush's 1994 upset victory over Ann Richards, in part by limiting the fledgling candidate's early exposure to the media.

Rove was a paid consultant to Phillip Morris until 1996, when he quit after reports he helped tobacco lobbyists deliver an industry poll to the governor's office in an effort to discredit the Democratic attorney general and head off the state's tobacco lawsuit. He denied any conflict but said he was "uncomfortable" representing both the governor and the tobacco industry.

In his 1998 reelection effort, Bush's largest campaign cost, excluding television advertising, was the services of Karl Rove & Co. From July to the end of December, the governor's reelection committee paid Rove's firm nearly $2.8 million and another $267,000 to the political strategist's Praxis List Company for use of its mailing lists. Rove, who has been described as a "mainframe computer living in a human body," said his work for the Bush campaign included direct mail, voter contact, phone banks, and computer services.

When Rove arrived in Texas in 1981, there were no statewide Republican officeholders. Almost twenty years later, he counted as clients the governor, attorney general, a Railroad Commission member, the agriculture commissioner, several members of the Texas Supreme Court, and a number of state senators.

After Bush won reelection in November 1998, the governor asked his "good friend" and "confidant" to sell his company and devote full-time attention to the budding presidential campaign as his chief political adviser. "Bush doesn't want my focus diluted," Rove contended. "If he's going to make the run, he'd like to have me available."

Mark McKinnon, who worked with President Clinton's advisers, James Carville and Paul Begala, and later headed the Bush campaign media effort (including the production of Bush's "documentary" videotapes), noted of Rove, "I've worked with some of the best political people in the business, but he is head and shoulders above the crowd."

An astute student of history, Rove also compared McKinleys' 1896 front porch campaign to the strategy he engineered for Bush. Ironically, the Ohio governor's political Svengali, an industrialist named Mark Hanna, kept McKinley on his home turf in Canton, while he accepted the entreaties of thousands of out-of-state supporters to enter the presidential race, thus avoiding a national tour Hanna thought "demeaned the office." The grassroots campaign worked in 1896 and Rove was determined to make sure history successfully repeated itself almost a hundred years later.

A classic example of Rove coordinating the steady stream of out-of-state politicos to Austin to help inflate the unofficial Bush presidential campaign, occurred on February 18, 1999, when the governor's political office in Texas issued the following news release: "As a courtesy, we are forwarding two press releases issued in South Carolina . . . and New Mexico." Both reported that sizable numbers of Republican legislators in the two states were urging Bush to enter the race for president.

Described as an "isolated, spontaneous outburst of support," the effort to garner loyalists in New Mexico was, in fact, attentively orchestrated by Rove from Austin, according to the leader of the effort there. "I called Rove and said, 'If you guys want to do something, give me a call. I'm ready to help,'" said Colin McMillan, a former assistant secretary of defense in the elder Bush administration. "I asked him what he wanted me to do. Rove said, 'Well, you might consider doing this,'" McMillan added, referring to the draft movement that snared more than three-quarters of the GOP members in the state Legislature.

A day later, fax machines at Bush's political office in Texas were whirring with the news release from McMillan and the one from South Carolina.

Within a week, Alabama joined the grassroots "Draft Bush" movement, with Attorney General Bill Pryor—a former Rove & Co. client and avowed Bush fan—heading the southern state's support. Pryor claimed he was inspired by what other states were doing, and decided to "follow the lead." While he said he needed no encouragement from Rove, Pryor acknowledged that he had talked with the political consultant about the governor, and he cited a "kind letter" from Bush that compelled him to "do something."

Dated January 29, 1999, the correspondence read, in part: "Karl told me of your kind words of encouragement to run for President. If I decide to seek higher office, I would very much appreciate your support." Adding that he would decide by spring, the Texas governor asked Pryor to "keep your powder dry until then."

"From Warming to the Task to Getting Pretty Hot"

On a Sunday afternoon in early March 1999, four months after he was reelected to a second term as governor of Texas and an even longer period of coy political theater, Bush officially unveiled the presidential exploratory committee that would help him raise and spend millions in campaign contributions without declaring his candidacy.

Flanked by a diverse group of high-profile Republicans and a row of American and Texas flags serving as a patriotic backdrop to his long-expected announcement, Bush opened the news conference with a stiffly delivered speech in which he said, "I do have a compelling reason to consider running for president: I want the twenty-first century to be one of prosperity, and I don't want anybody being left behind."

The multicultural composition of his exploratory committee also reflected the governor's "compassionate conservatism," which he said sought to embrace minorities and other nontraditional constituencies in the GOP. Bush's "Dream Team," as described by *San Antonio Express-News* columnist, Carlos Guerra, included U.S. Congressman J.C. Watts of Oklahoma who would help win over African-Americans and Congressman Henry Bonilla who would do likewise with Hispanics; U.S. Representative Jennifer Dunn, who had almost challenged Dick Armey for House majority leader in the wake of the 1998 Republican elections debacle, would be key to heading off Elizabeth Dole, the would-be presidential candidate's strongest opponent; Michigan Governor John Engler, a self-described "common sense, Midwestern conservative" would possibly ward off the regional challenge Reform Party populist Jesse Ventura could pose; and, finally, in an effort to demonstrate traditional Republican support, former Reagan Secretary of State George Schultz and southerner Haley Barbour, who served as chairman of the GOP National Committee, were naturals.

Questioned by dozens of national and international reporters, Bush declined to take specific positions on a number of critical issues such as taxes, Kosovo, Russia, and the Asian economic crisis, saying he would outline his platform in more detail once he began formally campaigning across the country in June with his wife. Although he said he wouldn't make a decision on whether to formally seek the presidency until later in the summer, the governor admitted, "I've gone from warming to the task to getting pretty hot."

Bush's explanation that he needed more time "to get comfortable with the idea" of running for the Republican nomination was yet another delay tactic. The governor's political strategists offered a number of reasons for why he wouldn't officially announce for an extended period of time: Bush would gain positive press and cut down on possible errors by giving three or four months worth of canned speeches to prepared crowds before getting into the primary battles; he anticipated some major legislative failures in Texas and needed time for damage control prior to announcing; and the governor didn't want any more press scrutiny than he was already getting as undeclared candidate.

While establishing an exploratory committee was a step short of actually announcing a presidential candidacy, Bush indicated in his press conference that he was serious about entering the race. Asked what could possibly change his mind, he said he might decide not to run "if we got out there and just heard a loud thud and huge yawn."

Bush's electability was by no means a given, and polls showing him with a significant lead over all potential Republican candidates, as well as Vice President Al Gore, could be a liability so early in the race. "It's like being Superman," said Republican consultant Mike Murphy. "You get to wear the red cape, but then people start expecting you to fly and lift up locomotives."

However, after getting skunked in the past two presidential elections and taking a pasting in the 1998 midterms, the GOP was desperate for a winner. "If we have to use smoke and mirrors to give the impression that Bush is not what a lot of people think he is, then we'll do whatever it takes," conceded a Republican strategist who frequently advised the Texas governor. "If we lose the White House in 2000, we'll lose another third of the federal judiciary and two more Supreme Court justices. And we'll lose the House. We're staring into the abyss, and lot of Republicans feel Bush is the only one who can save us," he said, adding that compared to Quayle, Elizabeth Dole, Buchanan, Bauer, Forbes, and the other candidates, "Bush is a giant walking onto the playing field."

★ 12 ★

Great Expectations

I haven't seen a candidate like this in my life.
It's like the Lord looked down on us Republicans and said,
"I really want to bless you for a change."

—Harry Dent, the architect of Richard Nixon's "Southern strategy"

No matter how much support you get from insiders, activists, fund-raisers, you still gotta run the gauntlet. You gotta earn it at the polls. That the beauty of the system.

—Charles Black, veteran Republican strategist

The land did it. It pretended to be poor because nobody knew how to work it right; and then, all at once, it worked itself. It woke up out of its sleep and stretched itself, and it was so big, so rich, that we suddenly found we were rich, just from sitting still.

—Willa Cather, *O Pioneers!*

The Same Song Sheet

Since announcing the formation of a presidential exploratory committee in March 1999, Bush hunkered down in Austin, Texas, hosting a string of likely supporters, journalists, and potential donors while collecting a long list of endorsements.

In April, the Texas chief executive and Rudolph Giuliani, mayor of New York City, met for more than an hour at the Governor's Mansion to talk policy and politics, then emerged to offer kind words about each other although they admitted to the press that they differed on abortion rights, gays rights, and gun control.

Giuliani, who only two days earlier had announced a Senate exploratory committee for a race that might pit him against First Lady Hillary Rodham Clinton, didn't endorse Bush for president but dismissed foreign policy critics of the Texas governor. In the weeks preceding their joint appearance, newspaper columnists and political observers had complained that Bush had been too tentative in expressing his opinion on NATO's involvement in Kosovo.

"When Ronald Reagan was elected president of the United States, one of the questions was: Did he have any foreign policy experience?" the mayor said. "If you look at the twelve years of the Reagan/Bush administration and compare that to where our foreign policy is today, a lot of Americans would say that maybe leadership is the real key to whether you can handle foreign policy well."

For his part, Bush praised Giuliani as "an excellent candidate" for the U.S. Senate, but when asked by reporters if the mayor might be a prospective vice presidential candidate, the Texas governor demurred. "It's too early to be talking about the vice president."

New York governor George Pataki had been seeking to raise his profile nationally with a series of out-of-state political trips. On one such journey to New Hampshire, Pataki had said he planned to consider running for the GOP presidential nomination. But the possibility of a Pataki presidential run seemed to generate little excitement. In addition, sixteen other GOP governors had already endorsed Bush and pressure had been mounting for Pataki, even from some New York Republicans, to follow suit.

The month following, the New York governor shelved his own presidential ambitions and threw his political muscle behind Bush. "He is an inclusive Republican who has reached out with his doctrine of 'compassionate conservatism' and in the process built a party that has supported him with overwhelming votes from the Hispanic community, from women, from African-Americans across Texas," Pataki announced in a live satellite hookup with Bush, who happily responded, "I'm honored to have you on my team."

Also in May, more than half of the 222 Republican members of the U.S. House of Representatives publicly pledged their support for Bush's presidential campaign, a display of solidarity Representative Henry Bonilla of Texas, called a "kick in the gut" to other would-be GOP candidates. "Endorsements are . . . a huge fundamental building block of a campaign."

One of those "other" candidates, former Vice President Dan Quayle, complained bitterly about the swarm of supporters. "I think it shows that there is a genuine nervousness in the Republican Party and they're trying to go with polls rather than ideas—and that is a colossal mistake. It may feel comfortable today, but down deep if you think you're going to win this on what public opinion polls say eighteen months out, I beg to differ," Quayle told the press. "When you show nervousness like that, you are in trouble."

Bush, in a prepared statement, expressed gratitude for the support from the House members, who represented both rural and urban congressional districts. "I'm particularly proud of these endorsements because the men and women supporting me are extraordinarily close to their constituencies and span the ideological spectrum of our party."

House leaders* viewed Bush's nomination as so inevitable that they began conducting informal meetings weeks earlier with the Texas governor as well as his advisers, including Karl Rove, his top strategist, to discuss a unified agenda on issues ranging from Social Security to taxes to education. They had also begun to discuss joint electoral and fund-raising strategies for the 2000 campaign.

The outpouring for Bush's candidacy was all the more striking because members of Congress traditionally preferred backing one of their own for the presidency. In supporting the Texas governor, they passed over Senators John McCain of Arizona and Bob Smith of New Hampshire, and Representative John Kasich of Ohio.

One top strategist to a Bush opponent explained: "They're panic-stricken

---

*House Speaker Dennis Hastert of Illinois had previously agreed to be the Bush campaign's chief House liaison, but stepped aside when he rose to the speakership.

on Capitol Hill, and they're afraid they're going to lose their five-seat majority. And they're looking for a savior. But in trying to preclude a contest from taking place before it's even started, they're putting an awful lot of eggs in the basket for a candidate they know absolutely nothing about."

House leaders involved in the agenda exploration sessions with Bush cautioned that they were only preliminary discussions. "He believes, as I believe, there's a great opportunity for us to come together around a common set of principles," announced Dick Armey of Texas, the second-ranking House Republican. "We'll work out the details through the basic legislative process. You will probably see a final distillation of all these ideas in a set of programmatic objectives that would not be announced formally until after he's the nominee."

"What's going on is the beginning of a coherent message-development process," said one GOP official involved. "You won't see Bush [and Congress] talking about the same issues in two weeks, but we're getting in the position to be on the same song sheet."

THE NEW HAMPSHIRE SESSION

Although the unprecedented policy agenda talks between the Bush campaign and GOP members were characterized by all parties as "private" and "informal," they were criticized by members of the press, Democrats, and Texas voters for taking up "too much of Bush's time back home."

"Governor George W. Bush says he will remain in Texas and not actively campaign for the Republican presidential campaign until the end of this session of the Legislature," wrote James Howard Gibbons in the *Houston Chronicle*. "His decision, however, seems to stem from his desire to avoid answering questions from the people and the press than from his duty to provide strong leadership for Texas."

In May, with the legislative session moving into its final days and Bush's "front porch" strategy about to come to an end, the governor's opponents intensified their attacks against the Republican presidential front-runner. Even though he had not been out of the state for national campaigning since forming his exploratory committee, Bush was criticized for focusing on his presidential ambitions and neglecting his gubernatorial duties.

"I don't know if I'd say he's been missing in action, but it's pretty close to that," noted State Representative Kevin Bailey of Houston, in a news conference with thirty other Democratic legislators. "He's a lot less involved than in the past."

Karen Hughes, the governor's communications director, dismissed the complaints. "[Bush's] fellow Republicans criticized him for not being in Iowa and New Hampshire and for keeping his word to the people of Texas, and now Democrats are criticizing him for whatever the issue of the day is."

However, after a *Houston Chronicle* review of Bush's office calendars indicated that the governor had had about half the personal involvement in the 1999 Legislature compared to the 1997 Legislature, Bush presidential campaign advisers voiced their concerns.

"We told the boss if bills on major issues on which he campaigned failed, that would give his opponents like Elizabeth Dole and Steve Forbes cause to attack him as an ineffective leader," admitted one top Bush campaign strategist.

The Texas governor vowed the next day to get most of what he asked for from the Legislature: school voucher programs, substantial property tax cuts, parental notification when minors sought abortions, salary increases for teachers, passage of the Religious Freedom Restoration Act, and even more stringent welfare reform.

With virtually all of his legislative agenda still pending only two weeks before the session adjourned, Bush paid his first visit to the Texas Senate in months. "It's been a while since I've been in the chamber," the governor admitted. "The reason I came by today is that we're heading toward the end of the session and it's a chance to make my presence felt." Bush added that it was merely coincidental his visit occurred the same day Republican members were attempting to rally sufficient support to amend a controversial school voucher program to a House bill.

On May 31, Memorial Day, when lawmakers completed their 140-day biennial Legislature—admittedly the most important of Bush's political career—they handed the governor his biggest defeat of the session: rejection of a pilot program to allow some students to use taxpayer-funded vouchers to pay private school tuition, which was a major reelection campaign promise made by the governor a few months earlier.

Opponents of the bill had complained that the provision allowing parents to transfer children into religious schools violated a constitutional prohibition against public funding of religious institutions. Critics also had warned that the program would have siphoned off much-needed funding as well as the most promising students from failing schools, leaving them worse off than they had been. The plan would have also had a disproportionately adverse effect on schools in Hispanic and African-American communities, NAACP leaders claimed.*

"I worked hard on the voucher issue," Bush said in the wake of the bill's defeat. "It just wasn't meant to be in this legislative session. I believe [vouchers are] an idea that frightens certain people."

The governor's "get-even-tougher" sanctions of a welfare reform bill, which opponents referred to as "draconian" proposals because of their severity, also failed. Under Bush's plan if a welfare recipient refused to show up for required work training or classes, not only would the recipient be sanctioned with benefit cuts, so would any dependents. He also advocated efforts to cut young mothers of small children off welfare rolls forever if their felony drug conviction was for possession of what amounted to a relatively small quantity of marijuana or cocaine. Lawmakers instead offered new incentives to aid in getting recipients off public assistance, such as training, transportation service, and even drug treatment. With the session coming to a close, bipartisan legislators in the House finally reached a compromise, but time ran out before the welfare reform package could be enacted.

Before the Legislature convened, the governor requested that lawmakers approve a $2 billion property tax cut that he had promised Texan voters during his reelection campaign in 1998. Hours before the session adjourned, the Republican-led Senate and Democratic-controlled House passed a compromise bill which was almost $1 billion less than Bush proposed. The governor called the tax cut "substantial," enough to claim as bragging rights in the presidential campaign.

The centerpiece of the Legislature's tax-reduction efforts was a major education reform law that gave teachers a $3,000-a-year pay raise, attacked social promotion in the public schools, and included a number of other public education improvements. The measure increased state aid to school districts in order to provide for school property tax cuts averaging six cents per $100 valuation, or about sixty dollars a year on a house taxed on $100,000 of its value. Actual tax savings, however, would vary widely from school district to school district throughout the state, based on a district's property wealth,

---

*Ironically, George W.'s brother Jeb was able to push a sweeping school voucher program through the 1999 Legislature of Florida, making the Sunshine State the first in the nation to offer a statewide program of vouchers to help parents of students in failing schools offset the cost of private education.

debt, and other factors. According to projections by the Legislative Budget Board, about 120 districts would not see any tax relief during the 1999–2000 school year, and some of these were actually considering raising their levy rates.

While low-income Texans in poor school districts might benefit, renters would not receive advantage from the lower school taxes, as was the case with the 1997 property tax package. Once again, the wealthiest Texans would benefit proportionately more than the poorest residents of the state. According to the Legislative Budget Board's analysis, the 1999 law would slash the state and local tax liability by 1.38 percent for Texans with annual incomes of more than $107,664, compared to less than 1 percent for most other income groups.

Unlike two years earlier, businesses would benefit from property tax cuts under the new law, realizing about three-fourths of the projected school tax savings during the next two years, according to the budget board. While the owner of a $100,000 house would save sixty dollars a year in a school district that reduced its tax rate by six cents, the owners of petrochemical or power plants in the same district would save hundreds of thousands of dollars. Also, landlords of apartment complexes and owners of other residential rental property were expected to save $174 million from the tax reductions in the first two years after the law's enactment, but they would not be required to pass any of those savings to tenants.

"It's important to be bold," Bush boasted after the bill's passage. "I took a message to the people of Texas. I said, 'Let's pay the teachers more money and let's substantially cut taxes.' This bill will do both."

At the start of the session, Bush also called for $600 million in tax cuts for businesses and consumers. Legislators, however, approved a bill that would cut business and sales taxes by $506 million over a two-year period. The budget board estimated that the two groups would share about evenly in the cuts the first year, but that businesses would receive about sixty percent of the benefits during the second year, when more of the business tax cuts and credits kicked in.

For consumers, the bill imposed a back-to-school sales tax holiday, eliminating the sales tax each year on nonathletic clothing and footwear items that cost less than $100 each. A family purchasing $1,000 worth of clothing from a Dallas retailer during the once-a-year sales tax holiday would save $82.

Bush described the overall tax relief plan as fair. "We did the best we could to make sure the tax cuts were widespread and felt by all Texans," he said, noting that he had previously vowed to call lawmakers back into special session if the tax cut and education bill failed.

Beleagured Texas oil producers also received a tax break at Bush's urgent request. The bill, the first to pass the Seventy-sixth Legislature, authorized a seven-month exemption from the 4.6 percent severance tax for marginal wells that produced no more than fifteen barrels a day and small gas wells that yielded no more than 90,000 cubic feet per day in late 1998. Estimates at the time indicated there were more than 140,000 eligible oil wells and more than 40,000 eligible gas wells.

Bush, feeling his West Texas roots, immediately signed the legislation, bypassing a bill to help pay for health insurance for children of the working poor, a proposal the Senate had passed and sent to the House several hours before the tax relief measure reached the Governor's desk. "It's about priorities," Representative Dale Tillery of Dallas told reporters. "I know a whole lot of uninsured children, but I don't know a lot of poor oilmen."

Bush said the tax break would keep small, semiproductive wells open, helping to preserve jobs and shore up the tax base in school districts that depended on oil related revenue. "These are tough times for the oil and gas industry,* and this legislation says our state is committed to helping this vital industry."

Opponents noted that though the governor and other lawmakers had pitched the tax break as a "helping hand for the little guy," the majority of the relief actually would go to large oil producers. Citing Texas Railroad Commission statistics showing that the largest thirty-four well operators made up less than one percent of the state's oil producers but controlled twenty-five percent of wells eligible for the exemption, critics demonstrated that oil giants like Chevron and Exxon would be the actual recipients of the severance tax exemption. According to other estimates, the typical small oil company would save only $5,600.

The chief proponent of the bill in the House—and an oilman who might expect to benefit from the new law—was Tom Craddick, a Republican representative from Midland and one of Bush's closest friends from his hometown in West Texas. According to Craddick's financial disclosure statement,

*In March 1999, when Bush signed the tax break bill into law, commodity prices averaged $15 per barrel of oil and $1.80 per thousand cubic feet for gas, the benchmarks for breaking even. In 1998, over four thousand oil and gas workers had been laid off in just the Houston area in the worst industry slump since the mid-1980s oil bust, while the number of production wells in the state fell forty-three percent.

the state lawmaker received between $11,000 and $34,997 in combined annual royalty income from three of the largest operators of affected oil wells.

Representative Kevin Bailey, who voted against the tax break, complained to reporters that Bush was being motivated by his potential White House run. "The governor's got to satisfy certain interests within the Republican Party as he tries to win the Republican nomination, and the oil interests are very strong among that group," the Democratic legislator stated. "Clearly, he's doing what he's got to do to curry favor with those who will influence the nomination for president."

Of particular interest to critical conservative voters in the upcoming Republican primaries was the passage of Bush's abortion notification bill, which required doctors to inform parents when their unmarried, school-aged daughters (eighteen or younger) sought an abortion procedure. It was the most significant piece of abortion-control legislation to be passed by the Texas Legislature since the U.S. Supreme Court *Roe v. Wade* decision legalized abortion in 1973. The far-right conservative elements of the GOP had sought the passage of the parental notification law for years and it was "Priority One" for the Christian Coalition in the 1999 legislative session.

"When a child is in crisis, parents should have a role and a voice," Bush announced. "They should be the first to help, not the last to know. I believe that life is valuable, even when it is unwanted, even when it is physically imperfect. I believe our society has a responsibility to defend the vulnerable and the weak."

As they did during an emotional debate on the bill in the Legislature, opponents warned afterward that the measure would force pregnant teens into dangerous back-alley abortions. They also cited statistics that showed most young people already involved their parents in the decision to seek an abortion—approximately 75 percent in states without parental notification laws. Among those who didn't, 30 percent reported or feared domestic violence.*

Additionally, the effects of parental notification laws in other states had been disastrous. In Massachusetts and Mississippi, two states with such a law, abortions had not decreased, but the number of minors crossing state lines to seek an abortion had increased dramatically. In Indiana, a young woman died from an illegal abortion she sought in order to avoid telling her parents about her pregnancy. In Idaho, a teenage girl was shot to death by

*Governor Bush was against an amendment to the bill that would have allowed grandparents, older aunts and uncles, or older siblings to be notified rather than parents.

her father when he learned she sought to terminate the pregnancy caused by his act of incest.

Although Bush attempted to portray himself as a centrist on the issue of abortion while on the presidential campaign trail, his fervent opposition to a woman's right to choose and his record as Texas governor contrast starkly with his moderate image. Since he was first elected in 1994, Bush has signed sixteen anti-choice provisions in the three legislative sessions—more than any other governor in the country. Among them:

- A waiting period for minors seeking abortion services.
- A law making it a felony for a grandparent to take his or her fourteen to sixteen-year-old grandchild out of state to obtain an abortion without notifying the parents, even if doing so might result in physical or emotional abuse or if her pregnancy is the result of incest.
- A law expanding Texas' abortion clinic regulations and imposing a $2,500 licensing fee on specified physicians' offices, which increased the cost of an abortion.
- A prohibition blocking school-based health care centers from providing reproductive health services, counseling, or referrals.
- A law prohibiting Children's Health Insurance Programs from covering reproductive services.
- A law denying tax exemptions to nonprofit organizations that perform, make referrals for, or assist specified organizations that perform or refer for abortions.
- A prohibition on family planning funding for organizations that dispense prescription contraceptives to minors without parental consent.

"George W. Bush's anti-choice policies harm those who deserve our compassion the most—the poor and young women in crisis," claimed Kate Michelman, president of the National Abortion and Reproductive Rights Action League (NARAL). "Despite the campaign rhetoric of 'compassionate conservatism,' his record reveals the true George W. Bush. He is anti-choice and hostile to the reproductive rights of American women." She added that the governor had tried to appear moderate by acknowledging that "America is not ready to ban abortion"—a stance that had gotten Bush into trouble with the right-wing of the Republican Party—but, Michelman said, his record showed that as president, he would "continue to chip away at the right to choose until there's nothing left."

Critics of Bush's "compassionate conservatism" also complained that the

Texas governor failed to take a leadership role on a hate crimes bill introduced in memory of James Byrd Jr., the black man dragged to death by white racists in Jasper, Texas in 1998. The measure, which President Clinton backed during a visit to Texas, identified specific groups, including homosexuals, for protection from crimes of prejudice. A law already on the books in Texas was so vague it was virtually unenforceable, according to legal experts.

The tougher hate crimes bill passed the Texas House, winning the vote of one of the most conservative members of that legislative body, Republican Representative Warren Chisum. But the bill failed in the Senate in a partisan struggle so emotional and bitter it shut down the chamber for most of one day and forced hundreds of other bills to die in the Legislature when their deadlines passed.

Bush's presidential campaign strategists argued that he would have faced a dilemma if the hate crimes bill had passed the Legislature. The governor, who had previously said he opposed same-sex marriages, would have angered GOP social conservatives by signing the bill into law. If he vetoed it, moderates would have accused him of playing to the right.

During the fractious debate in the Senate, Bush refused to say how he would handle the bill, but maintained his previous stand that stiff sentences were warranted for all crimes no matter the motivation. "Punish the deed," he said. "Most deeds are based upon hate." Referring to the shootings at Columbine High School in Colorado, the governor added, "What's the difference between the white man who got killed or the black man who got killed during that rampage?"

Fortunately for Bush, he was able to gingerly step around the legislative landmine when the Republican-led Senate succeeded in killing a compromise version of the bill. "There were a lot of things that we all knew the governor didn't want to have on his desk, hate crimes being part of it," GOP Representative Wayne Christian later told reporters.

After the bill's defeat, Bush publicly asserted that the sexual preference protected category had never been "a sticking point" for him, although previously he had voiced reservations concerning the inclusion. "No, my position was, first of all, this was a moral conscience vote on the Senate," he said during a press conference. "I stood back and said I was going to analyze the bill once it made it off the floor of the Senate. It never did. Some bills pass and some don't. Good people, good honest decent Texans couldn't come to an agreement."

Democratic candidate for president, former U.S. Senator Bill Bradley, said during a fund-raising trip to Texas, "We're not going to be able to legislate against hate, but we can certainly punish those people who commit crimes based upon race, gender, sexual orientation, ethnicity, or disability." Bradley added that he would ensure that the bill's defeat would come back to haunt the governor. "I think leaders have to step up, and no leader should be silent on this. If I get the Democratic nomination and the governor of Texas gets the Republican nomination . . . I will make this an issue in the general election."

Dr. Richard Murray, a political scientist at the University of Houston, predicted the same scenario in 2000. "I would expect it will be used selectively at least by the Democratic nominee because he [Bush] wouldn't make any effort to assist in its passage," Dr. Murray said. "And we might see a Byrd family member in that commercial."

Republican lawmakers in the state Legislature later admitted in interviews that they also shielded the governor from the politically contentious issue of gun control when they defeated a law that would have required mandatory background checks on buyers at gun shows. Afterwards, Bush created a stir with opponents of gun control, when he said he favored such a measure, especially in light of the Littleton, Colorado school shootings, but called it a "federal matter."

When the governor signed NRA-backed legislation limiting the ability of Texas' cities, counties, and local governments to sue firearm and ammunition sellers and manufacturers for the public costs associated with gun violence—a move his office said was meant to discourage frivolous lawsuits*—he immediately drew fire from Vice President Gore, a possible Democratic opponent for president in 2000.

"In this presidential race, there are some who believe the urgent matter

---

*A month after signing the bill, Bush's presidential campaign finance chairman in Maine abruptly resigned after the Associated Press exposed him as an assault weapons manufacturer being sued by a Los Angeles police officer wounded in a gun battle.

Richard E. Dyke, owner of Bushmaster Firearms in Windham, Maine, a company that makes automatic weapons for government agencies and semiautomatics that are sold to the public, told Don Evans, Bush's national finance chairman: "I just don't want to be any baggage. Young Bush doesn't have to justify why I was trying to help him."

Dyke's weapons manufacturing firm was one of nine makers of assault rifles that Los Angeles cop, Martin Whitfield, had sued after the officer was wounded in a shootout with bank robbers armed with such guns. The rifles were similar to the military's M-16, and Dyke's company advertised its sale of the civilian guns as "modified" to get around the 1994 ban on some types of assault weapons. The two robbers, armed with the rifles, had the police seriously outgunned when they wounded ten officers, including Whitfield and two civilians.

related to guns is the need to extend new protections to the gun manufacturers," the vice president said. "I believe it is time to have new protections for our children and our families. Some want concealed weapons. But they can't conceal the fact that they are doing the bidding of the National Rifle Association."

Nina Butts, a lobbyist for Texans Against Gun Violence, said Bush "is not a rootin'-tootin' cowboy, and I think he does have a sense of what's necessary and right to stop gun violence. But the NRA gets to him over and over, and he doesn't do what's right."

Bush makes no apologies for his record on gun control. "What people want to know is, does a candidate have a practical view of guns, and I do," he has stated in interviews. "I support the vigorous prosecution of people who break the law with guns. There ought to be vigorous prosecution of people who sell guns illegally as well."

In a form letter sent to concerned Americans who write to the Texas Governor's office in regard to his stance on firearms, Bush says, "I support tough laws and long sentences for those who use guns to commit crimes. Additional gun-control laws, such as requiring arbitrary waiting periods, do not achieve this goal."

When the Texas Legislature adjourned in June 1999, a *USA Today*/CNN/Gallup Poll found that 62 percent of Americans wanted stricter laws covering sales of firearms, and 77 percent said candidates' views on gun control would be an important factor when they voted. The survey also asked people which issues mattered most in their votes for Congress in 2000. Gun control came in fourth, after Social Security, health care, and Medicare.

Throughout the 1999 legislative session, Bush faced criticism—from admirers and detractors—for putting his budding presidential aspirations first, which overshadowed much of the session's work and often made legislators question the governor's—and each other's—motives. Publicly referring to the law-making body as "the New Hampshire session," many of the state legislators claimed "everything he has done was geared toward what would make him look good to run nationally."

"We're either going to care more about the voters in New Hampshire or Iowa, or we're going to care about the schoolchildren of Texas," Representative Domingo Garcia of Dallas complained during a debate pitting property tax cuts against funding for smaller school classes.

Bush responded by saying that his interest in the presidency was an easy scapegoat. "There's going to be people who figure out ways if something doesn't go their way or something's not perfect, they all blame presidential politics," the governor stated, adding that the "successful and substantial legislative session" approved the majority of his priority initiatives.

"I think he basically got his core agenda," bragged Texas Republican Chairwoman, Susan Weddington. "He was successful."

State Senator Rodney Ellis, a Democrat from Houston, who battled Bush—at least indirectly—on the hate crimes bill also said the governor "came out well."

Political scientist Allan Saxe of the University of Texas at Arlington, said Bush's front-runner status in the presidential race assured the governor would get much of the legislative proposals he sought. "It was preordained," Saxe asserted. "The Legislature was going to give him essentially what he needed to walk out and become a presidential aspirant. And that's what happened."

As for Bush himself, the governor had his own ideas about how the American public should view his legislative legacy. "I'm a person who sets clear goals. I try to do a few things and do them well," he said. "I hope people will say, 'This is a fella who knows how to lead, who is able to achieve results by working with others.' "

But it would be up to voters nationwide to decide whether Bush's priorities were theirs, too. Once he left the comfort of the front porch of the Texas Governor's Mansion for a shot at the White House, he would be running on the record he created as governor—wherever it would lead.

THE PHANTOM MENACE FINALLY APPEARS

After five months in Austin balancing the twin tasks of a presidential campaign and a legislative session, Bush finally began another key part of his bid for the presidency: actual campaign appearances. (The other GOP candidates nicknamed Bush "The Phantom Menace" because he continued to outdistance them by several percentage points in the polls even though he was the last Republican to make the journey to the key early caucus and primary states.)

"I want to look people in the eye and shake their hands and let them know what's in my heart and hear what they have to say as well," Bush told reporters as he prepared to leave for Iowa and New Hampshire and a month of nearly endless campaigning. "I understand polls and expectations are out of sight," he added. "As my daughter said, 'Hey, Dad, you're not nearly as cool as they think you are.' "

Michael Kranish, writing for the *Boston Globe,* addressed Bush's concerns: "So far, Bush has been the proverbial 'empty vessel,' and many people of all political persuasions have poured in their hopes and dreams for the type of person who will win the White House. The danger for Bush is that as he defines himself on an array of issues, some people might be disappointed."

Mark McKinnon, a Bush adviser, agreed. "We recognize that it is a real challenge that we have to go from zero to sixty in two seconds. The expectations are exponentially high, and it will be very difficult to meet the expectations."

On Saturday, June 12, Bush left Austin for Iowa on a 727 chartered jet aptly named "Great Expectations" and packed with more than one hundred reporters—even though he had not yet declared himself an official candidate for the Republican nomination for president. The governor's inner circle considered, then abandoned, the idea of "pool" (group) coverage at most stops. That's for presidents, not candidates, they concluded.

Joking with reporters on the campaign plane, Bush grabbed a microphone and announced, "Please store your expectations securely in the overhead bins, as they might shift during the trip and may fall and hurt someone—especially me."

However, the governor was visibly fatigued when he embarked for Iowa from Austin. "I only got six hours' sleep last night," he confessed, with a weary shake of his head. "I need more than that." Prior to the campaign inaugural trip to Iowa, fund-raising aides scheduled two closed events for Bush, one in St. Louis and another in Chicago. The fund-raisers garnered $1.5 million, but the Bush press staff was furious.

One top Bush political strategist admitted, "We didn't think it was a good way to start the campaign to have him going to two fat-cat fund-raisers that excluded the press" on the day before he left for Iowa and New Hampshire, states which would hold, respectively, the nation's first precinct caucuses and presidential primary early next year. A compromise was worked out between the two camps: the governor would go to the fund-raisers,* but he would also appear at a reading center and attend a baseball game.

---

*Bush was forced to enter and leave the hotels where the fund-raisers took place through the basement due to about fifty antigun protesters that stood outside the fund-raisers carrying signs reading, GO HOME GUNSLINGING GEORGE. "Bush has opened a Pandora's box he will never be able to close," said one of the protesters, Mike Robbins, a former Chicago police officer shot a dozen times with an assault weapon by an alleged gang member. "Guns are and have been for too long, too easy to get hold of in America, and it's politicians like Texas Governor George W. Bush that make it possible for these conditions to exist."

When Bush was finally informed of the gaffe, he went ballistic. "What you're telling me is that because you guys fucked up, I got to break my ass all day and won't get home until midnight?" Bush said. "We're going back to Plan A." The reading center and baseball game appearances were cancelled, but the governor still didn't return to Austin until 11 P.M., resulting in a tired candidate departing the next day for Iowa.

The television reporters likened Bush's arrival in the Hawkeye State to "a Texas twister" and featured close-ups of his Texas-style belt buckle and monogrammed cowboy boots with his business suit as he addressed about two hundred boisterous supporters and another one hundred reporters who greeted him at the Cedar Rapids airport.

"I'm ready," Bush told the sign-carrying (BUSH FOR 2000 and IOWA IS BUSH COUNTRY) throng as rousing movie theme songs and rock music blared in the background. "I know expectations are really high, but here's what you can expect from me. You can expect someone who will talk from the heart, you can expect someone who will talk straight. You can expect someone who will not take a single caucus vote for granted," Bush said. "I believe you can expect someone named George W. to win this nomination."

Finally, dropping all pretenses about his White House ambitions, Bush announced, "I intend to win this nomination the old-fashioned way and that is to earn it. Earn your respect. Earn your trust." Then, with his wife Laura at his side he waded into the lunging crowd of supporters, signing autographs and shaking hands.

Later, at a bratwurst-and-sauerkraut fund-raising luncheon for Republican U.S. Representative Jim Nussle, the Texas governor proclaimed, "I have come here today to say this—I'm running for president. There's no turning back, and I intend to be the next president of the United States." He later said he would make a formal "announcement" in the fall, but assured Iowans that already "I'm running, and I'm running hard."

Speaking in shirtsleeves to an audience of close to a thousand and sharing the dais at the historic Amana Colonies near Cedar Rapids with hay bales and a shiny red tractor that matched his tie, Bush reiterated the themes of personal responsibility, economic prosperity, and caring for the downtrodden that had proved extremely popular back in Texas.

The centerpiece speech, which aides had been composing and editing for months, would serve as the standard stump text for the summer campaign as the governor toured the other early-primary states—New Hampshire, South Carolina, California, Michigan, Virginia, Washington, Montana, Connecticut, and New Jersey. Bush would later add comments for local consumption and tack on a new twist or idea or proposal to give the press a fresh angle for their daily articles, but the thrust of the speech—nearly ninety percent—wouldn't change and emphasized social policy at the expense of economic and foreign policy. According to Fred Barnes in the *Weekly Standard,* it was all part of campaign strategist Karl Rove's plan to start with vague generalities and add details later.

"I am proud to be a 'compassionate conservative.' I welcome the label. And on this ground I will make my stand," Bush said, hammering away on his trademark theme. "Is compassion beneath us? Is mercy below us? Should our party be led by someone who boasts of a hard heart? I am running because my party must match a conservative mind with a compassionate heart."

His first goal, Bush said, would be to "usher in the responsibility era" in America, as he tried to do in Texas, with strong messages and "tough-love" juvenile justice laws designed to persuade young people to avoid drugs, alcohol, out-of-wedlock pregnancies, and other undesirable behaviors. "Some people think it's inappropriate to draw a moral line in the sand. Not me," he declared.

Bush also promised to rally the "armies of compassion"—the social and religious agencies that he believed were essential to assist the government in helping the wayward and needy—and to "lift the regulations that hamper them."

The Texas governor stated that he would see to it that every America child was educated, and promised that if elected president, he would provide the individual states with more flexibility and authority in establishing education policy.

Bush acknowledged that his "compassionate conservatism" theme had been criticized, but added that he was "confident that Americans view compassion as a noble goal, the calling of a nation where the strong are just and weak are valued."

Concluding his ten-minute speech, Bush promised a positive, inclusive campaign that "appeals to our better angels, not our darker impulses."

Like a lightning-quick summer storm, Bush left Iowa late that same Saturday to spend Sunday with his parents at the family's summer home in Kennebunkport, Maine before heading to New Hampshire. "It may have been a quick trip, but it was a productive trip,' Bush told his aides. An Associated Press poll taken after his one-day visit to America's heartland seemed to confirm his opinion. The survey gave Bush the backing of forty percent of Republican caucus voters. The governor was twenty-seven points higher than second-place finisher, Elizabeth Dole, who received thirteen percent. Third place went to multimillionaire publisher Steve Forbes, who got ten percent of the vote.

Sunday's front page of the influential *Des Moines Register* featured a large photograph of the Texas governor working a crowd of two thousand in full swoon at a local rally the night before. The headline: "Bush Pledges Fresh Start." On the same page, under a smaller heading "The Other Candidates," were diminutive pictures of GOP hopefuls Lamar Alexander, Dole, and John Kasich.

Bush's adulation-and-entourage-filled kickoff tour moved on to New Hampshire, where he continued to ride a wave of goodwill, endorsement, and hefty campaign contributions. Stop after stop—whether at town hall–style meetings with adults and children or shaking shift workers' hands at a manufacturing plant—the first-time presidential candidate generated the kind of enthusiasm and media attention that typically occurred in the closing days of a primary campaign.

Doubters of Bush's political star quality could only listen to how WMUR-TV, New Hampshire's largest station, reported the governor's arrival to the state: "With charisma rarely seen in national politics, George W. Bush exploded onto the scene." Or read the headline in Tuesday's edition of the *Union Leader,* the state's leading newspaper: "Exuberant Bush Sweeps Through NH." The welcome sign outside Madden's Family Restaurant in Derry, where the Texas governor grabbed a coffee pot and filled diners' cups, fittingly summed up Bush's presidential campaign debut: WOW! WHAT A START!

Although the Republican front-runner did not disappoint supporters with sky-high expectations, his four-day campaign blitz through Iowa and New Hampshire wasn't a flawless performance. After recycling his stump speech to more than three hundred supporters at an early morning rally on the fog-shrouded banks of the Atlantic Ocean, Bush was subjected to a traditional political initiation—the first news conference of his campaign. He was asked to outline his views on abortion, taxes, and affirmative action, and to detail the mistakes he had said he made when he was "young and irresponsible." The candidate answered some questions, fended off a couple more and promised specific proposals later on others. ("There's a lot of time for ten-point programs.")

Bush's rivals, looking for vulnerabilities in the candidate's campaign, immediately pounced on his comments and "Clinton-like" evasiveness.

"The idea that you can go through a campaign and just not say anything is not going to work," Forbes said, challenging Bush to a debate on the issues. "The last Republican convention in Philadelphia was 1948 when they nominated a governor from a big state who was ahead in the polls and looked like a sure winner," added Forbes, referring to Thomas Dewey, governor of New York who was defeated by President Harry Truman.

Lamar Alexander, the former Tennessee governor and U.S. education secretary, labeled Bush's "compassionate conservatism" as "weasel words." He explained to reporters that "weasels used to suck the good out of the eggs and leave nothing behind for the farmer but an empty shell."

Pat Buchanan, the conservative TV pundit making his third attempt for the presidency, complained that Bush was not "deep in the issues" and added, "I cannot see anything thus far that justifies elevating this young man to be the president of the United States and the leader of the Western World."

Elizabeth Dole questioned whether Bush would stake out a position and stand by it. "I think [voters] want people with the courage of their convictions. That's what I call 'courageous conservatism' and that's what I'm bringing to the table."

Dan Quayle, who prohibited his staff from using the words "compassionate conservatism," predicted the race for the White House would "tighten up" once "we find out what [Bush] is made of. . . . The American people are fixated with ideas. Ideas win elections."

Fearing that Bush was so far ahead that he would escape the intraparty fight and ensuing wounds that usually accompanied a closer, more bruising contest for the nomination, Vice President Al Gore officially announced his presidential effort on June 16—earlier than expected—in an effort to slow any momentum from Bush's national debut in Iowa and New Hampshire.

Gore promised he would keep prosperity going "the right way—not by letting people fend for themselves, or hoping for crumbs of compassion, but by giving people the skills and knowledge to succeed"—a not-so-veiled reference to Bush's watchword. Although never addressing Bush by name, the vice president repeatedly criticized those who protected gun manufacturers, jeopardized the environment, and had no foreign policy experience in the "complex" and "volatile" world of today.

In a speech before the centrist Democratic Leadership Council, Bill Clinton, with a boyish smirk and admitting that what he was about to say was not quite "presidential," lampooned Bush's campaign catch phrase. "This 'compassionate conservatism' has a great ring to it, and I've really worked hard to figure out what it means," he said. "And the nearest I can tell, here's what it means. It means, 'I like you—I do. And I would like to be for the patients' bill of rights. I'd like to be for closing of gun-show loopholes. And I'd like not to squander the surplus—you know, save Social Security and Medicare for the next generation. I'd like to raise the minimum wage. I'd like to do these things, but I just can't. And I feel terrible about it." The crowd laughed heartily.

Ann Richards, the former Texas governor who was ousted in 1994 by Bush, appeared on CNN's *Larry King Live* and complained that Vice President Gore's campaign lacked a central theme to combat Bush's "compassionate conservatism," which could make her successor tough to beat in the 2000 general election.

"When you run against George Bush, he is going to have one message," Richards, a Washington lobbyist and potent Democratic fund-raiser, told King. "He's going to say that message until the world gags and everybody else is going to be able to say it back," she said, adding that Gore's campaign was "all over the place. You know, one day it's mental health. The next day it's more money for cancer. All of these are real good causes, but you have got to have discipline. You have got to have focus."

"I am pleased that the Democrats are paying attention to me," Bush said, claiming that "they must be worried." As for his Republican rivals ("good and talented people"), who individually stated that they were not going to hand the nomination to Bush without a fight, the Texas governor admitted he was "taking nothing for granted. I know this race will be competitive."*

The day after Bush departed Iowa, Leon Panetta, former White House chief of staff under President Clinton, appeared on *Fox News Sunday* and predicted that the Republican front-runner would find campaigning rougher as people got to know him. "Look, the governor is a decent man; he's committed to public service. He has done a pretty good job as governor in Texas. But nobody knows what his positions are on national issues,"

---

*Bush's opponents—both Republican and Democrat—hired opposition researchers to search Texas state records, collect speeches, scour contributions, and quiz political friends and enemies in an effort to discover any negative information on Bush even before the governor had hit the presidential trail. Perhaps the strongest anti-Bush assault was mounted by wealthy GOP rival Steven Forbes, according to *Newsweek.* But the Bush team was well prepared in advance. According to former campaign spokesman David Beckwith, during the governor's 1998 reelection drive, Bush asked his personal lawyer, Dallas attorney Harriet Miers, to do a "survey of public records" so his campaign would be ready to answer questions about his background. Miers used paralegals from her firm and she remains the "repository of the record," claimed Bethwith.

Panetta said, concluding that Bush, especially at events with his Republican challengers, would be "running into a lot of land mines."

But that scenario would only occur if there were any GOP rivals left standing after Bush finished shattering presidential fund-raising records—soon collecting nearly ten times as much as his closest Republican opponent.

FOLLOW THE MONEY

When Bush swept into the nation's capital during the last week of June, the Republican Party establishment practically threw itself at his feet. At a private meeting on Capitol Hill with fawning GOP senators and representatives, he confidently told them, "I look forward to working with you." Afterwards, he predicted to the press, "I believe I'm going to be here to work with them for a better tomorrow. I know I've got a long way to go. But I'm pleased with the support I've received inside this building. The best way to convey my thanks is to look them each in the eye and say, 'Thank you very much.'"

Ironically, earlier in the day at a fund-raiser in Richmond, Virginia—where he collected $350,000 in contributions—he derided Vice President Gore as "a Washington, D.C. person. He thinks Washington has got all the answers. I believe the answers are found in our communities."

Later in the evening, thirty-six Republican senators, one hundred congressmen and two thousand well-tailored donors, many of them lobbyists*

*In the first three months of 1999—Bush raised nearly $800,000 from lawyers and lobbyists, nearly 12 percent of his total. Although he criticized Vice President Gore as a captive of the Washington establishment and presented himself as an outsider not beholden to special interests, the Texas governor turned to the capital city's biggest insiders—lobbyists—to generate support for his presidential candidacy on an Iowa Republican straw poll held on August 14.

A memo intercepted by the campaign of his rival, Steve Forbes, outlined Bush's plan to tap fifty Washington-based trade associations and companies to activate their Iowa contacts and turn out seven hundred Bush votes for the test ballot. The straw poll is typically a fund-raiser for the state party. Iowans pay $25 each to get in, then cast ballots. It is seen as an early test of a candidate's organizational strength and viability.

The Bush effort was being led by a Washington lobbyist for United Airlines. The list of supporters included BellSouth, Consolidated Edison, and Microsoft corporations, and trade groups including the U.S. Chamber of Commerce and the Associated Builders and Contractors. Many of the lobbyists on the list attended the fund-raiser in Washington, D.C.

When news organizations reported in July that Bush used unregulated out-of-state campaign contributions to rent prime space for the straw poll, a practice that tested the bounds of federal election laws, the money was replaced with cash from Bush's own campaign account. His aides initially insisted the so-called "soft money" donations were within the limits

"hoping to cement a White House connection," paid $1,000 apiece to eat hot dogs, hamburgers, and brownies, and listen to Bush give his standard campaign speech against a backdrop of twenty-six American flags. CNN called it "possibly the biggest presidential fund-raising day for a candidate that the nation's capital has ever seen."

Among the attendees, half had already contributed the maximum $1,000 to the Bush presidential campaign and were invited to attend. The event itself raised an additional $1 million in $1,000 donations. During an earlier interview, the candidate proposed lifting the $1,000 per person contribution limit in presidential races—a federal cap that was imposed in 1974 in the wake of the Watergate scandal—a suggestion that drew criticism from campaign finance reform advocates. Although he didn't say how much higher the limit should be set, he complained that it was difficult to solicit contributions $1,000 at a time.

Bush was raising money at an unprecedented pace, leaving his Republican challengers gasping, because as one Bush fund-raiser put it, "we're sucking the oxygen right out of the air."

"Governor Bush is taking in a whole bunch of money that other folks are not taking in," said Ron Kaufman, one of Bush's closest friends. "This man is drawing numbers and drawing money like nobody's ever seen before."

In the last eight days of June, Bush planned nearly a dozen more fundraisers, four in Pennsylvania, one near Detroit, Michigan, three in Florida where his brother Jeb was governor, and several more in California. According to campaign strategists, June 30, the cut-off date for the next campaign finance report candidates would file, was important because whichever presidential hopeful had raised the most money by then "would look like a winner," thus making it easier to attract even more campaign contributions.

During Bush's three-day tour through California, America's most populous state, fund-raising events outnumbered campaign events more than 2-to-1 on his itinerary. Plodding methodically from one $1,000-a-ticket meal to another, Bush delivered the same speech five times in thirty-six hours while visiting most of the state's media,* money, and political power centers:

---

of the law, but when they realized the obvious political problems, campaign manager Joe Allbaugh, a no-nonsense Texan, told them to quit bickering over complicated legal questions and directed aides to use campaign funds.

*Although nearly fifty reporters requested interviews with Bush, he granted only one, to the news program *Voz y Voto,* a co-production of *La Opinion,* a Spanish-language newspaper, and KMEX-34, the Univision affiliate in Los Angeles. The interview was conducted mostly in Spanish.

San Diego, Orange County, Los Angeles, Sacramento, San Francisco, Silicon Valley, and Fresno.

The Texas governor's actual meet-and-greet campaign events were limited but high-profile and packed with minority children. He strolled through the Plaza de Mexico, a heavily Hispanic area at the Del Mar County Fair; visited a school in a minority neighborhood of Los Angeles; and tossed around a football with kids in a Sacramento mentoring program. Photographs of Bush with black and Hispanic children appeared in newspapers across the country, including one on the front page of the *New York Times.*

But the main reason for Bush's trip to California was to spend plenty of time with wealthy Republicans and add another $4 million to his already swollen campaign coffers. On the second day of his three-day bus tour of the state, it was announced that the Texas governor had set a new presidential fund-raising record by assembling an astonishing $37 million in the first six months of 1999.* The amount was more than any candidate had ever raised for an entire primary race, much less the four months Bush had been soliciting contributions.

"I am humbled by the response," the governor told reporters at a news conference in Los Angeles. "I am, as you well can imagine, amazed at the outpouring of support. This is a campaign that has got a wide range of people who are willing to help people from all around the country. I'm gratified and that's that."

Appearing somewhat overwhelmed by the announcement, Bush was asked to explain the fund-raising record. "A wonderful personality," he joked. "Seriously, that's what the pundits are going to have to figure out. I've got a lot of friends."

"The outpouring for Bush is beyond belief," noted Larry Makinson of the Center for Responsive Politics, a nonpartisan group that tracks money in politics. "It really shows the power of the purse. The funders have decided who the next nominee is going to be six months before anyone casts a vote. The reality of these numbers has to be brutal for the other Republican candidates."

Based on an analysis of thousands of campaign contribution records, Makinson and his public interest organization also noted that the governor

*Lyndon Johnson spent $10.5 million to run for president in 1964. When adjusted for inflation, the amount is equivalent to $56 million in 1999 dollars. Even if Bush's fund-raising pace slows down, he still should pass Johnson's total by the end of 1999—a little less than a year away from Election Day 2000. Nor is Ross Perot's 1992 total of $67 million out of the Texas governor's reach—not even when adjusted to $79 million in current dollars.

received more contributions than his opponents from the top executives at American corporations in the Dow Jones Industrial Average. According to the group's database, thirty-one high-level executives of sixteen of the thirty companies in the Dow had donated $1,000 each to Bush's campaign.

Bush's fund-raising prowess had virtually dried up the pool of GOP money for his rivals, forcing them to lay off campaign staff workers and downsize their budgets in an effort to remain in the race. In response, the governor came under direct attack from some of his opponents.

"Look who's saying he can't lose—the pundits," Elizabeth Dole said in an interview. "The same pundits who said Bill Clinton would have to resign after the Monica Lewinsky affair. The same pundits who said Bush's father could never lose after the Persian Gulf War."

Lamar Alexander, who later dropped out of the presidential race after finishing poorly in the Iowa straw poll, argued: "This nomination is too important to be bought, too important to be inherited and it ought to be earned."*

Conservative GOP challenger Gary Bauer said: "If elections could be bought, Ross Perot would be ending his second presidential term. So I think, at the end of the day, ideas matter, and I think the ideas I have are much more in line with Republican voters than this sort of mushy comments we're hearing out of Austin, Texas right now."

"This level of fund-raising from lobbyists and special interests calls into question Governor Bush's ability to make the changes necessary in Washington," opined Bill Dal Col, the campaign manager for Steve Forbes, who spent $37 million of a self-financed campaign in 1996 and was running again for president. Dal Col called on Bush to return all his special-interest donations, adding: "He has sold his soul to the Washington lobbyists."

Noting that Vice President Gore had raised $18.5 million in the first six months of the campaign, compared to Bush's $37 million, even Bill Clinton had to offer a comment to reporters aboard Air Force One. "He's a governor of a state. His brother is a governor of a state. They want to win. They've got more money than we do," the president said. "I'm not at all surprised they've raised that kind of money.

---

*In the first negative television ad of the presidential campaign, the struggling and cash-strapped Alexander warned that "big money" was threatening the Republican contest. The thirty-second spot, which began showing in most Iowa TV markets during the last week of July, featured cigar-smoking Texans in black cowboy hats auctioning off the White House to the highest bidder. "Going once, going twice, I've sold it for fifty million dollars," said an auctioneer with a Southern accent in the TV commercial, which was clearly aimed at Texas Governor Bush.

"What did he raise in Texas—eleven million dollars?" the president asked. "When I ran in '92 . . . in a state of two and a half million people, with a lower per-capita income and not nearly as many millionaires, we raised four million dollars. That would be the equivalent of twenty million dollars or more in Texas."

As Clinton pointed out, the source of one-third of the $37 million generated for Bush's campaign war chest in the first half of 1999 was his home state of Texas,* where he tapped into a network formed during his father's career. "That has been very important," chief fund-raiser Don Evans acknowledged. The former president's contacts "enabled us to get into cities in the spring and get people energized. That played an important part in laying the foundation." (Bush also inherited his mother's infamous Christmas-card list, a list of contacts and financial supporters going back over thirty years. One of her son's first mass presidential campaign fund-raising letters sent out in 1999 went out with her signature attached.)

Although the Bush campaign boasted that a populist "grassroots organization" of 75,000 concerned Americans in all fifty states had contributed an average of $480 or less, the real force behind Bush's fund-raising machine was an elite tier of $100,000 fund-raisers known as "Pioneers." Because federal law limits individual contributions to $1,000, each Pioneer fulfilled a

---

*In the wake of Bush's announcement that he had raised a record-shattering $37 million in a few short months, the shock was felt throughout the political community. But to close observers of his fund-raising record as Texas governor, the news was less of a surprise.

When Bush began his 1998 gubernatorial reelection campaign, his report of campaign contributions was released on paper only, with the names of two contributors on each page. In order to get a complete list of the governor's donors, the interested citizen would have had to spend over a thousand dollars for a photocopy of the report. Using data compiled for the *Los Angeles Times* and CNN by the Campaign Study Group (an independent research firm that analyzes campaign finance), the California newspaper undertook the most detailed examination to date of Bush's fund-raising in his 1994 and 1998 campaigns for governor. In two statewide elections, Bush raised $41 million—more than any candidate for governor in U.S. history—and much of the money came from contributors with major stakes in state regulation, including oil and other large industrial companies opposed to mandatory pollution controls; businesses seeking relief from expensive civil suits and caps on damage awards; and conservatives advocating school vouchers.

The analysis identified the employers and occupations of more than 14,000 substantial contributors, grouped them by industry and interest, and checked that against the governor's legislative record. According to the survey, the financial sector gave the most with a total of $4.6 million. Energy and mining were next with $3.7 million followed by real estate and developers at $2.2 million. Unlike presidential elections, where individual contributions are limited to $1,000, there are no limits in Texas and donations often exceeded $100,000.

According to the *Times* reporter Alan C. Miller, "These longtime alliances with major Texas corporate interests are significant. Many of the large donors continue to back Bush as he pursues the presidency."

FUNDING SOURCE, STATE BY STATE

George W. Bush raised $37 million in the first six months of 1999 in his campaign for the Republican presidential nomination. Here's a look at where the money—individual gifts of $1,000 or less, as limited by federal law—came from, based on his formal report to Federal Election Commission on July 15, 1999:

State	Amount	State	Amount
Texas	$11,254,300	Utah	151,100
California	4,118,800	Oregon	127,100
Florida	2,995,800	New Mexico	123,000
New York	1,503,500	Mississippi	123,000
Michigan	1,374,000	Other*	120,200
Pennsylvania	1,343,100	Delaware	118,300
Virginia	1,334,800	Indiana	114,600
Connecticut	1,286,100	Kansas	110,200
Massachusetts	893,600	Arkansas	108,400
Illinois	880,200	Wisconsin	79,600
Missouri	722,900	Nevada	73,200
Maryland	701,300	Iowa	68,200
District of Columbia	662,800	Alaska	66,700
Georgia	622,200	West Virginia	65,600
New Jersey	587,000	North Dakota	58,700
Ohio	468,900	New Hampshire	57,300
North Carolina	415,300	Wyoming	50,500
Colorado	390,000	Puerto Rico	49,300
Louisiana	380,800	Idaho	45,100
Arizona	363,700	Rhode Island	38,300
Oklahoma	357,500	Maine	37,300
Minnesota	260,500	Montana	28,400
Kentucky	232,900	Nebraska	27,200
Washington	222,000	Vermont	14,800
South Carolina	221,800	South Dakota	11,000
Tennessee	193,000	Hawaii	9,400
Alabama	164,900	Virgin Islands	1,200

**Americans living abroad or residence unknown*

pledge to raise at least $100,000 for the Bush campaign by soliciting contributions of $1,000 from 100 people. The Pioneers' effort was a sizable chunk of the record $37 million Bush raised during the first six months of 1999.

The Texas governor wasn't the first to use a fund-raising system like the Pioneers. The members of his father's "Team 100" each collected $100,000 for the Republican Party in 1988, but the son employed it more effectively than any presidential candidate before him. The Bush campaign originally wouldn't say how many Pioneers there were, but the organization issued a statement asserting that 2,500 people promised to raise $10,000 or more.

"These are people who have decided to take time out of their lives to help me become president," Bush said of the Pioneers (so-named because they were blazing new trails in campaign finance). "And I am really grateful and humbled by their support."

A partial list of the volunteers obtained by the *Dallas Morning News* showed that Bush not only inherited his father's famous name, but his donor lists, as well. Among those on the list who had longstanding family ties to the Bushes were Dallas philanthropist Louis Beecherl, California agribusiness executive Howard Leach, Microsoft's executive vice president and CEO Robert Herbold, Austin high-tech entrepreneur Steve Papermaster, Dallas cosmetics executive Richard Heath, and former Texas Secretary of State George Bayoud Jr. Also listed were Bush's sister Dorothy Koch of Maryland, uncle Jonathan Bush of Connecticut, and Craig and Debbie Stapleton, Bush cousins.

For the first three-month reporting period, the largest single contribution, more than $172,000, came from donors with connections to the Houston-based law firm of Vinson & Elkins, where Thomas Marinis, a partner at the firm and longstanding Bush friend, served as a Pioneer to the campaign.

Edison Electric Institute president, Thomas Kuhn, who represented the electric utility in Washington, D.C. acknowledged to the press that he helped recruit several lobbyists in the capital to support Bush, his classmate at Yale. Kuhn conceded that some of the lobbyists, and the CEOs of the companies they represented, had become Pioneers, too.

Craig McDonald, director of the nonpartisan Texans for Public Justice, a group that monitors political spending, argued that the system of super-donors "evades the spirit" of the post-Watergate campaign-finance reforms and accused the Pioneers of using other people's money to buy political influence with Bush.

"The average American is not in a position to raise $100,000 for a political campaign," McDonald said in a letter to Bush, asking him to identify the fund-raisers and how much money they had assembled. "The limited number of Bush Pioneers who have been identified by the media comprise a Who's Who of the nation's powerful business and lobby elite. Many of these people have keen interests in the outcome of federal policies."

McDonald also noted that the Pioneers' fund-raising efforts were tracked by the campaign, adding "they know who they are, and that creates a class of donors who become the creditors for the campaign. It's skirting the spirit of the law that says you can only give $1,000."

In his letter to Bush, McDonald called the arrangement "a sophisticated bundling scheme," in which a single contributor boosted his influence by coordinating donations through others.

Meredith McGehee of the Washington chapter of Common Cause, agreed, saying many Washington lobbyists were eager to "bundle" for Bush so that if he was elected they could call in their favors for special interest clients. "What's happening is you have powerful Washington insiders who use their Rolodex and say, 'George W. is going to be the next president, so you'd be wise to pony up,'" McGehee said.

Although Bush publicly described the complaints about his fund-raising success as "sour grapes," his campaign staff—wary of accusations that their candidate was circumventing federal finance laws—said he would honor McDonald's request and release the previously secret list of big-money contributors.

"I can give you a pretty good start of names," Bush told reporters. "Just start with my best friends, all of whom would like to see me be president, and all of whom are anxious to help me become president."

When asked about claims that the Pioneers might receive more favorable treatment from a second Bush administration, the governor snapped back: "You either have somebody in the process who's honest or not honest."

The list of 115 well-connected people who had raised at least $13.7 million (forty percent of the record $37 million) for his presidential race included fifty-seven Texans. Several of the Pioneers had been supporters of Bush's father and assembled $100,000 or more from contributors as members of "Team 100" in 1988. Many others were developers and lawyers who helped Jeb Bush win office as governor of Florida in 1998. The list also included a multitude of Pioneers the Texas governor had appointed to key positions in state government and others who had helped make Bush a wealthy politician.

The list of $100,000 Pioneers included: Texas Utilities Chairman Erle Nye and Enron Corp. CEO Kenneth Lay, who were raising money for Bush while the 1999 Texas Legislature was voting on an electric industry deregulation bill, which the governor later signed into law; four of his partners in the Texas Rangers—Rusty Rose, Roland Betts, Bill DeWitt, and Mercer Reynolds (DeWitt and Reynolds were also Bush partners in Spectrum 7, an energy company); and Austin broadcast executive Steven Hicks, brother of Tom Hicks, who bought the Rangers in a $250 million deal in 1998 that produced $15 million for Bush.

Bush appointees to state boards and commissions who were also disclosed on the Pioneers list: Jim Francis, a longtime Bush friend and backer who headed the Public Safety Commission, the three-member board that oversees the Department of Public Safety and the elite Texas Rangers law enforcement division (Francis was also coordinator of the Pioneers program); chairman of the Texas Transportation Commission, David Laney; Texas Parks and Wildlife Commission Chairman Lee Bass; and four University of Texas System regents—oil company executive Tony Sanchez, consulting engineering firm executive Raul Romero, retired banker Dub Riter, and former Texas Congressman Tom Loeffler (a Washington lobbyist whose clients included Citicorp and Envirocare of Utah, which operated a low-level radioactive waste dump and was seeking to run a similar unit in Texas).

Bush's political friends who were listed as Pioneers, included: Michigan Governor John Engler (frequently mentioned as a possible Bush running mate); State Senator Teel Bivins; U.S. Representatives Joe Barton and Jennifer Dunn (who raised $130,000); Colorado Governor Bill Owens; former Senator Rudy Boschwitz of Minnesota; former Florida Governor Bob Martinez; and Fred Webber, head of the Chemical Manufacturers Association and a former senate liaison for Presidents Nixon and Ford, who had worked for every Republican presidential candidate since.

Jim Francis, head of the Pioneers program, boasted to the press after the list was released that as many as three hundred more Bush backers were working toward the $100,000 goal. If they were successful, he said, that would translate into an additional $30 million for the presidential candidate.

Craig McDonald, director of the citizen group that successfully sought the public release of the list containing the first 115 Pioneers, complained that it was incomplete in light of Francis comments. "Bush has fallen short of full disclosure," McDonald announced at a news conference. "There are three hundred more Pioneers who are bundling contributions for the campaign. The public has a right to know who these high rollers are and exactly how much they have delivered."

The Bush campaign declined to release further names of "power brokers" who had pledged to become Pioneers but had not yet actually raised $100,000. "We have made a list available of all those who have reached out to their friends and neighbors to raise $100,000," responded Bush communications director, Karen Hughes. "There may be additional people who are trying to raise this amount of money."

"Obviously the people responsible for raising $100,000 or more are in a position to have a very exclusive level of access and influence on the candidate," noted Paul Hendrie, spokesperson for the Center for Responsive Politics. "The money is speaking so loud, so early, that it may speak louder than voters. This thing may be decided long before the 2000 caucuses and primaries in Iowa and New Hampshire."

Two of Bush's Pioneers had been criticized in the past for treatment they received from the elder Bush's presidential administration. In an extensive 1992 investigation, *Common Cause Magazine* cited the case of Howard Leach (a wealthy California agricultural investor and member of President Bush's Team 100 contributors), who requested that the president reverse the Interior Department's plan to not release any water from the federally-subsidized Central Valley Project during the drought-stricken spring. Ten days later, President Bush released 326 billion gallons of low-cost federal water from the project, a massive system of dams and reservoirs, in a publicized effort to aid California farmers in the area. Others who benefited from Bush's emergency water allocation were Howard Marguleas and J.G. Boswell. Both agribusinessmen were friends of Leach's, two of the largest users of the Central Valley Project water, and fellow members of Bush's wealthy Team 100 contributors.*

Similarly, *Common Cause* also reported on benefits obtained by Heinz Prechter, president of the Michigan-based automobile customizing company American Sunroof Corporation, another Team 100 member and one of George W.'s Pioneers in later years. As chairman of the President's Export Council (a quasi-official panel that advised the White House on trade matters), Prechter helped persuade Bush to allow himself and twenty other top U.S. executives to accompany the president on his official trip to Japan in January 1992. While in the Asian country, Prechter closed a deal to supply sunroofs for Honda's American-made automobiles, wresting the contract from Japanese firms. Within three weeks of the trip, Prechter contributed a total of $60,000 in soft money to the Republican Party.

---

*The Administration cited heavy February rains as the reason for its reversal of the Interior Department's plan.

The six-month investigation by *Common Cause Magazine* noted that "while direct quid pro quos are inherently difficult to prove, a clear pattern of favorable treatment of Team 100 members involving questionable actions and policy reversals emerges from government records, corporate reports, interviews, and industry and press reports."

Not only were the various public-interest groups troubled by Bush's vast sum of campaign money and particularly by the way in which it was raised, they grew even more concerned when Bush announced in mid-July 1999 he would forgo public funds and thus wouldn't be bound by spending limits designed to limit the influence of contributions in presidential elections.

"After looking at the numbers, cash on hand of $30 million, I've decided not to accept federal matching funds during the course of this campaign," Bush told the press, adding that he wanted to "enjoy as much strategic flexibility as possible" in his race for the White House.

By passing the 1974 amendments to the Federal Election Campaign Act after the Watergate scandal, Congress intended to strip the influence of big money from political contests and redirect the focus back to voters. In an effort to prevent a White House race from becoming an open-ended money-arms-race, the law restricted the size of contributions and offered public funds for presidential campaigns. Traditionally, candidates accept money from the federal treasury, which "matches" a percentage of their own fund-raising. They then agree to abide by state-to-state spending caps.

Bush's decision—while not unexpected in light of the $37 million he raised in the first six months of his presidential run—meant he was passing up about $16.5 million in taxpayer-funded campaign money, but it also freed him from restrictions spelling out how much money a candidate could spend in the primary season.

"You've got limits that constrain a candidate," Bush said. "I want to be in a position to respond. I want to be in a position to plan, and I want to be in a position to plan according to need."

In exempting himself from spending limits, Bush, a student of history, clearly had learned from the last election cycle when multimillionaire Steve Forbes rejected matching funds. During the 1996 primary season, he poured considerable money into Iowa and New Hampshire TV advertising, but battered GOP front-runner, Bob Dole, was unable to respond in kind because he accepted federal funds and agreed to spending regulations that limited how much money he could collect from private donors. Dole secured the Republican nomination but ended up broke for months prior to the GOP convention. By then, President Clinton had an insurmountable lead in his bid for reelection.

In 1999, Forbes was once again running for president and sidestepping federal matching funds and the accompanying spending limits. "Competing against somebody in the primary who can write one check, I'm mindful of what happened in 1996 and I'm not going to let it happen to me," Bush told the press during an impromptu news conference alongside his campaign bus.

"If you've got it, spend it," Dan Quayle said on NBC-TV's *Today* program. "What Bush is doing is trying to win this campaign by money alone. He really believes in the school of old politics that money wins elections."

Although Quayle's campaign was operating in the red at the time, he was not the first casualty of the Y2K presidential race. During the same week that Bush announced he was forgoing federal matching funds, one Republican opponent changed political parties and another dropped out of the race completely.

Senator Robert Smith of New Hampshire, a conservative firebrand who badly trailed fellow GOP challenger Bush even in his home state, announced in a speech on the floor of the Senate that he was leaving the Republican Party over philosophical differences and changing his political registration to independent.

"The elitists of the party . . . believe that electing people with an 'R' next to their name is more important than principle," Smith said later that evening on CNN's *Larry King Live.* "I came to the Republican Party on principle, and I'm leaving on principle." The senator lambasted the Republican leader on the *Today* show: "Many who want to lead our party—specifically candidate Bush—won't take a position on the issues."

House Budget Committee Chairman John Kasich, another challenger for the GOP nomination who had shown negligible support in national polls and was plagued by lackluster fund-raising, abandoned his campaign for president the following day. The nine-term Ohio congressman also announced he had no plans to seek reelection to his seat in the House of Representatives.

At a news conference in Columbus and then later in a joint appearance with Bush at the Ronald Reagan International Trade Center in downtown Washington, Kasich formally dropped out of the presidential race and endorsed the Texas governor for nominee of the Republican Party.

In the congressman's view, Bush's "compassionate conservative" theme was closest to his own message. Kasich, author of a book about inspirational volunteers across the country, said community leaders rather than government programs were a key to solving social problems. Both men said religious charities and institutions should play a bigger role.

Stating that "you got to know when to hold 'em, you got to know when to fold 'em," Kasich quit the presidential race in large part because of the overwhelming early attention focused on Bush and the Texans' staggering fund-raising edge.

"Bush got the low-hanging fruit, the high-hanging fruit and all the fruit in between," admitted Ed Gillespie, one of Kasich's advisers. The Ohio congressman had recently kept his beleaguered presidential campaign afloat by transferring money from his House campaign committee.

Common Cause issued a scathing reaction predicting "the fund-raising—and potential corruption—will be out of control" during the year 2000 White House race. "We are a year and a half from the elections, and we already know who our likely two choices for president are going to be: George Bush vs. Al Gore. So much for the primaries and giving voters a choice," complained Meredith McGehee of the Washington chapter of Common Cause.

"I know campaign finance reform is not as sexy as Monica Lewinsky's dress, but until we send politicians a strong, clear message about their being accountable to the people they are representing and not to the power brokers with the biggest donations, we are going to see that we don't have much of a democracy," McGehee said, adding, "At least Bush is being honest about his greed—whatever it takes to win."

"I've learned that life doesn't end if you lose a campaign," Bush told 150 reporters on the lawn of his family's seaside summer home in Kennebunkport, Maine. The candidate had made a short pit stop during his presidential campaign to celebrate the seventy-fifth birthday of his father. "I've seen a really good man win, and I've seen a really good man come in second, but he never lost his perspective and his values."

Turning to the former president, who was smiling broadly at his side, Bush continued to explain—rather unconvincingly—that winning wasn't everything: "I will give it my best shot. I will speak from my heart. I will talk about a hopeful tomorrow. I'm not going to trash-mouth my opponents. I'm going to try to bring a level of dignity to the political process that many in this country long for, and we'll just see what happens."

Pausing momentarily, the son who had just embarked on his own quest for the White House seemed reflective as he scanned the Atlantic Ocean. "And if it works out, I'm ready, and if it doesn't work out, me and the old boy will spend a lot of time fishing together. The thing you learn from being George Bush's son is that life moves on."

Epilogue: Brand Name

Some folks are born made to wave the flag

—Creedence Clearwater Revival
"Fortunate Son"

With a commanding lead in the polls and a mountain of money in the bank, George W. Bush leads the GOP field nationally and is, by any measure, the favorite for the Republican presidential nomination in the year 2000. He even beats Vice President Al Gore, the putative Democratic nominee, in trial heats.

"High hopes can be troublesome," noted *Weekly Standard* editor Bill Kirstol, former chief of staff to Vice President Dan Quayle. "One need only recall George Romney's '68 campaign. There's a history of early front-runners faltering, never to be heard from again."

This particular bit of history, George Romney, won a landslide reelection as Michigan governor in 1966, and instantly became the favorite for the

1968 Republican presidential nomination. His campaign imploded, however, and didn't last through the first primary in New Hampshire when he unwisely commented that he had been "brainwashed" during a trip to Vietnam.

During the next presidential campaign in 1972, another White House hopeful, Democratic Senator Edmund Muskie, who had been the 1968 vice presidential nominee, looked in similarly strong shape as his party's leader. Many Democrats endorsed Muskie for the 1972 nomination early, much the same way the GOP virtually anointed Bush as the 2000 Republican nominee, more than a year before the national convention. Before the primaries, Muskie not only led the Democratic pack but beat President Nixon by five percentage points in the polls. When the press reported Muskie broke down in tears after an attack by a New Hampshire newspaper (he always insisted snowflakes had dampened his cheeks), his campaign ended practically overnight. The weakest candidate, George McGovern, won the nomination and was annihilated by Nixon in the general election. In the process, Democrats were left with a left-wing image that plagued them into the 1990s.

Romney and Muskie, and Edward Kennedy in 1980, looked like certain winners more than a year before the primaries and the presidential conventions. But eventually they had to campaign in other states, take a stand on the political issues, counter their opponents' charges, avoid blunders, and prove to the voters they had the prerequisite "fire in the belly" to run for president. The results proved disastrous to their campaigns.

Will the surging energy behind Bush's campaign propel him to the Oval Office once occupied by his father? Or will it meet with inglorious defeat as did the presidential aspirations of Romney, Muskie, and Kennedy? Bush's political consultants and strategists cite a half dozen reasons why they believe their candidate will end the Democrat's eight-year hold on the presidency:

1. **Brand name.** His is the second-best in Republican politics. Only Ronald Reagan is more admired among the GOP's faithful than former president Bush and his wife Barbara, George W.'s parents. "If his name was Governor Smith, he might not be so popular," asserted Bruce Buchanan, a political scientist at the University of Texas. "A lot of this is name recognition." In addition, many Americans now admit that they regret their vote for Bill Clinton over then-President Bush in 1992. A May 1999 Fox News-Opinion Dynamics Poll showed Governor Bush thrashing Clinton, 56 percent to 34 percent in a theoretical match-up. A second

Bush presidency offers voters an opportunity to seek repentance for the error of their ways.

2. **Bipartisanship.** Bush talks of changing the political culture of Washington and the country is eager to put an end to governmental shutdowns and party bickering. "Without question, he's the best governor I ever worked with," stated the late Democratic Lieutenant Governor of Texas, Bob Bullock, when he endorsed Republican Bush for reelection in 1998. Although Texas Democrats are more conservative than those he would face in the House of Representatives, Bush could plausibly claim to offer a fresh start as a Washington outsider.

3. **Clinton/Gore fatigue.** Despite one of the strongest peacetime economies, soaring stock prices, and violent crime numbers at the lowest level in twenty-five years of reporting, voters have grown weary of Monica Lewinsky, fund-raising controversies, Whitewater, Filegate, Travelgate, and a host of other White House scandals associated with the Clinton/Gore years. They're ready to throw the rascals out of the palace.

4. **Personality.** Bush projects his father's likability, draws strength from a crowd like Clinton, and smiles with Reagan's lopsided grin. Like the 1996 Republican vice presidential candidate, Jack Kemp, Bush's crossover appeal is high with women, African-Americans, Hispanics, and others in the Democratic Party's base, judging by the turnout for his landslide reelection to the governorship and, more importantly, by presidential preference polls.

5. **"Compassionate conservative."** In other words, Bush claims he is not the stereotypical right-wing extremist usually associated with the Republican Party. He is at times described as Reaganesque, blending fiscal and social conservatism, but with a more "communitarian" focus on society and government's role in helping the less fortunate. He'd rather talk about limited government, inclusion, and a new prosperity than abortion, race quotas, or immigration. Just as Clinton often talks like a moderate Republican while offering new government programs, Bush often sounds like a new Democrat, even when governing from the right in Texas. "What you're seeing, for the first time, is a primary campaign made up of tactics rather than ideology," noted Jay Severin, a New York-based Republican consultant who worked for conservative presidential

candidate Pat Buchanan in the 1996 election. "He's saying to conservative primary voters, with a wink, 'Trust me. You know I'm really one of you, but if I say that, I will damage myself such that I may not be able to win the general election."

6. **The Republicans will pull out all the stops to win.** "There is a very, very strong desire to win," said Whit Ayres, a GOP consultant in Atlanta. "We're tired of losing!" After two lost presidential races and the disastrous 1998 midterm congressional elections, the only litmus for a Republican candidate in 2000 is the ability to win elections and to raise significant amounts of campaign contributions, both of which Bush has proven quite convincingly that he is capable of doing.

It is somewhat ironic that the GOP could find itself turning to a man named Bush to reclaim the presidency after eight years of Democratic rule. After all, the elder Bush lost the White House to Clinton at a time when the Republican Party had made winning the presidency an almost routine event every four years.

Privately, however, Governor Bush has told aides and political strategists that his campaign won't be a rerun of his father's and that he won't surround himself with former advisers from the Bush White House. "I'm not interested in the people who lost my dad's election," Bush has said. "This is going to be my race, not my dad's."

And this is the great paradox with George W. Bush. This is a man who, had he not been George Herbert Walker Bush's son, would not now be the favorite for the Republican presidential nomination. Despite attempts to step out of his father's intimidating shadow over the years, his life has been one lucky break after another because of their relationship: acceptance and graduation from Ivy League schools; avoidance of serving in Vietnam; the rescue of his failed oil companies in West Texas; the Harken Energy Corporation stock sale; ownership in the Texas Rangers (which eventually transformed him into a multimillionaire when the baseball franchise was sold); and election and subsequent reelection to the governorship of the Lone Star State. The pattern continued to persist in mid-1999 when Bush set a new record for presidential campaign fund-raising, due mostly to the wealthy GOP connections of his father, a former chairman of the Republican Party.

The best investment strategy, of course, is to have a wealthy and influential father. Bush seems aware of that and has acknowledged on occasion that he is "a blessed person," but he doesn't quite seem to understand that with a different last name he could be just another Texan who failed in the oil business and now operates a shrimp boat in the Gulf of Mexico.

"I was born on second base but got to third on my own," the fortunate son professed to members of the press during the first summer of his presidential campaign. The next day, however, a poll was released indicating that Bush fared so well in nationwide presidential surveys primarily because respondents erroneously believed that his father was once again running for the White House.

Attempting to save face, George W. Bush made light of the confusion. "In politics, an easily recalled name is a very, very important thing."

Afterword

Trust but verify.

—Ronald Reagan

On August 4, 1999, Senate minority leader Tom Daschle publicly charged the press with giving George W. Bush a "free ride" in regards to the persistent rumors of past cocaine use, adding that it was "a legitimate question" to expect any presidential candidate to answer to determine if he or she was morally fit to hold the highest elected office in the United States.

In response to Senator Daschle's challenge, later that same day the *New York Daily News* asked Bush and his other eleven political rivals whether they had ever used cocaine. All of them—except for the presidential front-runner, who refused to answer the question—denied ever experimenting with the illegal drug. When the Associated Press asked the same group of candidates about the general use of drugs, eight said no, and two acknowledged trying marijuana. Once again, Bush refused to answer the question, contributing to the media's feeding frenzy regarding allegations of his prior drug use by evasively responding: "I've made mistakes in the past, and I've learned from my mistakes," branding such rumors "ridiculous and absurd," but declining to label them false.

The other presidential hopefuls called for Bush to end his obfuscation and candidly "tell the truth" to a "simple question that all the candidates should answer." His political opponents in both parties argued that the Texas governor had previously voiced no objection to revealing personal details, as long as they were of his own choosing. When President Clinton's extramarital affairs made headlines in 1998, Bush announced—without being asked by the media—that he'd been faithful to Laura, his wife of more than twenty years. He had also repeatedly recited his story of a "young and irresponsible" early life of excessive drinking followed by sobriety at age forty. Unlike drinking and infidelity, cocaine use is illegal and Bush testily refused to say whether he had ever experimented with the drug, stating at each campaign appearance that he was not going to participate in the "politics of personal destruction."

"We ought to be able to say with no hesitation that, 'No, we have not broken the drug laws of the United States,' and 'No, we have not used cocaine,'" asserted one of Bush's Republican presidential challengers, Gary Bauer, a former Reagan White House aide.

Even Oklahoma Governor Frank Keating, an early Bush supporter and chairman of the Republican Governors Association, told reporters in Washington that Bush should "address issues about private conduct. In today's world, everyone of us who serves in public office needs to answer questions about conduct that is arguably criminal."

Fresh from a first-place showing in the Iowa GOP straw poll on August 14, the Texas governor was forced to amend his stock message when Sam Attlesey of the *Dallas Morning News* asked whether, as president, Bush would insist that his appointees answer drug-use questions contained in the standard FBI background check. (As president, Bush would nominate candidates for the Supreme Court, other federal judges, cabinet secretaries, foreign ambassadors, and federal prosecutors. All would be required to answer questions "fully and truthfully" regarding illegal drug use on the questionnaire for national security decisions, a part of the FBI background check.)

After receiving advance word that the new slant on the drug question was going to be asked, Bush conferred with campaign finance chairman Don Evans, finance director Jack Oliver, media adviser Mark McKinnon, chief strategist Karl Rove, and communications director Karen Hughes.

"Imagine the ad our opponents could make if we didn't answer the question," said one Bush campaign adviser. "As president, George W. Bush would maintain a double standard when it comes to illegal drug use by White House employees—one for him and one for everybody else."

Bush's inner circle of campaign officials agreed that the leading presidential candidate should confirm to the *Dallas Morning News* that he would meet all the standards himself, a response that would "hopefully put a stake in the heart of the coke-use stories."

"As I understand it, the current form asks the question, 'Did somebody use drugs within the last seven years?' and I will be glad to answer that question, and the answer is 'No,'" Bush responded during a news conference he called to introduce his new state education commissioner.

However, the Texas governor once again refused to say whether he had ever used cocaine in particular and angrily claimed that his political enemies were peddling unsubstantiated rumors of illegal drug use. "I know they're being planted," Bush said, obviously irritated. "They're ridiculous, absurd, and the American people are sick of this kind of politics." Earlier, he had chided reporters for again raising the drug issue. "Somebody floats a rumor and it causes you to ask a question, and that's the game in American politics, and I refuse to play it," he stated. "That is a game. And you just fell for the trap."

The following day at another media event in Roanoke, Virginia, Bush decided to move the boundary markers yet again, volunteering that at the time his father was inaugurated in 1989 he could have passed even the fifteen-year background check in effect then, dating his drug-free years all the way back to 1974, when he was twenty-eight and a graduate student at Harvard.

But the presidential candidate suddenly drew the line and defined a statute of limitations for only the past twenty-five years after NBC's David Bloom noted that current White House appointees were required to list any drug use since their eighteenth birthday.

"I believe it is important to put a stake in the ground and to say enough is enough when it comes to trying to dig up people's backgrounds," Bush said, reverting to his previous position of firmly standing against "trash-mouth politics" and refusing to discuss details about his past. If voters didn't like that answer, he announced, "they can go find somebody else to vote for. I have told the American people all I'm going to tell them."

Later in the day, Bush continued his stonewall strategy, saying only that parents should counsel their children about the perils of alcohol and drugs. "I think a baby-boomer parent ought to say, 'I have learned from the mistakes I may or may not have made, and I'd like to share some wisdom with you, and that is: Don't use drugs. Don't abuse alcohol.' That's what leadership is about," the presidential front-runner told reporters while touring an Ohio homeless shelter that offered treatment for drug addicts.

"Bush has essentially admitted to *something*. But he refuses to say what, creating a political paradox," wrote the editors of *USA Today*. "If his offense is trivial, why hide it? Voters have shown little inclination to punish candidates for youthful drug use, at least in the case of marijuana. And if it's substantive, why should those voters be denied the facts?"

"He's been drawing all kinds of distinctions, rather than just giving an answer which will put these queries to rest for good," said Mark Rozell, a political scientist at Catholic University of America in Washington, D.C. "It's sort of a piecemeal, hoping-it-will-go-away approach. But this line of inquiry will not go away until he does what only he can do to end it: Tell the flat-out truth about what happened."

Bush's public flip-flops on the drug use question only heightened the mystery and invited deeper scrutiny by the media. On August 25, the on-line magazine *Salon* reported on allegations that "back in the late '60s or early '70s," Bush "was ordered by a Texas judge to perform community service in exchange for expunging his record showing illicit drug use and that this service was performed at the Martin Luther King, Jr., Community Center in Houston."

In response, Madgelean "Madge" Bush (no relation), the center's director for thirty-one years, stated to over fifty news organizations that she had "never heard of him [Bush] doing community services here at the agency." She did, however, note that as a gubernatorial candidate, Bush had publicly announced his welfare reform program from her agency's office.

In the wake of the *Salon* article, hundreds of reporters attempted to validate the allegation, but when nothing could be substantiated, the story died within days and only a few follow-up articles appeared in the magazine or in any other media outlet. But when *Online Journal* and MSNBC questioned why the presidential candidate had his Texas driver's license number changed in March 1995 for "security measures" (although his father, the former president and a Texas resident since January 1993, would seem to be at much more of a risk), the reporter's instinct in me wondered if Bush may have had something expunged from his driving record, which could have resulted in the issuance of a new license. Did Bush have something in his past to hide to cause him to purge the old record and number?*

As a biographer and a former investigative journalist, I always had nagging questions regarding Bush's tenure as a Project P.U.L.L. inner-city youth counselor for several months in 1972. It was like a jigsaw-puzzle piece you keep trying to push into place, but you know it will never quite fit because it's the wrong piece. At the time, the twenty-six-year-old Bush was flying planes part-time for the Texas Air National Guard on the weekends, while spending most of his days in Houston drinking heavily, chain-smoking, and, according to friends who partied with him in the early seventies, occasionally getting high on marijuana and snorting cocaine.

After working less than a year for an agricultural conglomerate owned by one of his father's longtime friends, the official campaign biography states that Bush's first notable full-time job was at Project P.U.L.L., an antipoverty charity program, of which his father was a "benevolent supporter" and honorary chairman. For several months, he counseled hardened African-American youth in Houston's tough third ward, played basketball with them, and took the teenagers on field trips to prisons. By the end of the year in 1972, he had left his position at P.U.L.L. and, before heading off to Harvard Business School, had a man-to-man, in-your-face confrontation with his father after driving drunk with his fifteen-year-old younger brother, Marvin, as a passenger.

Although I had completed *Fortunate Son* and was in the process of proofing galley pages of the Bush biography before it went to press, the August 1999 *Salon* article concerning allegations of a possible drug arrest and community service—and the reports on MSNBC and *Online Journal* of Bush's new driver's license—forced me to readdress my old concerns regarding the short period he spent mentoring young black men at Project P.U.L.L. Why would the carousing Bush, whose life seemed nothing more than one big

*Although Texas requires renewal of a driver's license every four years on one's birthday, Bush obtained a new number (a nine-digit 000000005) on March 31, 1995 as a renewal instead of on his birthday, July 6, which the Texas Department of Motor Vehicles called "highly unusual."

party, abruptly quit behaving "young and irresponsible" for a few months before returning almost as suddenly to an existence of "just living for the moment"?

Then I began to ask myself, "What if *Salon* magazine was right about the 'illicit drug use', but wrong about the location of Bush's community service?" If George W. had been court-ordered to work full-time at Project P.U.L.L. in 1972, it would explain why he steadily refused to discuss drug use prior to 1974. It might also explain why the future presidential candidate would purge his old driver's-license record and number and be issued a new one after he entered political life, as reported by MSNBC and *Online Journal.*

Although the manuscript to the Bush biography was finished and I had already begun conducting interviews for my next book, these new articles were akin to a punch in the gut. There was something here, a lead that I hadn't followed up on. I could sense it, and I felt compelled to learn the truth.

Acting on what can only be described as a reporter's hunch, I telephoned Houston's Martin Luther King, Jr., Community Center and asked to speak to its director of thirty-one years, Madge Bush, who was obviously not too enthusiastic about speaking to yet another probing journalist. When she came on the line, she immediately began complaining that she had been contacted by over fifty reporters and "told them the same thing. Newspapers in London and New York and—"

"Ma'am, I know Governor Bush wasn't ordered by a judge to perform community service at MLK Community Center for illegal drug use," I said, matter-of-factly, interrupting her seemingly well-rehearsed speech.

"Finally, someone believes me," she shot back with a detectable amount of relief in her voice. "Then if that's the case, what do you want to talk to me about?"

"I've done my homework and I know you also serve as a Texas state executive committee woman, precinct judge, and treasurer of the Harris County Democratic Party in Houston."

"You got a point to this call or is this where I hang up?" Ms. Bush asked, adding that she had "too many people—from a day old to a hundred years old—depending on the community center" for her to "sit on the phone all day listening to reporters ask a hundred questions."

"Yes, ma'am, I understand you've been hounded by the press and for that I'm truly sorry," I said, apologizing. "But I just want to know if a die-hard

Democrat like yourself would tell the truth about the governor if the right question was asked?"

She paused and I sensed her apprehension. "What do you mean by the 'right question'?"

At least she hadn't hung up on me at this point, which wouldn't have been surprising considering the numerous calls she had received from other persistent reporters. Although I could tell she dreaded what I was going to ask, I had to push forward if I was going to get to the truth.

"Did Governor Bush perform court-ordered community service at *another* agency in Houston or elsewhere in Texas other than the Martin Luther King, Jr., center?" I pointedly asked.

She paused once again, a little longer this time, as if she was weighing the consequences of her reply.

Then abruptly she issued a curt "no comment, because Madge Bush is not gonna talk to you," before adding, "I'm not getting off into anything about George except he's the governor of Texas. That's all I'm gonna say about George W. Bush." And then she hung up the phone.

More important than what Ms. Bush said was what she *didn't* say. I detected an unmistakable hint of regret in her voice, as if she was saying, "I wish I could tell you the truth, but I'm between a rock and a hard place because so many underprivileged people depend on me and this agency and I can't jeopardize the community center's existence."

The next call I made was to one of Bush's former Yale classmates, a family friend who also partied with the future Texas governor and presidential candidate in the late sixties and early seventies in Houston. For almost a year, he had graciously contributed his time, knowledge, and experiences while I worked on *Fortunate Son*. Believing that a definitive biography should be well-balanced and contain "both a man's halos and horns," he provided me with invaluable information only on the condition that he would not be identified in the book.

Never mentioning the *Salon* story or my conversation with Madge Bush, I asked him if George W. volunteered to work at Project P.U.L.L. in 1972 or if his involvement with the antipoverty youth program had been court-ordered.

"I was wondering when someone was going to get around to uncovering the truth," he replied, surprisingly unruffled by my direct approach. "Evidently, you kind of glossed over it in the book like a lot of other reporters have done in their newspaper and magazine articles. It doesn't fit, does it?"

Grudgingly, I had to admit I had doubts at the time I wrote that particular chapter, but facing an early May deadline for delivery of the manuscript to my publisher, I had decided to forego following up on my gut feeling.

"George W. was arrested for posession of cocaine in 1972, but due to his father's connections, the entire record was expunged by a state judge whom the elder Bush helped get elected," he explained. "It was one of those 'behind closed doors in the judge's chambers' kind of thing between the old man and one of his Texas cronies who owed him a favor. In exchange for successfully completing community service at Project P.U.L.L., where Bush senior was a heavy contributor and honorary chairman, the judge purged George W.'s record."

"Can you tell me more about the incident involving his arrest or give me a name of the police officer or, better yet, the judge?" I asked.

"I've told you enough already," he replied, sounding uncharacteristically apprehensive. "There's only a handful of us that know the truth. I'm not even sure his wife knows about it." Then he paused and added, "Just keep digging. But keep looking over your shoulder."

Bush's former Yale classmate and close friend was not someone who scared easily. After I hung up the phone, I sat at my desk for a few moments, trying to comprehend the ominous implications of our conversation. The whole thing seemed too unreal, but I couldn't help wondering about the importance of what I'd uncovered, and how far some might go to make this particular problem disappear. But to be honest, sitting there in my office, the dangers seemed vague and insubstantial. Whatever I'd found had me in its grip, and short of the grave, I was willing to follow wherever it might lead.

Another confidential source, a longtime Bush friend and unofficial political adviser, also acknowledged that Bush had indeed been arrested for cocaine possession in 1972 and had his record expunged by a Houston judge after George W. worked as a youth counselor for several months at Project P.U.L.L.

"Take this any way it sounds, but do you think George would take time out from speeding around town in his TR-6 convertible sports car, bedding down just about every single woman—and a few married ones—and partying like there's no tomorrow to go work full-time as a mentor to a bunch of streetwise black kids? Get real, man, this is a white-bread boy from the other side of town we're talking about."

Pressing once again for more details about the arrest and purging of Bush's record, my source explained: "Say you get a *D* in algebra for your last grade of the semester and now you're going to be required to repeat the class the following year, but your teacher says if you promise to be tutored during the summer by a friend of hers who's good in math, she'll change the *D* to a *C*. You spend a few hours a week during the summer vacation learning all about arithmetical operations and relationships, and then the teacher issues you a new report card, replacing the one on file in the principal's office. Now you're the only one possessing a copy of that original report card that had a non-passing *D* on it. Something akin to that scenario is what happened with Bush in 1972," he said, adding that Bush "did the community service and the judge, a good ol' Texas boy and friend of George's politically influential daddy, purged the record. It happened a lot in Texas years ago and George damn sure wasn't the first rich kid who got caught with a little snow and because of his family's connections had his record taken care of by the judge."

Although he told me that no one at Bush's office would answer any of my questions, he stated that their responses would prove interesting.

Presidential campaign spokesman Scott McClellan had previously told *Salon*, "We do not dignify false rumors and innuendoes with a response," after the on-line magazine asked him if Bush had ever performed community service at the Martin Luther King, Jr., Community Center in Houston in exchange for having his "illicit drug use" record expunged.

In the past, McClellan always seemed to be the consummate campaign spokesperson, always in control, never rattled by the sometimes raucous press corps and their continuous barrage of questions. But that impression was shattered when I queried McClellan about Bush's involvement at Project P.U.L.L. in 1972 as a condition of having his cocaine possession charge purged. There was a moment of electric silence, and then McClellan muttered an almost inaudible, "Oh, shit," and after hesitating for a moment, finally said, "No comment."

After McClellan abruptly terminated our conversation, I called the Bush presidential exploratory committee back, but a Megan Moran answered and informed me that either Karen Hughes or Mindy Tucker, two other Bush campaign spokespersons, would return my call. Neither one of them ever did.

I had one final source to telephone. I felt compelled to talk to the one person who had the access, connections, and resources to make or break my investigation: a high-ranking adviser to Bush who had known the presidential candidate for several years. In June 1999, he called me on my unlisted number and described himself as "a close associate of the governor concerned with making sure I got all the facts right in the biography." Although I told him I had already turned in the final draft of the manuscript to my publisher in May, he knowingly argued that I still could make "changes, corrections, and revisions" when the copyedited pages were returned to me. After negotiating where and when to meet for almost two weeks, we finally decided on Lake Eufaula, a massive man-made body of water with over six hundred miles of shoreline in Eufaula, Oklahoma, which was only a couple of hours drive-time from the Texas state line.

To be honest, I was more than a little timorous about going out in the middle of a lake on a boat with someone who obviously had his own agenda regarding my biography of Bush (my pregnant wife even asked if I should pack a gun). Although it now seems and proved to be ludicrous, one of the final scenes in *The Godfather, Part II,* in which Fredo Corleone is shot to death on a boat in Lake Tahoe kept being replayed over and over in my mind.

At his request, I agreed never to identify him or his actual position in the Bush campaign to anyone. Our discussions while fishing for bass for three days on Lake Eufaula would be only to confirm information that had been previously obtained elsewhere and to add some perspective to the manuscript I had already delivered to my publisher, which ended up being several additional pages. More importantly, he never told me anything that was incorrect, nor did he try to inflate his knowledge or show off his importance in the Bush circle of advisers. In addition to having access to the Texas governor's office and the presidential exploratory committee, my source had known Bush since the years he lived in Midland.* He seemed genuinely committed to helping me "fill in the blanks" in Bush's life and establishing the truth where other journalists had erred in their reporting.

When I called my "Eufaula Connection" in September 1999, to confirm the allegation of Bush's drug use and community service in exchange for his record being expunged in 1972, my source's nervousness was evident on the phone.

"I wish you hadn't called me."

"You told me to never contact you unless it was important and I think you would agree that this qualifies as important."

---

*The presidential candidate once boasted to the press that he maintained his campaign headquarters in the Texas capital of Austin instead of Washington, D.C., so that his aides and advisers wouldn't be tempted to leak information to reporters representing the national media.

After a long, uncomfortable silence, he said, "You're not on one of those goddamn cordless phones, are you?"

I assured him I wasn't. There was a pause, and then—

"I'll call you back in thirty minutes."

While I waited on him to return my call, the delay—which seemed like an hour—forced my mind to work overtime. Who else was he talking to in the interim? Would he tell Bush the nature of my call? Or perhaps he would never call me back and then what would I do?

Punctual as always, he phoned almost exactly thirty minutes later and immediately proceeded to lecture me. "Out on the boat, you arrogantly told me you had already finished the book," he began, "but if I wanted to provide the missing pieces of truth, you would ask all the questions and I would do all the answering. Isn't that correct?"

Fearing that I might be a target of disinformation by someone sent by Bush or his campaign staff, I determined it would be in my best interest to query him only on subjects which I could confirm with other sources.

I could see where the question was going, but I had to play along because, unfortunately, he was right. "Those were the ground rules we both agreed to," I said lamely.

"Then how the fuck did you let the Project P.U.L.L. part of his life slip past you? If you were half-ass as good a biographer as you think you are, you would have caught that flagrant inconsistency, asked me about it and in the process I would have confirmed the truth three months ago," the Eufaula Connection said.

"Better late than never. Besides, no one else has figured it out, yet."

My informed source said that Bush was arrested in 1972 in Houston for possession of cocaine, "a controlled substance or whatever the hell they called it almost thirty years ago," and the elder Bush worked out an agreement with the judge, a fellow Republican and elected official, to allow George W. to perform community service at Project P.U.L.L. in exchange for having the entire record regarding the incident expunged.

I asked him if the judge was still alive or if the arresting officer was still on the police force.

"I can't and won't give you any new names, but I can confirm that W.'s Dallas attorney remains the repository of any evidence of the expunged record. From what I've been told, the attorney is the one who advised him to get a new driver's license in 1995 when a survey of his public records uncovered a stale but nevertheless incriminating trail for an overly eager reporter to follow," he said, pausing occasionally to spit tobacco juice into the ever-present Styrofoam cup.

"Bush won't admit he's used drugs before 1974. Period. Because we're not talking about experimenting with a little pot like a lot of baby boomers did back then. Hell, for a significant number of us, drug use was a youthful indiscretion, a misguided rite of passage," he continued, "but W. got caught with cocaine in 1972 and because his daddy was oil rich and influential in Harris County politics, he got his son off with a little community service at a minority youth center instead of having to pick cotton on a Texas prison farm."

"Why didn't Bush just keep his mouth shut last month and refuse to answer questions on possible drug use, rather than establishing a statute of limitations at 1974?" I asked, citing the headlines in *The Hotline,* a daily digest of political news, which read: ZERO TO 26 YEARS IN 12 HOURS. GEORGE W. BUSH'S 2-STEP ANSWER.

"When he admitted that he could have passed even the fifteen-year FBI background check in effect when his father was inaugurated in 1989, George, along with some other top advisers, believed his response would finally lay the story to rest," the Eufaula Connection acknowledged. "I personally advised him to stay on course and never admit anything, believing the American public would get sick and tired of hearing about it. I said, 'George, once you start answering, you're never going to be able to stop. The press will trick you by claiming if you answer just one more question, they'll get off your ass. But he ignored my advice and now everybody wants to know why he won't rule out drug usage prior to 1974."

Sensing it might be our last chance to talk before the book was published—perhaps even our final conversation—I thanked him for sharing his information, recollections, and insight during the past few months.

"Be careful and watch your back every step of the way," he warned, speaking almost in a whisper. "Without sounding paranoid, I think I would be amiss if I didn't remind you that George's old man was once director of the CIA. Shit, man, they named the building after the guy not too long ago. Besides, W.'s raised almost a staggering sixty million dollars for his White House run in a matter of only a few months and his corporate sponsors and GOP fat cats aren't going to roll over and play dead when you expose the truth about their investment."

I swallowed hard, remembering what my other source had said about looking over my shoulder.

"You know what makes me sick about all this shit?" my source asked. "It's

Bush's hypocrisy. Cocaine use is illegal, but as governor of Texas, he's toughened penalties for people convicted of selling or possessing less than a gram of coke (a crime previously punished by probation), OK'd the housing of sixteen-year-olds in adult correctional facilities and slashed funding for inmate substance-abuse programs. Texas currently spends over one point four-five million dollars per day keeping drug offenders behind bars and another twenty-eight thousand dollars a day incarcerating young people on drug offenses," he said angrily.

"I've known George for several years and he has never accepted youth and irresponsibility as legitimate excuses for illegal behavior—except when it comes to himself."

Source Notes

The following chapter notes indicate the sources used by the author in writing each chapter of this book, including the documents examined, the published sources consulted, and the people interviewed. The author has respected the wishes of many interview subjects to remain anonymous and accordingly has not listed them, either here or elsewhere in the text.

The following summary is by no means all-inclusive, but it offers the reader a general review of other aspects of research involved in constructing the book. The archives and oral history collections of, among other institutions, The George Bush Presidential Library, the Texas State Archives, the libraries of Yale University, Harvard University, and the University of Texas yielded a wealth of information. In addition, there have been thousands of news reports and articles concerning George

Walker Bush and his family published over the years that served as source material for this book—far too many to cite here. More generally, publications that proved particularly useful included the *Dallas Morning News, Houston Chronicle, Houston Post, Dallas Times Herald, Austin American-Statesman,* and the *Midland Reporter-Telegram.* Other important sources included the Associated Press, Reuters, Knight-Ridder, and Gannett news wire services.

Prologue: Curious George

Among the books consulted on the presidential campaigns of Nelson Rockefeller and Edward Kennedy were: *America in Search of Itself: The Making of the President, 1956–1980,* by Theodore White, HarperCollins, New York, 1984; *The Last Brother,* by Joe McGinnis, Simon & Schuster, New York, 1993; *The Imperial Rockefeller: A Biography of Nelson A. Rockefeller,* by Joseph E. Persico, Simon & Schuster, 1982.

Newspaper and magazine articles referenced include "Poll Indicates Texans Back Gov. Bush but Can't Say Why," by R.G. Ratcliffe, *Houston Chronicle,* April 22, 1999; "Bush's Quick Rise Stuns Observers," by Sam Attlesey, *Dallas Morning News,* April 4, 1999; "Voters Know Bush by Name, Not Record," by Ken Herman, *Austin American-Statesman,* April 23, 1999; "For the Nation, Governor Has Some Explaining to Do," *Houston Chronicle,* June 3, 1999.

Television: "George W. Bush: The Son Also Rises, A & E Biography, June 9, 1999.

Chapter 1. The Founding Father

Several days spent at the following Texas-based archives and oral history collections provided the author with invaluable documentation and insight: The George Bush Presidential Library, College Station, Texas; the Texas State Archives, Austin, Texas; Permian Basin Petroleum Museum, Midland, Texas; Midland County Historical Museum; Texas Room, Houston Public Library; Center for American History, the University of Texas at Austin; Texas Historical Society, Houston, Texas; Public Service Archives, Woodson Research Center, Rice University; Library of Congress Microform Reading Room (to examine Zapata Petroleum annual reports); Haley Library and History Center, Midland, Texas; Yale University Library (examination of the Skull and Bones membership list, 1833–1950, printed 1949 by the Russell Trust Association, New Haven, Connecticut); Prescott S. Bush Papers, "Prescott Bush-biographical," Box 1, Manuscript & Archives Division, University of Connecticut at Storrs; H. Neil Mallon obituary in the *New York Times,* March 3, 1983; Thomas Ludlow Ashley Papers, MS-159, Center for Archival Collections, Bowling Green State University, Bowling Green, OH; Bush-Connally Folder, Yarborough Papers, Box ZR508, Eugene C. Barker Texas History Center, Austin; Prescott S.

Bush, Columbia Oral History Research Office, interviewed by John T. Mason Jr., 1966.

Books: *Profiles in Courage* (Reissue/Memorial edition), by John F. Kennedy, HarperCollins, New York, 1989; *American Presidential Families,* by Hugh Brogan and Charles Mosley, Macmillan, New York, 1993; *Flight of the Avenger: George Bush at War,* by Joe Hyams, Harcourt Brace Jovanovitch, New York, 1991; *Looking Forward,* by George Bush and Victor Gold, Doubleday, New York, 1987; *George Bush: A Biography,* by Nicholas King, Dodd, Mead & Company, New York, 1980; *George Bush: An Intimate Portrait,* by Fitzhugh Green, Hippocrene Books, New York, 1989; *George Bush: The Life of a Lone Star Yankee,* by Herbert S. Parmet, Charles Scribner's Sons, New York, 1997; *Barbara Bush: A Memoir* (paperback edition), by Barbara Bush, St. Martin's Press, New York, 1995; *Simply Barbara Bush: A Portrait of America's Candid First Lady* (paperback edition), by Donnie Radcliffe, Warner Books, New York, 1990; *Barbara Bush: A Biography,* by Pamela Kilian, St. Martin's Press, New York, 1992; *The Wise Men: Six Friends and the World They Made—Acheson, Boblen, Harriman, Kennan, Lovett, McCloy,* by Walter Isaacson and Evan Thomas, Simon & Schuster, New York, 1986; *Initiative in Energy: Dresser Industries, Inc. 1880–1978,* by Darwin Payne, Simon & Schuster, New York, 1979; *V Was for Victory,* by John Morton Blum, Harcourt Brace Jovanovich, 1976; *George Bush: His World War II Years,* by Robert B. Stinnett, U.S. Brassey's Inc., McLean, Virginia, 1992; *Midland: The Economic Future of a Texas Oil Center,* by Robert H. Ryan, University of Texas, Austin, 1959; *Land of the High Sky,* by John Howard Griffin, First National Bank of Midland, Midland, Texas, 1959; *Odessa: City of Dreams,* by Velma Barrett and Hazel Oliver, The Naylor Company, San Antonio, Texas, 1952; *Promises to Keep: My Years in Public Life, 1941–1969,* by Chester Bowles, Harper & Row, New York, 1971; *Wildcatters: A Story of Texas,* by Sally Helgesen, Doubleday, Garden City, NY, 1981; *Oil & Honor: The Texas-Pennzoil Wars,* by Thomas Petzinger Jr., G.P. Putnam's Sons, New York, 1987; *Imperial Texas: An Interpretative Essay in Cultural Geography,* by D.W. Meinig, University of Texas Press, Austin, 1976; *Friday Night Lights: A Town, a Team and a Dream,* by H.G. Bissinger, HarperCollins, New York, 1991.

Articles: "George Bush: How He Got Here," by Richard Ben Cramer, *Esquire,* June 1991; "The Day Bush Bailed Out," Allan Wolper and Al Ellenberg, *New York Post,* August 12, 1988; "Presidential Genealogy," by the Associated Press, October 1, 1992; "Britain-Presidential Pedigrees," by Associated Press, October 22, 1992; "Bush Opened Up to Secret Yale Society," by Bob Woodward and Walter Pincus, the *Washington Post,* August 7, 1988; "Team Player Bush: A Yearning to Serve," by Barry Bearak, *Los Angeles Times,* November 22, 1987; "George Bush on God, War and Ollie North," by David Frost, *U.S. News & World Report,* December 14, 1987; "No Scandals in Bush Finances," by David E. Rosenbaum, *New York Times,* June 6, 1988; "'Mom' Rogers Babysitter from West Texas Reunites with Former Employers at White House," by Steve Stein, *The Odessa American,* October 17, 1989; "War Story," by Sidney Blumenthal, *The New Republic,* October 12, 1992; "Barbara's Backlash," by

Marjorie Williams, *Vanity Fair,* August 1992; "Yale's Most Famous Graduate," *U.S. News & World Report,* October 16, 1989; "George Bush: Man and Politician," by Bob Woodward and Walter Pincus, *Washington Post,* August 7, 1988; "Sportsman Born and Bred," by George Plimpton, *New York Times,* July 11, 1994; "Yale First Baseman Once Caught Scouts' Eyes," by Jack Cavanaugh, *Sporting News,* November 7, 1988; "Life in Midland," by Seymour Freedgood, *Fortune,* April 1962; "George Bush, Plucky Lad," by Harry Hurt III, *Texas Monthly,* June 1983; "Who Would Have Dreamed?" by Susan Atchison, *City Life,* Fall 1995; "Long a Confidant, Bush Now Aspires to Commanding Role," by R.G. Ratcliffe, *Midland Reporter-Telegram,* May 15, 1994; "Another Bush in Line," by Sue Anne Pressley, *Washington Post,* May 9, 1997; "The Leading Man," by Alan Bernstein, *Houston Chronicle,* September 6, 1998; "President Bush's Son on a Roll," by Steven R. Reed, *Houston Chronicle,* July 2, 1989; "George W. Bush From the Golf Course to the Boardroom," by R.G. Ratcliffe, *Houston Chronicle,* October 30, 1994; "George Walker Bush, Driving on the Right," by Lois Romano, *Washington Post,* September 24, 1998; "A Dynasty Sign in Bush Sons' Rise," by Mary Leonard, *Boston Globe,* November 18, 1998; "I Was Young and Irresponsible," by Pete Slover and George Kuempel, *Dallas Morning News,* November 15, 1998; "The Hidden Life of Barbara Bush," by Kenneth Walsh, *U.S. News & World Report,* May 20, 1990; "Family First, Mrs. Bush Tells Friend and Foe at Wellesley," by Fox Butterfield, *New York Times,* June 2, 1990; "First Lady's Speech," by Rania Nagulb, *Los Angeles Times,* June 8, 1990; "Our Healthy Veep and Family," by Cory Servaas, *Saturday Evening Post,* October 1998; "Former Student in Limelight," by Frank P. Jarrell, *The News and Courier,* Charleston, South Carolina, February 10, 1980; "Barbara Bush Addresses Ashley Hall Graduates," by Patricia McCarthy, *The News and Courier,* Charleston, South Carolina, June 4, 1984; "Stalwart Hub of the Family—Barbara Bush: Loyal Wife Who's Reserved, Not Shy," by Cathleen Decker, *Los Angeles Times,* August 7, 1988; "Texas 1948: Some Fond Memories," by George Bush, *American West,* January–February 1986; "Well-Traveled Bush Grew Up in Oilfields," by Jean Becker, *USA Today,* April 15, 1988; "Hospital Visit Evokes Memories of Bushes' Tragedy," by Kathy Lewis, *Houston Post,* June 29, 1986; "The Bush Bunch," by David Maraniss, *Washington Post Magazine,* January 22, 1989; "Barbara Bush—First Lady, First Class," by Cindy Adams, *Ladies Home Journal,* November 1990; "Doing Well With Help From Family, Friends," Walter Pincus and Bob Woodward, *Washington Post,* August 11, 1988; "The Mexican Connection of George Bush," by Jonathan Kwitny, *Barron's,* September 19, 1988; "George W. Bush; Politics, Baseball and Life in the Shadow of the White House," by Diane Reischel, *Dallas Morning News,* February 25, 1990; "A Fresh Start and Struggles," by George Lardner, Jr. and Lois Romano, *Washington Post,* July 26, 1999; "Bush Camp is Getting into the Swing of Things," by Sam Attlesey, *Dallas Morning News,* July 18, 1999; "The Man from Midland," by Kenneth T. Walsh, *U.S. News & World Report,* June 7, 1999; "The Son Rises," by Pamela Colloff, *Texas Monthly,* June 1999.

Television: Chris Matthews interview with *Washington Post* reporter, Lois Romano, CNBC's *Hardball,* July 26, 1999; "George W. Bush: The Son Also Rises, A & E Biography, June 9, 1999.

Interview subjects include Billy Beck; Laura Stanton; Claire Bowie; Tim Fuller; Johnny Hackney; Bucky Bush; Diane King; OthaTaylor; and confidential interviews with two of the Bush family's former neighbors in Midland.

Chapter 2. Young and Irresponsible

Archives, oral history collections, and documents consulted include The George Bush Presidential Library, College Station, Texas; the Texas State Archives, Austin, Texas; Lyndon B. Johnson Presidential Library, Bush Folder, Box 611; Texas Room, Houston Public Library; Center for American History, the University of Texas at Austin; Zapata Petroleum annual reports, Library of Congress Microform Reading Room; Texas Historical Society, Houston, Texas; Skull and Bones membership list, 1833–1950, printed 1949 by the Russell Trust Association, New Haven, Connecticut, available through the Yale University Library; Prescott S. Bush Papers, "Prescott Bush-biographical," Box 1, Manuscript & Archives Division, University of Connecticut at Storrs; Thomas Ludlow Ashley Papers, MS-159, Center for Archival Collections, Bowling Green State University, Bowling Green, Ohio; Bush-Connally Folder, Yarborough Papers, Box ZR508, Eugene C. Barker Texas History Center, Austin; Prescott S. Bush, Columbia Oral History Research Office, interviewed by John T. Mason Jr., 1966; *Congressional Record,* August 11, 1967; Ehrlichman notes of meetings with the president, Fenn Gallery, Santa Fe; Public Service Archives, Woodson Research Center, Rice University.

Books: *Youth from Every Quarter: A Bicentennial History of Phillips Academy, Andover,* Phillips Academy, Andover, Mass., 1979; *America's Secret Establishment: An Introduction to the Order of Skull and Bones,* by Anthony C. Sutton, Liberty House Press, Billings, Montana, 1986; *Race and Class in Texas Politics,* by Chandler Davidson, Princeton University Press, Princeton, 1990; *Texas Rich,* by Harry Hurt III, W. W. Norton, New York, 1981; *Two-Party Texas,* by John R. Knaggs, Eakin Press, Austin, Texas, 1985; *The Lone Star: The Life of John Connally,* by James Reston, Jr., Harper & Row, New York, 1989; *Looking Forward* by George Bush and Victor Gold, Doubleday, New York, 1987; *George Bush: A Biography,* by Nicholas King, Dodd Mead & Company, New York, 1980; *George Bush: An Intimate Portrait,* by Fitzhugh Green, Hippocrene Books, New York, 1989; *George Bush: The Life of a Lone Star Yankee,* by Herbert S. Parmet, Charles Scribner's Sons, New York, 1997; *Barbara Bush: A Memoir* (paperback edition), by Barbara Bush, St. Martin's Press, New York, 1995; *Simply Barbara Bush: A Portrait of America's Candid First Lady* (paperback edition), by Donnie Radcliffe, Warner Books, New York, 1990; *Barbara Bush: A Biography,* by Pamela Kilian, St. Martin's Press, New York, 1992; *The Oil Follies of 1970–1980,* by Robert Sherrill, Anchor Press/Doubleday, New York, 1983; *The Selling of the Presi-*

dent, by Joe McGinnis, Penguin Books, New York, 1968; *Lone Star: A History of Texas and Texans,* by T.R. Fehrenbach, Macmillan, New York, 1968; *Dan Quayle: The Man Who Would Be President,* by Bob Woodward and David Broder, Simon & Schuster, New York, 1992; *Standing Firm,* by Dan Quayle, HarperCollins, New York, 1994; *Vietnam: A History,* by Stanley Karnow, The Viking Press, New York, 1983; *America's Longest War: The United States in Vietnam, 1950–1975,* (Second Edition), by George C. Herring, Alfred A. Knopf, New York, 1986.

Articles: "For George W. Bush, Early Life a Wrangle Between East, West," by Michael Kranish, *Boston Globe,* March 28, 1999; "The Ten Richest People in Houston," *Houston Post Magazine,* March 11, 1984; "Bush Cites Work, Rejects Rich-Boy Image," by Ken Herman, *Austin American-Statesman,* October 11, 1998; "Voices: Vietnam—Lady Bird Johnson, *Newsweek,* March 8, 1999; "The Woman George W. Bush Didn't Marry," by Tim Fleck, *Houston Press,* March 25–31, 1999; "Congressman's Son to Marry Rice Co-Ed," *Houston Chronicle,* January 1, 1967; "No Kiss and Tell," by Pete Slover, *Dallas Morning News,* April 1, 1999; "Well Son-of-a-Bush!" (The Bush Beat), *Texas Observer,* April 19, 1999; "Bush Jr. Wavers Over Revenge for His Father," by Hugh Davies, *London Telegraph,* November 5, 1998; "Bush: The Houston Years," by Alan Bernstein, *Houston Chronicle,* April 11, 1999; "Easygoing George W. Bush," by Stuart Eskenazi, *Houston Press,* October 29–November 4, 1998; "President Bush's Son on a Roll," by Steven R. Reed, *Houston Chronicle,* July 2, 1989; "Favorite Son," by Robert Draper, *GQ,* October 1998; "Downloading The Bush Files," by Michael King, *Texas Observer,* November 1998; "Out of Texas, a Familiar But Singular Brand," by Jill Lawrence, *USA Today,* September 8, 1998; "The Four Republicans," by Ronnie Dugger, *Texas Observer,* April 17, 1964; "The Substance of the Senate Contest," by Ronnie Dugger, *Texas Observer,* September 18, 1964; "Houston's Superpatriots," by Willie Morris, *Harper's Magazine,* October 1961; "President Frat Boy?" by Maureen Dowd, *New York Times,* April 7, 1999; "Long a Confidant, Bush Now Aspires to Commanding Role," by R.G. Ratcliffe, *Midland Reporter-Telegram,* May 15, 1994; "George W. Bush From the Golf Course to the Boardroom," by R.G. Ratcliffe, *Houston Chronicle,* October 30, 1994; "George Walker Bush, Driving on the Right," by Lois Romano, *Washington Post,* September 24, 1998; "George W. Bush Still Studying Options in Politics," by Steven R. Reed, *Midland Reporter-Telegram,* July 4, 1989; "Inside the Austin Fun House," by Molly Ivins, *The Atlantic,* May 1975; "Texans Downplay Military Issue," by John Gravois, *Houston Post,* August 19, 1988; "Quayle Guard Duty Clouds GOP Liftoff," by Cragg Hines, *Houston Chronicle,* August 18, 1988; "Bentsen III Denies Father Used Influence to Get Him into Guard in '68," by Michael Haederle, *Houston Post,* August 23, 1988; "Bush, Bentsen Sons Also Were in Guard," by Stephen Johnson, *Houston Chronicle,* August 20, 1988; "The Son Also Rises," by Evan Thomas, *Newsweek,* November 16, 1998; "Gramm Says Facts Will Show Quayle Did Nothing Wrong in Joining National Guard," by Robert Stanton, *Houston Post,* August 20, 1988; "Like Father, Like Son—Sort Of," by Ken Herman, *Houston Post,* November 7, 1993; "Bush: Any Past Illegal Drug Use Irrelevant to Gubernatorial Race," *Midland Reporter-Telegram,* May 4, 1994; "Understanding What the National Guard is All About: An Interview with Governor George W. Bush," by Zack Northrup, *National Guard Review,* Winter, 1998; "Republican National Convention/Debate Renewed Over Military Issues," by R.G. Ratcliffe, *Houston Chronicle;* "'I Was Young and Irresponsible,'" by Pete Slover, *Dallas Morning News,* November 15, 1998; "Bush Pledges Hint on 2000 Race in 2 Weeks," by R.G. Ratcliffe, *Houston Chronicle,* February 25, 1999; "Prospective Juror Bush Dismissed from DWI Case," by Kathy Walt, *Houston Chronicle,* October 9, 1996; "The Bush Brothers," by Howard Fineman, *Newsweek,* November 2, 1998; "Bush Says He's Learned from His Rowdy Past," by Jim O'Connell, *Rocky Mountain News,* July 26, 1998; "New Rules of the Road," by Richard Lacayo, *Time,* February 22, 1999; "Following His Father's Path—Step by Step by Step," by Lois Romano and George Lardner, Jr., *Washington Post,* July 27, 1999; "McCain's Next Battle," by James Carney, *Time,* July 5, 1999; "Bush Defends '78 Statement About Military Service," by Katie Fairbank, Associated Press, July 14, 1999; "Ex-Official Wants Bush's Testimony," by George Kuempel and Pete Slover, *Dallas Morning News,* July 28, 1999; "Friends: Barnes Was Asked to Help Get Bush in Guard," by George Kuempel and Pete Slover, *Dallas Morning News,* September 8, 1999; "Drug Rumours Haunt Bush Presidency," by David Wastell, *London Telegraph,* May 23, 1999; "At Height of Vietnam, Graduate Picks Guard," by George Lardner, Jr. and Lois Romano, *Washington Post,* July 28, 1999; "Name Gave Bush a Push in National Guard," by Richard A. Serrano, *Los Angeles Times,* July 4, 1999; "War-Service Critics Keep Bush in Sights," by Mike Ward and Ken Herman, *Austin American-Statesman,* July 17, 1999; "Here Comes the Son," by Howard Fineman, *Newsweek,* June 21, 1999; "Go East, Young Man," by Helen Thorpe, *Texas Monthly,* June 1999; "I've Made Mistakes . . ." by Nancy Gibbs, *Time,* August 30, 1999; "Bush Prolongs Drug Questions with Hem-and-Haw Tactics," *USA Today,* August 20, 1999; "Bush Says He Hasn't Used Drugs in Last Seven Years," by Scott Parks and Sam Attlesey, *Dallas Morning News,* August 19, 1999; "Questions Keep Flying at Bush," by Jill Lawrence, *USA Today,* August 20, 1999.

Television: "Lone Star Legend," produced by Phillips Productions, December 11, 1994; "Running for Governor . . . and Beyond," PBS NewsHour, October 27, 1998; "George W. Bush, the Dirt Digger," MSNBC, December 10, 1998; CNN interview with George W. Bush, February 2, 1999; Diane Sawyer interview with George W. Bush on ABC-TV's *Good Morning, America,* May 10, 1999; "George W. Bush: The Son Also Rises, A&E Biography, June 9, 1999; Diane Sawyer interview with George W. Bush, ABC's *Good Morning, America,* May 10, 1999.

On-line: "Fear of Nude Picture Rocks Campaign 2000 Star," the Drudge Report (www.drudgereport.com), February 28, 1999; "Bush Up to His Arse in Allegations!" by Amy Reiter (www.salonmagazine.com), August 25, 1999; "Bush Denies Using Any Illegal Drug During the Past 25 Years," CNN Interactive (www.cnn.com), August 19, 1999.

Interviews: Jimmy Keller; Clay Johnson; Buddy Jenkins; confidential interviews with Bush's former classmates at Andover and Yale; Cora Leonard; Joe Newell; Benny McKissick; confidential interviews with Bush family friends; Retired Maj. Gen. Thomas Bishop; Allen Gerson; John DeCamp; Sam Drogan; James Johnson; confidential interviews with Bush's flight school classmates at Moody Air Force Base in Valdosta, Georgia; Eddie Johnston; Leonard Freeman; confidential interviews with former residents of Houston's Chateaux Dijon apartment complex; Ernie Ladd; Edgar Arnold; Muriel Henderson; confidential interviews with former members of Winton "Red" Blount's U.S. Senate campaign staff; Diane King; Danny Freeman; "Junior" McDonald; confidential conversations with aides to Governor Bush and presidential campaign strategists.

Chapter 3. Ties That Bind

Archives and Oral History Collections: Incorporation records from the Texas Secretary of State's office regarding Arbusto Energy Inc., Bush Exploration, and Spectrum 7 Exploration Co.; 1978 campaign filings with the Federal Election Commission, Washington, D.C.; James N. Allison obituary in the *Midland Reporter-Telegram,* September 1, 1978; Gerald R. Ford Presidential Library, George Bush Files; The George Bush Presidential Library, College Station, Texas; the Texas State Archives, Austin, Texas; Texas Room, Houston Public Library; Center for American History, the University of Texas at Austin; Texas Historical Society, Houston, Texas; Thomas Ludlow Ashley Papers, MS-159, Center for Archival Collections, Bowling Green State University, Bowling Green, Ohio; Public Service Archives, Woodson Research Center, Rice University; Eugene C. Barker Texas History Center, Austin; Permian Basin Petroleum Museum, Midland, Texas; Midland County Historical Museum; Haley Library and History Center, Midland, Texas.

Books: *The Outlaw Bank: A Wild Ride Into the Heart of BCCI,* by Jonathan Beaty and S.C. Gwynne, Random House, New York, 1993; *With No Apologies: The Personal and Political Memoirs of United States Senator Barry M. Goldwater,* by Barry Morris Goldwater, William Morrow, New York, 1979; *Just As I Am: The Autobiography of Billy Graham,* by Billy Graham, Harper, San Francisco, 1997; *Looking Forward,* by George Bush and Victor Gold, Doubleday, New York, 1987; *George Bush: An Intimate Portrait,* by Fitzhugh Green, Hippocrene Books, New York, 1989; *George Bush: The Life of a Lone Star Yankee,* by Herbert S. Parmet, Charles Scribner's Sons, New York, 1997; *Barbara Bush: A Memoir* (paperback edition), by Barbara Bush, St. Martin's Press, New York, 1995; *Simply Barbara Bush: A Portrait of America's Candid First Lady* (paperback edition), by Donnie Radcliffe, Warner Books, New York, 1990; *Barbara Bush: A Biography,* by Pamela Kilian, St. Martin's Press, New York, 1992; *The Agency: The Rise and Decline of the CIA,* by John Ranelagh, Simon & Schuster, New York, 1987.

Among the published articles consulted: "Good Connections: Family Ties

Helped Fund Oil Venture That Began Bush's Business Career," by Richard A. Oppel Jr. and George Kuempel, *Dallas Morning News,* November 16, 1998; "Rangers' Bush Keeps Traditions Intact, Times Two," by Bob Porter, *Dallas Times-Herald,* May 23, 1991; "George W. Bush/Wealth Produced Via Stock Swaps and Bailouts," by Bob Sablatura, *Houston Chronicle,* May 8, 1994; "The Color of Money," by Stephen J. Hedges, *U.S. News & World Report,* March 16, 1992; "Oil Firms of Vice-President's Sons Also in Struggle to Survive," by Robert Reinhold, *New York Times,* May 4, 1986; "George W. Bush Blazing Own Trail," by R.G. Ratcliffe, *Houston Chronicle,* November 7, 1993; "Family Value$," by Stephen Pizzo, *Mother Jones,* September/October 1992; "The Family that Preys Together," by Jack Calhoun, *Covert Action Quarterly,* #41, Summer 1992; "The Saturday Profile: The Bush Clan, The Family That Plays Too," by Rupert Cornwell, *Independent,* November 7, 1998; "The Same Old Dirty Tricks," by David Corn, *The Nation,* August 23, 1988; "Bush Planning Run-Off Tactics," by Ed Todd, *Midland Reporter-Telegram,* May 10, 1978; "Bush, Hance Trying to Keep 'Big Names' Out of Race," *Midland Reporter-Telegram,* September 13, 1978; "GOP Candidate Bush Under Fire From Hance Camp," by Lana Cunningham, *Midland Reporter-Telegram,* November 3, 1978; "Bush Says Most Contributions Come From Within 19th District," by Lana Cunningham, *Midland Reporter-Telegram,* November 6, 1978; "Campaign Donations Favor Bush," *Midland Reporter-Telegram,* October 15, 1978; "George Bush Works the Hustings From Door to Door," by Linda Hill, *Midland Reporter-Telegram,* May 28, 1978; "It's Bush Over Reese in Election," by Lana Cunningham, *Midland Reporter-Telegram,* June 7, 1978; "Bush, Reese in Runoff for Mahon Seat," by Lana Cunningham, *Midland Reporter-Telegram,* May 7, 1978; "Bush (of Connecticut) Reveals His Single Regret," by Lana Cunningham, *Midland Reporter-Telegram,* June 2, 1978; "Innuendo Countered by Bush," *Midland Reporter-Telegram,* May 30, 1978; "Long Road to Victory; Questions Abound About Likely Race for Governor," by Sam Attlesey, *Dallas Morning News,* September 7, 1993; "George Bush Jr. Enters Race for Mahon's Seat," *Dallas Morning News,* July 20, 1977; "Candidate's Father is Runoff Issue," by Ron Calhoun, *Dallas Times-Herald,* June 1, 1978; "George W. Bush Trying to Hold Up Tradition in Runoff," by Carolyn Barta, *Dallas Morning News,* June 2, 1978; "Bush's Son Sees 'Victory' for Father," *Dallas Morning News,* January 13, 1980; "Bush Says Election of Republican Vital," by Lana Cunningham, *Midland Reporter-Telegram,* September 9, 1978; "Bush, Hance: A Hair's Difference," by Lana Cunningham, *Midland Reporter-Telegram,* October 6, 1978; "Bush-Backers Barbecue Looks Like 'Love Fest,'" by Lana Cunningham, *Midland Reporter-Telegram,* October 15, 1978; "Bush, Hance Focus on Inflation Ills," by Lana Cunningham, *Midland Reporter-Telegram,* October 26, 1978; "Our Future President a Man of Warmth," by Rollan Melton, *Reno Gazette-Journal,* January 19, 1989; "Allison 'Missing Man' in Bush's Formation," by Pete Roussel, *Midland Reporter-Telegram,* November 27, 1988; "Bush Stumps for Husband on Home Turf," by Tonie Millar-Uzzel, *Midland Reporter-Telegram,* May 12, 1994; "Out of Texas, A Familiar But Singular Brand," by Jill Lawrence, *USA Today,* September 8, 1998; "A

Dynasty Sign in Bush Sons' Rise," by Mary Leonard, *Boston Globe,* November 18, 1998; "George W. Bush; Politics, Baseball and Life in the Shadow of the White House," by Diane Reischel, *Dallas Morning News,* February 25, 1990; "Younger Bush Wasn't Surprised," by Lana Cunningham, *Midland Reporter-Telegram,* May 27, 1980; "Bush Cites Reagan Stamina, Class," by Lana Cunningham, *Midland Reporter-Telegram,* February 15, 1981; "President Bush's Son on a Roll," by Steven R. Reed, *Houston Chronicle,* July 2, 1989; "Another Bush in Line?" by Sue Anne Presley, *Washington Post,* May 9, 1997; "Downloading the Bush Files," by Michael King, *Texas Observer,* November 1998; "Arabs Bought into Bank with Connally Aid," by Kate Thomas and John Mecklin, *Houston Post,* August 3, 1991; "Feds Investigate Entrepreneur Allegedly Tied to Saudis," by Jerry Urban, *Houston Chronicle,* June 4, 1992; "Bush Beginnings/New First Lady's Quiet Life to Greet Thunder of Politics," by Cheryl Laird, Associated Press, January 15, 1995; "Lone Star Stars," by Julia Reed, *Vogue,* February 1999; "Faithful Have a Place in Politics, Says Bush," by R.G. Ratcliffe, *Houston Chronicle,* March 7, 1999; "Bush Cites Work, Rejects Rich-Boy Image," by Ken Herman, *Austin American-Statesman,* October 11, 1998; "Footnotes," *Houston Chronicle,* February 7, 1999; "Eldest Son May Seek Office," *Dallas Morning News,* December 23, 1991; "The Son Also Rises," by Evan Thomas, *Newsweek,* November 16, 1998; "'I Was Young and Irresponsible,'' by Pete Slaver and George Kuempel, *Dallas Morning News,* November 15, 1998; "George Walker Bush, Driving on the Right," by Lois Romano, *Washington Post,* September 24, 1998; "Favorite Son," by Robert Draper, *GQ,* October 1998; "Billy Graham/A Prophet with Honor," by Cecil Holmes White, *Houston Chronicle,* September 28, 1991; "Company Man," by Scott Armstrong and Jeff Nason, *Mother Jones,* October 1988; "Republicans Try to Get Their Act Together," by Tom Wicker, *New York Times Magazine,* February 12, 1978; "He Ran the GOP for Nixon, he Ran the CIA for Ford," by Alexander Cockburn and James Ridgeway, *Rolling Stone,* March 30, 1980; "Reading Laura Bush," by Skip Hollandsworth, *Texas Monthly,* November 1996; "Laura Bush Likes the Traditional Role She's Filled," by Claudia Feldman, *Houston Chronicle,* July 20, 1997; "A Run for the House," by Lois Romano and George Lardner, Jr., *Washington Post,* July 29, 1999; "A Shrub Grows in Midland," by Karen Olsson, *Texas Observer,* July 1999; "1986: A Life-Changing Year," by Lois Romano and George Lardner, Jr., *Washington Post,* July 25, 1999; "Bush Putting Faith to Fore in Public," by Deborah Kovach Caldwell, *Dallas Morning News,* May 12, 1999; "Longtime Friendship Drives Bush Campaign Fund-Raiser," by Laylan Copelin, *Austin American-Statesman,* March 3, 1999; "In Business, Bush Known for Strength of Personality," by Richard Alm and Mark Curriden, *Dallas Morning News,* July 30, 1999; "How George Got His Groove," by Eric Pooley and S.C. Gwynne, *Time,* June 21, 1999; "The Man from Midland," by Kenneth T. Walsh, *U.S. News & World Report,* June 7, 1999; "Go East, Young Man," by Helen Thorpe, *Texas Monthly,* June 1999; "Not So Great in '78," by Patricia Kilday Hart, *Texas Monthly,* June 1999; "George's Road to Riches," by Byron York, *American Spectator,* June 1999.

Television: CNN interview with George W. Bush, February 2, 1999; "Lone Star Legend," produced by Phillips Productions, December 11, 1994; Diane Sawyer interview with Laura Bush on ABC-TV's *Good Morning, America,* May 10, 1999; Chris Matthews interview with *Washington Post* reporter, Lois Romano, CNBC's *Hardball,* July 26, 1999; "George W. Bush: The Son Also Rises, A & E Biography, June 9, 1999; Diane Sawyer interview with George W. Bush, ABC's *Good Morning, America,* May 10, 1999.

On-line: "George W. Bush: Front-Runner for 2000," BBC Online Network (news.bbc.co.uk), October 2, 1998; www.bush98.com (See Biographies—Laura Welch Bush).

For this chapter, the author drew on conversations with Walt Holton, Jr.; Diane King; Tom Craddick; Don Evans; confidential interviews with U.S. intelligence operatives regarding concerns that bin Laden might attempt an assassination of Bush or his father in 1998; Frank Hobbs; Carl Barker; Bill Hammer; confidential interviews with Midland friends of Harold and Jenna Welch; Floyd Walker; Roger Newman; Jimmy Dolan; confidential interviews with friends and former Midland neighbors of George and Laura Bush; Pete Teeley; David Rosen; Dennis "Wemus" Grubb; Larry Makinson; confidential interviews with a former Texas Republican Party fund-raising consultant; Harvey Blocker; Jay Howard; Bill Barnes; confidential interview with members of the Billy Graham Evangelistic Association; Logan Gray, M.D.

Chapter 4. Home Run

Archives and Oral History Collections: The George Bush Presidential Library, College Station, Texas; the Texas State Archives, Austin, Texas; Texas Room, Houston Public Library; Center for American History, the University of Texas at Austin; Texas Historical Society, Houston, Texas; Thomas Ludlow Ashley Papers, MS-159, Center for Archival Collections, Bowling Green State University, Bowling Green, Ohio; Public Service Archives, Woodson Research Center, Rice University; Ronald Reagan Presidential Library; Eugene C. Barker Texas History Center, Austin; *Report of the Congressional Committees Investigating the Iran-Contra Affair,* 100th Congress, First Session, 1987; Report No. 100-433; *Final Report of the Independent Counsel for Iran-Contra Matters* by Lawrence Walsh (3 vols; Washington, D.C.: United States Court of Appeals for the District of Columbia Circuit, 1993).

Books: *Whose Broad Stripes and Bright Stars? The Trivial Pursuit of the Presidency 1988,* by Jack W. Germond and Jules Witcover, Warner Books, New York, 1989; *What It Takes: The Way to the White House,* by Richard Ben Cramer, Vintage Books, New York, 1993; *Turmoil and Triumph: My Years as Secretary of State,* by George P. Schultz, Charles Scribner's Sons, New York, 1993; *Compromised: Clinton, Bush and the CIA,* by Terry Reed and John Commings, S.P.I. Books, New York, 1994; *Guts and*

Glory, the Rise and Fall of Oliver North, by Ben Bradlee Jr., Donald I. Fine, New York, 1988; *Shadow Warrior,* by Felix Rodriguez and John Wiseman, Simon and Schuster, New York, 1989; *Veil: The Secret Wars of the CIA, 1981–1987,* by Bob Woodward, Simon and Schuster, 1987; *Honored and Betrayed,* by Richard Secord with Jay Wurts, John Wiley & Sons, New York, 1992; *Caveat: Realism, Reagan, and Foreign Policy,* by Alexander M. Haig, Jr., Macmillan, New York, 1984; *With Reagan: The Inside Story,* by Edwin Meese III, Regnery Gateway, Washington, D.C.; *For the Record: From Wall Street to Washington,* by Donald Regan, Harcourt Brace Jovanovich, New York, 1988; *George Bush: The Life of a Lone Star Yankee,* by Herbert S. Parmet, Charles Scribner's Sons, New York, 1997; *Barbara Bush: A Memoir* (paperback edition), by Barbara Bush, St. Martin's Press, New York, 1995; *Simply Barbara Bush: A Portrait of America's Candid First Lady* (paperback edition), by Donnie Radcliffe, Warner Books, New York, 1990; *Barbara Bush: A Biography,* by Pamela Kilian, St. Martin's Press, New York, 1992; *The Winning of the White House 1988,* by Donald Morrison (ed.), A Times Book, New York, 1988; *Dirty Politics: Deception, Distraction, and Democracy,* by Kathleen Hall Jamieson, Oxford University Press, New York, 1992; *Bad Boy: The Life and Politics of Lee Atwater,* by John Brady, Addison Wesley Publishing Company, New York, 1997; *Men of Zeal: The Inside Story of the Iran-Contra Hearings,* by Sens. William S. Cohen and George J. Mitchell, Viking, New York, 1988.

Articles: "Bush Waits and Hopes for Reagan Nod," by Jack Anderson and Dale Van Atta, *Washington Post,* August 18, 1986; "New Hampshire Chill," *Washington Post,* October 11, 1987; "Robertson Links Bush to Swaggart Scandal," *Washington Post,* February 24, 1988; "Bush Rumor Created Dilemma for Media," by Eleanor Randolph, *Washington Post,* October 22, 1988; "Vice President Sunbeam: The Man Who Isn't There," by Morton Kondracke, *New Republic,* March 30, 1987; "In Search of George Bush," by Randall Rothenberg, *New York Times Magazine,* March 6, 1988; "The Dirty Secrets of George Bush," by Howard Kohn and Vicki Monks, *Rolling Stone,* November 3, 1988; "In the Loop: Bush's Secret Mission," by Murray Waas and Craig Unger, *New Yorker,* November 2, 1992; "Spurious George," by Sidney Blumenthal, *New Republic,* November 5, 1984; "The Front-Runner," by Gerald M. Boyd, *New York Times Magazine,* February 23, 1986; "Playing Hardball," by Eric Alterman, *New York Times Magazine,* April 30, 1989; "George Bush on God, War and Ollie North," by David Frost, *U.S. News & World Report,* December 14, 1987; "Guess Who's in the Loop?" by Brian Duffy, *U.S. News & World Report,* October 5, 1992; "Book Concludes Bush Endorsed Iran Arms Sale," by Charles W. Corddry, *Baltimore Sun,* September 4, 1988; "Documents in North Trial Cast Bush in Key Contra Affair Role," Knight-Ridder Newspapers, April 7, 1989; "Significance of Bush's Diary in Arms Deal is Disputed," by David Johnston, *New York Times,* December 27, 1992; "The Man Behind the Message: Ailes," by Richard Stendel, *Time,* August 22, 1988; "The Republicans in '88," by William Schneider, *The Atlantic,* July 1987; "Getting Away with Murder," by Robert James Bidinetto, *Reader's Digest,* July 1988; "Bush's Most Valuable Player," by Jack E. White, *Time,* November 14, 1988; "Fighting the

Wimp Factor," by Margaret Warner, *Newsweek,* October 19, 1987; "The Making of Willie Horton," by Martin Schram, *New Republic,* May 28, 1990; "Bush Attacked; Dukakis Didn't," by David S. Broder, *Houston Chronicle,* August 14, 1989; "Son: Iran Affair a Problem for Bush," by Clay Robinson, *Houston Chronicle,* March 27, 1987; "Reagan: Bush Didn't Oppose Iran Arms Sale," by Cragg Hines, *Houston Chronicle,* March 20, 1987; "Bush Gets Most Early Oil-Patch Support," by William E. Clayton, Jr., *Houston Chronicle,* September 3, 1985; "Iran Controversy Poses Problem for Bush," by David Hoffman, *Washington Post,* November 25, 1986; "Republican National Convention/Bush's Eldest Son Relishes Task as a Texas Delegate," by Mark Toohey, *Houston Chronicle,* August 16, 1988; "Here Comes the Son," by Jeffrey H. Birnbaum, *Fortune,* June 22, 1998; "Bush is Linked to Iran-Contra by Memo," by Cragg Hines, *Houston Chronicle,* December 18, 1987; "CBS Producer Chronicles Bush-Rather Battle," by Phil McCombs, *Washington Post,* January 28, 1988; "Mauro Takes Shot at Bush in D.C. Visit," by Bennett Roth, *Houston Chronicle,* June 23, 1998; "Bush Helped Establish Houston Halfway House," by Clay Robinson, *Houston Chronicle,* September 8, 1988; "Midlander Bush Joining Father's Campaign," by Gary Ott, *Midland Reporter-Telegram,* February 1, 1987; "Clements' Support Not a 'Liability,' Bush Says," by Rick Brown, *Midland Reporter-Telegram,* December 29, 1987; "Make That George W., Please," *Houston Post,* October 12, 1987; "A Fiercely Loyal Son or Peevish Prince," by Julia Malone and Ken Herman, *Austin American-Statesman,* February 21, 1999; "Bush's Group Likely to Bid for Rangers," *Houston Post,* February 25, 1989; "AL Gives Approval to Sales of Rangers, Orioles," Associated Press, April 19, 1989; "President's Son May Buy Rangers," Associated Press, January 22, 1989; "Rangers' Chiles Close to Selling Team to Bush," Kurt Iverson, *Houston Post,* March 17, 1989; "Bush Group Will Buy Rangers," *Houston Chronicle,* March 18, 1989; "Chiles Announces Rangers' Sale Plans," by Bill Sullivan, *Houston Chronicle,* March 19, 1989; "Bush Administers Smooth Transition," by Denne H. Freeman, Associated Press, March 20, 1989; "Chiles to Sell Rangers to Bush," Associated Press, March 18, 1989; "Bush Group Signs Deal to Buy Rangers," *Houston Post,* March 19, 1989; "Rangers Have 20-Year Itch to Scratch," by Bill Sullivan, April 28, 1991; "Farewell to 'Mad Eddie,'" by Steven R. Reed, *Houston Chronicle,* August 29, 1993; "George W. Bush Moves Out of Father's Shadow," by Robert Suro, *New York Times,* April 26, 1992; "Could Young Bush Be Sending Signals?" by Alan Peppard, *Dallas Times-Herald,* February 11, 1989; "Young Bush's Reputation Blossoms at Flora Awards," by Nancy Smith, *Dallas Times-Herald,* April 14, 1990; "George W. and the Other Hubbies Livened Up the Leukemia Benefit," by Alan Peppard, *Dallas Morning News,* February 8, 1990; "Bush to Head Volunteer Auxiliary," *Dallas Times-Herald,* August 9, 1990; "Bush Brings His Soft Pitch to Hardball," by Ron Boyd, *Dallas Times-Herald,* April 26, 1989; "Barbara Bush Says Her Son is Not a Washington Man," by Steven R. Reed, *Houston Chronicle,* July 2, 1989; "Famous Names as Favorite Sons?" by Nene Foxhall, *Houston Chronicle,* February 5, 1989; "Bush's Son Delivers GOP Report Card," by Jane Ely, February 22, 1989; "Younger Bush Plans

9-City 'Lincoln Day' Speaking Tour of Texas," by John Gravois, *Houston Post,* February 6, 1989; "Gramm Sizes Up Bush vs. Richards," by Juan R. Palomo, *Houston Post,* January 28, 1989; "First Son Grooming for Race?" by Kathy Kiely, *Houston Post,* January 21, 1989; "Bush Won't Rule Out Political Race," by Rick Brown, *Midland Reporter-Telegram,* December 18, 1989; "Bush's Son Undecided About Whether to Build New Stadium," Associated Press, June 24, 1989; "George W. Bush, Partners Take Sporting Chance on Rangers," by Jimmy Patterson, *Midland Reporter-Telegram,* April 2, 1989; "Mattox, Bush Early Favorites in Poll Results," by Nene Foxhall, *Houston Chronicle,* May 7, 1989; "No Rush Bush's Son Still Undecided on Governor's Race," by John Gravois, *Houston Post,* June 23, 1989; "Younger Bush Unsure About Political Bid," by Susan Fahlgren, Associated Press, June 24, 1989; "Owner Sees Rangers at Close Range, George W. Bush Has Ring-Side Seat," *Houston Post,* July 26, 1989; "Bush's Eldest Sees No Politics for Now," Associated Press, January 19, 1989; "Bush's Son Rules Out Candidacy for Texas Governorship in '90," by Ron Calhoun, *Dallas Times-Herald,* August 2, 1989; "Bush's Son Rejects Gubernatorial Bid," by Cindy Rugeley and Mark Toohey, *Houston Chronicle,* August 2, 1989; "Governor's Race Opens Up Wide," by Nene Foxhall and Mark Toohey, *Houston Chronicle,* August 27, 1989; "Bush's Bow Sets Other Hopefuls Hopping," *Midland Reporter-Telegram,* August 4, 1989; "Republicans Differ on Bowout of Bush," By John Gravois, *Houston Post,* August 3, 1989; "Mom Says Bush Could Have Been Governor," Associated Press, March 29, 1990; "Bush Refuses to Make Pre-Primary Endorsement," by David Morris, *Midland Reporter-Telegram,* February 14, 1990; "Claydesta Millionaire Plans to Run for Governor," by Mary Lenz, *Houston Post,* March 18, 1989; "Williams Seeks Governship/Midland Man Willing to Spend 'Lifesavings' on Race," by Mark Toohey, *Houston Chronicle,* June 22, 1989; "George W. Bush Still Studying Options in Politics, With Rangers," by Steven R. Reed, *Midland Reporter-Telegram,* July 4, 1989; "Rangers' Bush is Key Player in Dallas Economic Revival," by David Jackson, *Dallas Morning News,* December 25, 1989; "Just One Man is Owning Up to Local Fans," by Randy Galloway, *Dallas Morning News,* October 4, 1990; "Purchase Seen as Good for Bush's Governor Pitch," by Arnold Stapleton, *Dallas Times Herald,* March 20, 1989; "The Governor's Sweetheart Deal," by Robert Bryce, *Texas Observer,* January 30, 1998; "More Than a Name to Rangers' New Manager," *Dallas Times Herald,* May 2, 1989; "Bush May Take Heat Over R-rated Film Ties," by R.G. Ratcliffe, *Houston Chronicle,* June 23, 1998; "Steady Barrage of Violence Partly to Blame, Bush Says," by Clay Robinson, *Houston Chronicle,* April 21, 1999; "How George Got His Groove," by Eric Pooley and S.C. Gwynne, *Time,* June 21, 1999; "George, Washington," by Evan Smith, *Texas Monthly,* June 1999; "Team Player," by Joe Nick Patoski, *Texas Monthly,* June 1999; "George's Road to Riches," by Byron York, *American Spectator,* June 1999.

Television: *CBS Evening News with Dan Rather,* January 25, 1988; NBC-TV's *Today,* July 30, 1997; CNN interview with George W. Bush, February 2, 1999; "Lone Star Legend," produced by Phillips Productions, December 11, 1994.

Information for this chapter was based in part on interviews with Alan Henning; John Carlson; Ted Keene; Frank Macassi; Pete Teeley; Jim Oberwetter; confidential conversations with former high-ranking officials in the Bush presidential campaign, Dallas friends of George and Laura Bush, and close family members.

CHAPTER 5. WINS AND LOSSES

Archives and Oral History Collections: The George Bush Presidential Library, College Station, Texas; the Texas State Archives, Austin, Texas; Texas Room, Houston Public Library; Center for American History, the University of Texas at Austin; Texas Historical Society, Houston, Texas; Thomas Ludlow Ashley Papers, MS-159, Center for Archival Collections, Bowling Green State University, Bowling Green, Ohio; Public Service Archives, Woodson Research Center, Rice University; Eugene C. Barker Texas History Center, Austin; Wal-Mart Visitor's Center and Museum, Bentonville, Arkansas; Securities and Exchange Commission records; Federal Election Commission filings.

Books: *The Outlaw Bank: A Wild Ride Into the Heart of BCCI,* by Jonathan Beaty and S.C. Gwynne, Random House, New York, 1993; *The Politics Presidents Make,* by Stephen Skowronek, Harvard University Press, Cambridge, Mass., 1993; *George Bush and the Guardianship Presidency,* by David Mervin, St. Martin's Press, New York, 1996; *Silverado: Neil Bush and the Savings and Loan Scandal,* by Steven Wilmsen, National Press Books, Washington, D.C., 1991; *Bare Knuckles and Back Rooms,* by Ed Rollins, Broadway Books, New York, 1996; *George Bush's War,* by Jean Edward Smith, Henry Holt and Company, New York, 1992; *The General's War: The Inside Story of the Conflict in the Gulf,* by Michael R. Gordon and General Bernard E. Trainor, Little, Brown, Boston, 1995; *Quest for the Presidency,* by Peter Goldman and Thomas DeFrank, Texas A&M Press, College Station, Texas, 1994; *Mad As Hell: Revolt at the Ballot Box, 1992,* by Jack W. Germond and Jules Witcover, Warner Books, New York, 1993; *George Bush: The Life of a Lone Star Yankee,* by Herbert S. Parmet, Charles Scribner's Sons, New York, 1997; *Barbara Bush: A Memoir* (paperback edition), by Barbara Bush, St. Martin's Press, New York, 1995; *Simply Barbara Bush: A Portrait of America's Candid First Lady* (paperback edition), by Donnie Radcliffe, Warner Books, New York, 1990; *Barbara Bush: A Biography,* by Pamela Kilian, St. Martin's Press, New York, 1992; *Sam Walton, Made in America: My Story,* by Sam Walton with John Huey, Doubleday, New York, 1992; *Citizen Perot: His Life and Times,* by Gerald Posner, Random House, New York, 1996; *Perot and His People: Disrupting the Balance of Political Power,* by Carolyn Barta, The Summit Group, Ft. Worth, Texas, 1993; *Campaign for President: The Managers Look at '92,* by Sharon Holman, Hollis Publishing, Hollis, N.H., 1994; *Ross Perot: The Man Behind the Myth,* by Ken Gross, Random House, New York, 1992; *A G-Man's Journal,* by Oliver "Buck" Revell, Pocket Books, New York, 1998; *Inside Job: The Looting of America's*

Savings and Loans, by Stephen Pizzo, Mary Fricker and Paul Muolo, HarperCollins, New York, 1991; *The Mafia, CIA and George Bush,* by Pete Brewton, S.P.I. Books, New York, 1992.

Published sources include "To a Son of Bush Won Bahrain Drilling Pact; Harken Energy Had a Web of Mideast Connections In the Background: BCCI—Entrée at the White House," by Thomas Petzinger, Jr., Peter Truell and Jill Abramson, *Wall Street Journal,* December 6, 1991; "Family Value$," by Stephen Pizzo, *Mother Jones,* September–October 1992; "Bush's Eldest Son Begins a Leave From Harken Posts," by Thomas Petzinger, *Wall Street Journal,* June 24, 1990; "Bush's Oldest Son Has a Stake in Persian Gulf," *Dallas Times Herald,* October 8, 1990; "Like Father, Like Son—Sort Of," by Ken Herman, *Houston Post,* November 7, 1993; "The Man Behind the Bahrain-Harken Deal," by Sam Fletcher, *Houston Post,* December 23, 1991; "The Color of Money," by Stephen J. Hedges, *U.S. News & World Report,* March 16, 1992; "George W. Bush/Wealth Produced Via Stock Swaps and Bailouts," by Bob Sablatura, *Houston Chronicle,* May 8, 1994; "Bush's Son Cautions GOP; Don't Make Issue of Democrats' 'Poor Judgement' on War, He Says," by Sam Attlesey, *Dallas Morning News,* March 6, 1991; "Oil in the Family," *Dallas Observer,* February 12, 1991; "So-Called Liberal Press Should be Whacking Bush," by Joe Conason, *New York Observer,* March 15, 1999; "The Bush Connection," by Allan Nairn, *The Progressive,* May 1987; "No Way to Sell a War; Press Critiques CNN's Attempted Rally on Iraq," by Neil deMause, *Extra!,* May–June 1998; "Crude Dealings; Business: Untangling the Business Associations That Bind George Bush Jr. and Harken Energy Corp.," by David Armstrong, *Dallas Observer,* August 8, 1991; "Good Connections," by Richard A. Oppel Jr. and George Kuempel, *Dallas Morning News,* November 16, 1998; "Who is David Edwards," by Micah Morrison, *Wall Street Journal,* March 1, 1995; "The Family That Preys Together," by Jack Calhoun, *Covert Action Quarterly,* Summer 1992; "Bush's Oldest Son Has Interests in Bahrain/Crisis in Gulf Threatens Company's Drilling Rights," by Pete Brewton, *Houston Post,* October 7, 1990; "Bush Cites Work, Rejects Rich-Boy Image," by Ken Herman, *Austin American-Statesman,* October 11, 1998; "Small Oil Companies Can Run Rings 'Round Big Ones for Foreign Deals," by Sam Fletcher, *Houston Post,* December 23, 1991; "Business, By George," *Dallas Observer,* February 27, 1997; "George W. Bush Blazing Own Trail," by R.G. Ratcliffe, *Houston Chronicle,* November 7, 1993; "Downloading The Bush Files," by Michael King, *Texas Observer,* November 1998; "Harken Stock Value Doubles/Interest in Bahrain Cited for Increases in Price," *Houston Post,* December 7, 1991; "Harken Energy Fortune Closely Tied to Result of Bahrain Drilling," Associated Press, July 6, 1992; "Bush's Eldest Son Linked to Stock-Sale Conflict," Associated Press, March 8, 1992; "Harken Energy Corp. Plugs Bahrain Well," by Sam Fletcher, *Houston Post,* March 6, 1992; "Easygoing George W. Bush," by Stuart Eskenazi, *Houston Press,* October 29–November 4, 1998; "Sale of Energy Stock Was Proper, Bush Says," by Ken Herman, *Houston Post,* October 9, 1994; "Richards Wants Letter Released," by John Gravois, *Houston Post,* October 11, 1994; "Richards Questions Thoroughness of Bush SEC Probe," by Ken Herman, *Houston Post,* October 12, 1994; "Bush Inquiry is Questioned by Richards," by R.G. Ratcliffe, *Houston Chronicle,* October 13, 1994; "SEC Papers Show Missteps by Bush," by Ken Herman, *Houston Post,* October 18, 1994; "SEC Files Raises Questions About Bush's Stock Dealings in Company," Associated Press, October 28, 1994; "SEC Data Cast Doubt on Bush's Stock Deal," by Rob Wells, Associated Press, October 28, 1994; "Report: Bush Son Sold Stock Before Decline," *New York Times,* March 9, 1992; "The Corruption of Neil Bush," by Steven Wilmsen, *Playboy,* June 1981; "A Crisis in the Family," by Ann McDaniel, *Newsweek,* July 23, 1990; "Inside the Silverado Scandal," by Stephen Hedges, *U.S. News & World Report,* August 13, 1990; "Who Lost Kuwait?" by Murray Waas, *Village Voice,* January 22, 1991; "Why Are We Stuck in the Sand?" by Christopher Hitchens, *Harper's Magazine,* January 1991; "Bush's Son Key to End of Sununu," by Bob Drummond, *Dallas Times Herald,* December 4, 1991; "Bush's Eldest Son Checks on Dad's Campaign," *Dallas Morning News,* April 10, 1992; "Perot's Swift Rise Draws GOP, Democratic Broadsides," *Los Angeles Times,* March 22, 1992; "Perot Tells Large Rally of Death Threat," by Michael Isikoff, *Washington Post,* November 8, 1993; "Bush Aims to Be Catalyst for Wide Change," by R.G. Ratcliffe, *Houston Chronicle,* January 15, 1995; "Sununu Paid Only Fraction of Flights' Cost," by Greg McDonald, *Houston Chronicle,* April 24, 1991; Sununu's Final Ticket One-Way," by John Gravois, *Houston Post,* December 4, 1991; "Beleaguered Sununu Quits, Cites 'Political Negatives,'" by Judy Wiessler Hines, *Houston Chronicle,* December 4, 1991; "Bush Siblings Have Grown Under National Spotlight," by Clifford Pugh, *Houston Post,* August 19, 1992; "Silverado's Name Exudes S&L Fiasco," Associated Press, September 23, 1990; "House Banking Panel Guts Bush S&L Bill," Associated Press, April 12, 1989; "Whitewashing the Bush Boys," by Stephen Pizzo, *Mother Jones,* March–April 1994; "My Three Sons," by Stephen Pizzo, *Mother Jones,* November–December 1992; "Oil Firms of Vice President's Sons Also in Struggle to Survive," by Robert Reinhold, *New York Times,* May 4, 1986; "The Saturday Profile: The Bush Clan That Plays Too," by Rupert Cornwell, *Independent,* November 7, 1998; "MOJO Updates," by Stephen Pizzo, *Mother Jones,* January 1993; "A Fiercely Loyal Son or Peevish Prince?" by Julia Malone and Ken Herman, *Austin American-Statesman,* February 21, 1999; "Bush's Secret Pals Network," by Kenneth T. Walsh, *U.S. News & World Report,* June 15, 1992; "George W. Bush/As Operative for His Father, Loyalty was the Foremost Watchword," by Cragg Hines, *Houston Chronicle,* May 8, 1994; "Bush Picks Longtime Associates for His Re-Election Effort," by Cragg Hines, *Houston Chronicle,* December 6, 1991; "Perot Blasts '92 Bush Camp, TV and Rap Music," *Dallas Morning News,* April 26, 1996; "Bush Brothers Grab Media Spotlight," by Clay Robinson, *Houston Chronicle,* November 18, 1998; "Convention '92/Some People to Watch as the Convention Unfolds/George W. Bush," *Houston Chronicle,* August 16, 1992; "This is a Rescue?" *Time,* March 12, 1990; "S&Ls," by Robert Sherrill, *The Nation,* November 19, 1990; "It's a Family Affair," *Time,* July 23, 1990; "Bush Signs 'Monster' S&L Rescue," by Gregory Seay, *Houston Post,* August 10,

1989; "Convention '92 Pulls Bush Clan into Limelight," by Ruth Rendon, *Houston Chronicle,* August 18, 1992; "Out of Texas, A Familiar But Singular Brand," by Jill Lawrence, *USA Today,* September 8, 1998; "Weakness of Bush, His Message, His Team Too Much to Overcome," by Terry Ellsworth, *Houston Post,* November 6, 1992; "George W. Bush is Adviser as Well as Son to President," *Houston Post,* August 30, 1992; "Ask Matalin/Only Woman on Bush Campaign Team an Oddball Whose Political Skill Translates into Clout," by Geraldine Baum, *Los Angeles Times,* May 24, 1992; "Presidential Election Defeat Took Bush by Surprise, Son Says," by R.G. Ratcliffe, *Houston Chronicle,* June 6, 1993; "White House Secrets Told/Ford Reportedly Tried to Get Quayle Dumped," by Jack Nelson, *Los Angeles Times,* August 13, 1995; "Complacency the Enemy, Bush's Son Tells GOP," by R.G. Ratcliffe, *Houston Chronicle,* December 8, 1991; "President's Son Campaigns with Confidence," by Darren J. Waggoner, *Midland Reporter-Telegram,* October 22, 1992; "Bush's Son Shows Interest in Bentsen's Senate Seat," by John Gravois, *Houston Post,* December 4, 1992; "Bentsen Remains Quiet, Possible Successors Aren't," by Gardner Selby and Mary Lenz, *Houston Post,* December 6, 1992; "The Clinton Cabinet/Bentsen Departure Leaves Political Power Vacuum," by R.G. Ratcliffe, Alan Bernstein, Ross Ramsey, and Nancy Mathis, *Houston Chronicle,* December 11, 1992; "President's Son Won't Run for Bentsen's Seat," by Alan Bernstein and R.G. Ratcliffe, *Houston Chronicle,* December 12, 1992; "Bush's Son, Staubach Out of Bentsen Derby," by Ken Herman, *Houston Post,* December 12, 1992; "Rangers Make Pitch for Tax, New Stadium," by Steven R. Reed, *Houston Chronicle,* January 13, 1991; "Critics Complain About Ballpark's $189 Million Financing," Associated Press, April 17, 1994; "Property Owners Sue Bush's Baseball Club," by Andrea D. Greene, *Houston Chronicle,* September 1, 1994; "Bush is Big Business," by Bill Addington, *Texas Observer,* June 19, 1998; "George W. Bush/Campaign Brings Renewed Scrutiny of Stadium Deal," by Bob Sablatura, *Houston Chronicle,* May 8, 1994; "Field of Dreams—Or Foul Ball?" by Ken Herman, *Houston Post,* March 31, 1994; "Bush Pushes Local Financing for a Stadium," *Houston Chronicle,* June 18, 1996; "Rangers Plan Stadium with That Touch of Texas," Associated Press, August 29, 1991; "The Governor's Sweetheart Deal," by Robert Bryce, *Texas Observer,* January 30, 1998; "What Price Baseball?" by Robert Bryce, *Austin Chronicle,* June 20–26, 1997; "Bush's Big Score," by Robert Bryce, *Dallas Observer,* February 9, 1998; "Bush the Businessman: Baseball Has Been Very Good to Him," by Ken Herman, *Houston Post,* October 9, 1994; "Bush Signs Name to Some 500 Bills—One Measure Will Limit Power to Houston's Sports Authority," by John W. Gonzalez, *Houston Chronicle,* June 20, 1999; "How George Got His Groove," by Eric Pooley and S.C. Gwynne, *Time,* June 21, 1999; "George, Washington," by Evan Smith, *Texas Monthly,* June 1999; "George's Road to Riches," by Byron York, *American Spectator,* June 1999.

Television: "Lone Star Legend," produced by Phillips Productions, December 11, 1994; *60 Minutes,* interview with Ross Perot, CBS, October 25, 1992.

Interviews: Phil Kendrick; Ed Martin; confidential conversations with Harken

Energy Corp. executives; Ben Moore; Kenneth Boone; Richard Thompson; confidential interview with a former SEC investigator; Stan Carmichael; Jack Harrington; Roger Martin; confidential interviews with former White House aides and Bush reelection campaign officials; Kevin Bates; Tracy Silverstein; Robert Lawson; Donald Morris; confidential interviews with Bush family members and close friends in Dallas; Roger King; Glenn Sodd.

Chapter 6. The Family Business

Archives and Oral History Collections: Texas Ethics Commission records; Federal Election Commission filings; The George Bush Presidential Library, College Station, Texas; the Texas State Archives, Austin, Texas; Texas Room, Houston Public Library; Center for American History, the University of Texas at Austin; Texas Historical Society, Houston, Texas; Public Service Archives, Woodson Research Center, Rice University; Eugene C. Barker Texas History Center, Austin.

Books: *The Thorny Rose of Texas: An Intimate Portrate of Governor Ann Richards,* by Mike Shropshire with Frank Schaeffer, Carol Publishing, New York, 1994; *Storming the Statehouse: Running for Governor with Ann Richards and Diane Feinstein,* by Celia Morris, Scribner, New York, 1992; *Claytie and the Lady: Ann Richards, Gener, and Politics in Texas,* by Sue Tolleson-Rinehart with Jeanie R. Stanley, University of Texas Press, Austin, Texas, 1994; *Citizen Perot: His Life and Times,* by Gerald Possner, Random House, New York, 1996.

Articles and other periodicals used as sources for this period include "Richards' Easygoing Charm Gives Her 'Star' Political Clout," by R.G. Ratcliffe, *Houston Chronicle,* January 28, 1990; "Politicos Reminisce About '90 Back Then, Williams Seemed a Sure Bet," Associated Press, September 5, 1994; "Favorite Son," by Robert Draper, *GQ,* October 1998; "Richards Rips Bush with Familiar Verve," by Rosaline Jackler, *Houston Post,* January 31, 1992; "George W. Bush May Run for Governor," Associated Press, June 6, 1993; "Possible Candidates Cite Chink in Richards' Armor," by R.G. Ratcliffe, *Houston Chronicle,* June 13, 1993; "GOP Pushes George W. Bush for Governor," Associated Press, August 19, 1993; "GOP Pair Decline Race Against George W. Bush," by Alan Bernstein and R.G. Ratcliffe, *Houston Chronicle,* August 31, 1993; "Bush Submits Forms to Run for Governor," by Ken Herman, *Houston Post,* September 16, 1993; "George W. Bush Files Campaign Papers," Associated Press, September 16, 1993; "Bush Takes Step Closer to Bid for Governor," by R.G. Ratcliffe, *Houston Chronicle,* September 16, 1993; "Rangers' Bush Says, 'I Can Win' Governor's Race," by Tonie Miller-Uzzel, *Midland Reporter-Telegram,* September 17, 1993; "George W. Bush to Play New Game," by Michael Holmes, Associated Press, November 6, 1993; "Bush to Announce Gubernatorial Candidacy Nov. 8," by Mary Lenz, Gardner Selby, and Ken Herman, *Houston Post,* November 11, 1993; "Barbara Bush Plans to Campaign for Sons," Associated Press, October 17, 1993; "Family Tradition, Family Values Drive Jeb Bush," by Cragg Hines, *Houston Chronicle,* October 27, 1994; "Another Branch of the Bushes Blooms in the South, Name a Blessing, Curse for Florida Gubernatorial Front-Runner," by Ken Herman, *Houston Post,* July 24, 1994; "George W. Bush Previews Strategy," by Sam Attlesey, *Dallas Morning News,* November 7, 1993; "George W. Bush Blazing Own Trail," by R.G. Ratcliffe, *Houston Chronicle,* November 7, 1993; "Eldest Son Kicks Off Governor Bid," by Alan Bernstein and R.G. Ratcliffe, *Midland Reporter-Telegram,* November 9, 1993; "Bush Kicks Off Governor's Race, Offers 'Modern-Day Revolution'," by Ken Herman and Mark Horvit, *Houston Post,* November 9, 1993; "Bush Drops in on Campaign Kick-off Tour," by Katherine Poteet, *Midland Reporter-Telegram,* November 10, 1993; "First, Get Specific About Which George Bush," by Jane Ely, *Houston Chronicle,* November 13, 1993; "A Little Bit Clinton, a Little Bit Nixon—It's George W. Bush," by Alan Bernstein, *Houston Chronicle,* November 14, 1993; "Targeting Crime, Bush Finds a Soft Spot in Record of Richards," by R.G. Ratcliffe, *Houston Chronicle,* November 14, 1993; "Richards, Bush Have Contrasting Views of Texas," by Sam Attlesey, *Dallas Morning News,* November 28, 1993; "Bush Promising a 'Revolution of Hope, Ideas," by Sam Attlesey, *Dallas Morning News,* December 5, 1993; "Candidates for Governor Put Spin on Stats," by Ken Herman, *Houston Post,* December 19, 1993; "Richards Looking Like 'New Democrat'," by Clay Robinson, *Houston Chronicle,* December 19, 1993; "Candidates for 2 Key races Tout Anti-Crime Plans," Associated Press, January 8, 1994; "Richards Criticized for Characterization, Candidate Bush Calls Remarks Unfair," by Robbie Morganfield, *Houston Chronicle,* January 30, 1994; "Campaigning Against Crime: Bush Targets Jeveniles, Richards Parolees," by Ken Herman and Matt Schwartz, *Houston Post,* January 6, 1994; "Bush Bashes Current System," by Katherine Poteet, *Midland Reporter-Telegram,* January 20, 1994; "For the Record: Richards, Bush and the Gubernatorial Nominations," *Houston Chronicle,* February 3, 1994; "Dems Cater to Women, GOPers Don't," by Jane Ely, *Houston Chronicle,* February 20, 1994; "Candidates for Governor to Release Their Tax Returns," by Ross Ramsey, *Houston Chronicle,* February 24, 1994; "Governor," by R.G. Ratcliffe, *Houston Chronicle,* February 27, 1994; "Richards, Bush Ready for Showdown," by Ken Herman, *Houston Post,* March 9, 1994; "Voter Turnout: The Turnoff and the Tuneout," by Alan Bernstein, *Houston Chronicle,* March 13, 1994; "It's Richards vs. Bush," by R.G. Ratcliffe, *Houston Chronicle,* March 9, 1994; "Crime Down 8.8 Percent, Governor Says," by Clay Robinson, *Houston Chronicle,* March 24, 1994; "Richards, Bush Paint a Picture of 2 States at Editors' Meeting," by Mark Horvit, *Houston Post,* March 22, 1994; "Richards Sees Jobs Progress as a Key to Her Re-Election," by Michael Holmes, Associated Press, April 13, 1994; "Candidates Report 6-Figure Incomes, But Bush's 5 Times That of Richards'," by Gardner Selby, *Houston Post,* April 16, 1994; "Ballpark Deal Draws Criticism," by Wayne Slater and David Jackson, *Dallas Morning News,* April 16, 1994; "George W. Bush Touts 'Innovative Ideas' Campaign in Permian Basin," by Gary Shanks, *Midland Reporter-Telegram,* April 23, 1994; "Bush to Petroleum Engineers: Let's 'Restore the Texas

Dream,'" by John Paul Pitts, *Midland Reporter-Telegram,* May 19, 1994; "Texas: A Tale of Two Candidates," by Dave McNeely, *Houston Post,* June 21, 1994; "'Phantom' Speakers for Richards, Bush Exchange Fire," by R.G. Ratcliffe, *Houston Chronicle,* April 22, 1994; "Richards Attacks Republican Policy," by R.G. Ratcliffe, *Houston Chronicle,* July 10, 1994; "Richards: Foe Isn't Prepared to be Governor,": by Ken Herman, *Houston Post,* July 13, 1994; "George W. Bush: 'I've come a Long Way'," by R.G. Ratcliffe, *Houston Chronicle,,* July 24, 1994; "Digging Up Dirt, Political Advisers' Skill at 'Opposition Research' in Demand in Texas," by Wayne Slater, *Dallas Morning News,* July 25, 1994; "Digging Dirt on Opponents/Skullduggery Becomes Practiced Art in Politics," by Mark Smith, *Houston Chronicle,* July 31, 1994; "The Best and Worst of Political Times," by Jane Ely, *Houston Chronicle,* August 3, 1994; "2 Campaign Aides Leaving Bush's Staff," by Ken Herman, *Houston Post,* August 11, 1994; "Bush's First TV Ad Attacks Richards with Damning Crime Statistics," by Ken Herman, *Houston Post,* August 16, 1994; "Bush's TV Ad Criticized by Richards Camp," by R.G. Ratcliffe, *Houston Chronicle,* August 16, 1994; "Richards Touts Teachers at Rally in Texarkana, Governor Calls Opponent a 'Jerk,'" by R.G. Ratcliffe, *Houston Chronicle,* August 17, 1994; "Bush Decries Richards as a 'Liberal,'" by R.G. Ratcliffe, *Houston Chronicle,* August 18, 1994; "Governor Downplays 'Jerk' Remark," by Ken Herman, *Houston Post,* August 18, 1994; "Getting to the Real Point—Is He a Jerk or Not?" by Molly Ivins, *Houston Post,* August 21, 1994; "Richards: Pull Plug on Bush Ad," by R.G. Ratcliffe, *Houston Chronicle,* August 3, 1994; "New Bush Ad assails Richards on Crime," by Wayne Slater, *Dallas Morning News,* August 23, 1994; "Ad Claims Flip-Flop by Governor," by Ross Ramsey, *Houston Chronicle,* August 24, 1994; "Candidates Seek Big Mo," by R.G. Ratcliffe, *Houston Chronicle,* August 28, 1994; "Bush Says Richards Ad Tries to 'Demean' Him," by R.G. Ratcliffe, *Houston Chronicle,* August 31, 1994; "Crime: The Richards Record: Is it Good Enough to Bag Another Election?" by Mary Lenz, *Houston Post,* September 4, 1994; Put on Your Helmets and Shin Guards, Folks," by Sam Attlesey, *Dallas Morning News,* September 4, 1994; "Bush Son May Have Florida Nomination in Hand Today," by Deborah Sharp, Gannett News Service, September 8, 1994; "DPS Finds Crime Still on Decline," by Christy Hoppe, *Dallas Morning News,* September 9, 1994; "State Dems Are Steering Clear of the President," by R.G. Ratcliffe, *Houston Chronicle,* September 11, 1994; "Governor's Race Becoming Point, Counterpoint," by Ken Herman, *Houston Post,* September 12, 1994; "Bush Defends Leaving Troubled Firm's Board," by Wayne Slater, *Dallas Morning News,* September 17, 1994; "Bush Takes Campaign to Farmers," Associated Press, September 20, 1994; "Weird is the Watchword of This Election," by Jane Ely, *Houston Chronicle,* September 21, 1994; "Richards' 'Comeback' Ad Touts Progress, Promises More," by Ken Herman, *Houston Post,* September 27, 1994; "New Richards Campaign Commercial Points Out Losses by Bush's Businesses," by Ken Herman, *Houston Post,* September 28, 1994; "Bush Says Richards' Attacks Getting Too Personal," by R.G. Ratcliffe, *Houston Chronicle,* September 28, 1994; "Bush Links Richards, Clinton," by Lori Stahl, *Dallas Morning News,* September 30, 1994;

"Bush the Businessman Believes Not Being Politician, Other Traits Important Assets," by Michael Davis, *Houston Post,* October 9, 1994; "Richards Wants Bush to Reveal Documents from SEC Inquiry," by Charlotte-Anne Lucas, *Dallas Morning News,* October 11, 1994; "Bush Accuses Foe of Mud-Ball Politics," Associated Press, October 14, 1994; "Richards' Latest Ad Dwells on Bush's Business Record," by Ken Herman, *Houston Post,* October 20, 1994; "Bush Quiet About Serving on Quinn Board," by Ken Herman, *Houston Post,* October 27, 1994; "Bush Bumped Himself from Seat on Board," by John Gravois, *Houston Post,* September 17, 1994; "Perot Backs GOP Nationwide, But Gives Richards Nod," by John Gravois, *Houston Post,* October 6, 1994; "Here's the Deal: Perot is Going to Help Richards," by John Gravois, *Houston Post,* October 15, 1994; "Bush, Richards Swap Charges, Challenger's Stock Sale Sparks Exchange of Negative TV Ads," by Wayne Slater, *Dallas Morning News,* October 20, 1994; "Richards, Bush See No Percentage in Discounting Perot in Close Race," by Ken Herman, *Houston Post,* October 24, 1994; "Richards, Bush Spar in TV Ads/Questions Continue Over Stock Sale," *Houston Chronicle,* October 20, 1994; "Key Dates in Bush's Business Career," *Houston Post,* October 9, 1994; "Richards, Bush Hammer Away at Familiar Themes," by Ken Herman, *Houston Post,* October 22, 1994; "Richards, Bush Step Up Attacks, Unveil Strategies," by Wayne Slater and Sam Attlesey, *Dallas Morning News,* October 23, 1994; "Gubernatorial Candidates Take the Gloves Off," by R.G. Ratcliffe, *Houston Chronicle,* October 22, 1994; "Bush, Richards Race Goes Down to Wire, by John Powers, *Midland Reporter-Telegram,* October 27, 1994; "Perot Backs Richards," by R.G. Ratcliffe and Robbie Morganfield, *Houston Chronicle,* November 2, 1994; "Perot Endorses Richards," by Ken Herman and Gardner Selby, *Houston Post,* November 2, 1994; "Bush Shrugs Off Perot's Support for Richards," by Gardner Selby and Mary Lenz, *Houston Post,* November 3, 1994; "Richards Placing Her Bet on the Perot Factor," by R.G. Ratcliffe, *Houston Chronicle,* November 3, 1994; "Richards Stumps for Bubba's Vote," by R.G. Ratcliffe, *Houston Chronicle,* November 4, 1994; "Richards, Bush Hunt Undecideds," by Ken Herman and Gardner Selby, *Houston Post,* November 4, 1994; "In Hopes for Future, Candidates Refer to the Past," by Robbie Morganfield, *Houston Chronicle,* November 6, 1994; "Richards Defends Her Tactics, Rips Challenger Bush—Again," by Robbie Morganfield and R.G. Ratcliffe, *Houston Chronicle,* October 30, 1994; "On the Issues: Crime, Education in Texas/Specifics Sparse in Governor's Contest," by Kathy Walt, *Houston Chronicle,* October 30, 1994; "Richards Focusing on Bush's Inexperience," by Ken Herman and Marty Graham, *Houston Post,* October 30, 1994; "Gubernatorial Candidates Speak Out on Issues," by Ken Herman, *Houston Post,* October 30, 1994; "Richards Derides Rival as Unqualified Unknown," by Ken Herman, *Houston Post,* October 17, 1994; "Former 1st Lady Defends Bush Amid Richards' Volleys," by Wayne Slater and Sam Attlesey, *Dallas Morning News,* October 27, 1994; "Bush, Richards Exchange Attacks in Ads," by Wayne Slater and Sam Attlesey, *Dallas Morning News,* October 29, 1994; "Richards, Bush Campaigns Focus on What's Lacking," by Sam Attlesey, *Dallas*

Morning News, October 30, 1994; "Ann W. Richards/She's a Hunter and a Motorcycle Mama, and Strikes a Chord with Many Texans," by R.G. Ratcliffe, *Houston Chronicle,* October 30, 1994; "Governor's Race: It's Still Close," by John Gravois, *Houston Post,* November 2, 1994; "Big Donors Fuel Governor's Race," by Wayne Slater, *Dallas Morning News,* November 3, 1994; "Bush Exuding Confidence as Race Nears End," by Sam Attlesey, *Dallas Morning News,* November 5, 1994; "Bush Sweeps by Richards," by R.G. Ratcliffe, *Houston Chronicle,* November 9, 1994; "Election '94: Nation/GOP Captures a Majority of Governorships," Associated Press, November 9, 1994; "A Major Triumph for GOP, Party Will Control House and Senate," by Cragg Hines, Bill Mintz, and Graeme Zielinskui, *Houston Chronicle,* November 9, 1994; "Bush-Whacking Just Didn't Fly with Voters," by Alan Bernstein, *Houston Chronicle,* November 9, 1994; "Voters Upset by Richards' Politicking," by Mark Horvit, *Houston Post,* November 9, 1994; "Governor/Richards Support from '90 Falls Off/Poll: Anglo, GOP Women Back Bush," by R.G. Ratcliffe, *Houston Chronicle,* November 9, 1994; "Former President Sits Tense on the Sidelines," by Kathy Lewis, *Dallas Morning News,* November 9, 1994; "Bush is in Business," by Ken Herman, *Houston Post,* November 9, 1994; "Dancing Bush Backers Revel in Win," by Mark Smith, *Houston Chronicle,* November 9, 1994; "That Sucking Sound, Democrats Across the Country Feel Voters' Anger," *Houston Post,* November 9, 1994 "Analysts, Exit Polls Credit Bush Tactics," by Sam Attlesey, *Dallas Morning News,* November 9, 1994; "2 Class Acts—Bush, Richards Deal Gracefully with Victory, Defeat," *Houston Post,* November 10, 1994; "GOP Gains in Texas Significant," by Clay Robinson, *Houston Chronicle,* November 10, 1994; "Bush Pulls Stunning Win," Associated Press, November 9, 1994; "George W. Bush: A Quick Ascent from Curiosity to Contender," by Ken Herman, *Houston Post,* November 9, 1994; "Jeb Bush Can't Match Big Brother's Feat: Younger Sibling Fails to Unseat Democratic Incumbent in Florida's Governor's Race," by George Rodriguez, *Dallas Morning News,* November 9, 1994; "Defections by Men Gave Edge to GOP," by Richard L. Berke, *New York Times,* November 11, 1994; "GOP's Broom Sweeps Clean," by Lori Rodriguez, *Houston Chronicle,* November 12, 1994; "That's Enough of Ross Perot," by Jack Germond and Jules Witcover, Tribune Media Services, November 14, 1994; "Gov-Elect Bush Cashes in on Oil, Gas Stock Shares," by Dan Fisher, *Bloomberg Business News,* December 29, 1994; "Reading Laura Bush," by Skip Hollandsworth, *Texas Monthly,* November 1996; "Transformation in Texas Politics," by Ross Ramsey, *Houston Chronicle,* January 15, 1995; "How George Got His Groove," by Eric Pooley and S.C. Gwynne, *Time,* June 21, 1999.

Television: "Lone Star Legend," produced by Phillips Productions, December 11, 1994; *Lifetime's Intimate Portrait* of Ann Richards, produced by Linda Ellerbee, narrated by Dan Rather, November 7, 1998.

Interviews: Ann Amalera; Stan Morris; Dick Karras; confidential conversation with former Richards and Bush campaign strategists and consultants; Matt Broyles; Chuck McDonald; B.B. Corn; Bill Walker; Robert Crager; Shirley Ackerman; Buck

Renfrew; Norman Wells; confidential interviews with Bush campaign aides, close friends of Barbara Bush, and family members provided collaborating details of the private telephone conversation between Geroge W. and his parents after being elected governor.

CHAPTER 7. "ANN DOESN'T WORK HERE ANYMORE"

Archives and Oral History Collections: Texas Ethics Commission records; Federal Election Commission filings; The George Bush Presidential Library, College Station, Texas; Texas Room, Houston Public Library; the Texas State Archives, Austin, Texas; Center for American History, the University of Texas at Austin; Texas Historical Society, Houston, Texas; Public Service Archives, Woodson Research Center, Rice University; Eugene C. Barker Texas History Center, Austin.

Books: *Reconstruction in Texas,* by Charles William Ramsdell, University of Texas Press, Austin, Texas, 1970; *Documents of Texas History,* by Ernest Wallace with George B. Ward and David M. Vigness, State House Press, Austin, Texas, 1994; *A Concise History of Texas* (Rev.), by Mike Kingston, Gulf Publishing Company, Houston, Texas, 1998; *Selena: The Phenomenal Life and Tragic Death of The Tejano Music Queen,* by Clint Richmond, Pocket Books, New York, 1995; *One of Ours: Timothy McVeigh and the Oklahoma City Bombing,* by Richard A. Serrano, W. W. Norton & Company, New York, 1998; *All-American Monster: The Unauthorized Biography of Timothy McVeigh,* by Brandon M. Stickney, Prometheus Books, Amherst, N.Y., 1996.

Among the published articles consulted: "The Bush Bash Brief Inauguration," by Ken Herman, *Houston Post,* January 15, 1995; "Bush Takes Austin Reins," by R.G. Ratcliffe and Clay Robinson, *Midland Reporter-Telegram,* January 18, 1995; "George W. Has Big Shoes to Fill," by Lynn Ashby, *Houston Post,* January 17, 1995; "A Nice, Quiet Day of Promise for Texas," by Jane Ely, *Houston Post,* January 18, 1995; "Barbecue, Bands, Balls Highlight Festivities," by Chip Brown, Associated Press, January 8, 1995; "Inauguration Inspires Vows of Cooperation," by R.G. Ratcliffe and Clay Robinson, *Houston Chronicle,* January 18, 1995; "Inaugural Words, Governor, Lieutenant Governor Start on Same Page," *Houston Chronicle,* January 18, 1995; "The Bush Bash/Many Corporate Sponsors Picking Up Tab for Festivities," by Ken Herman, January 15, 1995; "Elder Bushes Cheering from the Sidelines," by Alan Bernstein, *Houston Chronicle,* January 15, 1995; "Applause Also Follows Elder Bushes," by Alan Bernstein, *Houston Chronicle,* January 18, 1995; "Richards' Exit Graceful, Calm," by Dave McNelly, *Houston Post,* January 5, 1995; "Bullock Vows to Work with Bush to "Renew This State We All Love'," by Kathy Walt, *Houston Chronicle,* January 18, 1995; "'Just One of Guys': Bush Works for Good of Texans," by Bill Modisett, *Midland Reporter-Telegram,* June 10, 1995; "Bush Knows that Bills and Pictures Mix," by Jane Ely, *Houston Chronicle,* June 4, 1995; "Poll Finds Concealed Guns Supported," by Syliva Moreno, *Dallas Morning News,* February 3, 1995; "Devil in Details, Gov. Bush Restates 4 Campaign Goals for Lawmakers," *Houston Post,* February 8, 1995; "Bullock Says Concealed Guns Law Wouldn't Bring Wild West Back," Associated Press, February 25, 1995; "Study Doesn't Back Concealed Weapons Law," by Bill Mitchell, *Dallas Morning News,* March 12, 1995; "State's Law Officers Split on Concealed-Weapons Bill," by Lee Hancock, *Dallas Morning News,* March 14, 1995; "Senate Endorses Gun Bill, State Referendum on Issue Rejected," by Sylvia Moreno, *Dallas Morning News,* March 16, 1995; "Out of Sight, On the Mind: Concealed Weapon Law's Effects on Florida Crime are Unclear," by Sylvia Moreno, *Dallas Morning News,* March 21, 1995; "Selena's Fans Say Goodbye, Thousands in Corpus Christi Gather to See Singer's Casket," by Stephen Power, *Dallas Morning News,* April 3, 1995; "Gov. Bush Gets Good Marks All Around," by Jane Ely, *Houston Chronicle,* May 17, 1995; "Bush Adds Another Push to Proposal, Tells Lawmakers 5th Goal to State of State Speech: 'Pass the First Four,'" by Clay Robinson, *Houston Chronicle,* February 8, 1995; "Law Enforcement Group Blasts Bush Over Handgun Proposal" Associated Press, April 22, 1994; "Mayors Unlikely to Fight Concealed Weapons Bill/Most in Group Opposed But Stay Mum in Meeting" by Ken Herman, *Houston Post,* February 7, 1995; "Survey: 79% Want a Vote on Gun Law/Battle on Handguns Heats Up Statewide," by Clay Robinson, *Houston Chronicle,* February 3, 1995; "Better Get Set for Pistol-Packing Texans," by Clay Robinson, *Houston Chronicle,* March 3, 1995; "Both Sides in Gun Debate Point to Death of Selena," by Ken Herman, *Houston Post,* April 5, 1995; "Texans Split 50-50 on Handgun Bill," by R.G. Ratcliffe, *Houston Chronicle,* April 24, 1995; "Pay Back for the NRA?" by Susan Gates, *Houston Chronicle,* March 20, 1995; "Texas Jury Convicts Fan of Killing Selena," by Sam Verhovek, *New York Times,* October 23, 1995; "Former President Bush Angrily Resigns from NRA," by Armando Villafranca and Stephen Johnson, *Houston Chronicle,* May 11, 1995; "Oklahoma City Tragedy 'A Tough Moment' for Governor, Blast Claims Lives of Two Guards Linked to Bush Family," by R.G. Ratcliffe, *Houston Chronicle,* April 25, 1995; "Is He the Smoking Gun," by Matt Bai, *Newsweek,* January 5, 1999; "Florida Concealed Weapons Law: It's a Draw," by Ken Herman, January 22, 1995; "Study: Licensed Gun Owners in Texas Arrested 2,080 Times," Associated Press, March 23, 1999; "Bush Hints of One Term," *Houston Chronicle,* May 27, 1995; "Packing Pistols Won't Be Good for Texas," by Clay Robinson, *Houston Chronicle,* May 21, 1995; "NRA Takes Out Full-Page Ad Praising State Handgun Bill," Associated Press, June 9, 1995; "Gun Owners Target Lessons, Find None," by Norma Martin, Associated Press, May 28, 1995; "Bush Signs Handgun Bill," by R.G. Ratcliffe, Ross Ramsey and Kathy Walt, *Houston Chronicle,* May 27, 1995; "New Law Hits Too Close to Home," by John Williams, *Houston Chronicle,* May 17, 1995; "Oklahoma City Tragedy, Texans' Hearts Go Out to Neighbors to North," by R.G. Ratcliffe and John Williams, *Houston Chronicle,* April 21, 1995; "Bush Ad Won't Quite Let Go of Welfare," by Clay Robinson, *Houston Chronicle,* October 4, 1998; "Downloading the Bush Files," by Michael King, *Texas Observer,* November 1998; "Bush

Brothers' Welfare Plans Similar," by Ken Herman, *Houston Post,* March 26, 1994; "Bush Plan: Cut Welfare Spending," by Ken Herman, *Houston Post,* September 22, 1994; "Bush Ad Blasts Welfare Spending," by R.G. Ratcliffe, *Houston Chronicle,* September 22, 1994; "Bush: Survey Shows Welfare Changes Work," by Scott Greenberger, *Austin American-Statesman,* December 10, 1998; "Facts Can Mislead," *Houston Post,* September 24, 1994; "Bush Loses Points in Welfare Bill, Compromise Deletes Two Reform Measures," by Kathy Walt, *Houston Chronicle,* May 23, 1995; "State's Welfare Reforms Were Needed," by Lori Rodriguez, *Houston Chronicle,* June 3, 1995; "Easygoing George W. Bush," by Stuart Eskenazi, *Houston Post,* October 29-November 4, 1998; "Bush Touts Tort Reform, Answers Conflict Queries," by Ross Ramsey, *Houston Chronicle,* January 28, 1995; "Study Says Lawsuit Reforms May Affect Bush's Holdings," Associated Press, January 28, 1995; "Bush Says Tort Reform Would Be Key Project if Elected Governor," by Alan Bernstein, *Houston Chronicle,* October 21, 1994; "Richards Criticized on Tort Reform/Bush: Personal Injury Lawyers Influence Governor," by R.G. Ratcliffe, *Houston Chronicle,* September 14, 1994; "Bush Cites Work, Rejects Rich-Boy Image," by Ken Herman, *Austin American-Statesman,* October 11, 1998; "Legislature Fulfills Most Bush Promises," by R.G. Ratcliffe, *Houston Chronicle,* May 31, 1995; "The Leading Man/George W. Bush Has Pushed Most of the Popular Buttons as Governor," by Alan Bernstein, *Houston Chronicle,* September 6, 1998; "The 74th Legislature/Conservatism is Order of Day," by Clay Robinson, *Houston Chronicle,* May 30, 1995; "Bush Welfare Ads Mislead Public," by R.G. Ratcliffe, *Houston Chronicle,* September 23, 1994; "Plan to Cut Welfare Focuses on Paternity," by Mary Lenz, *Houston Post,* January 6, 1995; "Bush Signs Welfare Reform Bills and Cites 'Compassion'," by Kathy Walt, *Houston Chronicle,* June 14, 1995; "Gov. Bush's Easy Attitude Makes Him a Likable Guy Around Capitol," by Dave McNeely, *Houston Post,* April 8, 1995; "Away from the Spotlight," by R.G. Ratcliffe, *Houston Chronicle,* April 15, 1995; "Bush Puts His Signature on 217 Bills," by Ross Ramsey, *Houston Chronicle,* June 18, 1995; "Bush Outlining Own Welfare Reform Plan," by William Pack, *Houston Post,* April 19, 1994; "Bush Pushes Welfare Reform in Bid to Capture Governor's Office," by R.G. Ratcliffe, *Houston Chronicle,* March 26, 1994; "Bush Welfare Reform Plan Misleading," by Clay Robinson, *Houston Chronicle,* April 17, 1994; "Bush Would Require Welfare Fingerprints," by Robert Stanton, *Houston Post,* July 15, 1994; "Could Bush Ride the Tailwind to Re-Election?" by Ken Herman, *Houston Post,* January 20, 1995; "Bush Not Biting Dem Hands That Fed Him," by Clay Robinson, *Houston Chronicle,* May 5, 1995; "Favorite Son," by Robert Draper, *GQ,* October 1998; "Bush Calls for a New, Tougher Parole Law," by R.G. Ratcliffe, *Houston Chronicle,* February 26, 1994; "Bush Says Richards' Flip-Flopped on Parole," by R.G. Ratcliffe, *Houston Chronicle,* September 25, 1994; "Bush Would End Inmate Release Program," Associate Press, February 27, 1994; "Law Foils Bush on His Promise to End Early Release," by Clay Robinson and Kathy Walt, *Houston Chronicle,* April 4, 1996; "Bill to Limit Early Releases Gets Signature," *Houston Chronicle,* June 2, 1995; "More Teeth Sought for Penal Code, Hard

Time Urged for Repeat Felons," by Clay Robinson, *Houston Chronicle,* September 22, 1994; "End Abuse of Prisons' Good-Time Credit System," by Allan Polunsky, *Houston Chronicle,* March 15, 1995; "Mauro Criticizes Bush Over Inmate Releases," by R.G. Ratcliffe, *Houston Chronicle,* July 12, 1997; "Governor's Race Focus on Youth Crime," by Ken Herman and Mary Lenz, *Houston Post,* August 10, 1994; Richards Camp Responds to Bush Ad on Juvenile Crime," by Gardner Selby, *Houston Post,* September 7, 1994; "Bush Calls for Juvenile Justice Overhaul," by Ken Herman, *Houston Post,* February 8, 1995; "Crime in State, Houston on Decline/Juvenile Arrests, However, Are Increasing," by Clay Robinson, *Houston Chronicle,* September 9, 1994; "Talking Tough/Younger Criminals in the Crosshairs of Governor's Race," by R.G. Ratcliffe, *Houston Chronicle,* August 14, 1994; "More Youths Being Jailed," *Houston Chronicle,* November 21, 1995; "First Bush TV Ads Focus on Youth," by Stuart Eskenazi, *Austin American-Statesman,* April 24, 1998; "Reports Paint a Troubled Tableau of Youth," by Clay Robinson, *Houston Chronicle,* September 14, 1996; "Gun Law That Holds Parents Accountable is Lauded," by Clay Robinson, *Houston Chronicle,* June 27, 1995; "Bush Signs 'Tough Love' Juvenile Crime Bill," by Clay Robinson, *Houston Chronicle,* June 1, 1995; "The Bush Formula," by Eric Pooley, *Time,* November 16, 1998; "Cat is Out of the Bag: TEA is on Bush Hit List," by R.G. Ratcliffe, *Houston Chronicle,* October 19, 1993; "Bush Declares Education His No. 1 Priority," by Eric Hanson, *Houston Chronicle,* August 19, 1994; "Lawsuit Reform An Emergency, Bush Wants Action on Frivolous Cases," by Ross Ramsey, *Houston Chronicle,* January 21, 1995; "Bush Says Tort Reform Creates Jobs, Hopes to Curtail 'Junk' Lawsuits, Huge Rewards," by Mary Lenz, *Houston Post,* February 3, 1995; "Tort 'Reform' Effort Really Amounts to Tort Deform," by Juan R. Palomo, *Houston Post,* February 2, 1995; "The Last Don: Bob Bullock's Political Legacy," *Texas Observer,* January 31, 1997; "Bottom Line for Bob Bullock Was Making Government Work," *Houston Chronicle,* January 17, 1999; "Position of Power," by Terrence Stutz and George Kuempel, *Dallas Morning News,* December 27, 1998; "Bob Bullock Nears End of Four-Decade Career," by Clay Robinson, *Houston Chronicle,* January 17, 1999; "On the Record: Twelve Questions the National Media Should Ask Governor Bush," by Louis Dubose, *Texas Observer,* July 1999; "The W. Nobody Knows," by Paul Burka, *Texas Monthly,* June 1999.

On-line: www.bush98.com (See Accomplishments—74th Legislature); www.bush98.com (See Speeches); www.bush98.com (See News Releases); www.governor.statetx.us (See Legislative Information).

Interviews: Jack Allen: Kitty Pederson; James Henry; Brian Bailey; confidential conversations with aides to Governor Bush; Ed Martin; Tony Proffitt; Jack Brentwood; Don Cullen; Tommy Goodman; Sally Ellis; confidential conversations with housekeeping personnel employed at the Governor's Mansion; John Thomas; interviews with informed sources working for various Texas lawmakers; John Russi; Royce West; Tony Halsey; Charles Mayo; Hank Redman; confidential interviews with several state legislators.

CHAPTER 8. THE MEASURE OF THE MAN

Archives and Oral History Collections: Eugene C. Barker Texas History Center, Austin, Texas; the Texas State Archives, Austin, Texas; Sam Houston Regional Library and Research Center, Liberty, Texas; Sam Houston Memorial Museum, Huntsville, Texas; The George Bush Presidential Library, College Station, Texas; Texas Room, Houston Public Library; Center for American History, the University of Texas at Austin; Texas Historical Society, Houston, Texas; Public Service Archives, Woodson Research Center, Rice University.

Books: *Sword of San Jacinto,* by Marshall De Bruhl, Random House, New York, 1993; *Raven: A Biography of Sam Houston,* by James Marquis, University of Texas Press, Austin, Texas, 1988.

Articles: "The Leading Man—George W. Bush Has Pushed Most of the Popular Buttons as Governor," by Alan Bernstein, *Houston Chronicle,* September 6, 1998; "Bush Enjoys a Smooth Opening Day," by Ken Herman and Mary Lenz, *Houston Post,* January 19, 1995; "Day of the Dauphins," by Maureen Dowd, *New York Times,* November 4, 1998; "Texas' First Lady Laura Bush," by Bonnie Gangelhoff, *Houston Post,* December 4, 1994; "Father's Footsteps," by Wayne Slater and Sam Attlesey, *Dallas Morning News,* November 15, 1998; "Texas' First Lady Touts Her Causes Across the State," by Clifford Pugh, *Houston Chronicle,* October 18, 1995; "Bush: Daughters Will Go to Austin Private School," by R.G. Ratcliffe, *Houston Chronicle,* December 20, 1994; "Can He Save the Republicans?" by Kenneth T. Walsh, *U.S. News & World Report,* November 16, 1998; "Bush Says He's Learned from His Rowdy Past," by Jim O'Connell, *Rocky Mountain News,* July 26, 1998; "Favorite Son," by Robert Draper, *GQ,* October 1998; "Another Bush in Line," by Sue Anne Pressley, *Washington Post,* May 9, 1997; ". . . Speaking of Moves, Gov.-Elect Bush to Enlarge Office in Restored Capitol," *Houston Post,* January 14, 1995; "Reading Laura Bush," by Skip Hollandsworth, *Texas Monthly,* November 1996; "Property Tax Savings Analyzed: Average Dallas-Area Cut Under Bush Plan is 28%," by Chris Kelly, *Dallas Morning News,* February 23, 1997; "Few Respond to Inquiry on Bush Tax Proposal," by Barbara Powell, *Arlington Star-Telegram,* March 5, 1997; "Bush Proposes $2.8 Billion Cut in Property Tax," by Wayne Slater, *Dallas Morning News,* January 29, 1997; "Key Legislators Praise Property Tax Relief," by Terrance Stutz and Sylvia Moreno, *Dallas Morning News,* January 29, 1997; "Democratic Leader Says Bush Tax Plan Will Cost Average Texans, Benefit Rich," by Todd J. Gillman, *Dallas Morning News,* March 1, 1997; "Bush Defends Tax Plan: Study Says Affluent Would Benefit Most," by Wayne Slater, *Dallas Morning News,* February 20, 1997; "The Powers That Be: George W. Bush, Governor," by Wayne Slater, *Dallas Morning News,* January 12, 1997; "Comptroller Says Bush Tax Plan Falls $400 Million Short," by Jay Root, *Arlington Star-Telegram,* February 12, 1997; "Analyst Sees 3% Tax Cut in Plan," by Michelle Kay, *Austin American-Statesman,* February 19, 1997; "Bush Unwraps $84.7 Billion Budget," by Jay Root and Max B. Baker, *Arlington Star-Telegram,* January 30, 1997; "Tax

Plan Campaign Under Way," by Mark Wrolstad, *Dallas Morning News,* January 31, 1997; "Pauken Talkin'," *Texas Observer,* October 10, 1997; "Property Tax Relief Panel Appointed," by Carlos Sanchez, *Arlington Star-Telegram,* January 24, 1997; "Good for George," by Rebecca Mance, *Dallas Morning News,* February 13, 1997; "Bush Proposal Attacked as an Income Tax," by Jay Root, *Arlington Star-Telegram,* February 4, 1997; "Bush's Tax Plan Draws GOP Critics," by Jay Root, *Arlington Star-Telegram,* January 31, 1997; "Bush's Tax Plan to Be Scrutinized," *Dallas Morning News,* February 18, 1997; "School Property Tax Plan in Trouble, Bullock Prepares to Tell Governor," by Jay Root, *Arlington Star-Telegram,* March 5, 1997; "Wrongheaded," by Milton A. Braun, *Dallas Morning News,* February 2, 1997; "Texas Doesn't Need a Higher Sales Tax," by Pat Truly, *Arlington Morning News,* February 3, 1997; "Last Increase in Sales Tax Came in '90," by Christy Hoppe, *Dallas Morning News,* January 29, 1997; "Bush's Tax-Funding Plan for Schools Called Unfair," *Dallas Morning News,* December 7, 1996; "Downloading the Bush Files," by Michael King, *Texas Observer,* November 1998; "Bush Defends Tax Break Under Little-Used Law," Associated Press, November 10, 1995; "Fairness Questions Dog Bush's Tax Plan," by Clay Robinson, *Houston Chronicle,* February 2, 1997; "Tax Savings Probably Won't Reach Renters," by Clay Robinson, John Williams, and Ralph Bivins, *Houston Chronicle,* January 31, 1997; "Renters Question Tax Plan," by David Snyder and Christopher Lee, *Dallas Morning News,* February 4, 1999; "Bush Looks for New Way to Fund Education," by Melanie Markley, *Houston Chronicle,* October 3, 1995; "Alternative to School Property Taxes Sought," by John Makeig, *Houston Chronicle,* October 19, 1995; "Texas Tax System Hits Poor, Says Study," by Michael Holmes, Associated Press, June 27, 1996; "Bush: Turn the Heat Up on Legislators, Public Urged to Aid in Tax Reform Plan," by Clay Robinson, *Houston Chronicle,* September 21, 1996; "Tax Relief Issue Could Undo Bush's Aura," by Clay Robinson, *Houston Chronicle,* September 29, 1996; "Bush Plans $1 Billion Property Tax Cut, State Democratic Leaders Cautious About Proposal," by Clay Robinson, *Houston Chronicle,* November 14, 1996; "Back to Austin/Legislature Faces Important, Controversial Agenda," *Houston Chronicle,* January 12, 1997; "Bush Antes Up His Political Clout in Push to Lower Property Taxes," by Bob Tutt, *Houston Chronicle,* January 25, 1997; "Bush Touts Property Tax Cut," by Michael Kashgarian, *Midland Reporter-Telegram,* February 1, 1997; "Bush's Tax Cut Plan/System Needs Reform, But It Must Be Fair to All," by Carolyn Grafton Davis, *Houston Chronicle,* February 9, 1997; "Taking on the Devil," *San Antonio Business Journal,* February 24, 1997; "Bullock Says Bush Tax Overhaul Plan is in for a Rough Ride," by Clay Robinson, *Houston Chronicle,* March 5, 1997; "Governor's Tax Plan Numbers Just Don't Add Up," by State Rep. Kevin Bailey, *Houston Chronicle,* March 12, 1997; "Bush's Tax Plan: 'Devil is in the Details'," by Clay Robinson, *Houston Chronicle,* March 9, 1997; "Tax Plan Would Aid Rich Most," by Clay Robinson, *Houston Chronicle,* April 19, 1997; "Some Business Owners Fear 'Tax Relief' Proposal," by Clay Robinson, *Houston Chronicle,* April 14, 1997; "Lawmaker Doubts Bush's Tax Plan Will Help Fund Schools," by Clay Robinson, *Houston*

Chronicle, February 4, 1997; "Governor Fails in His Big Gamble to Secure State Property Tax Relief," by R.G. Ratcliffe, *Houston Chronicle,* May 25, 1997; "Legislature OKs Slim Tax Break for Homeowners," by Kathy Walt and R.G. Ratcliffe, *Houston Chronicle,* June 1, 1997; "Governor Doesn't Regret Acting 'Boldly' on Taxes," by Clay Robinson, *Houston Chronicle,* June 3, 1997; "Bush Signs Gutted Property Tax Cut Bill in Beaumont," by Juan B. Elizondo, Jr., Associated Press, June 5, 1997; "Sharp Raps Bush on Tax Proposals," by R.G. Ratcliffe, *Houston Chronicle,* June 4, 1997; "Despite Apathy, Tax Cut Likely to Win Aug. 9 Vote," by Clay Robinson, *Houston Chronicle,* July 13, 1997; "Tax Vote Big Step in Bush's Political Career," by Jane Ely, *Houston Chronicle,* August 6, 1997; "Property Tax Cut Wins Thumbs Up in Statewide Vote," by R.G. Ratcliffe, *Houston Chronicle,* August 10, 1997; "Bush Fears Tax Relief May Be Just Temporary for Some," by R.G. Ratcliffe, *Houston Chronicle,* August 11, 1997; "Texans Still Back Bush, Poll Finds/But Many Unaware of His Tax Relief Plan and Reasons for its Failure," by Clay Robinson, *Houston Chronicle,* August 30, 1997; "Gov. Bush Has Learned From His Past Losses," by David S. Broder, *Washington Post,* November 26, 1997; "The Issue is Not Dollars," by Jim Hightower, *Texas Observer,* June 19, 1998; "Business Associates Profit During Bush's Term as Governor," by R.G. Ratcliffe, *Houston Chronicle,* August 16, 1998; "Secrecy Cloaks $1.7 Billion in UT Investments," by R.G. Ratcliffe, *Houston Chronicle,* March 20, 1999; "Bush's Big Score," by Robert Bryce, *Dallas Observer,* February 9, 1998; "What Price Baseball?" by Robert Bryce, *Texas Observer,* June 20–26, 1997; "The Governor's Sweetheart Deal," by Robert Bryce, *Texas Observer,* January 30, 1998; "It's the Message," by Joe Gunn, *Texas Observer,* June 19, 1998; "Governor Gets His Pot of Baseball Gold from Sale of Texas Rangers," by R.G. Ratcliffe, *Houston Chronicle,* June 18, 1998; "'Diamond Brilliance'/Bush Mastered Art of the Deal in Building His Baseball Fortune," by R.G. Ratcliffe, *Houston Chronicle,* August 16, 1998; "Report Says Business Ties Profited Bush," Associated Press, July 31, 1994; "Out of Texas, a Familiar But Singular Brand," by Jill Lawrence, *USA Today,* September 8, 1998; "Teacher Pension Fund Had Big Loss in Building's Sale/Gov. Bush's Partners Made Deal with State-Run Retirement System," by R.G. Ratcliffe, *Houston Chronicle,* January 19, 1998; "Bush's Ally May Benefit from Privatization Plan," by Polly Ross Hughes, *Houston Chronicle,* February 25, 1997; "Richard Rainwater: The Invisible Man Behind One the Year's Biggest Deals," by John Morthland, *Texas Monthly,* September 1996; "Profit From Rangers Sale Has Bush Foes Pitching Fit," by Ken Herman, *Austin American-Statesman,* January 9, 1998; "The Bush Brothers," by Howard Fineman, *Newsweek,* November 2, 1998; "Bush's Financial Bases Left Loaded in Team Sale," by Kathy Walt, *Houston Chronicle,* January 9, 1998; "UT Regent Hicks Will Buy Rangers," *Austin American-Statesman,* January 7, 1998; "Stars Owner Hicks to Buy Rangers," by Christopher Lee and Todd J. Gillman, *Dallas Morning News,* January 7, 1998; "Deal to Surpass $230 Million, Source Says," by Gerry Fraley, *Dallas Morning News,* January 7, 1998; "Lone Star Stars," by Julia Reed, *Vogue,* February 1999; "Bush's Tax Tab: $3.77 Million," by R.G. Ratcliffe, *Houston Chronicle,* April 15, 1999; "Tax

Cut Proves Illusory," by Todd J. Gillman, *Dallas Morning News,* June 22, 1999; "Texas Anti-Tax Group Says Gov. Bush, Like Father, Broke Pledge," Associated Press, June 28, 1999; "Bush Revels True Picture of Wealth," Associated Press, July 3, 1999; "Team Player," by Joe Nick Patoski, *Texas Monthly,* June 1999; "George's Road to Riches," by Byron York, *American Spectator*, June 1999.

On-line: "Bush as Businessman: How the Texas Governor Made His Millions," by Brooks Jackson, CNN Interactive (www.cnn.com), May 13, 1999; www.bush98.com (See Biographies—Laura Welch Bush); "Common Cause Rejects Governor's Tax Proposals, Offers Four Options for Reform," (www.ccsi.com/~comcause/news/govtax1.html); www.bush98.com (See Accomplishments—75th Legislature); www.bush98.com (See Speeches); www.bush98.com (See News Releases); www.governor.statetx.us (See Legislative Information); "Who's That Man Behind George W. Bush?" by Jim Hightower (www.onlinejournal.com/Commentary/Rainwater/rainwater.html).

Interviews: Informed sources on the Governor's staff; Dick Lavine; Tom Pauken; John Weaver; Gary Spruce; Jess Rider; Dave Roberts; confidential conversations with several state lawmakers and their legislative aides.

Chapter 9. Crime and Punishment

Archives and Oral History Collections: Eugene C. Barker Texas History Center, Austin; the Texas State Archives, Austin, Texas; Texas Room, Houston Public Library; Center for American History, the University of Texas at Austin; Texas Historical Society, Houston, Texas; Public Service Archives, Woodson Research Center, Rice University.

Books: *Crossed Over: A Murder, A Memoir,* by Beverly Lowry, Alfred Knopf, New York, 1992; *The Confessions of Henry Lee Lucas,* by Mike Cox, Pocket Books, New York, 1991; *Henry Lee Lucas: The Shocking True Story of America's Most Notorious Serial Killer,* by Joel Norris, Kensington Publishing, New York, 1991.

Articles: "Lanier, Bush Applauded for Cime-Fighting Efforts," by Rad Sallee, *Houston Chronicle,* August 19, 1997; "State Leaves $182 Million in Fund for Crime Victims," by Christy Hoppe, *Dallas Morning News,* December 10, 1998; "Lost Stocks Turn Up for George W. Bush," by Wayne Slater, *Dallas Morning News,* September 22, 1989; "Reported Crime Up in First Half of 1996, Increase is State's First in Four Years," by Clay Robinson, *Houston Chronicle,* October 22, 1996; "Bush Wants Prison Exit Law Changed," by Clay Robinson, *Houston Chronicle,* November 23, 1996; "Convicts May Lose Mandatory Releases Under Veto Rule," by S.K. Bardwell, *Houston Chronicle,* January 12, 1997; "Mandatory Release, Bipartisan Bill Would Put an End to Senseless Policy," *Houston Chronicle,* January 24, 1997; "Early-Release Bill Heads to State House," by Kathy Walt, *Houston Chronicle,* January 13, 1997; "Inmate Release Measure Not a Done Deal," by Clay Robinson, *Houston Chronicle,* February

23, 1997; "Bush's 1994 Promise on Halting 'Early Releases' at Issue," by R.G. Ratcliffe, *Houston Chronicle,* Decembr 3, 1997; "Molester Still Behind Bars," by Stefanie Asin, *Houston Chronicle,* April 3, 1996; "Inmate Abuse Projects Lose Funding from State, Governor Decides Not to Renew Grants," by Kathy Walt, *Houston Chronicle,* September 1, 1995; "Bush Bitten by His Campaign Sound Bite," by Clay Robinson, *Houston Chronicle,* April 7, 1996; "Mauro Takes Shots at Bush in D.C. Visit," by Bennett Roth, *Houston Chronicle,* June 23, 1998; "Bush Calls Mauro Remark on Jasper Killing 'Shallow'," Associated Press, June 25 1998; "Jasper Pulled into the National Spotlight/Governor: Some People Have 'Hate in Their Hearts'," by Clay Robinson, *Houston Chronicle,* June 11, 1998; "Gov. Bush's Positions on Morals Illustrate the Republican Conflict," by Alan Bernstein, *Houston Chronicle,* June 21, 1998; "Jasper Working to Break Down its Racial Barriers," by Lee Hancock, *Dallas Morning News,* January 24, 1999; "Bush Urged to Back Tougher Hate-Crimes Law," Associated Press, January 27, 1999; "Legislators Back Tougher Hate Crimes Law," by Jamie Stockwell, *Houston Chronicle,* January 27, 1999; "Byrd's Family Past the Anger/Relatives of Dragging Victim Push Hate Crimes Bill," by Jamie Stockwell, *Houston Chronicle,* January 31, 1999; "Texas Year in Review," by David Snyder, *Dallas Morning News,* December 27, 1998; "Psychiatrist Says Convicted Killer 'A Continuing Threat,'" by Lee Hancock, *Dallas Morning News,* February 25, 1999; "Jasper Man Guilty of Murder," by Lee Hancock and Bruce Tomaso, *Dallas Morning News,* February 24, 1999; "One Night in East Texas," by Susan Lee Solar, *Texas Observer,* July 3, 1998; "Inmates' Releases Soar Under Bush, Governor Had Blasted Richards' Record in '94," by Christy Hoppe, *Dallas Morning News,* July 11, 1997; "First of Three Suspects in Texas Dragging Death Ready to Go to Trial," by Terri Langford, Associated Press, January 24, 1999; "Texas City Braces for Murder Trial," by Chairsse Jones, *USA Today,* February 16, 1999; "Watched by the World," by Lee Hancock, *Dallas Morning News,* January 24, 1999; "Defense Expects Inmates to Testify Plan Started in Prison," by Lee Hancock, *Dallas Morning News,* January 28, 1999; "Prosecutor Offers Graphic Description of Jasper Death," by Lee Hancock, *Dallas Morning News,* January 26, 1999; "Byrd Family Girds for 2 More Trials," by Bruce Tomaso, *Dallas Morning News,* February 26, 1999; "Dragging Victim's Pain Described," by Terri Langford, Associated Press, February 22, 1999; "Ex-Con Says Man Plotted Racial Killing," by Lee Hancock, *Dallas Morning News,* February 19, 1999; "Jasper Killer Becoming Extremists' Hero," by Lee Hancock, *Dallas Morning News,* March 7, 1999; "'She Was Sentenced to Death; She Needs to Die," by Kathy Walt, *Houston Chronicle,* December 13, 1997; "Spin Doctors Summoned as Needle Looms," by Jeff Millar, *Houston Chronicle,* December 14, 1997; "Execution May Haunt Texas, Tucker Case Likely to Bring Unprecedented Scrutiny," by Kathy Walt, *Houston Chronicle,* December 15, 1997; "Ritual Murder," *Texas Observer,* January 16, 1998; "Death Watch," *Texas Observer,* January 30, 1998; "'Moment of Truth'/Death Penalty Opponents Rally at State Capitol," by Kathy Walt, *Houston Chronicle,* January 18, 1998; "Excerpts from Karla Faye Tucker's Letter," *Houston Chronicle,* January 21, 1998; "Church Groups

Make Pleas for Clemency for Tucker," by Mike Ward, *Austin American-Statesman,* January 27, 1998; "Court Rejects Tucker Plea," by Kathy Walt, *Houston Chronicle,* January 29, 1998; "Death Penalty Dilemma," by Bob Herbert, *New York Times,* January 4, 1998; "Karla Faye's Last Chance," *Houston Chronicle,* February 1, 1998; "Fox News Airs Photos from Crime Scene," Associated Press, February 4, 1998; "The Execution of Karla Faye Tucker/Bush Prayed for Guidance Before Denying Tucker's Appeal," by R.G. Ratcliffe, *Houston Chronicle,* February 4, 1998; "Many Still Fighting to Stop Tucker's Execution," by Polly Ross Hughes and Stephen Johnson, *Houston Chronicle,* February 3, 1998; "Board Rejects Tucker's Plea for Clemency," by Kathy Walt and Polly Ross Hughes, *Houston Chronicle,* February 3, 1998; "Tucker Dies After Apologizing," by Kathy Walt, *Houston Chronicle,* February 4, 1998; "Texas Executes Tucker: Killer's Life Ends Amid Prayers, Calls for Justice," by Mike Ward and Rebeca Rodriguez, *Austin American-Statesman,* February 4, 1998; "The Execution of Karla Faye Tucker/TV Turns Last Day on Death Row into Media Marathon," by Ann Hodges, *Houston Chronicle,* February 4, 1998; "Bush Decision Unlikely to Have Political Fallout," by Ken Herman, *Austin American-Statesman,* February 4, 1998; "A Day Later, No Rush to Change Death Penalty Law," by Mike Ward and Rebeca Rodriguez, *Austin American-Statesman,* February 5, 1998; "For the Next to Die, Novelty's Gone," by Mike Ward, *Austin American-Statesman,* February 5, 1998; "Death Penalty's Support Plunges to a 30-year Low/Karla Faye Tucker's Execution Tied to Texans' Attitude Change," by Kathy Walt, *Houston Chronicle,* March 15, 1998; "Lucas Tearfully Denies Slaying That Landed Him on Death Row," by Jean Pagel, Associated Press, January 9, 1996; "Woman Believes Mother Was Not a Victim of Henry Lee Lucas," by Matt Curry, *Amarillo Globe-News,* April 3, 1998; "Prosecutor Urges Death Amid Vote on Lucas Reprieve," Associated Press, June 25, 1998; "Parole Board Recommends Lucas be Spared," by Kathy Walt, R.G. Ratcliffe, Alan Turner and Jim Henderson, *Houston Chronicle,* June 26, 1998; "Sparing Lucas' Life is Relief for Woman," by Chip Chandler, *Amarillo Globe-News,* June 26, 1998; "Kin of Lucas Victim 'Disappointed' in Bush," by S.K. Bardwell and Patty Reinert, *Houston Chronicle,* June 27, 1998; "'The Real Killers are Still Out There'/Henry Lee Lucas Able to Confuse Authorities and Then Beat Death," by Jim Henderson, *Houston Chronicle,* June 28, 1998; "Mauro: Bush Was Wrong to Grant Lucas Clemency," by R.G. Ratcliffe, *Houston Chronicle,* July 1, 1998; "Bush Explains Decision to Commute Lucas' Sentence," Associated Press, July 14, 1998; "Scapegoat Debate," *Texas Observer,* August 14, 1998; "6 Men Face Execution by State During 12-Day Period, 1998 May Become Second Most Active Year for Death Penalty in Texas," by Michael Graczyk, Associated Press, November 30, 1998; "Albright Asks Bush for Stay in Execution of Canadian," Associated Press, December 2, 1998; "Albright Joins Effort to Spare Canadian's Life," by Jim Henderson, *Houston Chronicle,* December 2, 1998; "Bush to Hold Off on Stay Decision, Reprieve for Canadian is Sought," by Clay Robinson and Jim Henderson, *Houston Chronicle,* December 4, 1998; "Bush Says Canadian Killer Getting Due Process," Associated Press, December 4, 1998; "On Death Row, Good

Defense Hard to Find," by Nan Aron, *USA Today,* December 7, 1998; "Death-Penalty Foes Urge Bush to Spare Canadian," Associated Press, December 8, 1998; "Delegation Pleads Canadian's Case, Group Asking Bush for Stay of Execution," by Renae Merle and Jim Henderson, *Houston Chronicle,* December 8, 1998; "Court's Ruling Unlikely to Delay Canadian's Death," by Dave Harmon, *Austin American-Statesman,* December 8, 1998; "Bush: Don't Threaten Governor," Associated Press, December 8, 1998; "Court Rules for Parole Board, Clears Canadian's Execution," by Pete Slover and Christy Hoppe, *Dallas Morning News,* December 9, 1998; "Texas Parole Board Denise Clemency," Associated Press, December 9, 1998; "Judge Halts Execution of Canadian," by Wayne Slater and Pete Slover, *Dallas Morning News,* December 10, 1998; "Canadian's Execution Put on Hold," by Michael Graczyk, Associated Press, December 10, 1998; "Judge Blocks Texas' Execution of Canadian," *USA Today,* December 10, 1998; "Supreme Court Delays Canadian's Execution," *USA Today,* December 11, 1998; "Justices Halt Execution," by Bruce Tomaso, *Dallas Morning News,* December 11, 1998; "Texas' System of Clemency Still Under Fire," Associated Press, December 11, 1998; "Supreme Court Halts Canadian's Execution," by Kathy Walt and Allan Turner, *Houston Chronicle,* December 11, 1998; "Test for Bush and Texas in Near-Execution," by Clay Robinson, December 13, 1998; "Bush Defends State Process for Clemency, Resists Changes," by Ken Herman and Mike Ward, *Austin American-Statesman,* December 19, 1998; "Morales Leaves with Death Penalty Questions," by Christy Hoppe, *Dallas Morning News,* December 20, 1998; "Clemency Debate Goes to Court," by Pete Slover, *Dallas Morning News,* December 22, 1998; "Final Arguments Heard on Texas' Clemency Policy," by Pete Slover, *Dallas Morning News,* December 23, 1998; "State Clemency System Ruled Constitutional," by Pete Slover, *Dallas Morning News,* December 29, 1998; "Hearing to Question Clemency," Associated Press, January 4, 1999; "Bush Says Clemency System Legal," Associated Press, January 5, 1999; "Attorneys Argue Clemency Hearings Should Be Public," Associated Press, January 6, 1999; "Jurist OKs Process for Clemency," by Clay Robinson, *Houston Chronicle,* January 9, 1999; "Texas Clemency Process Again Passes Muster," by Christy Hoppe, *Dallas Morning News,* January 9, 1999; "Controversy Dogs Actions of the State's Parole Board," by Jim Henderson, *Houston Chronicle,* January 10, 1999; "Parole Board Reviews Process on Clemency," by Bruce Tomaso, *Dallas Morning News,* February 5, 1999; "Clemency-Review Period Expanded," by Bruce Tomaso, *Dallas Morning News,* February 6, 1999; "State Parole Board Takes Step to Revise Rules for Clemency," by Allan Turner, *Houston Chronicle,* February 6, 1999; "Clemency Process Defended, Parole Official Says Overhaul Not Needed," by John W. Gonzalez and Jamie Stockwell, *Houston Chronicle,* March 3, 1999; "Parole Board Alters Policies on Clemency," by Bruce Tomaso, *Dallas Morning News,* April 1, 1999; "Inmates' Tales Told on Web," by David Snyder, *Dallas Morning News,* January 3, 1999; "U.N. Death Watch," by Michael King, *Texas Observer,* November 7, 1997; "Capital Irony," by Steve McVicker, *Houston Press,* June 25–July 1, 1998; "Death Penalty: Reforms Are Needed for the System to Be Fair,"

Dallas Morning News, December 20, 1998; "Bill May Open Door on Staff 'Conferences'/House Cuts Exception to Open Meetings Law," by John W. Gonzalez, *Houston Chronicle*, April 13, 1999; "Texas Gov. Bush Against Bill Banning Death Penalty for Retarded," by Jay Root, *Arlington Star-Telegram*, April 13, 1999; "Condemned Canadian's Appeal Denied," Associated Press, June 10, 1999; "Board Refused to Halt Canadian's Execution," by Bruce Tomaso, *Dallas Morning News*, June 17, 1999; "Canadian Executed in '75 Killing," by Bruce Tomaso, *Dallas Morning News*, June 18, 1999; "A Fatal Ride in the Night," by Sarah Van Boven and Anne Belli Gesalman, *Newsweek*, June 22, 1998; "Lies of a Serial Killer," by Daniel Pedersen, *Newsweek*, June 22, 1998; "Texas Gov. Bush Vetoes Measure on Lawyers for Poor," by Max B. Baker, *Fort Worth Star-Telegram*, June 21, 1999.

Television: Karla Faye Tucker interview CNN on *Larry King Live*, February 3, 1998; "A Question of Mercy: The Karla Faye Tucker Story," Court TV, January 27, 1998.

On-line: "Texas Sheriff 'Knew Somebody Was Murdered Because He Was Black,'" CNN Interactive (www.cnn.com), February 16, 1998; "Tucker Speaks Out on Prime-Time TV," BBC News Interactive (www.bbc.co.uk), January 23, 1998; "Governor Faces Death Row Dilemma," BBC News Interactive (www.bbc.co.uk), January 22, 1998; "A Crime That Shocked America," BBC News Ineractive (www.bbc.co.uk), January 23, 1998; Amnesty International report on human rights abuses directed at Texas for assessing the death penalty (www.rightsforallusa.org/info/report); "Texas v. Karla Faye Tucker: Writ of Habeas Corpus," Court TV Online (www.courttv.com/legaldocs/newsmakers.tucker/); "Execution Looms Even as State Admits Guilt 'Highly Improbable'," Death Penalty Information Center (www.commondreams.org/pressreleases/June98/061298a.htm)

Interviews: Confidential conversations with lawmakers, legislative aides, and gubernatorial assistants; Bob Deacon; Mike Braddock; Joe Baker; Thomas Edmonton; Pat Hardy; James Smith; Karla Faye Tucker; David Botsford; Richard Dieter; John Thomas; Bill McDougal; William Robert Walker; Ken Anderson; Norman Willis; Wilkie Collins.

Chapter 10. New Dog, Old Tricks

Archives and Oral History Collections: Eugene C. Barker Texas History Center, Austin; Texas Room, Houston Public Library; Center for American History, the University of Texas at Austin; the Texas State Archives, Austin, Texas; Texas Historical Society, Houston, Texas; Public Service Archives, Woodson Research Center, Rice University.

Books: *Blinded by Might: Can the Religious Right Save America?*, by Cal Thomas and Ed Dobson, Zondervan Publishing House, Grand Rapids, Mich., 1999; *The Soul of Politics: Beyond Religious Right and Secular Left*, by Jim Wallis, Harcourt Brace &

Company, New York, 1995; *Perfect Enemies: The Religious Right, the Gay Movement and the Politics of the 1990s,* by Christopher Bull with John Gallagher, Crown Publishing Group, New York, 1996; *Between Jesus and the Market: The Emotions That Matter in Right-Wing America,* by Linda Kintz, Duke University Press, Durham, N.C., 1997; *Why the Religious Right Is Wrong: About Separation of Church and State,* by Rob Boston, Prometheus Books, Amherst, N.Y., 1994; *The New Religious Right: Piety, Patriotism and Politics,* by Walter H. Caps, University of South Carolina Press, Columbia, S.C., 1995; *Who Speaks for God?: An Alternative to the Religious Right—A New Politics of Compassion, Community and Civility,* by Jim Wallis, Delacorte Press, New York, 1996; *Old Nazis, the New Right, and the Republican Party,* by Russ Bellant, South End Press, Boston, Mass., 1991; *Thunder on the Right: The Protestant Fundamentalists,* by Gary K. Clabaugh, Nelson-Hall, Chicago, Ill. 1974; *Beaches, Bureaucrats and Big Oil: One Man's Fight for Texas,* by Gary Mauro, Look Away Books, Austin, Texas, 1997.

Published articles include "What Exactly Does George W. Stand For?" by Tony Snow, *Jewish World Review,* February 11, 1999; "Millionaire's Influence Felt in Texas Politics," by Jeanne Russell, *San Antonio Express-News,* January 26, 1999; "Child Abuse Deaths Up 71% in '98, State Finds," by Christopher Lee, *Dallas Morning News,* January 6, 1999; "Low-Income Texas Residents Struggle More Than National Average, According to Survey," by Polly Ross Hughes and Jamie Stockwell, *Houston Chronicle,* January 31, 1999; "Prosperity Fails to Reach Many," by Diane Jennings, *Dallas Morning News,* February 12, 1999; "Critics: State's Fund Limit, Treatment Strategy Harm Kids," by Diane Jennings, *Dallas Morning News,* February 14, 1999; "Texas' Poor Need More Than Welfare Reform," by Clay Robinson, *Houston Chronicle,* April 4, 1999; "Bush's Vow of Compassion Has Its Critics," by Lori Stahl, *Dallas Morning News,* March 7, 1999; "Republican-Democratic Differences," by Jeff Strater, *Dallas Voice,* July 3, 1998; "Texas Ranks Low in Benefits for the Unemployed," by Lori Stahl, *Dallas Morning News,* April 14, 1999; "Legislature Urged to Expand Health Plan to Add 500,000 Children," by Jo Ann Zuniga, *Houston Chronicle,* February 28, 1999; "Bush Proposes Tougher Welfare Reform," by Clay Robinson, *Houston Chronicle,* September 30, 1998; "Others Not So Compassionate on Bush Label," by Clay Robinson, *Houston Chronicle,* February 5, 1999; "Lone Star Stars," by Julia Reed, *Vogue,* February 1999; "These Quotes Compassionate," by Alan Bernstein, *Houston Chronicle,* February 13, 1999; "Bush's Brand of Conservatism Gets Mixed Reception," by Jay Root, *Arlington Star-Telegram,* January 30, 1999; "Bush Just Took the 'C-Word' Away from the Liberals," by Marvin Olasky, *Houston Chronicle,* November 17, 1998; "GOP Presidential Hopefuls Say Adjective Saps Strength from True Conservatism," by Ken Herman, *Austin American-Statesman,* January 22, 1999; "'Compassionate Conservatism,' Bush Style," by Scott Baldaufs, *Christian Science Monitor,* January 19, 1999; "Evolution of a Term," *Austin-American Statesman,* January 22, 1998; "Weasel Words? Criticism of Compassion No Favor to Conservatism," *Houston Chronicle,* January 25, 1999; "What is Compassionate Conservatism?" by Myron Magnet, *Wall Street Journal,* February 5, 1999; "Bush is Republicans' Best Shot to Regain White House," by Jon Pepper, *Detroit News,* March 3, 1999; "Missteps of Youth Won't Haunt Bush Candidacy, Bennett Says," by Polly Ross Hughes and R.G. Ratcliffe, *Houston Chronicle,* April 1, 1999; "British View: How Dickens Inspires Bush," by Andrew Marshall, *Independent,* March 7, 1999; "Bush Puts His Brand on Texas Politics," by Dan Balz, *Washington Post,* March 21, 1999; "Bush's 'Compassionate' Label Taking a Beating," by Ken Herman, *Austin American Statesman,* January 22, 1999; "George W. Bush Breaks Out of Pack with 'Compassionate Conservatism,'" by Nate Blakeslee, *Texas Observer,* September 25, 1998; "Gov. Bush Still Defining 'Compassionate'?" by Clay Robinson, *Houston Chronicle,* November 29, 1998; "America Changing and So, Too, Are the Republicans," by E.J. Dionne, Jr., *Houston Chronicle,* March 21, 1999; "A Little More Light on Bush's Conservatism," by E.J. Dionne, Jr., *Houston Chronicle,* April 1, 1999; "Overseers Added in Senate Bill Allowing Welfare Privatization," by John Moritz, *Fort Worth Star-Telegram,* May 21, 1997; "Bush's Welfare Plan Nears Homestretch," by Bill Mintutaglio, *Dallas Morning News,* May 18, 1997; "The Rich Get Richer . . ." by Molly Ivins, *Texas Observer,* August 29, 1997; "The Issue is Not Dollars," by Jim Hightowher, *Texas Observer,* June 19, 1998; "Improve the Lives of Ordinary Texans," by Glenn Maxey, *Texas Observer,* June 19, 1998; "Mauro: Give Top HMO Care to Texans," by Ken Herman, *Austin American-Statesman,* May 1, 1998; "Choking on Pork," *Texas Observer,* June 19, 1998; "Groups Criticize Bill on Privatizing Welfare," *Fort Worth Star-Telegram,* May 15, 1997; "Get Over Clinton, Candidates Wooing Conservatives Say," by Jill Lawrence, *USA Today,* January 22, 1999; "The Bush Brothers," by Howard Fineman, *Newsweek,* November 2, 1998; "State Has Failed to Spend $100 Million Set Aside for Housing, HUD Report Says," Associated Press, August 3, 1998; "Business Forum/Bush's Patient Protection Measure Veto was Unwise," by Dr. Richard J. Hausner, *Houston Chronicle,* September 22, 1996; "Bush's Veto is Blasted," *Houston Chronicle,* June 24, 1997; "Families Should Share Medicaid Cost, Bush Says," by Bennett Roth, *Houston Chronicle,* December 13, 1995; "Health Care Frustrations Escape Bush, Mauro Says," by Todd J. Gillman, *Dallas Morning News,* April 19, 1998; "Mauro to Take 'Doctor Choice' Issue to TV Airwaves, by Clay Robinson, *Houston Chronicle,* April 23, 1998, "Mauro Hits Bush Over Cancer Care," by R.G. Ratcliffe, *Houston Chronicle,* May 1, 1998; "Texan Mauro Tries Democrats' Health Care Election Theme in Snipe at Bush," by Brian Carlson, *Washington Post,* June 23, 1998; "Bush, Mauro Disagree Over Regulating HMOs" by Alan Bernstein, *Houston Chronicle,* March 5, 1998; "Playing Politics with Kids' Health," by Annette Fuentes, *In These Times,* February 22, 1998; "Governing Texas," by Michael King, *Texas Observer,* December 5, 1997; "Who's Poisoning Texas? Part One: Why the State's Biggest Polluters Won't Clean Up Their Act," by Michael King, *Texas Observer,* April 24, 1998; "Who's Poisoning Texas? Part Two: Voluntary Grandfathering and Big Dirty Secrets" by Michael King, *Texas Observer,* May 8, 1998; "Governor Has Fallen Short as Leader of All Texans," by Bob Ray Sanders, *Fort Worth Star-Telegram,* March 4,

1999; "Bush Backs Election of State Judges, Minorities Urged to Embrace GOP," by Clay Robinson, *Houston Chronicle,* December 1, 1994; "Bush's Appointments Resemble Himself," Associated Press, *Houston Chronicle,* August 22, 1995; "Dems Assail Bush Failure to Blacks on UT Board," by Clay Robinson, *Houston Chronicle,* March 2, 1999; "Gov-Elect to Minorities: Join GOP," by Ken Herman, *Houston Post,* December 1, 1994; "Bush Declines Pardon for Man in Rape Case Despite DNA Evidence," *Dallas Morning News,* September 14, 1997; "Bush Stingy with Pardons but Still Fuels Debate Over Choices," by Jay Root, *Arlington Star-Telegram,* September 22, 1997; "Bush Insists Race Not Tied to Pardons/Statistics Show No Blacks Among 14 He's Granted," by John Makeig and R.G. Ratcliffe, *Houston Chronicle,* September 25, 1997; "Racial Issues in Arlington/Is it Fair or Foul?" by Steven R. Reed, *Houston Chronicle,* August 1, 1993; "Accusations Fly in Austin Over Nuclear Dump Proposal," by R.G. Ratcliffe, *Houston Chronicle,* May 23, 1995; "Texas Lobbies to Receive Nuclear Waste," by Michelle Mittelstadt, Associated Press, October 19, 1997; "Nuclear Waste Site Inspires Radioactive Debate," by John W. Gonzalez, *Houston Chronicle,* April 19, 1998; "Mexican Lawmakers Decry W. Texas Nuclear Dump," by Lori Rodriquez, *Houston Chronicle,* June 19, 1998: "Judges Recommend Against Sierra Blanca N-Waste Site," by John W. Gonzalez, *Houston Chronicle,* July 8, 1998; "Agency Says N-Waste Plan 'Very Much Alive'," by Clay Robinson, *Houston Chronicle,* July 9, 1998; "Loophole: Texas; Backyard Shouldn't Be a Dumpsite for Other States," *Houston Chronicle,* July 28, 1998; "Democrats Deride Nuclear Dump," by Juan Elizondo, Jr., Associated Press, August 2, 1998; "Texas Nuked," *Texas Observer,* August 14, 1998; "Clinton Pushed to Veto Plan for Texas N-Dump," by Bennett Roth, *Houston Chronicle,* September 2, 1998; "Should a Nuclear Waste Disposal Facility be Built in Texas?" by Olive Hersey, *Houston Chronicle,* September 20, 1998; "Senate Passes Nuke-Waste Site for West Texas/Governor 'Very Pleased' by Vote," by Bennett Roth, *Houston Chronicle,* September 3, 1998; "Officials from Mexico Urge Texas Not to Build Radioactive Waste Site," by John W. Gonzalez, *Houston Chronicle,* October 8, 1998; "With Nowhere to Go, Nuclear Waste Piles Up," by Kathryn Winiarski, *USA Today,* December 31, 1998; "Bill Would Let Company Operate Texas Nuclear Waste Dump," by George Kuempel, *Dallas Morning News,* January 23, 1999; "Firm Mounts Lobbying Offensive for Nuclear Waste Pact," by George Kuempel, *Dallas Morning News,* February 7, 1999; "W. Texas Residents Fighting Waste Site," by Christi Harlan, *Austin American-Statesman,* February 6, 1998; "Nuke Tour," by Gary Oliver, *Texas Observer,* September 26, 1997; "Bush to EPA: Don't Meddle in State Affairs," by John Williams, *Houston Chronicle,* April 13, 1995; "Pollution Tied to Lack of Permits/Exempt Plants Cause Most Air Problems," by Bill Dawson, *Houston Chronicle,* March 31, 1997; "Smoggy Air Apparent?" by Bill Dawson, *Houston Chronicle,* November 7, 1997; "Mauro Criticizes Bush with Polluted Research," by Alan Bernstein, *Houston Chronicle,* August 6, 1998; "A Call for Cleaner Air," *Houston Chronicle,* November 24, 1998; "Environmentalists Ask Bush to Tighten Clean-Air Measure," Associated Press, November 24, 1998; "Study Challenges Governor's Claims About Pollution

Reduction," by Bill Dawson, *Houston Chronicle,* December 4, 1998; "Environmentalists Want State Authority Revoked," by Randy Lee Loftis, *Dallas Morning News,* January 14, 1999; "Report Says Students Could Face Air Pollution Risk," by Randy Lee Loftis, *Dallas Morning News,* January 21, 1999; "Four Groups Criticize Pollution Exemptions," by Bill Dawson, *Houston Chronicle,* January 21, 1999; "Air Pollution Panel Lists Battle Plan Against Smog," by Bill Dawson, *Houston Chronicle,* February 27, 1999; "Plant-Pollution Exemption Bills Ready to Rumble," by Bill Dawson, *Houston Chronicle,* March 29, 1999; "EPA Cites Beaumont-Port Arthur Air Pollution," by Bill Dawson, *Houston Chronicle,* April 7, 1999; "Battle Brewing Over Factory-Emissions Bills," by Randy Lee Loftis, *Dallas Morning News,* April 11, 1999; "Green George? Bush Needs to Improve His Environmental Record," by Timothy O'Leary, *Dallas Morning News,* April 12, 1999; "Activists Calling on Bush to Slash Plant Exemptions," by Armando Villafranca, *Houston Chronicle,* April 13, 1999; "Industries Seeking Pollution Exemption Gave Heavily to Campaigns, Report Says," by Jim Vertuno, Associated Press, April 14, 1999; "Senate Leaves Open Clean-Air Loophole," by Clay Robinson, *Houston Chronicle,* April 14, 1999; "Religious Rights Bill Raises Concerns; Critics Fear On-Job Proselytizing," by John Moritz, *Arlington Star-Telegram,* January 29, 1999; "Cover Boy," *Dallas Morning News,* April 11, 1999; "Bush's Slogan Just a Fig Leaf for Intolerance," by Susan Estrich, *Houston Chronicle,* April 5, 1999; "Bush: America Isn't Prepared To End Abortion," by Wendy Benjaminson, *Houston Chronicle,* March 9, 1999; "Bush Backs School Prayer Amendment," by Bennett Roth, *Houston Chronicle,* November 21, 1994; "Bush Wants Hate Crime Bill Shelved, Say House Members," by Dennis Vercher, April 5, 1999; "Good News and Bad News for the Governor," by Mark Davis, *Fort Worth Star-Telegram,* April 10, 1999; "Bush Opposes Adoptions by Gays," by Wayne Slater, *Dallas Morning News,* March 23, 1999; "Gay-Rights Groups Critical of Bush's Adoptions Stance," Associated Press, March 24, 1999; "Bill Would Bar Gay Foster, Adotive Homes," by Christopher Lee, *Dallas Morning News,* March 28, 1999; "Bill Would Ban Gay Texans From Adopting Children," by Polly Ross Hughes, *Houston Chronicle,* December 11, 1998; "Anti-Sodomy Law Becomes Issue in Race Between Richards, Bush," by Ken Herman, *Houston Post,* January 14, 1994; "Governor Urges Abstinence," by R.G. Ratcliffe, *Houston Chronicle,* June 18, 1996; "Quiet Doctor's Issues, Money Put Him High in GOP's Texas," by Dave Harmon, *Austin American-Statesman,* January 17, 1999; "Here Comes The Son," by Jeffrey H. Birnbaum, *Fortune,* June 22, 1998; "Enron Gets Religion," *Texas Observer,* January 16 & 30, 1998; "Conservative Leaders Defend Bush's Abortion Stand," *Dallas Morning News,* March 21, 1999; "Bush: Faith Can Aid Reverse Downhill Path of U.S. Culture," *Dallas Morning News,* March 7, 1999; "Last Thing Texas Needs is a Religious Supremacy Act," by Marci A. Hamilton, *Houston Chronicle,* March 19, 1999; "Lawmaker Proposes New Prayer Amendment, by Katharine Q. Seelye, *New York Times,* March 24, 1997; "Christian Coalition Considers Changes for Direct Political Activity," by Ruth Marcus, *Washington Post,* January 5, 1998; "State Approved 'Christ-Centered' Rehabilitation Program for

Inmates," by Christy Hoppe, *Dallas Morning News,* November 15, 1996; "Churches' Role in Social Services Debated—Bush's 'Faith-Based' Agenda Draws Share of Accolades, Criticism," by Bill Minutaglio, *Dallas Morning News,* April 6, 1997; "Anti-Gay Provision Not Appropriate for Hate Crime Bill, Bush Says," by R.A. Dyer, *Arlington Star-Telegram,* March 22, 1999; "Bush Take Compassion Message to Christian TV," by Bud Kennedy, *Fort Worth Star-Telegram,* February 15, 1999; "High in the Polls and Close to Home, Bush Navigates by the Center Line," by Richard L. Berke, *New York Times,* April 9, 1999; "Bush Wows New Hampshire Right," by Alan Bernstein, *Houston Chronicle,* February 7, 1999; "Gay Leaders Criticize Bush Over Stance on Hate Crimes," by Bennett Roth, *Houston Chronicle,* March 24, 1999; "Back in the Amen Corner," by Howard Fineman and Matthew Cooper, *Newsweek,* March 22, 1999; "Top Baptists Show Confidence in Bush," by Kim Sue Lia Perkes, *Austin American-Statesman,* March 3, 1999; "Faithful Have a Place in Politics, Says Bush," by R.G. Ratcliffe, *Houston Chronicle,* March 7, 1999; "Father's Footsteps, Part One," by Wayne Slater, *Dallas Morning News,* November 15, 1998; "Conservative Sees U.S. Cultural War," by Ron Fournier, Associated Press, February 17, 1999; "Bush Backs Bill Restricting Limits on Religious Practice," by Wayne Slater, *Dallas Morning News,* January 12, 1999; "Bush, Legislators Gather to Support Religious Freedom," by R.G. Ratcliffe, *Houston Chronicle,* January 12, 1999; "Bush Runs on Record, Not Pedigree," by Scott Baldauf, *Christian Science Monitor,* December 5, 1997; "The Christians Very Much Like the Lions," by Jane Ely, *Houston Chronicle,* June 15, 1994; "Democrats Push Bush on GOP Battle," by R.G. Ratcliffe, *Houston Chronicle,* June 8, 1994; "Unity is Elusive as Religious Right Ponders 2000 Vote," by Gustav Niehbuhr and Richard L. Berke, *New York Times,* March 7, 1999; "This Country's Party of God? Republicans Attempt to Meld Church, State in Baptist Smelter," by Don S. Wilkey, *Houston Post,* September 20, 1992; "Conservatives Face New Hurdles," by Jill Lawrence, *USA Today,* November 13, 1998; "Bush Staying Out of Party Dispute, He doesn't Condone Battle with Gays," *Dallas Morning News,* June 11, 1998; "Presidential Light to Shine on Bush/Conservatives With Clout Will Toast Governor," by Cragg Hines, Clay Robinson and R.G. Ratcliffe, *Houston Chronicle,* April 4, 1997; "Gap Between Growth Numbers and Texas Wallets," by Bernard L. Weinstein, March 17, 1997; "A Trail of Green Money and Brown Air," by Molly Ivins, *Fort Worth Star-Telegram,* April 19, 1999; "'Armies of Compassion' in Bush's Plans," by Dan Balz, *Washington Post,* April 25, 1999; "Businessman Invests Capital in His Causes/Leininger's Millions Helped Conservatives Make Gains," by R.G. Ratcliffe, *Houston Chronicle,* September 21, 1997; "Polluters Puff Money to Political Campaigns," by Clay Robinson, *Houston Chronicle,* June 10, 1998; "Running on Empty: The Truth About George W. Bush's 'Compassionate Conservatism'," by Louis Dubose, *The Nation,* April 26, 1999; "Candidates Offer Plans as Bush's Platform Remains Work in Progress," by Dan Balz, *Washington Post,* April 25, 1999; "What "W" Stands For: Wishy-Washy or Wise?" by Dana Milbank, *New Republic,* April 26–May 3, 1999; "About Our Governor; Forget About Bush's Past; What About His Issues?"

by Molly Ivins, *Fort Worth Star-Telegram,* April 3, 1999; "Texans Support Hate-Crimes Law by a Wide Margin, Poll Indicates," by Clay Robinson, *Houston Chronicle,* April 26, 1999; "Activists Challenge Bush on Old Plants: Grandfathered Polluters Seen as Test in Run for President," by Ralph K.M. Haurwitz, *Austin American-Statesman,* April 27, 1999; "Bush Putting Faith to Fore in Public," by Deborah Kovach Caldwell, *Dallas Morning News,* May 12, 1999; "Bush Still Has Something to Prove on the Border," by Judy Keen, *USA Today,* May 27, 1999; "Activists Accuse Bush of Taking Polluter 'Payoff,'" by R.G. Ratcliffe, *Houston Chronicle,* May 1, 1999; "Sierra Club, Bush Differ on Texas Air," by Bill Dawson, *Houston Chronicle,* May 25, 1999; "Compromise Will Urge Older Plants to Reduce Emissions Voluntarily," by Bill Dawson and Clay Robinson, *Houston Chronicle,* May 31, 1999; "Bills May Mold Bush's Record on Environment," by R.G. Ratcliffe, *Houston Chronicle,* May 20, 1999; "Bush Will Skip Chance to Meet with 6,000 Journalists," by Sam Fulwood III, *Los Angeles Times,* July 8, 1999; "Texas Too Rich to Leave Its Poor Children Behind," by Sen. Lloyd Bentsen and Lan Bentsen, *Houston Chronicle,* May 2, 1999; "Rev. Falwell Sees Bush as Next President," by Jim Jones, *Fort Worth Star-Telegram,* June 14, 1999; "Arrested Drug Officer Had Been Pardoned," by Eric Garcia, *Dallas Morning News,* December 15, 1995; "Ecology Growing as Issue in Race," by Ralph K.M. Haurwitz, *Austin American-Statesman,* July 18, 1999; "Bush Signs Religious Freedom Bill," Associated Press, June 11, 1999; "Byrd's Daughter Meets Privately with Bush," by Terrence Stutz, *Dallas Morning News,* May 7, 1999; "Challenge Offered on Legislation, Clinton Urges Bush to Ink Hate-Crimes Bill," by Greg McDonald, R.G. Ratcliffe, and Alan Bernstein, *Houston Chronicle,* May 8, 1999; "Pastor at Bush's Church Backs Hate-Crimes Bill," *Dallas Morning News,* May 13, 1999; "Political Donors Have the Money, and Get the Time," by R.G. Ratcliffe and Alan Bernstein, *Houston Chronicle,* May 23, 1999; "Group Blasts State's Beach Monitoring," by Scott S. Greenberger, *Austin American-Statesman,* July 16, 1999; "Corporate Polluters Escape Bush's Big Stick," by Clay Robinson, *Houston Chronicle,* May 2, 1999; "Bush Pledges Tax Breaks to Aid the 'Armies of Compassion,'" by Richard Benedetto, *USA Today,* July 23, 1999; "Indianapolis Mayor Taps Experience to Advise Bush," by Ken Herman, *Austin American-Statesman,* July 22, 1999; "Debating Separation of Faith and State," by Scott S. Greenberger, *Austin American-Statesman,* July 29, 1999; "Bush Backs Funds for Church Groups to Help Needy, Sick," by Christy Hoppe, *Dallas Morning News,* July 23, 1999; "Sound Bites," *Entertainment Weekly,* September 3, 1999.

Television: Lesley Stahl interview with Pat Robertson, CBS' *60 Minutes,* May 16, 1999.

On-line: "Why I Am Not a (Compassionate) Conservative," by Stephen Moore, (IntellectualCapital.com) March 18, 1999; www.bush98.com (See News Releases); "Clinton Urges Expansion of Hate Crime Law," CNN Interactive, April 6, 1999; www.bush98.com (See News Releases); "I'm a Uniter, Not a Divider," by David Horowitz (www.salon.com) May 6, 1999; "The Muteness of Prince George," by William Saletan (www.slate.com) March 11, 1999.

Interviews: Beatrice Lacey; Hank Owens; Dr. Cathy Smith; confidential conversations with informed sources on Governor Bush's staff; Harry Gudger; Deborah Burstion-Wade; Brian Berry; Norma Chavez; Norberto Corella Gil Samangiego; Lloyd Doggett; Tom "Smitty" Smith; Mark Davis; Daryl Verrett; Elizabeth Birch; Bonita Alvarez; Keith Stafford.

Chapter 11. Walk, Don't Run

Archives and Oral History Collections: Eugene C. Barker Texas History Center, Austin; Texas Room, Houston Public Library; Center for American History, the University of Texas at Austin; Texas Historical Society, Houston, Texas; the Texas State Archives, Austin, Texas; Public Service Archives, Woodson Research Center, Rice University.

For this chapter, the author consulted the following published articles: "Like Father, Like Son—Sort Of," by Ken Herman, *Houston Post,* November 7, 1993; "Another Bush in Line?" by Sue Anne Pressley, *Washington Post,* May 9, 1997; "Bush Announces Bid for Re-Election in '98/Question of Presidential Race Remains," by R.G. Ratcliffe, *Houston Chronicle,* July 10, 1997; "Bullock: Bush Can't Be Beaten/To Try Might Hurt Democrats, He Warns," by R.G. Ratcliffe, *Houston Chronicle,* July 26, 1997; "Gov. Bush Turns Lukewarm Shoulder to Presidential Talk," by John C. Henry, *Houston Chronicle,* September 4, 1997; "Perceptions Count, and Gov. Bush Knows It," by Clay Robinson, *Houston Chronicle,* September 7, 1997; "Bush to Focus on Re-Election, Put Presidency Plans on Hold," by R.G. Ratcliffe, *Houston Chronicle,* October 31, 1997; "Up in the Air with Gary Mauro," by Michael King, *Texas Observer,* October 24, 1997; "Bullock Endorses Bush Over His Friend Maruo," by R.G. Ratcliffe, *Houston Chronicle,* November 21, 1997; "Bush Keeps His Focus on '98 Race for Governor, Not Presidential Bid," by Clay Robinson, *Houston Chronicle,* November 23, 1997; "Another Bush Administration?" by David S. Broder, *Washington Post,* November 26, 1997; "Mauro Must Define Himself or Bush Will," by Clay Robinson, *Houston Chronicle,* November 30, 1997; "Candidates Begin Filing for 1998 Elections," Associated Press, December 4, 1997; "Citing His Leadership, Bush Seeks Re-Election," by R.G. Ratcliffe, *Houston Chronicle,* December 4, 1997; "Bush Kicks Off Re-Election Bid," by Richard Enos, *Midland Reporter-Telegram,* December 4, 1997; "Bush Targets 2nd Term in Midland Visit," by Mella McWeen, *Midland Reporter-Telegram,* September 13, 1997; "Mauro by Maruo," by Lucius Lomax, *Texas Observer,* October 24, 1997; "Bush Cadres Primed to Aid George W.," by Cragg Hines, *Houston Chronicle,* January 25, 1998; "President Bush?" by Paul Kurka, *Texas Monthly,* July 1998; "Bush: Twins 'Kind of Like Their Life in Texas'," by Ken Herman, *Austin American-Statesman,* October 7, 1998; "Polls Indicates Bush to Be Re-Elected," by R.G. Ratcliffe, *Houston Chronicle,* October 21, 1998; "Bush, Mauro Keep Eyes on House," by Ken Herman and Mike Ward, *Austin American-Statesman,* October 31, 1998; "Bush Sets 60% of the Vote as His Goal for Re-Election," by Ken Herman and Mike Ward, *Austin American-Statesman,* October 29, 1998; "Junell Endorses Bush for Governor," by Marla Dial and Steve Ray, *San Angelo Standard-Times,* March 13, 1998; "Bush is Thinking About Texas Instead of Washington," by Katie Fairbank, Associated Press, April 21, 1998; "For Now, Bush Wants to 'Win Big' in Texas," by Dan Balz, *Washington Post,* May 4, 1998; "How Bush's Presidential Rumblings Play at Home," by Scott Baldauf, *Christian Science Monitor,* May 12, 1998; "Mauro Takes Shots at Bush in D.C. Visit," by Bennett Roth, *Houston Chronicle,* June 23, 1998; "The Next Bush Presidency," by Cal Thomas, *Los Angeles Times,* July 6, 1998; "GOP Insiders expect Bush Bid," by Ron Hutcheson and Max B. Baker, *Arlington Star-Telegram,* July 18, 1998; "Hagel Endorses Texas Gov. George Bush for President in 2000," Associated Press, August 10, 1998; "Pulling No Punches: Garry Mauro on Policy and Politics," *Texas Observer,* August 14, 1998; "Democrat is Upbeat in Uphill Fight Against Governor Bush," by Rick Lyman, *New York Times,* August 20, 1998; "Bush Pushing GOP's Hot buttons," *Houston Chronicle,* August 23, 1997; "The Race for Governor, Relishing the Challenge," by Alan Bernstein, *Houston Chronicle,* September 6, 1998; "Gov. Bush Reconsiders Desire to be President," Reuters, September 17, 1998; "Benefits to Incumbency Amid Good Times," by Clay Robinson, *Houston Chronicle,* September 20, 1998; "George Walker Bush, Driving on the Right," by Lois Romano, *Washington Post,* September 24, 1998; "Favorite Son," by Robert Draper, *GQ,* October 1998; "Bush Ponders Presidential Stage," by Jaime Castillo, *San Antonio Express-News,* October 6, 1998; "Bush Outspends Mauro About 13-to-1," by Ken Herman and Juan B. Elizondo, Jr., *Austin American-Statesman,* October 6, 1998; "Mauro Makes Mark with Loyalty, Timing," by Ken Herman, *Austin American Statesman,* October 11, 1998; "Bush Cites Work, Rejects Rich-Boy Image," by Ken Herman, *Austin American-Statesman,* October 11, 1998; "Bush Derides Talk That He Fears 2000 Run," by Dan Balz, *Washington Post,* October 15, 1998; "Mauro Prods Bush to Decide on Presidency," by R.G. Ratcliffe, *Houston Chronicle,* October 17, 1998; "Mauro, Bush Go Face to Face," by Ken Herman, *Austin American-Statesman,* October 17, 1998; "Bush Says No Third, Probably," by Ken Herman, *Austin American-Statesman,* October 23, 1998; "Bush Can't Avoid Presidential Talk," by Wayne Slater, *Dallas Morning News,* October 25, 1998; "The Final Hours," by Bruce Davidson, *San Antonio Express-News,* October 30, 1998; "Bush Is Star of GOP's Visit to Round Rock," by Scott Greenberger, *Austin American-Statesman,* September 13, 1998; "Bush Urges Tall City Faithful to Get Out and Vote," by Mella McEwan, *Midland Reporter-Telegram,* October 30, 1998; "The Bush Brothers," by Howard Fineman, *Newsweek,* November 2, 1998; "Governor Appealed to Broad Base, Analysts Say," by Sam Attlesey, *Dallas Morning News,* November 3, 1998; "Bush Wins Landslide Re-Election," by R.G. Ratcliffe, *Houston Chronicle,* November 3, 1998; "Governor Plans 'Private Time' to Weigh Presidential Bid," by Wayne Slater, *Dallas Morning News,* November 3, 1998; "Governors: George W. Bush Is Re-Elected; His Brother Jeb Is Victorious in Florida," by David E. Rosenbaum, *New York*

Times, November 4, 1998; "Bush to Focus on Agenda, Wrestle with Presidential Question," by R.G. Ratcliffe, *Houston Chronicle,* November 4, 1998; "Bush Leads Statewide GOP Blitz," by R.G. Ratcliffe, *Houston Chronicle,* November 4, 1998; "Bush Wins by Landslide, Boosts National Standing," by Wayne Slater and Terrence Stutz, *Dallas Morning News,* November 3, 1998; "By George, GOP Sweeps," by Ken Herman, *Austin American-Statesman,* November 4, 1998; "American Elections: Bush Brothers Steal the Show," by Andrew Marshall, *Independent,* November 5, 1998; "Hint of Newt vs. George W. in GOP Ranks," by Robert Novak, *Chicago Sun-Times,* November 5, 1998; "Election Aftermath/Bush Revels in Afterglow," by R.G. Ratcliffe, *Houston Chronicle,* November 5, 1998; "Bush Ready to Tackle 2nd Term," by Wayne Slater, *Dallas Morning News,* November 5, 1998; "Good News for Gore; Warning for the G.O.P.," by R.W. Apple, Jr., *New York Times,* November 5, 1998; "Bush's Win Proves Wooing Hispanics Worth the Effort," by Victor Landa, *Houston Chronicle,* November 13, 1998; "Election Math: Debate Lingers About Bush's Hispanic Support," by Sam Attlesey, *Dallas Morning News,* November 15, 1998; "Newt Hits the Shows," by Howard Fineman and Matthew Cooper, *Newsweek,* November 16, 1998; "Now Hear This," by Richard Lacayo, *Time,* November 16, 1998; "Not Sure What 'Compassionate Conservative' Means," by Bonnie Erbe, *Houston Chronicle,* November 19, 1998; "Gov. Bush's 2 Daughters Oppose Run for President," by Clay Robinson, *Houston Chronicle,* November 20, 1998; "Bush Says Ideal GOP Candidate for 2000 Race Should be Upbeat," by Wayne Slater, *Dallas Morning News,* November 20, 1998; "Governor Asked to Clarify Remarks on Religion," by Ken Herman, *Austin American-Statesman,* December 1, 1998; "Can George W. Bush Save the GOP?" by Bill Thompson, *Fort Worth Star-Telegram,* December 2, 1998; "Bush Fields Questions About Faith Upon Return from Trip to Israel," by Clay Robinson, *Houston Chronicle,* December 4, 1998; "Bush Restates Views on Heaven, Religion," by Ken Herman, *Austin American-Statesman,* December 4, 1998; "Dark Side of the White House," by Damian Whitworth, *London Times,* December 5, 1998; "Bush Presidential Run Could Have Big Impact on State," by Sam Attlesey, *Dallas Morning News,* December 6, 1998; "A Father's Concern," *Newsweek,* December 7, 1998; "Bush-Watchers See Presidential Preparations," by Ken Herman, *Austin American-Statesman,* December 23, 1998; "Texas Year In Review," by David Snyder, *Dallas Morning News,* December 27, 1998; "Changing of the Guard," by Clay Robinson, *Houston Chronicle,* January 3, 1999; "Bush Sets White House Strategy for Rich Backers," Reuters, January 11, 1999; "Bush Studying the Presidency," by Alan Bernstein, *Houston Chronicle,* January 13, 1999; "Bush Plans," *USA Today,* January 12, 1999; "Bush Family Not Keen on 2000 Run," Associated Press, January 18, 1999; "Bush Worried About White House Bid," by Ron Fournier, Associated Press, January 20, 1999; "Californians Urge Texas Governor to Run for President," Associated Press, January 21, 1999; "Politics," *USA Today,* January 21, 1999; "Bush: 2000 May Be My Only Shot," by Ken Herman, *Austin American-Statesman,* January 21, 1999; "For Bushes, Question is a Big One," by R.G. Ratcliffe, *Houston Chronicle,* January 21, 1999; "The

Question: Bush is Saddled with Presidential Curiosity," *Houston Chronicle,* January 21, 1999; "Bush Lays Foundation of Campaign for Presidency," by Jill Lawrence, *USA Today,* January 19, 1999; "A Certain Uncertainty in Bush Speculation," by Jane Ely, *Houston Chronicle,* January 24, 1999; "Bushes Discuss Pros, Cons of Possible Life as 1st family," by Sam Attlesey, *Dallas Morning News,* January 24, 1999; "Courtship of Hispanic Voters Paid Off for Bush," by R.G. Ratcliffe, *Houston Chronicle,* February 28, 1999; "Texas' First Lady Wouldn't Fight Run for White House," by Todd J. Gillman, *Dallas Morning News,* February 1, 1999; "Dirty Politics Called Factor in Bush Decision on 2000," by Carolyn Barta, *Dallas Morning News,* February 7, 1999; "Iowa Republican Legislators Urge Bush to Run for President," by R.G. Ratcliffe, *Houston Chronicle,* February 9, 1999; "Molinari Urges Bush to Run in 2000," by Marc Humbert, Associated Press, February 9, 1999; "Iowa GOP Rallies Support for Bush," by Wayne Slater, *Dallas Morning News,* February 9, 1999; "Republican Officials Make Push for Bush Candidacy," by Cragg Hines, *Houston Chronicle,* February 10, 1999; "Bush Faults Cover Story on Chelsea," Associated Press, February 10, 1999; "Bush Priority on State Business Makes Sense," by Clay Robinson, *Houston Chronicle,* February 12, 1999; "Video's Out, But Bush Still Mum on Whether He'll Run for President," *Houston Chronicle,* February 13, 1999; "Visits Highlight Potential GOP Presidential Rivalry," by Christopher Lee, *Dallas Morning News,* February 13, 1999; "Bush Sends Video to Iowa Activists," by Mike Glover, Associated Press, February 12, 1999; "Ain't Quite Beating About the Bush, Y'all," by Boris Johnson, *London Telegraph,* February 15, 1999; "Now the Damage Assessment," by Richard Bendetto, *USA Today,* February 16, 1999; "World Dignitaries Stream to Austin," by John W. Gonzalez, *Houston Chronicle,* February 17, 1999; "Bush Says He is 'Warming to Task' of Running in 2000," by Wayne Slater, *Dallas Morning News,* February 18, 1999; "Stream of Politicians Visit Gov. George Bush," by Michael Holmes, Associated Press, February 18, 1999; "Bush Lining Up Team to Raise Money for Possible 2000 Bid," by Wayne Slater, *Dallas Morning News,* February 20, 1999; "Bush Ducks Spotlight at D.C. Gathering," by Gary Martin, *San Antonio Express-News,* February 20, 1999; "Signs Show Bush Ready for Campaign," by Ken Herman, *Austin American-Statesman,* February 21, 1999; "Texas Governor a Star at National Session," by Scott S. Greenberger, *Austin American-Statesman,* February 21, 1999; " 'He'd Make a Great President,' Parade of Republican Governors Endorses Bush for White House," by David S. Broder, *Washington Post,* February 21, 1999; "Bush Delivers Candidate-Like Performance," by Richard Wolf, *USA Today,* February 22, 1999; "Gov. Bush Collects Endorsements," by Bennett Roth, *Houston Chronicle,* February 22, 1999; "Trust in Bush to Run in 2000," by Robert Novak, *Chicago Sun-Times,* February 22, 1999; "Governors Urge Bush to Run," by Ron Fournier, Associated Press, February 23, 1999; "Bush Not Using Dad's Top Aides," by Wayne Slater and Catalina Camia, *Dallas Morning News,* February 24, 1999; "The World's Premier Undeclared Candidate," by Jane Ely, *Houston Chronicle,* February 24, 1999; "Bush Backers a Bit Too Quick to Crow," *Houston Chronicle,* February 24, 1999; "Bush Pledges Hint on 2000 Race in 2

Weeks," by R.G. Ratcliffe and John C. Henry, *Houston Chronicle,* February 26, 1999; "'Grassroots' Push for Bush Carefully Crafted in Austin," by Jay Root, *Arlington Star-Telegram,* February 28, 1999; "George W. Bush Gets Organized," by Matthew Rees, *Weekly Standard,* March 1, 1999; "Bush Moving a Step Closer to Ending Guessing Game," by R.G. Ratcliffe, *Houston Chronicle,* March 1, 1999; "Carolina Delegations Back Bush," by Wayne Slater, *Dallas Morning News,* March 2, 1999; "Bush May Announce Committee Tuesday," by Michael Holmes, Associated Press, March 1, 1999; "A State-by-State Look at Bush Supporters," *Austin American-Statesman,* March 2, 1999; "Gov. Bush Gets Ready to Run," by Ken Herman, *Austin American-Statesman,* March 3, 1999; "Bush Introduces His Presidential Exploratory Team," by Wayne Slater and Sam Attlesey, *Dallas Morning News,* March 8, 1999; "Top Bush Aide Brings Aggressive Style to Effort," by Wayne Slater, *Dallas Morning News,* March 21, 1999; "Bush Plans to Travel to Key Primary States," by Cragg Hines and R.G. Ratcliffe, *Houston Chronicle,* April 7, 1999; "GOP's Savior in 2000?" by Jill Lawrence, *USA Today,* March 8, 1999; "Bush's Latest Committee Offers More Prospecting Than Exploration," by Alan Bernstein, *Houston Chronicle,* March 7, 1999; "Cheering Bush On: Fund-Raisers, Colorado Leaders Visit Governor," *Dallas Morning News,* February 25, 1999; "Republican Factions Increasingly Agree on One Point: Bush in 2000," by Richard L. Berke, *New York Times,* March 1, 1999; "Bush Will Have a Key Role at Convention," by Bennett Roth, *Houston Chronicle,* May 2, 1996; "96 Republic National Convention/Though He Has High-Profile Role, Gov. Bush Low-Key About Future," by Clay Robinson, *Houston Chronicle,* August 12, 1996; "Bush Saga Echoes at Convention, Former President Introduced by Son," by Alan Bernstein, *Houston Chronicle,* August 13, 1996; "Bush Keeps Observers Guessing About 2000," by Paul Duggan, *Washington Post,* January 19, 1999; "Bush's Speech Seeks Audience Beyond Texas/Possible Presidential Candidate Talks of Diversity and Morality," by Clay Robinson, *Houston Chronicle,* January 20, 1999; "Bush's Speech Focuses on Value; Governor Likely to Seek Presidency," *Washington Times,* January 20, 1999; "State of State: Dual Audiences for Message from Gov. Bush," *Houston Chronicle,* January 28, 1999; "Florida's Jeb Bush Likely to Take Governorship Second Time Around," by Dick Polman, Knight Ridder Tribune News, *Houston Chronicle,* May 24, 1998; "Bush Brothers," *Texas Observer,* June 5, 1998; "Bush Brothers on Texas Money Trail," by Ken Herman, *Austin American-Statesman,* January 27, 1998; "Like His Brother, Jeb Bush Reaches Out to Democrats," by Kim Cobb, *Houston Chronicle,* July 12, 1998; "Election '98: Gubernatorial Races—Florida, Bush is Leaving No Base Untouched," by Mike Williams, *Atlanta Journal and Constitution,* October 18, 1999; "Bush's Performance is Mother-Approved," by Lucy Morgan, *St. Petersburg Times,* October 21, 1998; "Brothers Bush: Studious Jeb, Relaxes George Lead Their Races," by Ken Herman, *Austin American-Statesman,* October 25, 1998; "Issues May Belong to His Foe, But Jeb Bush Has the Appeal," by Jill Lawrence, *USA Today,* October 27, 1998; "'The Other' Bush's Heading for Florida Governorship, He Credits Brother George for Teaching Him Humility," by

Carolyn Barta, *Dallas Morning News,* October 28, 1998; "Bush Brothers, Victors, Continue a Legacy," by Rick Lyman and Mireya Navarro," *New York Times,* November 4, 1998; "The Sons Also Rise," by Evan Thomas, *Newsweek,* November 16, 1998; "Can He Save the Republicans," by Kenneth T. Walsh," *U.S. News & World Report,* November 16, 1998; "Lone Star Stars," by Julia Reed, *Vogue,* February 1999; "Two for Texas," by Paul Burka, *Texas Monthly,* October 1998; "Texas: Race for No. 2 Captivates State," by B. Drummond Ayres, Jr., *New York Times,* October 26, 1998; "The Southwest: Texas," *Washington Post,* November 1, 1998; "Perry Wins Bitter Fight Over Sharp," by John W. Gonzalez, *Houston Chronicle,* November 4, 1998; "Perry to Take Office as Senate Novice with Seasoned Support," by John W. Gonzalez, *Houston Chronicle,* January 18, 1999; "Both Parties Know Hispanic Vote Could Swing Election," by Mary Lenz, *Houston Post,* November 2, 1994; "Hispanic Vote Becoming More Conservative, Study Finds," *Houston Post,* November 19, 1994; "San Antonio Wants Cash, Clout of GOP Convention/Growing Hispanic Vote Issued as Enticement for 2000," by Thaddeus Herrick, *Houston Chronicle,* June 28, 1998; "San Antonio Wows Republicans/City Hopes to Attract Convention in 2000," Associated Press, June 30, 1998; "GOP Would Do Well to Elect San Antonio for 2000," *Huston Chronicle,* August 3, 1998; "Bush Ads Aim for Big Share of Hispanic Vote/Governor Speaks Spanish in Radio Spots," by R.G. Ratcliffe, *Houston Chronicle,* August 15, 1998; "Bush Campaign Ads Aimed at Hispanics Start Monday," by R.G. Ratcliffe, *Houston Chronicle,* September 26, 1998; "Hispanic Vote Seen as Political Earthquake in Making," by Stewart M. Powell, Hearst News Service, October 11, 1998; "Is All of GOP Reading from the Same Text," by Carlos Guerra, *San Antonio Express-News,* October 12, 1998; "Upbeat Bush Predicting Win in El Paso Area," by R.G. Ratcliffe, *Houston Chronicle,* October 19, 1998; "Bush, Mauro Predict Big Wins," by Ken Herman, *Austin American-Statesman,* October 30, 1998; "Could Border Area Upset the GOP Apple Cart?" by Carlos Guerra, *San Antonio Express-News,* November 2, 1998; "Philadelphia Gets GOP Convention," by Richard Benedetto, *USA Today,* November 6, 1998; "Mixed Messages to Hispanics Exposes Republican Rift," by Jill Lawrence, *USA Today,* November 25, 1998; "The Fastest Growing Minority in America," by Tad Szulc, *Parade Magazine,* January 3, 1999; "Immigration Population Up 51% Since '90, Census Says," Associated Press, January 20, 1999; "Gov. Bush 'Very Interested' In White House Run," Reuters, February 3, 1999; "The Candidate: Latinos Have Good Reason to be Wary," by Barbara Renaud Gonzalez, *Houston Chronicle,* March 7, 1999; "Dilapidated Colonias Border on Change, Yet Strides Toward Progress Show Miles of Work to Go," by Thaddeus Herrick, *Houston Chronicle,* March 7, 1999; "Al Looking for Some Salsa?" *Newsweek,* April 26, 1999; "Bush Names Gonzalez for High Court," by Clay Robinson, *Houston Chronicle,* November 13, 1998; "Bushes are Touted as Being Leaders of 'New Republicans'," by Polly Ross Hughes, *Houston Chronicle,* November 8, 1998; "Special Yo! Election Report/Will He Branch Out/Bush Leaves Other Candidates in the Dust," *Houston Chronicle,* November 12, 1998; "Election Uncovered a Real Gem," by William Raspberry, *Denver*

Post, November 8, 1998; "GOP Moderates Gain Influence," by Donald M. Rothberg, Associated Press, December 7, 1998; "Republican Heartthrobs," by Peter Beinart, *New Republic,* December 28, 1998; "Midterm Elections' End Marks Start of White House Race," by Stewart M. Powell, *Washington Times,* November 4, 1998; "GOP Power Tilting to Governors," Associated Press, November 22, 1998; "Can the GOP Do Anything Right?" by Jill Lawrence, *USA Today,* February 19, 1999; "The Speaker's Silence," by Major Garrett and Michael J. Gerson, *U.S. News & World Report,* November 16, 1998; "Middle of the Road Led to Victory in Races for Governor," by David E. Rosenbaum, *New York Times,* November 5, 1998; "Bush Can Handle 'Part-Time' Governor Tag," by Clay Robinson, *Houston Chronicle,* April 26, 1998; "Democrats Call Trip Presidential Posturing," by Jay Root, *Arlington Star-Telegram,* April 20, 1998; "Larry King's People: News and Views," *USA Today,* January 11, 1999; "2000 Elections Full of Possibilities, Richard Benedetto, *USA Today,* February 22, 1999; "Like Father, Like Sons: Bush Brothers Fire Up GOP Fund-Raising," by Ruth Marcus and Terry M. Neal, *Washington Post,* June 18, 1998; "Bush Brothers on Texas Money Trail," by Ken Herman, *Austin American-Statesman,* January 27, 1998; "Southern Straw Polls Participants Seek Bush for President in 2000," by Jack Elliot, Jr., *Austin American-Statesman,* March 2, 1998; "This Branch of Bush Family Tree is Green, Too," by Ken Herman, *Austin American-Statesman,* February 21, 1998; "Campaign Fund-Raisers Quietly Raise Millions: Solicitors Help Fill Presidential Hopefuls' Coffers," by Wayne Slater, *Dallas Morning News,* May 4, 1992; "Bush Rakes in Bucks at Record Pace," by Ken Herman, *Austin American-Statesman,* January 16, 1998; "House GOP Proposes Sales, Business Tax Cuts," by Christy Hoppe, *Dallas Morning News,* April 7, 1999; "House Halts Bush Proposal," by Juan B. Elizondo, Jr., *Austin American-Statesman,* April 15, 1999; "Bush Names Williams to Railroad Commission," by R.G. Ratcliffe, *Houston Chronicle,* December 21, 1998; "Arlington Man Named to State Post," by Jay Root, *Arlington Star-Telegram,* December 21, 1998; "7th Texas Legislature/Plan Would Limit Eligibility for Private School Vouchers," by Kathy Walt, *Houston Chronicle,* March 25, 1999; "76th Texas Legislature/Voucher Fight Heading for a Showdown," by Kathy Walt, *Houston Chronicle,* April 12, 199; "Senate GOP Offers School Proposal," by Terrence Stutz, *Dallas Morning News,* April 22, 1999; "Bush Agenda," *Dallas Morning News,* January 10, 1999; "The Texas Agenda," by Terrence Stutz, *Dallas Morning News,* January 10, 1999; "Bush Urges Legislators to Set Example," by Wayne Slater, *Dallas Morning News,* January 28, 1999; "Bush Speech to Take Aim at Tax Cut, Education/Address to Legislature May Draw National Media," by Clay Robinson, *Houston Chronicle,* January 27, 1999; "Brother, Can You Spare Some Dimes?" by Evan Smith, *Texas Monthly,* October 1998; "Off and Running," by Michael Rust, *Insight,* April 5–12, 1999; "A Place at U.S. Table for Latinos in 2001?" by Juan R. Palomo, *USA Today,* March 24, 1999; "The Wins of the Father Are Visited Upon the Son," by Adam Nagourney, *New York Times,* June 14, 1998; "Expectations May Be Too High for George W. Bush," by Alan Elsner, Reuters, November 6, 1998; "Watch Out for Hurricane W," by Howard Fineman, *Newsweek*, May 17, 1999; "Bush Awaits 'the Responsibility Era'," by Judy Keen, *USA Today*, May 10, 1999; "Gloom and Doom on the Campaign Trail," by George Hager, *Washington Post*, June 8, 1999; "The Bush Rolodex," by Michael Duffy, *Time*, March 29, 1999; "Bush Listened and Learned from Bullock," by Clay Robinson, *Houston Chronicle*, June 27, 1999; "Hundreds Bid Farewell to Bullock," by Clay Robinson, *Houston Chronicle*, June 21, 1999; "Governor Signs Bill to Help Colonias," Associated Press, June 18, 1999; "Bush and Hispanics," by Paul Leavitt, *USA Today*, July 27, 1999; "Who Chose George?" by Michael Duffy and Nancy Gibbs, *Time*, June 21, 1999.

Television: "First in the Nation: The New Hampshire Primary," CNN, February 2, 1999; Newt Gingrich on *The Tonight Show with Jay Leno*, January 5, 1999; Roundtable segment with Cokie Roberts, Sam Donaldson, George Will on ABC TV's *This Week*, November 8, 1998; "Predictions for 1998" with Linda Douglass, George Stephanopoulos, George Will, Sam Donaldson on ABC-TV's *This Week*, December 28, 1997; "Evans, Novak, Hunt & Shields," interview with Steve Largent and future of the Republican Party, CNN, November 7, 1998; "Inside Politics," CNN, November 9, 1998; "ABC News Special: The '98 Vote," with Peter Jennings, Cokie Roberts, Lynn Sherr, November 3, 1998; "George W. Bush's Impressive Victory," with Peter Jennings and Dean Reynolds, ABC-TV's *World News Tonight*, November 4, 1998; C-SPAN interview with George W. Bush, January 25, 1999.

On-line: www.bush98.com (See News Releases); "Texas Gov. Bush Stays Mum on Presidential Run," by Michael Holes, Associated Press, CNN Interactive (www.cnn.com), November 5, 1998; "Calif. Lawmaker Urges Bush to Run," Associated Press, Yahoo! News (www.dailynews.yahoo.com), January 20, 1999; "Secret Service Concerned Over Chelsea Clinton Cover Story," CNN Interactive (www.cnn.com), February 5, 1999; "Guy Molinari Urges Bush to Run in 2000," by Marc Humbert, Associated Press, CNN Interactive (www.cnn.com), February 8, 1999; "Bush Sends Video to Iowa Activists," by Mike Glover, Associated Press, CNN Interactive (www.cnn.com), February 12, 1999; "GOP Governors Rally Toward One of Their Own—George W. Bush," Associated Press, CNN Interactive (www.cnn.com), February 21, 1999; "Ex-President Ford Touts Gov. Bush," by Craig Horst, Associated Press, CNN Interactive (www.cnn.com), February 24, 1999; "Bush Builds Campaign Brain Trust," by Michelle Mittelstadt, Yahoo! News (www.dailynews.yahoo.com), February 25, 1999; "Bush Set to Move Toward Presidential Campaign," by Hillary Hylton, Yahoo! News (www.dailynews.yahoo.com), March 2, 1999; "Prodigal Son," by Jake Tapper, Salon News, (www.salonmagazine.com), April 9, 1999; "Texas Gov. Bush Unveils Exploratory Committee for 2000 GOP Bid," CNN Interactive (www.cnn.com), March 7, 1999; "Bush, Buchanan Plan Presidential Announcements," CNN Interactive (www.cnn.com), March 2, 1999; "Democrats Celebrate, Republicans Search for Direction After Election Night," CNN Interactive (www.cnn.com), November 3, 1998; "Bush Celebrates a Lone Star Victory," by John F. Yarbrough (ABCNews.com), November 4, 1998; "Bush, Gore Set Sights on 2000

Campaign," by Alan Elsner, Reuters (www.foxnews.com); "Not the Hispanic Vote, But the Hispanic Votes," by Roger Hernandez, Hispanic Link News Service (www.latinolink.com); "Candidate George W. Bush Aces His "Hispanic Test," by Victor Landa, Hispanic Link News Service (www.latinolink.com); "George W. Bush: Front-Runner for 2000," BBC Online Network (www.news.bbc.co.uk), October 29, 1998; "Bush Brothers Celebrate," BBC Online Network (www.news.bb.co.uk), November 4, 1998; "Texas Gov. George W. Bush Wins in Landslide," CNN Interactive (www.cnn.com), November 3, 1998; "Bush's Hispanic Support Debated," by David Koenig, Associated Press, Yahoo! News (www.dailynews.yahoo.com), February 2, 1999; "Bush Sworn in as Texas Governor, Eyes White House," by Alan Elsner, Reuters, Yahoo! News (www.dailynews.yahoo.com) January 20, 1999; "Jeb Bush Wins Big in Florida," CNN Interactive (www.cnn.com), November 3, 1998; "Jeb Bush: Third Way Republican," BBC News Online (www.news.bbc.co.uk), October 30, 1998; www.bush98.com (See Initiatives).

Author interviews include D.H. Johnson; Jim Paulson; Ray Kennedy; Robert Whitney; William Howell; Sam McKenzie; confidential interviews with key political strategists in the Bush and Mauro campaign organizations; Tommy Paulson; Mike Merle; Joe Harris; George Calloway; Dave Albert; Mitch Caesar; Harry Brenner; Dick Jackson; Phil Duncan; confidential conversation with Republican advisers on the Bush Presidential Exploratory Committee; Mark McKinnon; and James Elliot.

Chapter 12. Great Expectations

Archives and Oral History Collections: Barker Texas History Center, Austin, Texas; Texas Room, Houston Public Library; Center for American History, the University of Texas at Austin; Texas Historical Society, Houston, Texas; Public Service Archives, Woodson Research Center, Rice University.

The author also consulted the book *O Pioneers!*, by Willa Cather, Houghton Mifflin Co., New York, 1997, for the opening chapter quotation.

Published articles consulted include "Bush Ink: Manufacturing a President" by Michael King, *Texas Observer,* July 1999; "Bush's Dash for Cash," by Susan B. Glasser, *Washington Post,* April 7, 1999; "New York's Mayor Gives Bush a Boost," by R.G. Ratcliffe, *Houston Chronicle,* April 14, 1999; "Texas Governor, NY Mayor Trade Compliments," by Wayne Slater, *Dallas Morning News,* April 14, 1999; "Pataki Backs Bush for President," by Marc Humbert, Associated Press, May 24, 1999; "Bush Already Exploring a United Agenda with House," by Richard L. Berke, *New York Times,* May 7, 1999; "For Bush and Rivals, a Race to Define His Image," by Dan Balz, *Washington Post,* May 31, 1999; "Over Half of House's Republicans Vow to Support Bush for President," by Steve Lash, *Houston Chronicle,* May 27, 1999; "Bush Not Shy with the Public But the Press Another Matter," by R.G. Ratcliffe, *Houston Chronicle,* May 13, 1999; "Bush Visits Senate with Most of Agenda Pending," by Kathy Walt, *Houston*

Chronicle, May 21, 1999; "Time for President-in-Waiting to Lead Texas," by James Howard Gibbons, *Houston Chronicle,* April 19, 1999; "On Welfare, Legislature Goes for Carrot, Not Stick," by Polly Ross Hughes, *Houston Chronicle,* May 28, 1999; "Bush's Tax Savings Won't be Seen by Many Texans," by Clay Robinson, *Houston Chronicle,* July 11, 1999; "Legislature OKs School Bill, Property Tax Cuts," by Kathy Walt and John W. Gonzalez, *Houston Chronicle,* May 31, 1999; "Bush Signs Abortion Notification Bill," by Todd J. Gillman, *Dallas Morning News,* June 8, 1999; "Bush Signs Bill Giving Tax Cut to Oil Industry," by Christopher Lee, *Dallas Morning News,* March 12, 1999; "Tax Break Signed to Help Owners of Marginal Wells," by John W. Gonzalez, *Houston Chronicle,* March 12, 1999; "Legislative Session Pleases Bush," by Paul Duggan, *Washington Post,* June 1, 1999; "Bush Faces Criticism From Democrats," by Peggy Fikac. *Washington Post,* June 22, 1999; "Lawmakers Hail Tax Relief as Session Ends," by Kathy Walt and John W. Gonzalez, *Houston Chronicle,* June 1, 1999; "Leaders Tout Session's Focus on Education," by Terrence Stutz, *Dallas Morning News,* June 1, 1999; "Gore Takes Shots at Gun Lobby, Bush," by Scott Shepard, *Austin American-Statesman,* July 16, 1999; "Dems Hope Bush Stance Backfires," by Judy Keene, *USA Today,* July 20, 1999; "Governor Brushes Off Criticism Over Hate Crimes Bill," by Todd J. Gillman, *Dallas Morning News,* May 16, 1999; "Bradley Challenges Bush on Hate Crime Bill," by Laura Tolley, *San Antonio Express-News,* March 12, 1999; "Hate Crime Bill Fails," by Terrence Stutz, *Dallas Morning News,* May 14, 1999; "Bush Goes on the Stump Fresh from Tax-Cut Victory," by Michael Holmes, *USA Today,* June 1, 1999; "Two Campaigns, Two Divergent Styles in Iowa," by Judy Keen and Jill Lawrence, *USA Today,* July 21, 1999; "Governor Touts Session Successes," by Wayne Slater, *Dallas Morning News,* May 30, 1999; "Bush to 'Test the Waters' for White House Run," Reuters, June 2, 1999; "Legislators OKs School Bill, Property Tax Cuts," by Clay Robinson and R. G. Ratcliffe, *Houston Chronicle,* May 31, 1999; "Bush Pledges to Show His 'Heart and Mind' to Nation," by Thaddeus Herrick and Clay Robinson, *Houston Chronicle,* June 2, 1999; "Bush Cramming Before Campaigning," by Michael Kranish, *Boston Globe,* June 6, 1999; "Bush Eager to Hit Campaign Trail," by Ron Fournier, Associated Press, June 1, 1999; "Caution: Entering Campaign," *Newsweek,* June 14, 1999; "Iowa Takes its Time on Candidates," by Judy Keen, *USA Today,* June 28, 1999; "George W. Flips Stetson in Ring," by Thomas M. DeFrank, *New York Daily News,* June 13, 1999; "School Voucher Plan Signed Into Florida Law," Reuters, June 22, 1999; "Bush's Dilemma: Forgo Federal Funds or Accept with Strings," by Jonathan D. Salant, Associate Press, March 26, 1999; "Gov. Bush Can Show the Way on Campaign Spending," by Glenn Moramarco, *Houston Chronicle,* July 12, 1999; "Bush's Six-Month Total: $37 Million," by Jonathan D. Salant, Associated Press, July 15, 1999; "Bush 'Pioneers' Insist Fund Raising by 115 is a Grassroots Effort," by R.G. Ratcliffe and Alan Bernstein, *Houston Chronicle,* July 21, 1999; "Group Says Bush List Incomplete," Associated Press, July 21, 1999; "List of Fund-Raisers Includes 'My Best Friends,' Bush Says," by Ken Herman and Scott S. Greenberger, *Austin American-Statesman,* July 21, 1999; "Bush Proposes Lifting Political Donor Limits," by Wayne Slater, *Dallas Morning News,* April 15, 1999; "Texas Corporate Interests Financed Bulk of Bush Races," by Alan C. Miller, *Los Angeles Times,* July 14, 1999; "Costly Speech," by Myriam Marquez, *Orlando Sentinel,* July 22, 1999; "Bush's Money Team: Making of a Juggernaut," by Ken Herman and Scott S. Greenberger, *Austin American-Statesman,* July 4, 1999; "Bush Assembles Heavy-Hitting Team," by Jonathan D. Salant, Associated Press, July 21, 1999; "Bush Releases Donors' Names to Quell Critics," by Laura Tolley *San Antonio Express-News,* July 19, 1999; "Bush Says Complaints Are Foes' 'Sour Grapes,'" by Wayne Slater, *Dallas Morning News,* July 20, 1999; "Races Just Getting Warm; Fund-Raising Red-Hot," by Jim Drinkard, *USA Today,* July 15, 1999; "Clinton Says Ideas, Not Bush's Money, Will Earn Presidency," by Nancy Mathis, *Houston Chronicle,* July 2, 1999; "Texas Gov. George W. Bush Has Refused Public Funds for the Primaries," by Suzanne Sataline, *Philadelphia Inquirer,* July 18, 1999; "Bush Says He'll Forgo Matching Funds," by Mike Glover, Associated Press, July 15, 1999; "Bush Bonanza Leaves Little for Others," by Jim Drinkard, *USA Today,* July 16, 1999; "Kasich Dropping Race for President," by Jill Lawrence, *USA Today,* July 14, 1999; "Candidate Leaves with Jab at Front-Runner," by Cragg Hines, *Houston Chronicle,* July 14, 1999; "Gore Campaign Staff Seeking to Slow Bush Train, Aides Say," by Susan Feeney, *Dallas Morning News,* June 3, 1999; "Bush Raises $35.5M, Outpaces Others," by Ron Fournier, Associated Press, June 30, 1999; "Bush Breaks Fund-Raising Record," by Jill Lawrence, *USA Today,* July 1, 1999; "Clinton Says He's Not Letting Up," by Susan Page and Mimi Hall, *USA Today,* July 2, 1999; "Redefining Bush-League Fund-Raising," by Adam Clymer, *New York Times,* July 4, 1999; "Calif. GOP Rallies for Bush for President, and the Party," by Jill Lawrence, *USA Today,* June 29, 1999; "Iowa's Lone Star," by Sam Attlesey, *Dallas Morning News,* June 24, 1999; "Likely Bush Foes Peek at His Past," by Wayne Slater and Sam Attlesey, *Dallas Morning News,* May 24, 1999; "Bush Prepares for the Blitz," *Newsweek,* July 12, 1999; "Bush Reaches Out to Minority Voters," by Jill Lawrence, *USA Today,* July 2, 1999; "Bush Taps D.C. for Iowa Help," by Jim Drinkard, *USA Today,* June 24, 1999; "Running on His Own: Gore Officially Joins Race," by Jill Lawrence, *USA Today,* June 17, 1999; "Cautious Bush Watches His Step as He Begins Run," by Jill Lawrence, *USA Today,* June 11, 1999; "DNC Launches Early Strike Against Bush," by Richard Benedetto, *USA Today,* June 11, 1999; "Gore Makes It a Family Affair," *Newsweek,* June 28, 1999; "Bush Rivals: Race Still On," by Jill Lawrence, *USA Today,* June 28, 1999; "Bush Makes Campaign Official," by Clay Robinson and John C. Henry, *Houston Chronicle,* June 13, 1999; "Bush Campaign Greeted with Questions, Protests," by David Jackson, *Dallas Morning News,* June 15, 1999; "Bush Cooks Up Support at N.H. Eatery," by Holly Ramer, Associated Press, June 15, 1999; "Steve Forbes Blasts Rivals," by Mike Glover, Associated Press, July 12, 1999; "George W. Bush on a Roll, But Dangers Lurk," by Susan Estrich, *Houston Chronicle,* June 12, 1999; "Bush Ends First Campaign Trip to Rave Reviews," Reuters, June 16, 1999; "Bush Looks for Votes in South Carolina," by Sam Attlesey, *Dallas Morning News,* June 22, 1999; "Bush's List of $100,000 Solicitors is Released," by Ken

Herman, *Austin American-Statesman,* July 20, 1999; "Anti-Gun Protesters Attack Bush's Views," Associated Press, June 12, 1999; "Bush Fields, Fends Off Queries in N.H.," by Judy Keen, *USA Today,* June 15, 1999; "Texas Gov. Bush Wows Voters in East," by Ron Hutcheson, *Fort Worth Star-Telegram,* June 15, 1999; "Alexander Ad Rips Bush, 'Big Money,'" Associated Press, July 28, 1999; "2 Weeks Before Iowa Poll, Big Money is a 'Big Issue,'" by Jim Drinkard and Judy Keen, *USA Today,* July 29, 1999; "Weapons Maker Leaves Bush Campaign," by Larry Margasak, *Washington Post,* July 22, 1999; "Three Aides Keep Bush on Track in Another Campaign," by Ron Fournier, Associated Press, July 25, 1999; "Clinton Jeers Bush's 'Compassion' Theme," by Richard Benedetto, *USA Today,* July 15, 1999; "NARAL: Bush's Actions Contrast With His Image on Abortion," U.S. Newswire, June 22, 1999; "Elder Bush Says Presidential Campaign is Son's to Run," by Wayne Slater, *Dallas Morning News,* June 14, 1999; "Bushes Celebrate 'Darned Good Start' to Campaign," by Judy Keen, *USA Today,* June 14, 1999; "Blithe Bush 'Sky High' Before New Hampshire," by Ralph Z. Hallow, *Washington Times,* June 14, 1999; "Campaign Diary," by David Von Drehle, *Washington Post,* June 14, 1999; "Who Chose George?" by Michael Duffy and Nancy Gibbs, *Time,* June 21, 1999; "Here Comes the Son," by Howard Fineman, *Newsweek,* June 21, 1999.

Television: Ann Richards interview, CNN's *Larry King Live,* July 27, 1999.

On-line: "Bush Visits New Hampshire," CNN Interactive, June 14, 1999; "Bush Jr: Style Minus Substance," (www.cbs.com) June 15, 1999; "Bush Tops Iowa GOP Presidential Preference Poll," CNN Interactive, June 28, 1999; "New Polls Shows Bush Holding Lead," CNN Interactive, June 15, 1999; "All Things to All Checkbooks," by Anthony York, (www.salonmagazine.com) July 1, 1999; "Forbes Challenges Bush to Debates," CNN Interactive, June 14, 1999; "Bush Welcomes Attention From Opposition," by Walter R. Mears, CNN Interactive, Kasich Won't Seek Re-Election to House Seat," by Jack Torry (www.toledoblade.com) July 14, 1999, June 15, 1999; "Bush Sounds 'Compassionate Conservative' Theme in Iowa," CNN Interactive, June 12, 1999; "Smith Resigns from GOP," CNN Interactive, July 13, 1999; "Kasich Drops Out of GOP Race," CNN Interactive, July 14, 1999; "Bush to Forgo Federal Matching Funds, CNN Interactive, July 15, 1999; "It May Be a Record: Gov. Bush Raises $2 Million in D.C.," CNN Interactive, June 23, 1999; "'No Turning Back' From White House Bid, Bush Says," CNN Interactive, June 12, 1999; "Bush Fund-Raising Overwhelms Republicans and Democrats," CNN Interactive, July 16, 1999; "Bush Money Machine Raised Huge Money in Gubernatorial Campaigns," by Judy Woodruff, CNN Interactive, July 13, 1999; "Bush to Make His First Trip to Capitol as GOP Presidential Front-Runner," by David Espo, CNN Interactive, June 21, 1999; "Bush Begins Long-Awaited Campaign Swing," CNN Interactive, June 11, 1999; "Bush Using Texas to Build Record," by Ron Fournier, CNN Interactive, May 7, 1999; "Man of Substance?" by Gayle Tzemach (www.ABCNEWS.go.com) May 19, 1999; "Candidate Bush Gathers Steam as Texas Legislature Winds Down," CNN Interactive, May 28, 1999; "Bush Quietly Signs NRA-Backed Gun Bill," by Jane Caplan,

CNN Interactive, June 18, 1999; "Democrats: Bush Too Busy for Texas," Cnn Interactive, May 12, 1999; "Bush Contributors," by Rex Nutting (www.cbsmarketwatch.com) July 24, 1999; "On the Road with George W. Bush," by Jake Tapper (www.salonmagazine.com) June 16, 1999.

Interviews: Confidential sources associated with the Bush's campaign staff, aides to U.S. House Republicans, and officials representing campaigns of other GOP presidential contenders.

Epilogue: Brand Name

The half dozen reasons cited why Bush should win the presidency were obtained through confidential interviews with key political consultants associated with his campaign staff.

America In Search of Itself: The Making of the President, 1956–1980, by Theodore White, HarperCollins, New York, 1984, was a book that proved particularly useful regarding one-time presidential front-runners George Romney and Edmund Muskie and their 1968 and 1972 campaigns, respectively.

Articles consulted include "The Man to Beat," by Kenneth T. Walsh, *U.S. News & World Report,* March 15, 1999; "McCain's Substance Gets Lost in the Buzz Over Bush," by Walter Shapiro, *USA Today,* June 23, 1999; "'W' Bush: A GOP Centrist Similar in Style and Substance to Clinton," by Clarence Page, *Salt Lake Tribune,* July 8, 1999; "Only GOP Test: Can You Win?" by Linda Feldman, *The Christian Science Monitor,* May 4, 1999; "For George W. Bush, the Name's a Big Part of the Game," by Steve Kraske, *Kansas City Star,* May 2, 1999; "The Most Important Question Bush Needs to Answer," by David S. Broder, *Washington Post,* June 13, 1999; "Please Not So Fast to Proclaim Bush as the Nominee," by Marianne Means, *Houston Chronicle,* March 7, 1999; "Who Chose George?" by Michael Duffy and Nancy Gibbs, *Time,* June 21, 1999.

Television: Chris Matthews interview with *Washington Post* reporter, Lois Romano, CNBC's *Hardball,* July 26, 1999.

On-Line: "Bush Coronation is Almost Complete," by Jeanne Meserve, CNN Interactive, May 27, 1999.

Afterword

Articles consulted include "I've Made Mistakes . . ." by Nancy Gibbs, *Time,* August 30, 1999; "Bush Prolongs Drug Questions with Hem-and-Haw Tactics," *USA Today,* August 20, 1999; "Bush Says He Hasn't Used Drugs in Last Seven Years," by Scott Parks and Sam Attlesey, *Dallas Morning News,* August 19, 1999; "Questions Keep Flying at Bush," by Jill Lawrence, *USA Today,* August 20, 1999; "Devil May Care," by

Tucker Carlson, *Talk,* September 1999; "Bush: No Drugs in 25 Years," by Timothy J. Burger, *New York Daily News,* August 20, 1999; "Bush Zips Lip Again: Refuses to Reply to Drug-Use Questions," by Thomas M. DeFrank, *New York Daily News,* August 21, 1999; "Bush Won't Reveal If He's Used Cocaine," by Timothy J. Burger, *New York Daily News,* August 5, 1999; "Bush Hits Rumors: Sez Foes Selling Tale of Coke Use," by Timothy J. Burger, *New York Daily News,* August 19, 1999.

On-Line: "Bush Up to His Arse in Allegations!" by Amy Reiter (www.salonmagazine.com), August 25, 1999; "Bush Denies Using Illegal Drug During the Past 25 Years," CNN Interactive (www.cnn.com), August 19, 1999; "Why Did Bush Change His License?" by Jeannette Walls (www.msnbc.com), August 30, 1999; "What is George Dubya Hiding," by Linda L. Starr and Ben Conover (www.onlinejournal.com/Commentary/Dubya_Hiding/dubya_hiding.html).

Interviews: Confidential conversations with a former Yale classmate and close friend of George W. Bush; and "deep background" discussions with two of Bush's top aides and high-ranking campaign strategists.